G000167714

DIASPORA FOR DEVELOPMENT IN AFRICA

DIASPORA FOR DEVELOPMENT IN AFRICA

Sonia Plaza and Dilip Ratha
Editors

THE WORLD BANK
Washington, D.C.

© 2011 The International Bank for Reconstruction and Development / The World Bank
1818 H Street NW
Washington DC 20433
Telephone: 202-473-1000
Internet: www.worldbank.org

All rights reserved

1 2 3 4 14 13 12 11

This volume is a product of the staff of the International Bank for Reconstruction and Development / The World Bank. The findings, interpretations, and conclusions expressed in this volume do not necessarily reflect the views of the Executive Directors of The World Bank or the governments they represent.

The World Bank does not guarantee the accuracy of the data included in this work. The boundaries, colors, denominations, and other information shown on any map in this work do not imply any judgement on the part of The World Bank concerning the legal status of any territory or the endorsement or acceptance of such boundaries.

Rights and Permissions
The material in this publication is copyrighted. Copying and/or transmitting portions or all of this work without permission may be a violation of applicable law. The International Bank for Reconstruction and Development / The World Bank encourages dissemination of its work and will normally grant permission to reproduce portions of the work promptly.

For permission to photocopy or reprint any part of this work, please send a request with complete information to the Copyright Clearance Center Inc., 222 Rosewood Drive, Danvers, MA 01923, USA; telephone: 978-750-8400; fax: 978-750-4470; Internet: www.copyright.com.

All other queries on rights and licenses, including subsidiary rights, should be addressed to the Office of the Publisher, The World Bank, 1818 H Street NW, Washington, DC 20433, USA; fax: 202-522-2422; e-mail: pubrights@worldbank.org.

Library of Congress Cataloging-in-Publication Data

Diaspora for development in Africa / edited by Sonia Plaza and Dilip Ratha.
   p. cm.
 Includes bibliographical references and index.
 ISBN 978-0-8213-8258-5 — ISBN 978-0-8213-8619-4
 1. African diaspora—Economic aspects. 2. Africans—Foreign countries—Economic aspects. 3. Economic development—Finance—Africa. 4. Africa—Emigration and immigration—Economic aspects. 5. Emigrant remittances—Africa. 6. Entrepreneurship—Africa. 7. Migration for Development in Africa (Program) I. Plaza, Sonia. II. Ratha, Dilip.
 DT16.5.D536 2011
 304.82096—dc22

                                                                                    2011013214

ISBN: 978-0-8213-8258-5
eISBN: 978-0-8213-8619-4
DOI: 10.1596/978-0-8213-8258-5

Cover illustration by: Diana Ong/SuperStock by Getty Images
Cover design by Drew Fasick

Contents

Boxes

Figures

Tables

Foreword

The diaspora of developing countries can be a potent force for development for their countries of origin, through remittances, but also, importantly, through promotion of trade, investments, research, innovation, and knowledge and technology transfers. This book brings relevant experience from both developed and developing countries to bear on issues confronting today's governments in linking with their diaspora. The chapters present different approaches used by countries that have tried to maximize the possible gains from migration by engaging more comprehensively with different diaspora groups and individuals.

A sizable amount of research has been conducted on the topic of migration over the last several years. Early studies on immigration policy assumed that migrants leave their countries, settle in a new country, start integrating in their new society, and abandon their ties with their country of origin. Today, however, it is possible for immigrants to remain connected with—and give back to—their native countries while residing abroad, thus diminishing their loss of identity and separation from their countries of origin.

There has been a shift in the discussion from seeing the emigration of skilled people as a loss, to seeing skilled migration as an opportunity to get remittances, trade, investment projects, and new knowledge. China; India; Israel; Japan; the Republic of Korea; and Taiwan, China are examples of economies that have tapped into their diasporas as a source of knowledge. In addition, there has been a new emphasis on including both skilled and unskilled migrants as contributors to host and home country development.

To expand our knowledge about diaspora, the World Bank organized an International Conference on Diaspora and Development, held on July 13–14, 2009, in Washington, DC. The conference aimed to consolidate research and evidence on these issues with a view to formulating policies in both sending and receiving countries. The chapters in this volume present the findings of 10 papers chosen out of 32 presented at the conference.

Some African countries are pursuing policies to develop links with Africans abroad, either to encourage them to return or to use their skills, knowledge, or financial capital to foster African development. The book discusses concrete examples of diaspora initiatives that are being implemented in Africa. There are comprehensive reviews on how the diaspora can promote trade and investment linkages. Some developing countries are using dual citizenship to deepen ties with their diaspora. The book directly addresses the issues of remittances-linked financial instruments, investments by the diaspora, diaspora bonds, contributions of skilled and unskilled diaspora in transferring knowledge, analytical research on return migration, and concrete circular migration experiences. There is a need to have a better understanding of these initiatives and to see whether they can be scaled up or replicated in other countries worldwide.

The focus of the book is on Africa. However, the chapters should be of interest more broadly to other regions, as well.

Otaviano Canuto
Vice President
Poverty Reduction and Economic Management
World Bank

Acknowledgments

The editors wish to acknowledge the invaluable contributions that many individuals made to the publication of this book.

The papers in this volume were presented at the International Conference on Diaspora and Development on July 13–14, 2009, in Washington, DC. The papers selected for publication were prepared under the direction of the editors.

The contributors who presented papers at the conference and who subsequently worked with the editors in revising their papers are Chukwu-Emeka Chikezie, Michael A. Clemens, Jonathan Crush, Valeria Galetto, Flore Gubert, Suhas L. Ketkar, David Leblang, Ndioro Ndiaye, Christophe J. Nordman, Marion Panizzon, Lars Ove Trans, and Ida Marie Vammen.

We would like to express our thanks to all the participants in the International Conference on Diaspora for Development. Special thanks to all the members of the team who were particularly helpful in organizing the conference: Manka Angwafo, Virgina Barreto, Claudia Carter, Sohini Chatterjee, Jacqueline Irving, Farai Jena, Hazel Macadangdang, Seifu Mehari, Sanket Mohapatra, Maria Mbono Nghidiwa, Neil Ruiz, and Ani Silwal. We would also like to thank all the panelists, presenters, and participants for their excellent presentations and discussions.

The papers were reviewed by their peers, the other contributors to this volume, and by William Shaw. The editors thank them for their helpful comments and suggestions.

The editors are most grateful for the time devoted by the representatives of embassies and diaspora associations who participated in the interviews conducted in 2009 in Abu Dhabi; London; Paris; Pretoria; and Washington, DC.

Special thanks to Farai Jena and Neil G. Ruiz for their contributions to developing the embassy questionnaire, identifying embassy contacts, and participating in the interviews. Tola Oni and Carly Petracco provided excellent research assistance.

This report was made possible with the financial support of the African Development Bank; the Canadian International Development Agency; the Department of International Development; the French Ministry of Immigration, Integration, Asylum and Solidarity Development; the Danish Ministry of Foreign Affairs; the International Fund for Agricultural Development; and the Swedish International Development Cooperation Agency.

Book design, editing, and production were coordinated by Susan Graham, Stephen McGroarty, and Nora Ridolfi of the World Bank Office of the Publisher.

Contributors

Chukwu-Emeka Chikezie cofounded the African Foundation for Development (AFFORD) in London in 1994. AFFORD's mission is to expand and enhance the contribution Africa's diaspora makes to Africa's development. Mr. Chikezie served as its first Executive Director from 1999 to 2009. He also cofounded a sister organization, AFFORD-Sierra Leone, in 2008. After having been an active member of the African diaspora for nearly two-and-a-half decades, Mr. Chikezie now spends most of his time as a diaspora returnee working in Sierra Leone as a consultant for **Up!**-Africa Ltd, which concentrates on diaspora for development and private sector development assignments. A particular passion of his remains private-sector-led job creation in Africa, achieved through leveraging African diaspora and other resources.

Michael A. Clemens is a senior fellow at the Center for Global Development, where he leads the Migration and Development initiative. His current research focuses on the effects of international migration on people from and in developing countries. Mr. Clemens joined the Center after completing his PhD in Economics at Harvard, where his fields were economic development and public finance, and he wrote his dissertation on economic history. His writings have focused on the effects of foreign aid, determinants of capital flows, and the effects of tariff policy in the 19th century, and the historical determinants of school system expansion. Mr. Clemens has served as an Affiliated Associate Professor of Public Policy at Georgetown University, and as a consultant to the World Bank, Bain & Co., the Environmental Defense Fund, and the United Nations Development Programme. He has lived and worked in Brazil, Colombia, and Turkey.

Jonathan Crush is Professor of Global Development Studies and Director of the Southern African Research Centre at Queen's University, Kingston, Ontario, Canada. He holds an Honorary Professorship in the Department of Environmental and Geographical Science at the University of Cape Town and is Director of the Southern African Migration Program. His most recent books on the theme of African migration and development are *Surviving on the Move: Migration, Poverty and Development in Southern Africa*, with Bruce Frayne (Idasa Publishing and Development Bank of Southern Africa 2010); and *Zimbabwe's Exodus: Crisis, Migration, Survival* (Southern African Migration Program and International Development Research Centre 2010).

Valeria Galetto is a Fellow at the San Francisco office of Hispanics in Philanthropy, a transnational network of grant makers committed to strengthening Latino communities across the Americas. Ms. Galetto has conducted research on international migration and local development in Mexico for many years. Her work has focused on the factors that favor or hinder productive investment in migrants' communities of origin and on how these factors change over time and differ across communities. She has also studied the dynamics of social capital accumulation in migrant networks and the role of migrant networks in facilitating economic development in Mexico. She is working on a new project that examines how individual characteristics, community resources, and migratory experience in the United States jointly shape the ways people perceive and define poverty in rural areas of Mexico. Ms. Galetto received a PhD in Development Studies from the University of Wisconsin, Madison, in 2009.

Flore Gubert is a research fellow at the Institute of Research for Development in Paris, France, and Associate Professor at the Paris School of Economics. She has been working on migration issues for many years, with a strong focus on the migration and development nexus in Western Africa.

She is currently coordinating two projects on Senegal, one examining the link between migration and development using matched data on Senegalese migrants and their origin households in Senegal, and the other focusing on the political and economic impact of collective remittances.

Suhas L. Ketkar, a recognized expert on emerging markets of Asia, Europe, and Latin America, is Professor of Economics at Vanderbilt University. For 25 years, he worked as a financial economist and strategist with several Wall Street firms, including Credit Suisse First Boston, Marine Midland Bank, and RBS Greenwich Capital. He was also Director of Sovereign Research at Fidelity Investments and has been a consultant to the World Bank. In recent years, he has taught economic development, emerging markets finance, and international economics at New York University and Vanderbilt University. He has published widely on many topics in economics, and his current research is focused on innovative ways of raising development finance. He holds a PhD in economics from Vanderbilt University.

David Leblang is the J. Wilson Newman Professor of Governance and Chair of the Politics Department at the University of Virginia. He previously taught at the University of Colorado and the College of William and Mary. He has served as a research fellow at the International Monetary Fund and at the Directorate of Economics and Finance of the European Commission. He is currently working on two projects, one examining the causes and consequences of global labor flows, and the other dealing with the political and economic implications of global commodity prices. Dr. Leblang's articles, which focus on the political economy of global finance, have been published in the *American Political Science Review*, the *American Journal of Politics*, and the *International Organization and International Studies Quarterly*. His book *Democratic Politics and Financial Markets: Pricing Politics* (with William Bernhard) was published by Cambridge University Press in 2006. He received his PhD from Vanderbilt University in 1993.

Susanne Melde studied in Argentina and Germany and received a Bachelor's degree in International Relations from the University of Technology in Dresden, Germany. She obtained a Master's degree in Human Rights with a specialization in migration and development from the University of Sussex in the United Kingdom. Ms. Melde worked on migration and development issues at the headquarters of the International Organization for Migration (IOM) in Geneva, Switzerland, from 2007 to 2010. There she authored background documents for the Global Forum on Migration and Development in 2008, and coauthored a publication on IOM's Migration for Development programs in 2009 and a paper on Migration and Development in the Least Developed Countries in 2010. She was also a Research Officer on the team that wrote the IOM's 2010 *World Migration Report*. Since July 2010, she has been the Research Officer of the Observatory on African, Caribbean, and Pacific Migration based in Brussels, Belgium.

Ndioro Ndiaye is one of the first African women to pass the concours de l'agrégation, the highest competitive examination for teachers, in France, specializing in odontology and stomatology. In 1988, Professor Ndiaye was appointed to the position of Minister for Social Development. On behalf of the Government of Senegal, she coordinated humanitarian activities during the crisis between Senegal and Mauritania in 1989. As the supervising Minister, Professor Ndiaye designed and implemented practical solutions to assist both Senegalese and Mauritanian migrants displaced by the conflict. She was responsible for dealing with population movements arising from the situation in Casamance, where there has been a conflict for over 20 years. From 1990 to 1995, Professor Ndiaye was Minister for Women's, Children's and Family Affairs. Thereafter, and until her appointment as Deputy Director-General of the International Organization for Migration (IOM), she resumed her numerous activities at the Cheikh Anta Diop University of Dakar, where she was instrumental in reforming tertiary education in Senegal. Professor Ndiaye is currently president of the Dakar, Senegal-based Alliance for Migration, Leadership and Development (AMLD), a nongovernmental organization she founded after serving her term as the Deputy Director-General at the IOM from 1999 to 2009. She has published numerous scientific papers and has written several works and studies on social and political issues. Professor Ndiaye initiated the *Migration for Development in Africa Experience and Beyond* book and the Diaspora Dialogues. She is Commandeur des Palmes académiques and Chevalier dans l'ordre de la Légion d'Honneur in France, and Commandeur de l'Ordre du Lion du Sénégal.

Rougui Ndiaye-Coïc obtained her Masters in Geopolitics from the French Institute of Geopolitics, in Paris in 2005, with special mention, and a BA in international relations from the Institut des Hautes Études en Relations

Internationales, Paris. During her studies, Ms. Ndiaye-Coïc wrote about migration management in West Africa. Prior to her current consultancy for the Swiss National Centre of Competence in Research (NCCR) in Bern, Switzerland, where she is a researcher with the NCCR Trade Regulation, Ms. Ndiaye-Coïc worked as a project officer at the International Organization for Migration (IOM) in Geneva. At the IOM, Ms. Ndiaye-Coïc contributed to the drafting of various reports on migration and development and coauthored the IOM publication *The MIDA Experience and Beyond,* published in January 2010. Ms. Ndiaye-Coïc's experience in dealing with projects on development for migration has convinced her that all parties—the migrants, their countries of origin, and their countries of destination—need to be involved in migration management issues.

Christophe J. Nordman is a research fellow at the Institute of Research for Development (IRD), currently assigned as an economist at Développement, Institutions et Mondialisation (DIAL), a research center on development economics in Paris. Previously he was a research officer of Skills, Knowledge and Organisational Performance (SKOPE) at the University of Oxford, a research center on education, skills, and labor, where he is an associate research fellow. His research focuses on the functioning of labor markets in developing countries, and more specifically on human capital formation and diffusion, the formation of earnings inequalities across gender and ethnic groups, informal sector and employment vulnerability, and the labor market consequences of international migration. His research is published in books and international academic journals of development and labor economics. He is currently involved in the design and improvement of labor force surveys and surveys on the formation and labor market effects of social networks in Vietnam and West Africa. He has served as a consultant for various international organizations, including the World Bank, the International Labour Organization, and the Organization for Economic Co-operation and Development. He received a PhD in Development Economics from University of Paris 1 Panthéon-Sorbonne in 2002.

Marion Panizzon is Assistant Professor of Law at the University of Bern and a Senior Research Fellow at the World Trade Institute in Bern, Switzerland. She lectures regularly at the United Nations Institute for Training and Research, in Geneva, Switzerland; and at the Trade Policy Training Centre in Africa, in Arusha, Tanzania, where she teaches about the interface of migration and trade. Her commissioned research includes projects for the

Institut du Développement Durable, in Paris; the Swiss Agency for Development and Cooperation; the International Organization for Migration; the IDEAS Centre, in Geneva; the Friedrich Ebert Foundation, in Geneva; and, most recently, the International Trade Department of the World Bank. Her books include *Good Faith in the Jurisprudence of the WTO*, with Thomas Cottier and Petros C. Mavroidis (Hart Publishing 2006); *Intellectual Property: Trade, Competition, and Sustainable Development* (University of Michigan Press 2003); *GATS and the Regulation of International Trade in Services*, with Pierre Sauvé (Cambridge University Press 2008); and *Migration and Mobility Partnerships*, with Sandra Lavenex and Rahel Kunz (Routledge 2011).

Sonia Plaza is a Senior Economist in the Development Economics Prospects Group of the World Bank. She has worked on science and technology projects in Latin America and coauthored a major analytical survey of migration and development for the Bank's Africa Region. She was a core member of the group that produced the book *Africa's Silk Road: China and India's New Economic Frontier* (World Bank), and wrote chapter 5, which includes sections on market information through ethnic networks and migration, and diaspora contributions in innovation, technology, and skills transfer, regional trade agreements, and bilateral agreements dealing with labor mobility. She works on the international mobility of students and the impact of the Bologna Process and the Lisbon Agenda in developing countries. She advises many universities on the transfer of skills and tapping into their diasporas. Ms. Plaza attended the University of Lima and earned a degree in economics, after which she joined Chase Manhattan Bank. She was then invited to join the Peruvian Ministry of Trade as a manager responsible for countertrade and debt swap agreements. She negotiated Peruvian external debt and trade agreements. She was Professor of Economics (International Economics) at the Peruvian School of Foreign Service and at the University of Lima in Peru, and was adjunct faculty (Microeconomics and Macroeconomics) at The American University in Washington, DC. She has a dual degree from Yale University and the University of Pennsylvania in International Economics and Development. Her research interests include international migration, labor mobility, trade, and the future of labor. She joined the Institute for the Study of Labor as a Research Fellow in February 2010.

Dilip Ratha is a Lead Economist and the Manager of the Migration and Remittances Unit at the World Bank in Washington, DC. He acts as a focal point for the Bank's activities and international partnerships on migration and development. Mr. Ratha also leads the Migrating out of Poverty research consortium, a multidisciplinary collaboration among six universities and research institutions in Africa, Asia, and Europe. He has advised many governments and international forums, including the Global Forum on Migration and Development, the Global Remittances Working Group, and the World Economic Forum Global Agenda Council on migration. His expertise includes migration, remittances, and innovative financing. Prior to joining the World Bank, he was a regional economist for Asia at Credit Agricole Indosuez, Singapore; an assistant professor of economics at the Indian Institute of Management, Ahmedabad; and an economist at the Policy Group, New Delhi. He has a PhD in economics from the Indian Statistical Institute, New Delhi.

Lars Ove Trans is a PhD candidate in the Department of Cross-Cultural and Regional Studies at the University of Copenhagen, Denmark. His background is in anthropology and his research interests include migration, remittances, transnational politics, and citizenship. He previously worked at the Danish Institute of International Studies, where he completed a study of African diaspora associations in Denmark and their involvement in development activities. He has also conducted research on Mexican hometown associations, which was published in the peer-reviewed journal *Diálogos Latinoamericanos*. His current research focuses on Oaxacan pan-regional migrant associations in the United States and their relations with the state of origin.

Ida Marie Vammen is a research assistant at the Danish Institute for International Studies in Copenhagen, Denmark. She has conducted research on migrant associations and their development activities and on the role of migrants' transnational religious engagement. She is currently working on a project that investigates the presumptions about migration and development that have framed current migration policy making in Great Britain and the Netherlands, including toward what end policy initiatives have been directed and how they have been implemented. She is in the early stages of PhD research that will focus on the new migration flows from West Africa to Latin America. The research will explore how religious affiliation shapes alternative strategies for migrants' livelihoods in Latin America and how it is related to new opportunities, as well as to failures and constraints.

Abbreviations

AU	African Union
CPIS	Coordinated Portfolio Investment Survey
CRPO	Contracts of Reinsertion in the Country of Origin, Contrats de Réinsertion dans le Pays d'Origine
DCI	Development Corporation for Israel
DKr	Danish krone
EDPRS	Economic Development and Poverty Reduction Strategy
EU	European Union
FDI	foreign direct investment
GCIM	Global Commission on International Migration
GDP	gross domestic product
HTA	hometown associations
ICAPM	International Capital Asset Pricing Model
IntEnt	Internationalisation of Entrepreneurship
IOM	International Organization for Migration
LDCs	least developed countries
MIDA	Migration for Development in Africa
MIIINDS	Ministry of Immigration, Integration, National Identity and Solidarity Development, Ministère de l'immigration, de l'intégration, de l'identité national et du développement solidaire

MIREM	Collective Action to Support the Reintegration of Return Migrants in their Country of Origin
MS	Danish Association for International Co-operation, Mellemfolkeligt Samvirke
NGO	nongovernmental organization
OECD	Organisation for Economic Co-operation and Development
OFII	Bureau for Immigration and Integration, Office Français de l'Immigration et de l'Intégration
OSIM	Organizations of International Solidarity for Migration, Organisations de Solidarité International Issues des Migrations
PATC	Project Advice and Training Centre
pS-Eau	Water Solidarity Network, Programme solidarité eau
PSF	Priority Solidarity Funding
PTA	Preferential Trade Agreement
RISE	Regional Initiative in Science and Education
RQN	Return of Qualified Nationals programs
SBI	State Bank of India
SEC	Securities and Exchange Commission (United States)
SMEs	Small and medium enterprises
TOKTEN	Transfer of Knowledge through Expatriate Nationals program of the United Nations Development Programme

Harnessing Diaspora Resources
for Africa

Sonia Plaza and Dilip Ratha

African countries, including those in North Africa and Sub-Saharan Africa, have over 30 million international migrants. The size of the African diaspora, including unrecorded migrants and second- and third-generation migrants, is significantly larger. Migrant remittances to Africa exceeded US$40 billion in 2010, providing a lifeline to the poor in many African countries. The potential contribution of the diaspora to the continent's development goes much beyond personal remittances. Those contributions range from collective remittances that assist in philanthropic activities to knowledge exchange, increased trade links, and better access to foreign capital markets. It is estimated that the African diasporas save US$53 billion annually, most of which is currently invested outside Africa and which could potentially be mobilized for Africa via instruments such as diaspora bonds.

This book is an attempt to understand various ways—investments, trade links, skill and technology transfer—in which diaspora resources (other than remittances) can potentially be mobilized for the development of Africa.

This volume is the outcome of the International Conference on Diaspora and Development, held at the World Bank headquarters in Washington, DC, on July 13–14, 2009, as part of the 2008–11 Africa Migration Project. All the chapters in this volume were originally papers presented at the conference. The papers served as background material for a joint regional report of the African Development Bank and the World Bank entitled "Leveraging Migration for Africa: Remittances, Skills, and Investments" (released in March 2011). Collectively, these chapters provide the unique perspective of African and other countries on initiatives to maximize the benefits of diaspora engagement and their contributions.

The four sections of this overview will discuss the following areas:

- Where the African diaspora is located
- Benefits of the disapora, such as remittances, trade, various kinds of investment (including foreign direct investment, investment by households, investments in capital markets, investment funds, and diaspora bonds), collective remittances, and the transfer of technology facilitated by diasporas
- Policies that African and destination countries should consider to increase the diasporas' contribution to development
- Conclusions.

Locating the African Diaspora

Estimating the size of the African diaspora is difficult because of incomplete data and differences in defining both migrants and diasporas (see box 1). In this overview, we use the narrow but convenient definition of diaspora as "foreign-born population." According to the *Migration and Remittances Factbook 2011*, the stock of international emigrants from African nations totaled 30.6 million in 2010 (World Bank 2011).

African Diasporas Within Africa

Countries within Africa are the main destinations for Sub-Saharan African migrants. For other African migrants (including those from North Africa), destination countries outside Africa are equally important. According to the *Migration and Remittances Factbook 2011*, African diasporas living in Africa accounted for over 14 million people, or nearly half of all African diasporas. For example, large numbers of immigrants from Burundi and the Democratic Republic of Congo

BOX 1

Defining Diasporas

A diaspora can be defined as people who have migrated and their descendents who maintain a connection to their homeland.

The U.S. State Department defines diasporas as those migrant groups who share the following features:

- Dispersion, whether voluntary or involuntary, across sociocultural boundaries and at least one political border
- A collective memory and myth about the homeland
- A commitment to keeping the homeland alive through symbolic and direct action
- The presence of the issue of return, though not necessarily a commitment to do so
- A diasporic consciousness and associated identity expressed in diaspora community media, creation of diaspora associations or organizations, and online participation (Department telegraph 86401, U.S. State Department).

This is different from the definition used by the African Union, which defines the African diaspora as "consisting of people of African origin living outside the continent, irrespective of their citizenship and nationality and who are willing to contribute to the development of the continent and the building of the African Union."[a]

Estimating the size of a diaspora is complicated by several factors such as place of birth, time of emigration, citizenship, and questions of identity (Ionescu 2006). For example, estimates of U.S.-based diasporas are constructed using the "place of birth for the foreign-born population" available from the U.S. census. Most European Organisation for Economic Co-operation and Development (OECD) countries, Japan, and the Republic of Korea classify immigrants based on the ethnicity of the parent, which results in higher estimates of the stock of immigrants compared with a classification based on place of birth. Temporary immigrants may be considered

(continued next page)

BOX 1 (continued)

as part of a diaspora but may not be captured in immigration statistics. Origin countries also use different definitions of diasporas. For example, India uses three categories: nonresident Indian, person of Indian origin, and overseas citizenship of India.

As mentioned, in this overview we use a narrow but convenient definition of the diaspora as "foreign-born population." Such data capture only first-generation migrants, thus excluding children and grandchildren who may have ties to the origin country. Yet, the conclusions of this overview should hold, irrespective of the definition of diaspora.

Source: See African Union 2005.
Note: a. The African Union considers its diaspora as the sixth regional economic community; see "Statement at the African Union Consultation with the African Diaspora in the U.S.: Building Bridges across the Atlantic"; http://www.unohrlls.org/en/orphan/791/.

continue moving to Tanzania; Somalis are still living in Kenya; and many migrants from Lesotho, Mozambique, and Zimbabwe are living in South Africa.

Traditional migration configurations in West Africa have changed in recent years. For example, Côte d'Ivoire and Nigeria were traditionally key destinations. But the disruption in Côte d'Ivoire and the economic crisis in Nigeria have diminished the number of immigrants into these countries, although these countries still have large stocks of immigrants. Ghana has been one of the major host countries in the subregion. Senegal has been both a receiving and sending country (ECA 2006). Kenya continues to be the main destination in East Africa, although about 84 percent of Burundian emigrants are in Tanzania and 79 percent of Rwandan emigrants are in Uganda. South Africa is also a major pole of attraction not only for African immigrants in southern Africa but for immigrants from other parts of Africa (for example, the Democratic Republic of Congo and Somalia), and for immigrants from China, India, and European countries. South Africa is also a sending country; Germany, the Netherlands, the United Kingdom, and the United States are important destinations for South Africans.

African Diasporas Outside Africa

Former colonies continue to send significant numbers of emigrants to what used to be the mother country. But the importance of colonial ties has weakened over time as new destinations for African migrants have emerged. Italy, Qatar, Spain, and the United Arab Emirates have become new countries of destination for some African emigrants. Meanwhile, the African diaspora in the United States is relatively small. Nigerians are the largest group, followed by Ethiopians and Egyptians (see figure 1). In Canada, the top 12 source countries (South Africa, the Arab Republic of Egypt, Morocco, Algeria, Kenya, Somalia, Tanzania, Ghana, Ethiopia, Uganda, Nigeria, and the Democratic Republic of Congo) make up 75 percent of African migrant stock (Crush 2010a).

Benefiting from Diasporas

Several authors have written about how migrants contribute to the economic development of their countries of origin through transferring resources other than remittances. Much of the literature on diaspora contributions focuses on skilled migrants and how trade, technology, and

FIGURE 1
Top Sources of African Immigrants in the United States, 2010

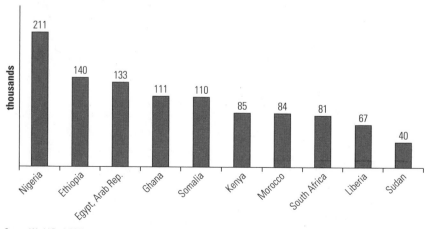

Source: World Bank 2011.

capital formation are facilitated by those with higher degrees of education. But both low-skilled and high-skilled diaspora members make contributions to their homeland. A growing body of research suggests that *skilled* diasporas and country networks abroad are an important reservoir of knowledge.[1] Other studies highlight the contributions of all migrants, including low-skilled diasporas.[2]

Research by others has analyzed how members of the African diaspora contribute to their countries of origin.[3] In chapter 1, "Diasporas of the South: Situating the African Diaspora in Africa," Jonathan Crush points out that internationally and within Africa itself, the African diaspora is generally seen as living outside the continent. Diaspora engagement strategies for development are therefore targeted at Africans living in Europe and North America. At the same time, the growing interest in South-South migration shows that these migration movements are extremely significant and have major development impacts on countries of origin and destination. This chapter argues that the concept of diaspora development needs to be redefined to include migrants who move to other countries within Africa. A consideration of the South African case shows that the African diaspora within the country has more significant development engagement and impacts than the South African diaspora abroad.

According to the authors, definitions of the African diaspora tend to focus on the development contributions of the highly skilled, educated, and networked members of diasporas in the North. However, African diasporas within Africa contribute to the development of origin and destination countries. Their contribution to countries of destination is often downplayed or minimized; migrants are rarely seen as a development resource in African countries of destination. More often, they are viewed as a threat to the interests of citizens, as takers of jobs, bringers of crime, consumers of scarce resources, and drainers of wealth.

Different types of diasporas have different potentials and propensities for involvement in development activities that benefit their countries of origin. An important point to underscore is that the African migration to South Africa has undoubtedly mitigated some of the negative impacts of the South African brain drain. The contribution of the diaspora in South Africa to the development of their countries of origin is also important. Further research is needed to understand the potential contributions of diaspora engagement to South African development and how the contributions of both diasporas can be maximized for the development of receiving and sending countries.

Remittances

African migrants sent US$40 billion in remittances to African countries in 2010. Migrant remittances are the most tangible and the least controversial link between migration and development (Ratha and Shaw 2007). Remittances tend to be relatively stable, and may also behave countercyclically with respect to the economic cycle of the recipient country. Surveys indicate that relatives and friends often send more remittances in response to negative shocks or a general downturn, and more affluent migrants' portfolio choices are affected by exchange rate movements. Remittances can also serve as an important support for a country's creditworthiness and can improve access to international capital markets (World Bank 2006).

Remittances play an important role in reducing the incidence and severity of poverty. They help households diversify their sources of income while providing a much needed source of savings and capital for investment. Remittances are also associated with increased household investments in education, entrepreneurship, and health, all of which have a high social return in most circumstances (World Bank 2006).

Trade

There are two channels through which migration can affect trade. First, immigrants have a preference for their native country's goods and services (supporting "nostalgic trade" in ethnic products) (Light, Zhou, and Kim 2002). The importance of this effect is difficult to evaluate, because if the emigrants had stayed in their country of origin, they presumably would have demanded the same products (Gould 1990, 1994). The effect is further clouded because the migrants likely have more income than they would have had in the origin country, but their relocation to the destination country reduces the efficiency with which the good is supplied (for example, by adding transport costs).

More important, migrants can increase the availability of market information essential for trade by helping origin-country exporters find buyers, improve their knowledge of the market, and comply with government requirements and market standards. Migrants facilitate bilateral trade and

investment between host and source countries because they help to overcome information asymmetries and other market imperfections (Black and
others 2004). For example, transnational networks can help producers of
consumer goods find appropriate distributors, and assemblers to find the
right component suppliers. Sharing the same language or a similar cultural
background eases communication and facilitates better understanding of
transport documents, procedures, and regulations.

Recent literature emphasizes the role of ethnic networks in overcoming
inadequate information about international trading opportunities, thus
driving down trade costs.[4] Gould (1994) and Rauch and Casella (1998) find
that ethnic networks promote bilateral trade by providing market information and by supplying matching and referral services. Empirical studies covering Australia, Canada, Spain, the United Kingdom, the United States, and
countries in the Organisation of Economic Co-operation and Development
(OECD) generally find that immigration increases bilateral trade flows.[5] But
these effects differ by type of good (for example, differentiated goods compared to more uniform commodities) and the skill level of the migrants.
Estimates of the size of these effects also vary widely, and it is difficult for the
models used to account for endogeneity. Studies for the United States
(Bandyopadhyay, Coughlin, and Wall 2008; Dunlevy 2004; Dunlevy and
Hutchinson 1999; Gould 1994; Herander and Saavedra 2005; Rauch 1999)
and for Canada (Head and Ries 1998) find a positive relationship between
trade flows and migration, although export and import elasticities vary
across countries and products.

Some governmental agencies and private firms in African countries
are tapping their diasporas to provide market information. Activities
include the establishment of Diaspora Trade Councils and participation
in trade missions and business networks. African embassies (of Ethiopia,
Kenya, and Uganda) in London and Washington, DC, support business
and trade forums to attract diaspora investors and to try to match suppliers with exporters. There are some case studies of activities in Sub-
Saharan Africa, but there has not been a proper assessment of whether
additional exports are generated through these contacts.

Countries tend to trade more with countries from which they have
received immigrants. Using Dolman's methodology (Dolman 2008),
figure 2 shows a positive relationship between the level of bilateral
merchandise trade between OECD countries and all African trading
partners (for which data are available) and the size of migrant populations living within these OECD countries. This positive relationship

FIGURE 2
Migration and Trade Go Hand in Hand

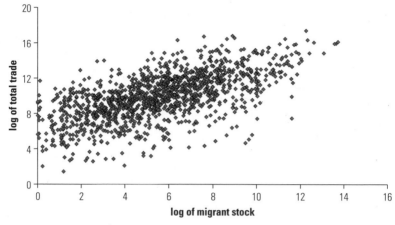

Source: Data on the stocks of migrants are taken from the Bilateral Migration Matrix 2010 (World Bank 2011). The trade data are for 2007 from the World Integrated Trade Solution.

could be due to other variables that affect trade flows between the OECD and Africa.[6]

Direct Investment

Members of diasporas can increase investment flows between sending and receiving countries because they possess important information that can help identify investment opportunities and facilitate compliance with regulatory requirements. Language skills and similar cultural backgrounds can greatly contribute to the profitability of investment in unfamiliar countries.[7] Diasporas may use the information they have regarding their countries to invest directly. Alternatively, investors can improve their profitability by tapping the expertise of a diaspora member.

A major barrier for a multinational or foreign firm setting up a production facility in another country is uncertainty and lack of information regarding the new market. For example, professionals and managers from Taiwan are very much sought after by multinationals such as Ciba, Nestle, and Phillips for their operations in China (*Business Asia* 1994). Members of a diaspora may be more willing than other investors to take on risks in their origin country because they are better placed to evaluate investment opportunities and possess contacts to facilitate this process (Lucas 2001).

According to Nielsen and Riddle (2007), emotion, sense of duty, social networks, strength of diaspora organizations, and visits to the origin country are important determinants of diaspora investment.

Some studies have found a significant relationship between migrants, particularly skilled ones, and investment inflows to origin countries. Kluger and Rapoport (2005); Docquier and Lodigiani (2007); Javorcik and others (2006); and Murat, Pistoresi, and Rinaldi (2008) have found that migration facilitates foreign direct investment.

Chapter 2, "Another Link in the Chain: Migrant Networks and International Investment," by David Leblang, addresses the question of what explains cross-national patterns of international portfolios and foreign direct investment. While current explanations focus on the credibility of a policymaker's commitment, Leblang emphasizes asymmetries of information between the borrower and lender. The author hypothesizes that migrant networks—connections between migrants residing in investing countries and their home country—decrease information asymmetries and increase cross-national investment. This hypothesis is tested using dyadic cross-sectional data, and the results are robust to a variety of specifications. The analysis concludes by suggesting that countries of emigration provide their expatriate communities with voting rights in order to harness their investment potential.

In Africa, government agencies are attempting to improve their contacts with diasporas to generate investment opportunities for origin-country firms. Ethiopia, Ghana, Kenya, Nigeria, Rwanda, and other African countries are looking to tap into their diasporas for investments in their homeland countries. For example, the East African Community recognizes the need to create a suitable mechanism to encourage diaspora members to channel remittances toward investment projects in partnering states, so they are developing a proposal to attract diaspora financing.[8] Both government and the private sector have supported business forums to attract diaspora investors. One of the new roles of African Investment Promotion Agencies, for example, in Ehtiopia, Ghana (Riddle 2006), Nigeria, and Uganda, is to provide accurate information and linkage opportunities to investors, including from diasporas.

Some private firms and African diaspora associations also provide information on investment opportunities and sourcing in their homeland countries and facilitate contacts between traders in destination and origin countries.

Investments by Households

Many migrants transfer funds to households in origin countries for the purpose of investment. Data from household surveys reveal that households receiving international remittances from OECD countries have been making productive investments in agricultural equipment, building a house, business, land purchases, improving the farm, and other investments (36 percent in Burkina Faso, 55 percent in Kenya, 57 percent in Nigeria, 15 percent in Senegal, and 20 percent in Uganda; see figure 3). Households receiving transfers from other African countries also are investing in business activities, housing, and other investments in Kenya (47 percent), Nigeria (40 percent), Uganda (19.3 percent), and Burkina Faso (19.0 percent).

Osili (2004, 844) uses a data set from Nigeria to analyze migrants' housing investments in their communities of origin. She finds that older migrants are more likely to invest in housing in their hometown and to devote a larger share of household income to these housing investments. She concludes that "housing investments may be the first stage of a

FIGURE 3

Investments in Business and Housing Funded by Remittances from Within and Outside Africa

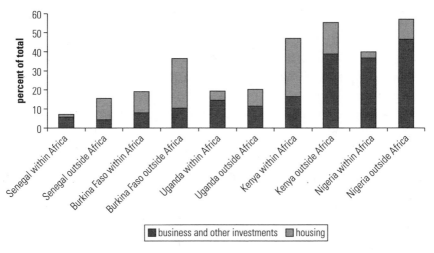

Source: Africa Migration Project Household surveys in Burkina Faso, Kenya, Nigeria, Senegal, and Uganda in second half of 2009 (Plaza, Navarrete, Ratha 2011).
Note: Other investments include agricultural equipment, investment in agriculture, land purchases, and livestock purchase.

broader investment relationship between migrants and their countries of origin." Survey data indicate similar patterns of investment by households receiving transfers from abroad in Latin America (de Haas 2005), with the difference that Latin American migrants and their family members invest in agriculture and other private enterprises, as well.[9] The evidence from household surveys for Africa of investment in agricultural equipment is somewhat limited.

African migrants in other African countries set up small businesses such as restaurants and beauty salons, or invest in housing. In other cases, the African diaspora has invested in service sector activities such as import/export companies, telecommunications, and tourism and transport companies (for example, Celtel, Sudan; Databank, Ghana; Geometric Power Limited, Nigeria; and Teylium, Senegal).

Some governments have eased restrictions on foreign land ownership to attract investments from diasporas. For example, the Ethiopian government allowed holders of a yellow card (the identification card for the Ethiopian diaspora) to lease land parcels at low rates for the construction of residences in Addis Ababa. Because of the high demand for land, the city of Addis Ababa officially suspended allocation of residential land for the diaspora in 2008. The Rwanda Diaspora General Directorate allows groups of 15 or more people to acquire land in Kigali for the purpose of house construction, provided the project is approved by the Kigali City Council based on the Kigali Master Plan.[10] Credit Financier de Cameroon offers a housing loan to migrants to attract investment in real estate.[11]

There is some evidence that returning migrants tend to use savings accumulated while abroad to invest in small businesses (Ahmed 2000; Gitmez 1988; King 1986; Massey and others 1987; McCormick and Wahba 2003; Murillo Castaño 1988; Murphy 2000).

In chapter 3, "Return Migration and Small Enterprise Development in the Maghreb," Flore Gubert and Christophe J. Nordman analyze returnees' entrepreneurial behavior using original surveys conducted among return migrants from Algeria, Morocco, and Tunisia during 2006–07. The authors also present the findings from the surveys, which contain detailed information on the returnees' conditions before migration, the returnees' experience abroad, and the returnees' post-return conditions in the country of origin.

Descriptive analyses of the database show that one-third of returnees did invest in projects and businesses after return, although this share strongly varies among countries. Algeria stands apart, with both a lower share of returnees being either employers or self-employed and a lower share of returnees being investors. In addition, entrepreneurs among returnees are more likely to be male, younger, and to have medium education levels.

The determinants of becoming an entrepreneur after return are then disentangled using a probit econometric model. The probability of becoming an entrepreneur seems to be higher for returnees with a first experience as employers or self-employed, for those who received vocational training while abroad, and for those who independently and freely chose to return. Surprisingly, there is no clear correlation between migration duration and entrepreneurship, even after controlling for the potential endogeneity of migration duration. Entrepreneurs do not form a homogenous group, though, and sharp differences emerge when employers and self-employed are considered separately. Overall, returnees show a high ability to create small or medium businesses and to generate jobs. For Africa, the authors find that one-third of returnees to Algeria, Morocco, and Tunisia (based on surveys conducted in 2006) invested in businesses. However, they do not find a correlation between migration duration and entrepreneurship.

Black and Castaldo (2009) find that more than half of Ghanaian and 23 percent of Ivorian returnees interviewed (in a survey of 302 returnees conducted in 2001) reported returning with more than US$5,000 in savings. Both of these studies suggest that many return migrants invest in business activity and that prior work experience is important for opening a business upon return. Maintaining communication with friends and family while the migrant is away facilitates the establishment of business back home. Cassini (2005) also concludes that the most successful Ghana-based businesses of Ghanaian migrants were owned by migrants who visited home frequently and developed social networks.

Investments in Capital Markets

Members of diasporas can act as catalysts for the development of financial and capital markets in their countries of origin by diversifying the investor base (the capital markets of many countries are dominated by investments from government and large companies), by introducing new financial products, and by providing a reliable source of funding. Diaspora connections with markets in destination and origin countries are important. The following discussion presents estimates of the savings of the African diaspora and then describes two vehicles—diaspora bonds and diaspora investment funds—to encourage diaspora investments in Africa.

Wealth and Assets of the African Diaspora in Host Countries

It is difficult to estimate the savings that members of the African diaspora could devote to investments in countries of origin. Ketkar and Dora (2009) use New Immigration Survey data from the United States to determine the wealth and asset diversification behavior of recent immigrants from Asia, Latin America, the Middle East and North Africa, and Sub-Saharan Africa. They find that the region of origin is not a significant determinant of savings levels once length of stay, educational attainment, and number of children are taken into account. In the United States, migrants from Africa tend to have lower levels of savings than immigrants from Asia and Latin America, largely because they have been in the country for a shorter period of time and have lower levels of education.

Ratha and Mohapatra (2011) estimate the potential annual savings of the African diaspora to be about US$53 billion (table 1), of which US$30.5 billion (approximately 3.2 percent of GDP) is attributable to the diaspora of Sub-Saharan African countries.[12] These estimates are based on the assumptions that members of the African diaspora with a college degree earn the average income of their host countries, the migrants without tertiary education earn a third of the average household incomes of the host countries, and both skilled and unskilled migrants have the same personal savings rates as in their home countries. Understandably, savings are higher for the countries that have more migrants in the high-income OECD countries. These savings are currently mostly invested in the host countries of the diaspora. It is plausible that a fraction of these savings could be attracted as investment into Africa if proper instruments and incentives (for example, diaspora bonds, as discussed below) can be designed by African countries.

Diaspora Bonds

In chapter 4, "Diaspora Bonds: Tapping the Diaspora during Difficult Times," Suhas L. Ketkar and Dilip Ratha contribute to the literature on how the access of diaspora members to information, and their relatively

TABLE 1

The Potential for Diaspora Savings in African Countries, 2009

	Emigrant stock (millions)	Potential migrants' savings (US$ billions)	Potential migrants' savings (% of GDP)
Morocco	3.0	9.6	10.5
Egypt, Arab Rep.	3.7	6.0	3.2
Algeria	1.2	4.2	3.0
South Africa	0.9	3.8	1.3
Nigeria	1.0	3.5	2.0
Tunisia	0.7	2.0	5.1
Ghana	0.8	2.0	7.5
Ethiopia	0.6	1.9	6.5
Kenya	0.5	1.8	6.1
Somalia	0.8	1.8	—
Zimbabwe	1.3	1.6	34.4
Sudan	1.0	1.3	2.3
Congo, Dem. Rep.	0.9	1.1	10.5
Senegal	0.6	0.9	7.0
Angola	0.5	0.9	1.1
Cameroon	0.3	0.8	3.8
Uganda	0.8	0.6	4.0
Mauritius	0.1	0.6	7.2
Liberia	0.4	0.6	66.8
Côte d'Ivoire	1.2	0.6	2.6
Others	10.2	7.1	2.5
Total	30.5	52.7	3.6
Memo			
North Africa	8.7	22.3	4.3
Sub-Saharan Africa	21.8	30.4	3.2

Source: Ratha and Mohapatra 2011.
Note: — = not available.

smaller concern over currency devaluation (where they hold local currency liabilities), can make them an attractive target for the so-called diaspora bonds issued by public or private sector entities. Chapter 4 discusses the rationale and potential for issuing diaspora bonds as instruments for raising external development finance, mostly drawing on the experiences of India and Israel. The Government of Israel has nurtured this asset class since 1951 by offering a flexible menu of investment options to keep members of the Jewish diaspora engaged. Indian authorities, in contrast, have used this instrument opportunistically to raise financing during times when they had difficulty accessing international capital markets (for example, in the aftermath of their nuclear testing in 1998).

Factors that facilitate the issuance of diaspora bonds include having a sizable and wealthy diaspora abroad and a strong and transparent legal system for contract enforcement at home. Absence of civil strife is a plus. In addition, earmarking proceeds from diaspora bonds for specific projects should also help improve their marketability (Okonjo-Iweala and Ratha 2011). While not a prerequisite, the presence of national banks and other institutions in destination countries would facilitate the marketing of bonds to the diaspora. Clarity is needed on regulations in the host countries that allow diaspora members to invest or that constrain them from investing in these bonds. A pertinent question in this context is: should these bonds be nonnegotiable or should there be efforts to develop a secondary market for these bonds? An argument can be made for the latter on the grounds that tradability in the secondary market would improve the liquidity and pricing of these bonds.

Diaspora Investment Funds

There is a shortfall of private equity capital in developing countries, especially in Sub-Saharan Africa. Ratha, Mohapatra, and Plaza (2009) report that portfolio equity flows to Sub-Saharan Africa have gone mainly to South Africa. Foreign investors appear to be averse to investing in Africa because of lack of information, severe risk perception, and the small size of the market (which makes stocks relatively illiquid assets). One way to encourage greater private investment in these markets could be to tap the African diaspora.

Several African investment funds have been proposed to attract investments from wealthy African migrants abroad.[13] Such funds can take the form of regional funds, mutual funds, and private equity to be invested in African companies and pension funds.[14] These investment funds are equity investments, unlike diaspora bonds discussed above. However, persuading diaspora investors to invest in African diaspora funds may require strengthening investor protections to ensure proper management of the funds. Some of the same mechanisms for building diaspora investors' confidence proposed by Aydagul, Ketkar, and Ratha (2010) apply to the investment funds:

- Management of funds by a state agency
- Management of funds by a private company[15]
- Management of funds by a combination of a private company with the participation of members of the diaspora.

Collective Remittances

The African diaspora has begun to contribute financial and nonfinancial resources to its homeland countries, although large-scale investments have not yet emerged. Organizations have been created in Europe, the United States, and some African countries, based on religion, ethnicity, or geographic ties. These groups include hometown associations (HTAs), ethnic associations, alumni associations, religious associations, professional associations, nongovernmental organizations, investment groups, national development groups, welfare and refugee groups, and Internet-based virtual organizations.

In contrast to similar groups of Asian (particularly Filipino) and Latin American diasporas, little is known about the scope, scale, patterns, and impact of African diaspora associations. Data are not collected on contributions sent by formal migrant associations, and there is no information on collective remittances by undocumented immigrants. HTAs and other voluntary associations of migrants from the same geographic area have provided substantial funds to some African communities—often as much or more than the municipal budget for public works, particularly in towns with small populations (Orozco 2003).

The number of associations appears to be correlated with the size of the diaspora in each country.[16] There are some twinning projects, in which, for example, Burundians in a town in France partner with a town in Burundi (Turner and Mossin 2008). Diaspora organizations are also active in African countries, for example, Somalis in Kenya, Zimbabweans in South Africa, and various groups in Côte d'Ivoire. Zimbabwe's associations contributed food, fuel, and medicines to their origin country during the economic crisis through the Global Zimbabwe Forum.[17]

To obtain a better understanding of the contributions of diaspora associations, country studies should be conducted in host countries. Chapter 5, "African Diaspora Associations in Denmark: A Study of Their Development Activities and Potentials," by Lars Ove Trans and Ida Marie Vammen, discusses the experience of African diaspora associations in Denmark. Since the early 1990s, an increasing number of African migrants have gone to Denmark, where they have formed a large number of migrant associations. The chapter presents selected findings from a comprehensive survey of African diaspora associations in Denmark and focuses specifically on their transnational engagement in development activities in their countries of origin.

The survey, which included 123 associations in 22 countries and three pan-regions in Africa, and 18 associations with regional coverage, shows that while most of these associations carry out a range of activities connected with the migrants' current life and situation in Denmark, 57 percent of the associations have also been involved in development activities in their native countries. However, the intensity and scale of the development activities vary considerably among the associations, which are divided into four prototypes based on their shared characteristics and capacity for undertaking projects.

The study also reveals that almost three-quarters of these associations have received some kind of financial support and aid from external sources to carry out their projects, and that although the Danish funding framework enables many associations to become involved in development activities, it also poses a number of obstacles for associations that want to undertake larger projects. These challenges are addressed in the policy recommendations in the final part of the chapter, where emphasis is put on alternative application procedures, capacity building, and further collaboration between Danish nongovernmental organizations and African diaspora associations. Nevertheless, it is also necessary to take into account that migrants often tend to focus only on their particular home regions and that the projects initiated by the migrants might sometimes seem to reflect more their own wishes and aspirations than the most pressing needs of the local population.

Interviews conducted for this book provide the following additional information on collective remittances from the African diaspora:[18]

- Networks of families and friends pool resources and support their villages or friends. In some cases, they send funds for development purposes such as for constructing a school, providing supplies to schools or hospitals, supporting orphans, and training new migrants arriving in the destination country.[19] In other instances, they send funds to support funerals or weddings. These transactions are not documented.
- These organizations rely on the skills of members, volunteers' time, donations, and fund-raising events for project financing.
- Collective remittances appear to be motivated by the migrants' sense of identity and feeling of solidarity with their home countries, and by sociocultural and political bonds or the feeling of being useful and powerful (similar conclusions are reached by Guarnizo [2003]).

- According to the survey cited by the authors of chapter 5, the most frequent activity of African diaspora organizations in Denmark is the shipment of used equipment in containers, typically destined for schools, universities, orphanages, or hospitals (41 associations), followed by the sending of collective remittances (27 associations), and educational campaigns such as increasing awareness of HIV/AIDS, the prevention of female circumcision, and the advancement of civil rights. Other projects involve construction of or support for schools, orphanages, or activity centers, and small-scale projects such as the construction of wells, implementation of farming or smaller business projects, and provision of microcredit loans. In some cases the money goes to private entities and, in other cases, to public institutions.[20]

It is difficult to properly gauge the impact of diaspora-financed development projects based on these case studies and surveys. Most of the projects involved are small and have not been evaluated in terms of their economic impacts. Many organizations appear to lack the capacity, funds, leadership, and information required to manage effective projects and to understand and navigate both their origin and destination countries' procedures. Such problems are not unique to Africa. For example, these findings are similar to the conclusions of Paul and Gammage (2004) on Salvadoran associations in the United States. The interviews also underline the difficulties facing development work in Africa: a poor investment climate, inadequate ports and customs facilities, excessive red tape, and lack of trust in governments.

Governments in a number of large labor-sending countries have attempted to develop schemes to channel collective remittances into public revenue, investment, or community development. Given the private nature of these transactions, policy interventions have focused either on appropriating some of the flow, largely without success, or on creating incentives to change individual or household behavior. For example, a few governments have offered matching grants for remittances from diaspora groups or HTAs to attract funding for specific community projects. The best known of these matching schemes is Mexico's 3-for-1 program, under which the local, state, and federal governments all contribute US$1 for every US$1 of remittances sent to a community for a designated development project. Colombia, according to the International Organization for Migration in Bogotá, also provides government funding to match migrant group funds for local projects benefiting vulnerable populations.

Little evaluation of the impact of these programs has been done. Resources have gone primarily to rural areas, where they have increased the supply of essential services (health, education, roads, and electricity). In certain cases, HTAs fund the construction of soccer fields and community halls but do not fund the ongoing maintenance of these facilities. It is difficult to assess whether these investments—and the matching grants— have gone to the highest-priority projects or have been diverted from other regions with a great need of assistance from fiscally constrained governments (World Bank 2005). Meanwhile, proponents argue that HTA involvement ensures that programs are focused on community needs, and that the associations promote increased accountability and transparency of local and national authorities (Page and Plaza 2006).

Three limitations on the potential for HTAs to serve as conduits for broader development projects also apply to HTA initiatives in Africa:

- They may not have the best information on the needs of the local community, or they may have different priorities
- The capacity of HTAs to scale-up or form partnerships is limited by the fact that their members are volunteers and their fundraising ability is finite[21]
- They can become divided and weaken their own advocacy potential (Newland and Patrick 2004; World Bank 2006).

In the context of Africa, support based on regional ties may exacerbate income disparities, particularly since, in many African countries, outmigration is concentrated in a few areas. Finally, volunteer initiatives are often driven by individuals, and a lack of institutionalized support could threaten the sustainability of projects.

Transfers of Technology and Skills

A diaspora can be an important source and facilitator of research and innovation, technology transfer, and skills development. Japan, the Republic of Korea, and Taiwan, China are examples of economies that have relied on their diasporas as knowledge sources. The governments in these economies promoted the return of foreign-educated students or established networks of knowledge exchange with them (Pack and Page 1994).

Other developed countries with large, skilled emigrant populations have also been able to tap their expatriates and develop some form of mentor-sponsor model in certain sectors or industries.

Diaspora involvement in origin countries' economies can take several forms (Kuznetsov 2006; Plaza 2008a):

- Licensing agreements to facilitate the transfer of technology and know-how between diaspora-owned or -managed firms in origin and destination countries
- Direct investment in local firms as a joint venture
- Knowledge spillovers, as when diaspora members assume top managerial positions in foreign-owned firms within their country of origin
- Involvement in science or professional networks that promote research in destination countries directed toward the needs of origin countries
- Temporary or virtual return, through extended visits or electronic communication in professional fields such as medicine and engineering
- Return to permanent employment in the sending country after work experience in the host country.

There has been a shift in the discussion from viewing emigration of skilled people as a loss for a country to viewing skilled migration as an opportunity to get trade and investment projects and new knowledge. Chapter 6, "The Financial Consequences of High-Skilled Emigration: Lessons from African Doctors Abroad," by Michael Clemens, contributes to the literature on analyzing the migration of skilled people as an opportunity for a country, or what is called the diaspora model. The idea is not to keep skilled people at home but to encourage those nationals abroad to participate in the development of their countries both at home and abroad. The chapter discusses how the departure of skilled professionals from developing countries is frequently suspected of producing a range of losses to their countries of origin.

The chapter also addresses the financial portion of those suspected losses. It uses new data on African physicians in North America to establish the following key facts relevant to the alleged financial loss that their residence abroad imposes on their countries of origin:

- About half of these physicians received their medical degrees outside of their home countries

- Those trained in their home countries typically spent more than five years rendering service in those countries before departing
- The typical African-trained physician who is a long-term emigrant to North America has remitted at least roughly twice the cost of his or her medical training to people in the home country (including those who remit nothing).

These facts suggest that there should be a reconsideration of the most common policy recommendations to mitigate the financial effects of high-skill emigration. Many of the skilled migrants contribute by sending collective remittances to construct hospitals and by returning for short-term visits to perform surgeries.

The term "diaspora knowledge networks" is often used by social scientists to refer to vast numbers of "skilled personnel who migrate every year from their home countries to join thousands and millions of their country-men and women residing in countries other than their own" (Mahroum, Eldridge, and Daar 2006, page 26).[22] There are three types of diaspora knowledge networks:[23]

- *Scientists and research and development personnel networks,* which provide knowledge, mentoring expertise, and finance (venture capital).
- *Professional and business networks,* which are regional or local networks of skilled diaspora members located in larger cities (Saxenian 2002a, 2002b). Arora and Gambardella (2004) and Commander and others (2004) describe the role of diasporas in the software industry. Indian professionals helped to promote India as an outsourcing destination, for example. Relevant associations provide technical assistance and organize conferences, investment forums to match investors with counterparts at home, and recruitment fairs. African examples include the Ghanaian Doctors and Dentists Association–UK and the Association of Kenyan Professionals in Atlanta, Georgia.
- *Global knowledge networks,* which are transnational networks linking global regions with diasporas' origin country.[24] Several African countries are attempting to organize their diasporas in order to gain more benefits from nationals abroad. Diaspora members sometimes maintain residences in both their origin and destination countries. In other cases, migrants have a primary residence abroad but return to their origin countries yearly to support specific activities. These movements and exchanges of knowledge and skills benefit those who reside in the

origin countries (Easterly and Nyarko 2008). Increasing these benefits will require efforts to survey diasporas' human resources, create active networks, and develop specific activities and programs. For example, there are some small pilot initiatives that invite diaspora members to teach courses in African universities.[25]

An Emerging Policy Agenda to Maximize the Benefits of Diasporas

Both sending and receiving countries are beginning to implement policies to boost flows of financial resources, information, and technology from diasporas. Several developing countries (for example, China, India, the Philippines, and several African countries) have set up agencies and initiatives to engage with diasporas. Elsewhere, such efforts and initiatives have met with little success (for example, in Armenia, Colombia, Mexico, Moldova, Peru, and South Africa). Some initiatives have lost momentum and faded away (Chaparro, Jaramillo, and Quintero 1994; Dickinson 2003) (for example, Conectandonos al Futuro, El Salvador; Red Caldas, Colombia; and Red Cientifica Peruana, Peru). The South African Network of Skills Abroad has also experienced a reduction in the number of new members since its inception in 1998 (Marks 2004).

Several high-income countries (for example, Australia, Ireland, Israel, and the United Kingdom) have implemented initiatives to strengthen engagement with their diasporas (Finch, Andrew, and Latorre 2010; Kingslye, Sand, and White 2009). In addition, the governments of high-income countries (for example, France, Italy, the Netherlands, Spain, the United Kingdom, and the United States) are working with developing-country diaspora groups not only to promote the development of origin countries, but also to further the destination country's foreign policy objectives. Often such initiatives (for example, the French codevelopment policy or the European mobility partnership agreements) aim to "better manage migration flows, and in particular to fight illegal migration."[26]

Dual or Multiple Citizenship

Holding dual or multiple citizenship provides an important link between diasporas and their home countries (Ionescu 2006). It can also improve both a diaspora's connection with its origin country and its integration into the destination country.[27] Citizenship and residency rights are important determinants of a diaspora's participation in trade, investment, and technology transfer with its origin country (Cheran 2004), and make it easier to travel and own land. Origin countries that allow dual citizenship also benefit because their migrants are then more willing to adopt the host country's citizenship, which can improve their earnings and thus their ability to send remittances and invest in the origin country.[28]

Immigrants from some countries that allowed dual citizenship during the 1990s and 2000s (Brazil, Colombia, Costa Rica, the Dominican Republic, and Ecuador) have experienced a rise in earnings in the United States (Mazzolari 2007), because they acquired legal status and can have access to better jobs. Mazzolari's findings indicate that immigrants from countries that were granted dual citizenship during the 1990s experienced a 3.6-percentage-point increase in the probability of full-time work relative to other Latin American immigrant groups. They also experienced relative earnings gains and relied less on welfare (Mazzolari 2007). Destination countries can also benefit by providing dual citizenship, which can help foster the assimilation of their immigrants.

Origin countries have increased their acceptance of dual citizenship. For example, 10 Latin American countries—Brazil, Colombia, Costa Rica, the Dominican Republic, Ecuador, El Salvador, Mexico, Panama, Peru, and Uruguay—passed new laws in the 1990s and 2000s on dual nationality or citizenship (Jones-Correa 2001). In some cases, the acceptance of such laws was under pressure from diaspora groups (for example, India and Kenya).[29] Some countries, however, have historically been opposed to dual citizenship status (for example, most of the former Soviet republics). About half of the African countries with available information allow for dual citizenship (see table 2). Interest has also increased in providing dual citizenship to the children or grandchildren of migrants, in order to encourage their ties to origin countries. But the potential gains for origin countries are limited because dual citizenship is not permitted in many destination countries.

Chiswick (1978) was the first to show a positive impact of naturalization on earnings. Recent studies show that the integration of migrants in destination countries amplifies their involvement in the development of their countries of origin (de Haas 2006). Studies for Canada and the United States seem to support the existence of a citizenship premium for both countries, while European studies show mixed results (Bevelander and Pendakur

TABLE 2
Countries Permitting and Prohibiting Dual Citizenship for Adults

Country	Dual citizenship Yes	Dual citizenship No	Country	Dual citizenship Yes	Dual citizenship No
Algeria	X		Libya		X
Angola	X		Madagascar		X
Benin	X		Malawi		X
Botswana		X	Mali		X
Burkina Faso	X		Mauritania		X
Burundi	X		Mauritius	X	
Cameroon		X	Morocco	X	
Cape Verde	X		Mozambique		X
Central African Republic	X		Namibia	X	
Chad	—	—	Niger		X
Comoros	—	—	Nigeria	X	
Congo, Dem. Rep.		X	Rwanda	X	
Congo, Rep.		X	São Tomé and Principe	—	—
Côte d'Ivoire	X		Senegal		X
Djibouti		X	Seychelles		X
Egypt, Arab Rep.	X		Sierra Leone	X	
Equatorial Guinea		X	Somalia		X
Eritrea		X	South Africa	X	
Ethiopia		X	Sudan	—	—
Gabon		X	Swaziland		X
Gambia	X		Tanzania	X[a]	
Ghana	X		Togo	X	
Guinea		X	Tunisia	X	
Guinea-Bissau	—	—	Uganda	X	
Kenya	X		Zambia (in draft constitution)		X
Lesotho		X	Zimbabwe		X
Liberia		X			

Sources: Compilation by Sonia Plaza and Dilip Ratha based on Brown (2009). Information for Africa was collected from interviews conducted by Plaza and Ratha with African countries' embassies and consular services in London; Paris; Pretoria; and Washington, DC. Other sources: http://www.multiplecitizenship.com/countrylist.html;
http://www.cic.gc.ca/english/resources/publications/ dual-citizenship.asp; and
http://allafrica.com/stories/201001200400.html.
a. In process.
— = Not available.

2009). According to Cheran (2004), the status of diaspora members is relevant, and citizenship or residency rights are important in determining their participation in trade, investment, and knowledge transfer.

Some origin countries do not allow dual citizenship but offer identification card schemes in destination countries. In certain cases, these cards grant visa rights to diasporas. For example, Ethiopia, India, and Mexico offer special identification cards that entitle migrants to specific rights.

Mexico issues a *matrícula consular* to Mexicans living in the United States for identification, and India issues a Person of Indian Origin card that allows for entry without a visa during the period of its validity.[30] The Ethiopian government enacted a law in 2002 to permit Ethiopian migrants with foreign citizenship to be treated as nationals if they hold a Person of Ethiopian Origin card, locally known as the "yellow card." The yellow card entitles its holder to most of the rights and privileges of an Ethiopian citizen, such as entry into Ethiopia without a visa, the right to own residential property, and the right to live and work in the country without additional permits. But yellow-card holders may not vote, be elected to political office, or be employed in national defense, security, or foreign affairs (*Federal Negarit Gazeta* 2002).

Voting Rights

Origin countries can strengthen diaspora ties by allowing their citizens who reside abroad to vote without returning. Some countries give nationals abroad voting rights, and some reserve a specific number of seats in parliament for diaspora representatives. African countries have different modalities for voting. Some countries allow their citizens to vote abroad for presidential and legislative elections. Others allow their citizens living abroad to vote, but only in person. Others do not allow citizens to vote while they are abroad.

Some African countries that confer voting rights on their diasporas require advanced registration or allow voting in person only. In other countries, voting by postal ballot is also possible. Those who permanently live abroad can register with an embassy or consulate in the country of their permanent residence and can vote there. But the costs involved in registration may be high. For example, South Africa approved voting rights for Global South Africans in 2009, but was unable to register voters in most foreign countries for the 2009 elections. Only some 16,000 voters (out of the estimated 1.2 million South African citizens living abroad) who had been registered well in advance were able to participate in the 2009 elections. Similarly, members of the Nigerian diaspora requested the Independent National Electoral Commission to register Nigerians abroad so they could participate in the 2011 elections.[31] The extent of participation also depends on whether voting is required (for example, Peru) or voluntary (for example, Argentina).

Interviews with diaspora groups and individuals showed that granting voting rights to the diaspora is an important means of encouraging greater engagement with origin countries. Rwanda provides a useful example of an effort to engage the diaspora through reaching out and encouraging voting by foreign citizens.[32]

Destination Countries' Support for Diasporas

Some destination countries are devoting resources to helping diasporas promote the development of their countries of origin. Canada, France, Germany, Italy, Spain, the United States, and the European Union, among other governments and institutions, are becoming more interested in working with the diasporas residing in their countries.

Some of their initiatives are at the initial stage of implementation and remain to be assessed. Other programs, such as those promoting return, have not been successful at all.[33] One area of focus has been the reduction in fees for transferring remittances (see chapter 2). But there are few well-defined programs that facilitate diaspora trade, investment, and technology operations apart from small grants or matching grants initiatives (for example, the Development Marketplace for the African Diaspora in Europe, the African Development Marketplace, and the Joint Migration and Development Initiative).

There is little information on initiatives and few external evaluations of their effectiveness (de Haas 2006). For example, the White House has focused on engaging with diaspora communities as a "core element" of U.S. foreign policy, with an emphasis on the role that diasporas can play in their origin countries (for example, Haiti relief). The U.S. State Department and the U.S. Agency for International Development have a new initiative called the Diaspora Networks Alliance.[34]

Canada, France, the Netherlands, and the European Commission have funded development projects executed by diaspora groups. The Netherlands has awarded grants to projects aimed at building migrant organizations' capacity.

In 2007, France added cofunding of diaspora projects to its menu for codevelopment. At the 25th Annual Africa-France Summit, participating heads of state decided "to place the African diasporas living in France at the center of the migration and development strategies, promoting their involvement in the economic and social development of their country of origin by means of codevelopment programs, encouraging migrant business projects, and mobilizing their savings for social and productive investment."[35]

Incentives to Return Offered by Migrant-Receiving Countries

Since the 1970s, some European countries (Germany since 1972, the Netherlands since 1975, France since 1977, and Spain since 2008)[36] have encouraged return migration by providing money to immigrants and financing projects to employ returnees (Constant and Massey 2002). But few migrants have participated, and most projects have not been successful.

For example, most projects undertaken by the French Development Program of Local Migration (Programme Developpement Local Migration) to employ Malian and Senegalese returnees could not be sustained over the long term (Lacroix 2003). The assumption that migrants would return home permanently and establish new firms has not proved correct, either. Several of developed countries' policies have been too tightly conditioned on the migrant's permanent return or have assumed that all the migrants are entrepreneurs. The new focus is more on the mobility of the migrants, which implies virtual, short-term, and permanent return, but also gives freedom to diaspora individuals to go home and to return to their host country without losing their legal status or their citizenship.

In the late 1990s, there was a change in this approach to encouraging the return of not only the unskilled, but also the skilled, diaspora. The approach shifted to encourage circular migration, codevelopment, reintegration of temporary workers in their home countries, and the return of skilled migrants back to Africa. For example, France's pact on concerted migration management with Senegal seeks the voluntary return of medical doctors and other health professionals in France by offering research equipment or the prospect of joint university appointments.[37] In addition, the new mobility partnership agreements also establish circular migration schemes for professional education and expert missions by members of the diaspora.

In chapter 7, "France's Codevelopment Program: Financial and Fiscal Incentives to Promote Diaspora Entrepreneurship and Transfers," Marion Panizzon analyzes France's codevelopment policy. Starting out as a cofunding scheme, France would financially match the diaspora's financial transfers to their countries of origin with development aid. In so doing, codevelopment seeks to associate a migrant-receiving country with migrants' transnational engagements.

The chapter describes the evolution of codevelopment policies and the involvement of the diaspora, and identifies five phases:

- Assisting with the integration of migrants
- Encouraging migrants to leave
- Providing aid with the goal of reducing migratory pressures
- Cofinancing diaspora contributions to public goods in countries of origin
- Promoting savings and tax breaks for investment in home countries.

Thus, a particular focus of this chapter is on understanding what motivated France to incentivize migrants to increase their savings by encouraging the use of banks; how the provision of tax breaks on migrants' revenues (defiscalization) contributes to source-country development; and what their effects on migratory flows are.

In terms of policy, we find that the strategy of encouraging the use of banks is nationality-neutral compared to the classic diaspora cofunding scheme, which had often relied on a specific diaspora's postcolonial ties to France. In addition, financial service providers can tap into new migrants' clients, offering attractive interest rates and promoting a better use of migrants' savings than if collected by the diaspora.

Increasing participation of financial service providers and providing tax breaks for migrants' savings are codevelopment actions that could be replicated on a more global scale. However, the previous codevelopment funding mechanism (matching funds) turned out to be a mixed success, because it was too tightly conditioned on the migrant's voluntary return. The two recent schemes (savings accounts and tax breaks) have not been evaluated yet, although there are only very few new migrant savers since migrants have to prove that they are legal migrants in France.

Temporary labor migration is seen by origin countries as a way for migrants to acquire skills abroad and bring them back home when they return. Examples include France's new pact with Benin and Senegal's government-run Retours vers l'agriculture plan, which includes an initiative to reintegrate returning migrants (Retours des immigrés vers l'agriculture, cofunded by the European Union and Spain in the amount of €20 million).

European governments, often in cooperation with the International Organization of Migration, have been implementing assisted voluntary return programs for almost three decades. Chapter 8, "The Migration for Development in Africa Experience and Beyond," by Ndioro Ndiaye, Susanne Melde, and Rougui Ndiaye-Coïc, presents the evolution of the Migration for Development in Africa (MIDA) program implemented by the International Organization of Migration. The program is a capacity-building initiative whose purpose is to promote development goals through the participation and contribution of members of the African diaspora. The author presents examples of MIDA projects on how to use the expertise, knowledge, and skills of diaspora members in their communities of origin. The initial objective of MIDA programs was to encourage permanent return. Since the objective was not achieved, the focus shifted to encouraging short, repeated visits and virtual return. However, there is a lack of impact evaluation of this program.

Governments are realizing the potential role migrants can play in providing lucrative networks with their native countries. In an effort to tap into these unique resources and facilitate remittances, knowledge sharing, and technology transfer, some source countries are creating policies designed to encourage long-term and long-distance linkages between emigrants and their countries of origin. Steps such as these enable immigrants to take part in the economic development of their countries of origin without having to return home. Temporary, virtual, and permanent return programs also offer alternatives to tap into the diaspora. The emphasis is on encouraging connections with their home country through visiting diaspora to share their knowledge. For example, the MIDA Great Lakes project involves missions, workshops, and roundtables to facilitate the exchange of knowledge between institutions in Burundi, the Democratic Republic of Congo, and Rwanda with the diaspora in Belgium.[38]

The United Nations Development Programme's Transfer of Knowledge through Expatriate Nationals (TOKTEN) projects support three-week to three-month development assignments for expatriates, at much lower costs than hiring professional consultants. But a recent evaluation of a TOKTEN program in Sri Lanka indicates that these services have not had a significant impact on the local institutions because the expatriates' involvement was not sustained (TOKTEN provides two visits at most) (Wanigaratne 2006). Similarly, an evaluation of the

Rwandan TOKTEN program in 2005–07, which involved visits by 47 volunteers to teach and provide technical assistance, emphasized that an average stay of less than two months and the variety of responsibilities constrained the transfer of knowledge to counterparts in host institutions (Touray 2008).

According to the OECD (2009), diaspora knowledge flows could increase if barriers to short-term and circular mobility were removed. There has been an increase in mobility partnership pacts between European Union countries and diasporas' origin countries. For example, an agreement with Cape Verde focuses on visa and border-control policies, while India has initiated discussions with the European Union focusing on the export of high-skilled professionals (Plaza 2009b). But more data and research are required to develop effective policies to encourage circular migration. The Swedish government has appointed an independent parliamentary committee to examine the connection between circular migration and development, with a report to be presented in March 2011 (Swedish Ministry of Justice 2010).

Return Initiatives by Sending Countries

A number of origin countries have introduced measures to encourage return by skilled migrants. The more successful efforts have been in Asia. One example is the Taiwan, China government's Hsinchu Industrial Park initiative, which in 2000 alone attracted more than 5,000 returning scientists (Saxenian 2002a, 2002b, 2006). Thailand has offered generous research funding and monetary incentives for return (Pang, Lansing, and Haines 2002). China has offered attractive salary packages, multiple-entry visas (in case a migrant has lost Chinese citizenship), and access to foreign exchange. Many programs to encourage return have met with only limited success, however, and studies of return migration suggest "that those who return may be those that have performed relatively poorly when abroad, while those who stay are the best and the brightest" (Lodigiani 2009).

Less information is available on African policies to encourage return. A study on return migrants in Côte d'Ivoire and Ghana found that policies that favor returnees above those who never left the country are likely to be counterproductive and to cause resentment (Ammassari 2006).

Experience from many of the government initiatives implemented by developing countries in Africa, Asia, and Latin America (for example, Mexico, Pakistan, Peru, and Turkey) have demonstrated that it is difficult to promote return, and particularly permanent return. Some returnees were not able to reenter local labor markets at a level appropriate for their skills and knowledge. For example, a lack of laboratories and equipment makes it difficult for scientists and researchers to keep up to date on the latest scientific developments worldwide. Some members of the diaspora may return with unrealistic expectations or may find it hard to readjust to local norms (OECD 2010).

African Governmental Initiatives to Engage the Diaspora

African governments are reaching out to the diaspora. Ghana, Nigeria, Senegal, and South Africa have launched several plans to incorporate their diaspora communities as partners in development projects. Several African countries (among them Ethiopia, Ghana, Mali, Nigeria, Rwanda, Senegal, Tanzania, and Uganda) have established institutions (at the agency or ministerial level) to interact with the diaspora.

These initiatives have taken various forms, ranging from the creation of dedicated ministries to deal with migrant communities to adding specific functions to the ministry of foreign affairs, ministry of interior, ministry of finance, ministry of trade, ministry of social affairs, ministry of youth, and so on. In addition, some governments have established institutions such as councils or decentralized entities that deal with migrant community issues. However, several of these initiatives have not maintained their momentum or have been discontinued with a change of government.[39]

To date, the interest of African governments in their diasporas has focused largely on those residing in countries outside Africa, such as in the OECD countries. Conferences and investment seminars, either at home or in the major capitals in OECD countries, are targeted to the diaspora outside Africa.

Chapter 9, "Reinforcing the Contributions of African Diasporas to Development," by Chukwu-Emeka Chikezie, offers some guidance to African governments seeking to make productive use of the resources of "their" diasporas for developmental gain. The guidance is drawn from the first 10 years of operation of the African Foundation for Development.

African governments would be wise to pay attention to the following four principles when trying to engage the African diaspora to contribute to their home country development:

- Try to be as inclusive as possible, since Africans in the diaspora often have different relationships and connections with their home countries depending on how and why they left their country, issues of identity, and their degree of trust in the government. For that reason, governments engaging with their diasporas must include everyone and not just the politically connected or those belonging to certain groups or elites.
- When governments look for the support of the diaspora, it is advisable to propose activities oriented toward developmental and results-oriented outcomes (enterprise development and job creation, health, education, infrastructure).
- Governments need to "know" and understand their diasporas in order to engage effectively with them.
- Governments need to be strategic in addressing needs, priorities, and strengths while not exacerbating capacity constraints. The objective is to focus diaspora efforts on their country's needs, and the activities supported must be demand-driven.

Diasporas not only contribute with remittances sent back home, but they also contribute with other forms of tangible and intangible capital. According to the author, there are five forms of diaspora capital, or what the author calls the "5Cs":

- Intellectual capital
- Financial capital
- Political capital
- Cultural capital
- Social capital.

By also factoring in diaspora motivations, chapter 9 argues that engaging diasporas in development efforts is not a one-way street, and it is vital for governments to pay attention to what is in it for diasporas as well. A key thrust of this chapter is that tapping into diasporas' resources does not let African governments off the hook in terms of marshalling leadership, good governance, and effective management, or of devising sound policies for development overall.

African governments typically face certain capacity constraints within state structures and institutions, and these constraints frame the development challenges they face. African diaspora groups also face a number of organizational constraints: most operate on a purely voluntary basis, so members must balance family and work obligations; organizations are not necessarily formally constituted as development organizations; and organizations often have multiple agendas.

While the growing interest of African governments in engaging the African diaspora as a development resource is logical, the diaspora is neither the silver bullet of development nor a panacea for all Africa's ills. Indeed, tapping into the African diaspora's resources does not reduce the need for home-grown solutions, sound leadership, effective management, and good governance as the absolute cornerstones of development in the 21st century. Rather, if anything, reinforcing the contributions of diasporas to development and taking them to a new level makes new and additional demands on African governments. Chapter 9 offers a number of specific recommendations for African governments and regional bodies, such as the African Union, and for what African governments can do to engage with their diaspora, given the capacity constraints that hamper most of their efforts.

There have been some proposals to take a more harmonized and integrated approach to the diaspora within each regional economic community. For example, there is a proposal for the creation of a regional diaspora office within the East African Community. The Economic Community of West African States has proposed establishing a dedicated financial instrument at a regional level to facilitate business contributions of the diaspora to the region. These proposals are more focused on the diaspora outside Africa. However, there are also some initiatives for establishing an integrated approach to cross-border payment systems, including the transfer of remittances in the Economic Community of West African States and in the Economic and Monetary Community of Central Africa.

Government institutions abroad, especially embassies and consulates, can play a key role in reaching out to the diaspora (Ionescu 2006). However, the survey conducted by Sonia Plaza and Dilip Ratha of embassies in Abu Dhabi; London; Paris; Pretoria; and Washington, DC, indicates a need to improve African governments' capacity and resources to sustain the activities of the ministries and institutions dealing with their communities abroad (box 2). Steps that could improve the engagement of embassies with diasporas include outreach programs to gain more information, the training of embassy staff in contacting diaspora members and facilitating investment and trade contacts, and the use of embassies as a vehicle for marketing investment and financial mechanisms such as diaspora bonds.

BOX 2

The Role of Embassies in Enabling Diasporas

Authors Sonia Plaza and Dilip Ratha conducted 48 interviews with government officials and diplomats of embassies in London; Paris; Pretoria; and Washington, DC to understand the role embassies are playing in enabling their diasporas to make economic contributions to their countries. The interviews revealed that there are few differences among embassies, whether from developed or developing countries, in this respect, and that most origin countries had only a limited engagement with the diaspora, although some embassies are implementing initiatives to reach their diaspora. Embassies provide consular services (for example, renewal of passports, visas, notary services) to their expatriate community but provide little information on trade and investment opportunities. Some of the difficulties embassies face in reaching their diasporas include:

- Lack of coordination among departments, especially between the embassy and consular offices
- Lack of adequate information on the number of migrants in a diaspora (especially since registration is optional)
- Migrants from politically unstable countries are less likely than those from stable countries to engage with the embassy
- Inadequate staff dedicated to working with the diaspora
- Need for capacity building in order for embassies to be able to reach out to their diasporas and facilitate investment, trade, and skill transfers.

Source: Plaza 2009a.

African governments are also working through the African Union (AU) on diaspora issues, which has resulted in the following:

- In 2003, at the AU's Executive Council, the AU agreed to actively engage the African diaspora.[40]
- In 2005, the AU formally designated the African diaspora as the "sixth region" of the AU's structure.
- In September 2008, the African Union Commission launched the Africa Diaspora Health Initiative to provide a platform by which health experts for the African diaspora can transfer information, skills, and expertise to their counterparts in Africa.
- The AU allocated 20 seats for the African diaspora in the AU Economic, Social and Cultural Council.
- The African Union Commission created the African Citizens Directorate to deal with overarching issues in the relationship between overseas diasporas and homeland governments.

The World Bank is supporting many of the diaspora activities of the AU and African governments. The World Bank's African Diaspora Program (launched in September 2007) partners with the AU, client countries, donors, and African Diaspora Professional Networks and hometown associations to enhance the contributions of African diasporas to development of their home countries.[41]

The AU's approach is to enable the diaspora to organize itself with AU support within the framework provided by executive organs of the AU, the Executive Council, and the Assembly, with the guidance of Member States. Despite these efforts, the mechanisms and the process for diaspora engagement are still being worked out. This is causing some frustration among diaspora communities, which in recent forums have expressed a reluctance to wait for AU directions before organizing themselves.[42]

The Business Environment

As with other potential investors and trading partners, migrants seeking to invest in or trade with African countries are often constrained by the poor business environment. Interview results stress the impediments of excessive red tape and customs delays. The diaspora requires a conducive business environment, a sound and transparent financial sector, rapid and efficient court systems, and a safe working environment

(Page and Plaza 2006). de Haas (2005) emphasizes that bad infrastructure, corruption, red tape, lack of macroeconomic stability, trade barriers, a lack of legal security, and a lack of trust in government institutions affect migrants' decisions to invest in their home countries and to return.

In chapter 10, "Migration and Productive Investment: A Conceptual Framework," Valeria Galetto presents a new theoretical framework for conceptualizing the relationship between migration and productive investment in migrants' communities of origin. Based on a detailed review of the literature and original empirical research, the author argues that investment is contingent on four main proximate factors:

- A minimum amount of money remitted or saved
- A minimum level of local development
- The presence of suitable investment opportunities
- The existence of specific household arrangements.

The framework offered in the paper:

- Explains low and high levels of productive investment in migrants' communities of origin
- Points to the mechanisms that generate those outcomes
- Helps identify the distal causes of productive investment
- Accounts for the disparate findings reported in the literature.

The chapter illustrates the proposed framework by applying it to the analysis of contrasting investment patterns of two migrant communities in western Michoacán, Mexico.

An examination of studies according to their reported level of productive investment (low or high) reveals several clear trends. One of the most important is that migration-driven investments are less likely to occur in communities that have poor public services, substandard infrastructure (lack of passable roads, schools, banks, and so forth), few natural resources (in particular, agricultural land), and a rudimentary economic structure. However, the inverse conditions do not seem to be sufficient for investment to occur; in addition to a minimal infrastructure and rich natural resources (in the case of rural areas), residents tend to invest in their communities of origin when they meet certain individual and household characteristics.

A survey of skilled South African migrants identified crime, the cost of living, taxation, and the quality of public and commercial services as the main barriers to conducting business (Plaza 2008a). Black and Castaldo (2009) report policies, laws, and regulations as the biggest obstacles to establishing a business by diaspora members and return migrants. According to the findings of case studies and interviews with members of the African diaspora, procedures governing business licenses, registrations, and exports and imports remain complicated. Indeed, some diaspora associations reported barriers to even shipping donated goods, citing, for example, cumbersome import procedures for donated books. That said, it is necessary that all merchandise meant for charity purposes fulfill the same inspection, quality-control, and certification processes required for other imports.

Governments can help facilitate diaspora networks through the Internet, professional associations, embassies abroad, and cultural events. Some origin countries are supporting long-term and long-distance linkages between emigrants and their countries of origin (Ghai 2004). In some countries, encouraging the growth of private sector networks may be more effective than direct government involvement in establishing links to the diaspora.

Some African governments are providing incentives to attract investment from the diaspora. For example, as mentioned, Ethiopia grants a yellow card to diaspora members, granting them the same benefits and rights as domestic investors. Additional investment incentives for both foreign investors and the diaspora include income tax exemptions for two to seven years, 100 percent duty exemption on the import of machinery and equipment for investment projects, and 100 percent customs exemption on spare parts whose value does not exceed 15 percent of the total value of capital goods imported (*Federal Negarit Gazeta* 2003).

Such policies have encouraged many in the Ethiopian diaspora to invest in small businesses in Ethiopia. Investments at this level include those in cafes, restaurants, retail shops, and transport services in big cities and small towns that were otherwise restricted to Ethiopian nationals living in the country (Chakco and Gebre 2009).[43] Some countries are considering having one window at a government institution for the diaspora in which all the paperwork for the different administrative levels can be handled. This could facilitate diaspora access to investment opportunities at home.

The treatment of potential diaspora investors remains controversial. Some diaspora members have complained that certain countries (for example, Burundi) have more favorable policies for foreign investors than for members of the diaspora. It may be better to provide efficient procedures for all investors, without requiring proof of the investor's origin and nationality. However, origin countries still could benefit from focusing their scarce resources on providing services to members of the diaspora and on moving beyond consular services to a broader range of support for diaspora investors.

Savings and Social Security Schemes

Governments can also mobilize resources from diasporas by encouraging their participation in social security, housing, and microfinance programs. The Philippines, for example, allows its citizens to enroll in or continue their social security coverage while abroad. Workers from the Philippines can also continue contributing to the Pag-IBIG Fund (Home Development Mutual Fund). Migrant workers can access this fund through diplomatic offices abroad (ADB 2004). Bangladesh has created a number of schemes tailored to investors and nonresidents, such as savings accounts in foreign currencies. Some of these initiatives could be implemented in Africa to generate savings.

Conclusions

This volume covers a diverse range of diaspora issues and provides a number of experiences that are relevant for policy makers in both developed and developing countries. The main findings are as follows:

- *Efforts to understand the size and characteristics of the diaspora should be a high priority for developing countries interested in harnessing diaspora resources.* Lack of adequate data on the diaspora impairs efforts to improve the contributions the diaspora can make to the origin country. The size of the African diaspora is larger than the official estimate of 30.6 million migrants. Many migrants are not counted in national surveys, especially within the African continent itself, and many descendants of migrants still have emotional ties to the country of their ancestors. Case studies indicate that networks of diaspora families and friends send funds for development purposes such as constructing schools, providing supplies to schools or hospitals, supporting orphans, and supporting small-scale projects. However, little is known about the scale or impact of such activities.

- *Diasporas facilitate cross-border trade, investment, and access to advanced technology and skills.* Diaspora networks play an important role in cross-border exchanges of market information about trade and regulations. Diaspora members may also invest directly in origin countries or provide their expertise to assist investments by multinational firms.

Compared with other foreign investors, members of diasporas may accept lower interest rates on loans to home countries, because

- ○ They have emotional ties to home countries
- ○ Better access to information may allow them to lower risk premium compared to other foreign investors
- ○ They may have local currency liabilities that makes them less worried than other investors about the potential for currency devaluation or the forced conversion of assets denominated in foreign currencies to local currencies. Diaspora bonds targeted to nationals residing abroad can open opportunities for investment and facilitate investment in their home countries.

Diasporas may provide origin countries access to advanced technology and scarce skills. While the role of the diaspora in technology transfer is well documented in many countries, particularly China and India, the evidence for African countries is limited.

- *Harnessing diaspora contributions in the areas of trade, investment, and technology requires a supportive business climate.* Property rights, security, elimination of red tape, and good infrastructure encourage diasporas to invest back home. Diaspora members may be more willing than other investors to take risks in their own country, but such investments require favorable working conditions. Providing voting rights and dual citizenship to migrants can help maintain their ties to origin countries, and dual citizenship can encourage trade and investment by enabling migrants to avoid constraints on business activities faced by foreigners. The devotion of more embassy staff to diaspora issues, and adequate training of these staff, would facilitate better services and enhance linkages. In addition, better coordination among different departments within embassies and governments will increase efficiency in building relationships with diasporas and their networks.

- *Finally, more economic and multidisciplinary analysis is required to guide policy.* Even with all the solid empirical studies and the evaluations of the impact of migration programs and policies available, many questions remain unanswered.

Notes

1. See, for example, Barre and others (2003); Khadria (1999); Kuznetsov (2006); Meyer and Brown (1999); Pack and Page (1994); Saxenian (2002a, 2002b, 2004, 2006); Westcott (2006); and Wickramasekara (2009).
2. See, for example, Crush (2010b); Lowell and Genova (2004); Lucas (2004); Orozco (2003, 2006a, 2006b); and Portes, Escobar, and Radford (2007).
3. See, for example, Bakewell (2008); Chikezie (2000); Mohan and Zack-Williams (2002); and Mohamoud (2003, 2010).
4. See Rauch (2001) for a review on business networks.
5. A growing body of research suggests that diasporas and country networks abroad are an important reservoir of knowledge of trade and investment opportunities. This literature emphasizes that trade and migration are complements as opposed to substitutes. See Bandyopadhyay, Coughlin, and Wall (2008); Bardhan and Guhathakurta (2004); Bettin and Turco (2008); Blanes (2005); Blanes and Martin-Montaner (2006); Blanes Cristobal (2004); Bryant and Law (2004); Co, Euzent, and Martin (2004); Combes, Lafourcade, and Mayer (2003); Dolman (2008); Dunlevy (2003, 2006); Dunlevy and Hutchinson (1999); Foad (2008); Girma and Yu (2002); Gould (1990, 1994); Head and Ries (1998); Helliwel (1997); Herander and Saavedra (2005); Hutchinson and Dunlevy (2001); Light, Zhou, and Kim (2002); Morgenroth and O'Brien (2008); Rauch (2003); Rauch and Trindade (1999, 2002); Wagner, Head, and Ries (2002).
6. Countries that are far apart trade much less than countries that are nearby. Colonial ties are important. Landlocked countries trade less.
7. Transnational companies make investments based on their ethnic ties (Aykut and Ratha 2004). For example, some ethnic Korean companies invest in Kazakhstan and some ethnic Chinese companies invest in the East Asia and Pacific Region.
8. http://www.eac.int/invest/index.php?option=com_content&view=article&id= 53:eac-diaspora&catid=39:global-east-africans.
9. Data from African household surveys conducted in Burkina Faso, Kenya, Nigeria, Senegal, South Africa and Uganda do not indicate that African migrants invest in agricultural equipment (Plaza, Navarrete and Ratha 2011).
10. http://www.rwandandiaspora.gov.rw/rwanda-investment/housing.html.
11. http://www.slideshare.net/ifad/vincent-okele.
12. This updates the previously available estimates for Sub-Saharan Africa in Ratha, Mohapatra, and Plaza (2009).

13. For example, the Liberian Diaspora Social Investment Fund, the Rwandan Diaspora Mutual Fund, and the Zambia First Investment Fund.

14. Several diaspora investment funds have been created or are in the process of creation and registration, such as the Diaspora Unit Trust Funds Schemes, a collective investment scheme licensed by the Capital Markets Authority of Kenya, under section 12 of Regulations 2001. See http://www.mobilepay.co.ke/tangaza/2010/04/kenyans-abroad-to-benefit-from-the-diaspora-investment-fund/.

15. A private company, PHB Asset Management Limited, a subsidiary of Bank PHB Plc, has been selected to manage the US$200 million diaspora investment fund. This fund was set up by the Nigerians in Diaspora Organisation Europe in 2008. See http://timbuktuchronicles.blogspot.com/2008/03/diaspora-investment-fund.html.

16. For example, the countries with the largest numbers of Ghanaians are the United Kingdom and the United States (about 100,000 migrants each), Germany (34,000), Italy (50,000), and the Netherlands (20,000). Accordingly, there are about 100 Ghanaian associations in the United Kingdom (Van Hear, Pieke, and Vertovec 2004), 200 in the United States (Orozco 2006c), 21 in Germany, and 70 in the Netherlands.

17. The forum, a nonprofit organization formed in June 2005 in South Africa, is a network of about 40 Zimbabwean organizations (http://www.zimcsoforum .org/index.php).

18. Those interviewed include members of diaspora organizations in Denmark, South Africa, the United Kingdom, and the United States, and embassy officials in France, South Africa, the United Arab Emirates, the United Kingdom, and the United States.

19. Research interviews with African diaspora organizations in the United States were also conducted. The interviews covered 10 groups from Ethiopia, Liberia, Mali, Nigeria, and two organizations covering Africa.

20. Trans and Vammen (2008) describe an association that sends regular donations to the Eritrean state to support development projects.

21. Interviews with African diaspora organizations in the United States from Ethiopia, Liberia, Mali, Nigeria, and two with continental coverage indicated that their members volunteer their time and work for the diaspora association's activities after normal work hours. To raise funds, these associations sponsored runners in marathons and organized sales of arts and crafts and other events. Membership fees are small, so they cannot fully cover the associations' activities.

22. See also Kuznetsov (2006) and Meyer and Quattiaus (2006). Meyer and Brown (1999) categorize the involvement of diasporas into three types: (a) student networks, (b) local associations of skilled expatriates, and (c) scientific diaspora networks.

23. For example, associations of Chinese and Indian immigrant scientists and engineers exchange information and collaborate in research and development

projects with scientists in their countries of origin (Saxenian 2002a, 2002b). Financing local sabbatical stays for researchers living abroad and the opportunity to teach short courses or workshops are good measures to promote exchange. African associations under this category include the International Society of African Scientists (Delaware) and the Ethiopian Scientific Society (Washington, DC).

24. See Plaza (2008a, box 1) for a description of Chile Global.

25. For example, the Carnegie-Institute for Advanced Study Regional Initiative in Science and Education (RISE) aims to strengthen higher education in Sub-Saharan Africa by increasing the number of qualified faculty teaching in Africa's universities. The diaspora can contribute by teaching short courses, hosting RISE students at labs abroad, and engaging in collaborative research. The Nelson Mandela Research Center hosts professors from the diaspora to teach in African universities.

26. "Circular migration and mobility partnerships between the European Union and third countries," European Union press release, May 16, 2007; http://europa.eu/rapid/pressReleasesAction.do?reference=MEMO/07/197.

27. A person can acquire citizenship by place of birth (the *jus soli* rule of citizenship), by descent according to blood kinship (*jus sanguinis*), or by naturalization. Most countries apply one or a combination of the three rules. Canada and the United States are the only developed countries that still offer birthright citizenship to tourists and undocumented people.

28. Becoming a citizen appears to result in increased earnings in the United States (Chiswick 1978), although studies on European citizenship show mixed results (Bevelander and Pendakur 2009).

29. For Kenya, see http://www.cnn.com/2010/WORLD/africa/08/05/kenya.elections/index.html.

30. The Person of Indian Origin card also allows a person who holds an Indian passport access to all facilities in the matter of acquisition, holding, transfer, and disposal of immovable properties in India except in matters relating to the acquisition of agricultural or plantation properties. This card does not allow the holder to vote.

31. See http://www.afriqueavenir.org/en/2010/08/03/nigerians-in-the-diaspora-demand-voting-rights-in-2011-election/.

32. In preparation for the elections, a delegation of the National Electoral Commission visited various countries (Belgium, Burundi, Denmark, France, Germany, Kenya, Norway, Sweden, Switzerland, and Uganda) to inform émigrés about the electoral process. Foreign citizens participated in Rwandan presidential elections in August 2010 for the first time since the civil war. Of the 17,824 registered voters in the diaspora, 14,242 (78 percent) cast valid votes (http://global.factiva.com/redir/default.aspx?p=sta&ep=AE&an=AFNWS00020100810 e68a000n7&fid=300516908&cat=a&aid=9JOI000500&ns=53&fn=diaspora&ft= g&OD=V2AUbjNaqd6b6yKMegonfnoY9oOdATkhWR19knPBTvmljPNVjs% 2fEl5nw%3d%3d%).

33. See the Reintegration of Emigrant Manpower and the Promotion of Local Opportunities for Development (REMPLOD) research project (Van Dijk and others 1978).
34. http://www.usaid.gov/our_work/global_partnerships/gda/remittances.html.
35. http://www.ambafrance-uk.org/France-Africa-Summit-conclusions.html.
36. https://blogs.worldbank.org/peoplemove/volunteers-wanted-will-spain-success fully-entice-unemployed-migrants-to-leave.
37. Sénat, Le Co-développement à l'essai, Travaux Parlementaires, Rapports d'information, Co-development pilot, Parliamentary work; http: www.senat .fr/rap.
38. http://www.migration4development.org/content/mida-migration-development-africa.
39. Nigeria launched a dialogue with Nigerians abroad to incorporate their views into national development policies. A 2003–05 Ghanaian poverty reduction strategy paper proposed establishing a Non-Resident Ghanaian Fund for poverty projects, but it was never implemented. A 2007 Kenya diaspora bill, designed to increase benefits from the diaspora, was never passed.
40. This mandate led to the adoption of a new Article 3: "to invite and encourage the full participation of the African diaspora as an important part of our continent, in the building of the AU" (Legwaila 2006).
41. The World Bank's strategy to engage the African diaspora has three pillars: (a) working with the African Union Commission, (b) working with country governments to assist in creating "enabling environments" for diaspora engagement, and (c) working with development partners to support diaspora development projects in Africa. In July 2008, the Bank signed an agreement with the AU.
42. See the report from an AU–UN gathering of the diaspora in New York, October 20–21, 2010; http://kingdomzx.net/forum/topics/report-from-recent-african?xg_ source=activity.
43. Paper presented at the Diaspora for Development Conference, World Bank, Washington, DC, July 2009.

References

ADB (Asian Development Bank). 2004. "Technical Assistance for the Southeast Asia Workers' Remittance Study." http://www.adb.org/Documents/TARs/REG/tar-stu-38233.pdf. Accessed February 18, 2011. TAR: STU 38233.

African Union. 2005. "Report of the Meeting of Experts from Member States on the Definition of the African Diaspora." Addis Ababa, April 11–12.

Ahmed, S. 2000. *Strange Encounters: Embodied Others in Post-Coloniality.* London: Routledge.

Ammassari, S. 2006. "From Nation-Building to Entrepreneurship: The Impact of Elite Return Migrants in Cote d'Ivoire and Ghana." Paper presented at the International Workshop on Migration and Poverty in West Africa, University of Sussex, United Kingdom, March 13–14.

Arora, Ashish, and Alfonso Gambardella, 2004. "The Globalization of the Software Industry: Perspectives and Opportunities for Developed and Developing Countries." NBER Working Papers 10538, National Bureau of Economic Research, Cambridge, MA.

Aydagul, B., Suhas Ketkar, and Dilip Ratha. 2010. "Diaspora Bonds for Funding Education." Draft Paper presented at a meeting of the Soros Foundation, New York.

Aykut, Dilek, and Dilip Ratha. 2004. "South-South FDI Flows: How Big Are They?" *Transnational Corporations* 13 (1): 149–76.

Bakewell, Oliver. 2008. "In Search of the Diaspora within Africa." *Africa Diaspora* 1 (1): 5–27.

Bandyopadhyay, Subhayu, Cletus C. Coughlin, and Howard J. Wall. 2008. "Ethnic Networks and U.S. Exports." *Review of International Economics* 16 (1): 199–213.

Bardhan, Ashok Deo, and Subhrajit Guhathakurta. 2004. "Global Linkages of Subnational Regions: Coastal Exports and International Networks." *Contemporary Economic Policy* 22 (2): 225–236.

Barré, Remi, V. Hernández, J.-B. Meyer, and D. Vinck. 2003. "Diasporas scientifiques. Comment les pays en développement peuvent-ils tirer parti de leurs chercheurs et de leursingénieurs expatriés?" Institute de Recherche pour le Développement, IRD éditions, Paris.

Bettin, Giulia, and Alessia Lo Turco. 2008. "A Cross Country View On South-North Migration And Trade: Dissecting the Channels." (Revised March 31, 2010.) http://ssrn.com/abstract=1233544.

Bevelander, P., and R. Pendakur. 2009. "Citizenship, Co-ethnic Populations and Employment Probabilities of Immigrants in Sweden." Working Paper No. 4495, Institute for the Study of Labor, Bonn.

Black, R., and A. Castaldo. 2009. "Return Migration and Entrepreneurship in Ghana and Côte d'Ivoire: The Role of Capital Transfers." *Tijdschrift voor Economische en Sociale Geografie* 100 (1): 44–58.

Black, R., K. Koser, K. Munk, G. Atfield, L. D'Onofrio, and R. Tiemoko. 2004. *Understanding Voluntary Return.* Home Office Online Reports. London: Home Office.

Blanes, J. V. 2005: "Does Immigration Help to Explain Intra-Industry Trade? Evidence for Spain." *Review of World Economics* 141 (2): 244–70.

Blanes, J. V., and J. A. Martín-Montaner. 2006. "Migration Flows and Intra-Industry Trade Adjustment." *Review of World Economics* 142 (3): 568–85.

Blanes Cristóbal, José Vicente. 2004. "Does Immigration Help to Explain Intra-Industry Trade? Evidence for Spain." Economic Working Papers at Centro de Estudios Andaluces E2004/29, Centro de Estudios Andaluces, Seville.

Brown, Jan H. 2009. "Dual Citizenship: Living on Both Sides of the Global Fence." *NYSBA International Law Practicum* 22 (Autumn): 2.

Bryant, J., and D. Law. 2004. "New Zealand's Diaspora and Overseas-born Population." Working Paper 04/13, Wellington, New Zealand Treasury. http://www.treasury.govt.nz/publications/research-policy/wp/2004/04-13.

Business Asia. 1994. "Human Reunification." 26: 5–6.

Cassini, S. 2005. "Negotiating Personal Success and Social Responsibility: Assessing the Developmental Impact of Ghanaian Migrants' Business Enterprises in Ghana." International School for Humanities and Social Sciences. Master's thesis, University of Amsterdam.

Chakco, E., and P. Gebre. 2009. "Leveraging the Diaspora for Development: Lessons from Ethiopia." Paper presented at the International Conference on Diaspora for Development, World Bank, Washington, DC, July 13–14.

Chaparro, Fernando, H. Jaramillo, and V. Quintero 1994. "Role of Diaspora in Facilitating Participation in Global Knowledge Networks: Lessons of Red Caldas in Colombia." Report prepared for the Knowledge for Development Program of the World Bank, Bogotá.

Cheran, R. 2004. "Diaspora Circulation and Transnationalism as Agents for Change in the Post-conflict Zones of Sri Lanka." Policy paper submitted to the Berghof Foundation for Conflict Management, Berlin.

Chikezie, Chukwu-Emeka. 2000. "Africans Help their Homelands." *West Africa* 13 (November): 12–4.

Chiswick, Barry. 1978. "The Effect of Americanization on the Earnings of Foreign-born Men." *Journal of Political Economy* 86 (5): 897–921.

Co, Catherine Y., Patricia Euzent, and Thomas Martin. 2004. "The Export Effect of Immigration into the USA." Applied Economics 36 (6): 573–83.

Combes, Pierre-Philippe, Miren Lafourcade, and Theirry Mayer. 2003. "Can Business and Social Networks Explain the Border Effect Puzzle?" Centre for Economic Policy Research Discussion Papers 3750, London.

Commander, Simon, Rupa Chanda, Mari Kangasniemi, and Alan Winters. 2004. "Must Skilled Migration Be a Brain Drain? Evidence from the Indian Software Industry." IZA Discussion Paper No. 1422, Institute for the Study of Labour, Bonn.

Constant, Amelie, and Douglas Massey. 2002. "Return Migration by German Guestworkers: Neoclassical versus New Economic Theories." *International Migration* 40: 5–38.

Crush, Jonathan. 2010a. "Diaspora Networks at Work in SADC." Presentation at the conference "Africa's New Frontier: Innovation, Technology, Prosperity," Ottawa, February 4.

————. 2010b. "Diasporas of the South: Situating the African Diaspora in Africa." In *Diaspora for Development*, ed. Sonia Plaza and Dilip Ratha. Washington, DC: World Bank.

de Haas, Hein. 2005. "International Migration, Remittances and Development: Myths and Facts." *Third World Quarterly* 26 (8): 1269–1284.

————. 2006. *Engaging Diasporas: How Governments and Development Agencies Can Support Diaspora Involvement in the Development of Origin Countries.* Oxford, U.K.: International Migration Institute.

Dickinson, D. 2003. "How Networking Can Help Mitigate the Brain Drain." Science and Development Network SciDevNet. http://unpan1.un.org/intradoc/groups/public/documents/APCITY/UNPAN022377.pdf. http://scidev.net/11/24/2003.

Docquier, Frédéric, and Elisabetta Lodigiani. 2007. "Skilled Migration and Business Networks." Development Working Papers 234, Centro Studi Luca d'Agliano, University of Milano, Milan, Italy.

Dolman, B. 2008. "Migration, Trade and Investment." Productivity Commission Staff, Working Paper, Canberra, February.

Dunlevy, James. A. 2003. "Interpersonal Networks in International Trade; Evidence on the Role of Immigration in Promoting Exports from the American States." Paper presented at the 7th Annual Meeting of the International Society for New Institutional Economics, Budapest, September 12.

————. 2004. "Interpersonal Networks in International Trade: Evidence on the Role of Immigrants in Promoting Exports from the American States." Working Paper, Department of Economics, Miami University, Miami, FL.

————. 2006. "The Influence of Corruption and Language on the Pro-trade Effect of Immigrants: Evidence from the American States." *Review of Economics and Statistics* 88 (1): 182–86.

Dunlevy, James A., and William K. Hutchinson. 1999. "The Impact of Immigration on American Import Trade in the Late Nineteenth and Early Twentieth Centuries." *The Journal of Economic History* 59 (04): 1043–62.

Easterly, W., and Yaw Nyarko. 2008. "Is the Brain Drain Good For Africa?" Brookings Global Economy and Development Working Paper 19, Brookings Institution, Washington, DC.

ECA (Economic Commission of Africa). 2006. *International Migration and Development – Implications for Africa.* New York: United Nations.

Federal Negarit Gazeta of the Federal Democratic Republic of Ethiopia. 2002. "Proclamation No. 270/202. Providing Foreign Nationals of Ethiopian Origin with Certain Rights to Be Exercised in Their Country of Origin Proclamation." Addis Ababa. February 3, p. 1710.

————. 2003. Proclamation No. 84. Addis Ababa.

Finch, Tim, Holly Andrew, and Maria Latorre. 2010. "Global Brit: Making the Most of the British Diaspora." Institute for Public Policy Research Publication, London, June.

Foad, Hishman. 2008. "FDI and Immigration: A Regional Analysis." http://papers
.ssrn.com/sol3/papers.cfm?abstract_id=1092286.

Ghai, D. 2004. "Diasporas and Development: The Case of Kenya." Global Migration Perspectives No. 10. Global Commission on International Migration. Geneva. http://www.gcim.org/attachements/GMP%20No%2010.pdf.

Girma, Sourafel, and Zhihao Yu. 2002. "The Link between Immigration and Trade: Evidence from the United Kingdom." *Review of World Economics* 138 (1): 115–30.

Gitmez, A. S. 1988. "The Socio-economic Re-integration of Returned Workers: The Case of Turkey." In *International Migration Today,* ed. C. Stahl. Paris: UNESCO.

Gould, David. 1990. "Immigrant Links to the Home Country: Implications for Trade, Welfare and Factor Returns?" PhD Dissertation, Department of Economics. University of California, Los Angeles.

———. 1994. "Immigrants' Links to the Home Country: Empirical Implications for U.S.-Bilateral Trade Flows." *Review of Economics and Statistics* 76 (2): 302–16.

Guarnizo, L. 2003. "The Economics of Transnational Living." *International Migration Review* 37 (3): 666–699.

Gubert, Flore, and Christophe Nordman. Forthcoming. "Return Migration and Small Enterprise Development in the Maghreb." In *Diaspora for Development,* ed. Sonia Plaza and Dilip Ratha. Washington, DC: World Bank.

Head, Keith, and John Ries. 1998. "Immigration and Trade Creation; Econometric Evidence from Canada." *Canadian Journal of Economics* 31 (1): 47–62.

Helliwell, J. 1997. "National Borders, Trade and Migration." *Pacific Economic Review* 2 (3): 165–85.

Herander, Mark, and Luz A. Saavedra. 2005. "Exports and the Structure of Immigrant-Based Networks: The Role of Geographic Proximity." *The Review of Economics and Statistics* 87 (2): 323–35.

Hutchinson, W., and J. Dunlevy. 2001. "The Pro-trade Effect of Immigration on American Exports during the Period 1870 to 1910." Vanderbilt University Department of Economics Working Papers, No. 0125, Nashville.

Ionescu, Dina. 2006. "Engaging Diasporas as Development Partners for Home and Destination Countries: Challenges for Policymakers." Migration Research Series No. 26, International Organization for Migration, Geneva.

Javorcik, Beata S., Caglar Ozden, Mariana Spatareanu, and Cristina Neagu. 2006. "Migrant Networks and Foreign Direct Investment." Policy Research Working Paper Series 4046, World Bank, Washington, DC.

Jones-Correa, Michael. 2001. "Under Two Flags: Dual Nationality in Latin America and Its Consequences for Naturalization in the United States." *International Migration Review* 35 (4): 997–1029.

Khadria, Binod. 1999. *The Migration of Knowledge Workers: Second-Generation Effects of India's Brain Drain*. New Delhi: Sage.

Ketkar, Suhas L., and Manoj K. Dora. 2009. "Wealth of Recent Immigrants to the United States." Paper presented at the International Conference on Diaspora for Development, World Bank, Washington, DC, July 13–14.

King, Russell. 1986. *Return Migration and Regional Economic Problems*. London: Croom Helm.

Kingsley, Aiking, Anita Sand, and Nicola White. 2009. "The Global Irish Making a Difference Together: A Comparative Review of International Diaspora Strategies." The Ireland Funds, Report, Dublin.

Kluger, M., and H. Rapoport. 2005. "Skilled Emigration, Business Networks, and Foreign Direct Investment." CESIFO Working Paper 1455, Center for Economic Studies, Munich.

Kuznetsov, Y. 2006. *Diaspora Networks and the International Migration of Skills: How Countries Can Draw on Their Talent Abroad*. Washington, DC: World Bank.

Lacroix, Th. 2003. "Espace transnational et territoires: les réseaux Marocains du développement." Unpublished PhD thesis, Université de Poitiers, Poitiers, France.

Leblang, D. 2011. "Another Link in the Chain: Migrant Networks and International Investment." In *Diaspora for Development*, ed. Sonia Plaza and Dilip Ratha. Washington, DC: World Bank.

Legwaila, L. J. 2006. *The Role of the Diaspora in Support of Africa's Development*. London: African Leadership Diaspora Forum.

Light, Ivan, M. Zhou, and R. Kim. 2002. "Transnationalism and American Exports in an English-Speaking World." *International Migration Review* 36 (3): 702–25.

Lodigiani, Elizabettai. 2009. "Diaspora Externalities as a Cornerstone of the New Brain Drain Literature." CREA Discussion Paper 2009-03, Center for Research in Economic Analysis, University of Luxembourg.

Lowell, L., and S. Gerova. 2004. *Diasporas and Economic Development: State of Knowledge*. Washington, DC: World Bank.

Lucas, R. 2001. "Diaspora and Development: Highly Skilled Migrants from East Asia." Institute for Economic Development Working Paper Series 120, Boston University Department of Economics, Boston.

———. 2004. *International Migration and Economic Development: Lessons from Low-Income Countries*. UK: Edward Elgar.

Mahroum, S., C. Eldridge, and A. S. Daar. 2006. "Transnational Diaspora Options: How Developing Countries Could Benefit from Their Emigrant Populations." *International Journal on Multicultural Societies* 8 (1): 25–42.

Marks, Jonathan. 2004. "Expatriate Professionals as an Entry Point into Global Knowledge-Intensive Value Chains: South Africa." Report prepared for the Knowledge for Development Program, World Bank Institute, Washington,

DC. http://siteresources.worldbank.org/EDUCATION/Resources/278200-1126210664195/1636971-1126210694253/South_Africa_Diasporas.pdf.

Massey, D. S., R. Alarcon, J. Durand, and H. Gonzalez. 1987. *Return to Aztlan: The Social Process of International Migration from Western Mexico.* Berkeley: University of California Press.

Mazzolari, Francesca. 2007. "Dual Citizenship Rights: Do They Make More and Better Citizens?" IZA Discussion Paper 3008, Institute for the Study of Labor, Bonn.

McCormick, B., and J. Wahba 2003. "Return International Migration and Geographical Inequality: The Case of Egypt." *Journal of African Economies* 12 (4): 500–32.

Meyer, J. B., and M. Brown. 1999. "Scientific Diasporas: A New Approach to the Brain Drain." Discussion Paper Series 41, United Nations Educational, Scientific and Cultural Organization, Paris. http://www.unesco.org/most/meyer.htm.

Meyer, J. B., and J. P. Quattiaus. 2006. "Diaspora Knowledge Networks: Vanishing Doubts and Increasing Evidence." *International Journal on Multicultural Societies* 8 (1): 4–24.

Mohamoud, Awil. 2003. "African Diaspora and Development of Africa." Report for the African Diaspora Summit in the Netherlands, Felix Meritis European Centre for Art, Culture and Science, Amsterdam, December 16.

Mohamoud, Awil, ed. 2010. "Building Institutional Cooperation between the Diaspora and Homeland Governments in Africa. The Cases of Ghana, Nigeria, Germany, USA, and the UK." African Diaspora Policy Initiative, Africa Diaspora Policy Centre, The Hague, the Netherlands.

Mohan, Giles, and A. B. Zack-Williams. 2002. "Globalisation From Below: Conceptualising the Role of the African Diaspora in Africa's Development." *Review of African Political Economy* 92: 211–36.

Morgenroth, E., and M. O'Brien. 2008. "Some Further Results on the Impact of Migrants on Trade." Working Paper, DYNREG26, Economic and Social Research Institute, Dublin.

Murat, M., B. Pistoresi, and A. Rinaldi. 2008. "Italian Diaspora and Foreign Direct Investment: A Cliometric Perspective." University of Modena and Reggio Emilia. Paper presented at the Economic History Society Annual Conference, University of Nottingham, U.K. March 28–30, 2008. http://www.eco.unc.edu.ar/ief/workshops/2008/24abril2008_Murat_Pistoresi_Rinaldi_EHR.pdf.

Murillo Castaño, Gabriel. 1988. "International Labor Migration and Refugees in the Americas: Issues for Hemispheric Cooperation." *In Defence of the Alien* 10: 182–213.

Murphy, Rachel. 2000. "Migration and Inter-household Inequality: Observations from Wanzai County, Jiangxi." *The China Quarterly* 164: 965–82. doi:10.1017/S0305741000019251.

Newland, K., and E. Patrick. 2004. *Beyond Remittances: The Role of Diaspora in Poverty Reduction in Their Countries of Origin.* A Scoping Study by the Migration Policy Institute for the Department of International Development, Washington, DC.

Nielsen, T. M., and L. Riddle. 2007. "Why Diasporas Invest in the Homelands: A Conceptual Model of Motivation." http://papers.ssrn.com/sol3/Papers .cfm?abstract_id=987725.

OECD (Organisation of Economic Co-operation and Development). 2009. "The Global Competition for Talent: Mobility of the Highly Skilled." Policy Brief, OECD, Paris.

————. 2010. "The Contribution of Diaspora Return to Post-Conflict and Fragile Countries: Key Findings and Recommendations." Partnership for Democratic Governance, Organisation of Economic Co-operation and Development, Paris.

Okonjo-Iweala, Ngozi, and Dilip Ratha. 2011. "Homeward Bond." *New York Times*, Op-Ed, March 11. http://www.nytimes.com/2011/03/12/opinion/12ratha .html?_r=1.

Orozco, M. 2003. "The Impact of Migration in the Caribbean and Central American Region." Focal Policy Paper FPP-03-03, Canadian Foundation for the Americas, Ottawa. http://www.focal.ca/pdf/migration.pdf.

————. 2006a. "Conceptualizing Diasporas: Remarks about the Latino and Caribbean Experience." Paper presented at the International Forum on Remittances, Inter-American Development Bank, Washington, DC. http://idbdocs .iadb.org/wsdocs/getdocument.aspx?docnum=561695.

————. 2006b. "Diaspora and Development: Some Considerations." June, Inter-American Dialogue, Washington, DC. http://www.thedialogue.org/page.cfm? pageID=32&pubID=1010&s=.

————. 2006c. "Migrant Hometown Associations (HTAs): The Human Face of Globalization." In *World Migration Report 2005*. Geneva: International Organization for Migration.

Osili, U. 2004. "Migrants and Housing Investments: Theory and Evidence from Nigeria." *Economic Development and Cultural Change* 52 (4): 821–49.

Pack, H., and John Page. 1994. "Accumulation, Exports, and Growth in the High Performing Asian Economies." *Carnegie-Rochester Conference Series on Public Policy* 40 (1): 199–235.

Page, John, and Sonia Plaza. 2006. "Migration, Remittances and Economic Development: A Review of Global Evidence." *Journal of African Economies* 15 (2): 245–336.

Pang, T., M. Lansing, and A. Haines. 2002. "Brain Drain and Health Professionals." *British Medical Journal Online*.

Panizzon, V. 2010. "France's Co-development Program: Financial and Fiscal Incentives to Promote Diaspora Entrepreneurship and Transfers." In *Diaspora for Development*, ed. Sonia Plaza and Dilip Ratha. Washington, DC: World Bank.

Paul, Alison, and Sarah Gammage. 2005. "Hometown Associations and Developoment: The Case of El Salvador." Working Paper No. 3, Destination, D.C.

Paulson, A., and U. Okonkwo Osili. 2007. "Immigrants' Access to Financial Services and Asset Accumulation." Working Paper. http://www.econ.yale.edu/ seminars/labor/lap07/osili-paulson-071105.pdf.

Plaza, Sonia. 2008a. "Mobilizing the Diaspora: Creating an Enabling Environment for Trade, Investment, Knowledge Transfer and Enterprise Development." In *Africa's Finances: The Contribution of Remittances*, ed. Raj Bardouille, Muna Ndulo, and Margaret Grieco. UK: Cambridge Scholars Publishing.

———. 2008b. "Volunteers Wanted: Will Spain Successfully Entice Unemployed Migrants to Leave?" People Move Blog (cited September 23, 2008). https://blogs .worldbank.org/peoplemove/volunteers-wanted-will-spain-successfully-entice-unemployed-migrants-to-leave.

———. 2009a. "Promoting Diaspora Linkages: The Role of Embassies." Conference on Diaspora and Development, July 14, World Bank, Washington, DC.

———. 2009b. "Labor Mobility and Circular Migration: What Are the Challenges of the Stockholm Program?" People Move Blog (cited November 2, 2009). https:// blogs.worldbank.org/peoplemove/labor-mobility-and-circular-migration-what-are-the-challenges-of-the-stockholm-program.

Plaza, Sonia, Mario Navarrete, and Dilip Ratha. 2011. "Migration and Remittances Household Surveys in Sub-Saharan Africa—Methodological Aspects and Main Findings." World Bank, Washington, DC.

Portes, A., C. Escobar, and A. W. Radford. 2007. "Immigrant Transnational Organizations and Development: A Comparative Study." *International Migration Review* 41 (1): 242–81.

Ratha, Dilip. 2010. "Diaspora Bonds for Development Financing during the Crisis." People Move blog, October 26, 2010. World Bank, Washington, DC.

Ratha, Dilip, and Sanket Mohapatra. 2011. "Preliminary Estimates of Diaspora Savings." Migration and Development Brief 14, World Bank, Washington, DC.

Ratha, Dilip, Sanket Mohapatra, and Sonia Plaza. 2009. "Beyond Aid: New Sources and Innovative Mechanisms for Financing Development in Sub-Saharan Africa." In *Innovative Financing for Development*, ed. Dilip Ratha and Suhas Ketkar. Washington, DC: World Bank.

Ratha, Dilip, and William Shaw. 2007. "South-South Migration and Remittances." World Bank Development Prospects Group Working Paper 102, World Bank, Washington, DC.

Rauch, James. 2001. "Business and Social Networks in International Trade." *Journal of Economic Literature* 39 (December): 1177–203.

———. 2003. "Diasporas and Development: Theory, Evidence, and Programmatic Implications." Department of Economics, University of California, San Diego. USAID/TESS–funded project. http://www.tessproject.org/products/ special_studies/diasporas.pdf.

Rauch, James, and Alessandra Casella. 1998. "Overcoming Informational Barriers to International Resource Allocation: Prices and Group Ties." NBER Working Paper 6628, National Bureau of Economic Research, Cambridge, MA.

Rauch, James, and Victor Trindade. 1999. "Ethnic Chinese Networks in International Trade," NBER Working Paper 7189, National Bureau of Economic Research, Cambridge, MA.

———. 2002. "Ethnic Chinese Networks in International Trade." *Review of Economics and Statistics* 84 (1): 116–30.

Riddle, Liesl. 2006. "Export and Investment Promotion Organizations: Bridges to the Diaspora Business Community?" Paper presented at the UN Expert Convocation "Strengthening the Business Sector and Entrepreneurship in Developing Countries: The Potential of Diasporas," New York, October 5. http://www.un.org/esa/ffd/business/msc/tie/Riddle.ppt.

Saxenian, A. L. 2002a. "Brain Circulation: How High-Skill Immigration Makes Everyone Better Off." *Brookings Review* 20 (1): 28–31.

———. 2002b. "The Silicon Valley Connection: Transnational Networks and Regional Development in Taiwan, China and India." *Science Technology and Society* 7 (1): 117–49.

———. 2004. "Taiwan's Hsinchu Region: Imitator and Partner for Silicon Valley." In *Building High Tech Clusters: Silicon Valley and Beyond.* Cambridge, UK: Cambridge University Press.

———. 2006. *The New Argonauts: Regional Advantage in a Global Economy.* Cambridge, MA: Harvard University Press.

Swedish Ministry of Justice. 2010. "Sweden's Committee for Circular Migration and Development." Fact Sheet, July–September, Stockholm.

Touray, Katim S. 2008. *Final Evaluation of the Support Project to the Implementation of the Rwanda TOKTEN Program.* Final Report for the UNDP Evaluation Center. http://erc.undp.org/evaluationadmin/reports/viewreport.html;jsessionid=7CB6512829832D08DEA79BA3E36245B5?docid=1814.

Trans, Lars Ove, and Ida Marie Vammen. Forthcoming. "African Diaspora Associations in Denmark: A Study of their Development Activities and Potentials." In *Diaspora for Development*, ed. Sonia Plaza and Dilip Ratha. Washington, DC: World Bank.

Turner, S., and B. Mossin. 2008. "Diaspora Engagement in Post-conflict Burundi." World Bank report, World Bank, Washington, DC.

U.S. Department of State. Telegraph 86401. Washington, DC.

———. 2010. "Engaging with Diaspora Communities. Focus on EAP, EUR, and NEA." Summary Report, Foreign Service Institute Leadership and Management School Policy Leadership Division and the Global Partnership Initiative, Foreign Policy Institute, Office of the Secretary of State, Washington, DC.

Van Hear, N., Frank Pieke, and Steven Vertovec. 2004. "The Contribution of UK-based Diasporas to Development and Poverty Reduction." A report by the ESRC Centre on Migration, Policy and Society (COMPAS), University of Oxford for the Department for International Development. April 2004. Oxford. UK.

http://www.compas.ox.ac.uk/fileadmin/files/pdfs/Non_WP_pdfs/Reports_and_Other_Publications/DFID%20diaspora%20report.pdf.

Van Dijk, P. J. C., R. W. Koelstra, Paolo De Mas, Rinus Penninx, Herman van Renselaar, and Leo van Velzen. 1978. REMPLOD Project. Slotconclusies en Aanbevelingen. NUFFIC/IMWOO REMPLOD, The Hague.

Wagner, D., K. Head, and J. Ries. 2002. "Immigration and the Trade of Provinces." *Scottish Journal of Political Economy* 49 (5): 507–525.

Wanigaratne, R. D. 2006. "An Evaluation of the UNDP Transfer of Technology through Expatriate National Program (TOKTEN)." Evaluation Report. http://erc.undp.org/evaluationadmin/reports/viewreport.html;jsessionid=C2765F527 5DEBAF69935903CCEE56D57?docid=1863.

Westcott, C. G. 2006. "Harnessing Knowledge Exchange among Overseas Professionals of Afghanistan, People's Republic of China and Philippines." Labour Migration Workshop (UNITAR, UNFPA, IOM, ILO), New York, March 15.

Wickramasekara, Piyasiri. 2009. "Diasporas and Development: Perspectives on Definitions and Contributions." Perspectives on Labour Migration No. 9, International Labour Office, Social Protection Sector, International Migration Programme, International Labour Office, Geneva.

World Bank. 2005. *Global Economic Prospects 2006: Economic Implications of Remittances and Migration*. World Bank: Washington, DC.

———. 2006. *Diaspora Networks and the International Migration of Skills: How Countries Can Draw on Their Talent Abroad*. Edited by Yevgeny Kuznetsov. World Bank: Washington, DC.

———. 2011. *Migration and Remittances Factbook 2011*. Washington, DC: World Bank.

CHAPTER 1

Diasporas of the South: Situating the African Diaspora in Africa

Jonathan Crush[1]

The African diaspora is increasingly viewed as a key to realizing the development potential of international migration (de Haas 2006a; Nyberg-Sørensen 2007; Van Hear, Pieke, and Vertovec 2004). At the same time, there remains considerable confusion about who exactly constitutes the diaspora and which groups should be targeted for "diaspora engagement" (Bakewell 2009a). For some, the diaspora consists of all migrants of African birth living outside Africa. The African Union's definition of the African diaspora, for example, "comprises people of African origin living outside the continent, irrespective of their citizenship and nationality" (African Union 2005:7). The World Bank goes a step further to distinguish between an involuntary and a voluntary, and a historical and a contemporary, component of the diaspora: "Over four million voluntary immigrants of African origin reside in the West. This 'voluntary' Diaspora is distinct from the vastly larger 'involuntary' Diaspora that populates North America, Europe, the Caribbean, and Brazil. On matters of African development, however, the interests of both groups often intersect" (World Bank 2008).

Despite differences of emphasis, most definitions of the African diaspora in the migration and development literature agree on two things. First, the African diaspora is located outside the continent, usually in several different countries or regions but primarily in the North. Second, membership of the African diaspora is predicated on an interest or involvement in African development. Former South African President Thabo Mbeki, for example, argued at the 2007 African Ministerial Diaspora Conference that "there is an urgent need for knowledge sharing and economic cooperation between Africa and the Diaspora" (Mbeki 2007). The African Union (2005:7) similarly notes that members of the Diaspora must be "willing to contribute to the development of the continent and the building of the African Union."

Clearly, the African Union and African governments have little interest in engaging with those who have turned their backs on Africa for a new life elsewhere. From that standpoint, a definition of the diaspora that demands actual or potential engagement in African development makes perfect sense. What does not make sense is the idea that diaspora individuals and groups are located exclusively outside Africa. Perhaps, as Bakewell (2009a:3) notes, this is not surprising for "these tend to be wealthier, better-educated and more organized groups" with easier access to donor and African government officials and business groups across the globe. This may well be true, but it is also elitist, ignoring the much larger number of ordinary migrants whose "hidden" contributions to development go largely uncelebrated and unrecorded (except perhaps in aggregate remittance statistics). There is no reason why the African diaspora should not include all migrants who maintain links with Africa, and the many migrants from Africa who live and work in other African countries (Bakewell 2008a).

This chapter argues for a spatially inclusive definition of the African diaspora that encompasses all migrants of African origin with a development-related "interest" wherever they live so long as they are outside their country of origin. This would include people of African origin (not just first-generation migrants) resident in the North, in the South and, crucially, in Africa itself. There are, in other words, African diasporas outside Africa and African diasporas within Africa, and the two are often closely connected. Accordingly, this chapter:

- Discusses the development rationale for a revised definition of the African diaspora, which encompasses African migrants living in other countries within the continent
- Discusses the case of South Africa, which is a major African migrant country of origin and destination
- Compares the African diaspora in South Africa and the South African diaspora outside South Africa
- Reflects on the general relevance of the South African case study for our understanding of the role of the diaspora in African development.

Diasporas of the South

The migration and development debate initially tended to imply that the only stream of relevance to African development was migration from South to North (Crush 2006). One line of analysis argued that the North should encourage economic development in origin countries to reduce the pressure for out-migration from regions such as Africa (de Haas 2006b; Bakewell 2008b). Another sought to encourage (skills) migration from the South to the North while simultaneously avoiding charges of promoting a debilitating "brain drain" by emphasizing the positive diaspora feedback mechanisms of out-migration (remittances, investment, knowledge transfers, and so on) (Clemens 2007). China and India are held up as exemplars of diaspora-fed development (Bhargava and Sharma 2008; Geithner, Johnson, and Chen 2004). The curious feature of this debate is that it ignores the long-standing reality that South-South migration is numerically more important than South-North migration and continues to grow in volume and economic importance (Ratha and Shaw 2007).

At an aggregate level, South-South migration has generated an estimated 45 percent of the current global migrant stock compared to only 37 percent for South-North migration (table 1.1). There is considerable uncertainty about how to configure South-South migration within the global migration-development debate (Bakewell 2009b). By tacking on the activities of migrants in the North to other North-South "development" linkages, (for example, by constructing graphs comparing flows of remittances with aid flows and foreign direct investment), the emphasis on South-North linkages is maintained. Ironically, the sizable contribution of South-South remittances—estimated at 30 percent of the total by Ratha and Shaw (2007:12)—is usually "hidden" in aggregated global flows.

TABLE 1.1

Cumulative Global Migration Flows, 2005

Origin	Destination			
	North		South	
North	25 million	14%	8 million	4%
South	64 million	37%	87 million	45%

Source: Calculated from Global Migrant Origin Database v4, updated March 2007; http://www.migrationdrc.org/research/types ofmigration/Global_Migrant_Origin_Database_Version_4.xls.

While there is growing awareness of the role of South-South migration in development, the term "diaspora" is rarely used in this new literature. In their pathbreaking analysis of South-South migration and remittances, for example, Ratha and Shaw (2007:17) use the term only once, to refer to the dispersal of African groups within the interior of Southern Africa in the 19th century. The irony of this use of the term to describe the movement of people *within* Africa will not be lost on those who agree with the fundamental premise of this chapter. There is thus a need to develop a conversation between the new literature on South-South migration and the growing analysis of diaspora engagement with Africa.

Bakewell (2009b:58) notes that "African diasporas within Africa are absent from the picture" of migration and development. There are five basic reasons why the definition of the African diaspora should be expanded to include migrants who have relocated to other countries within Africa.

First, consistent with the general argument made above about South-South migration, Africa itself is the most important destination for African migrants. The latest United Nations–Democratic Republic of Congo figures for global migrant stock indicate that the main destinations for African migrants are Africa itself (13 million, or 53 percent of the total), Europe (7.3 million, or 30 percent), the Middle East (2.6 million or 10 percent), and North America (1.2 million, or 5 percent) (table 1.2). Nearly two-thirds

TABLE 1.2
Global African Migrant Stock by Region

	Number	Percent
NORTH		
Europe	7,337,542	29.4
North America	1,239,722	5.0
Australasia	223,095	0.9
Subtotal	8,800,359	35.3
SOUTH		
Africa	13,181,759	52.8
Middle East	2,595,856	10.4
Asia	339,014	1.3
Latin America	58,273	0.2
Subtotal	16,174,902	64.7
TOTAL	24,975,261	100.0

Source: Calculated from Global Migrant Origin Database v4, updated March 2007; http://www.migrationdrc.org/research/typesofmigration/Global_Migrant_Origin_Database_Version_4.xls.

of African migration is to countries of the South. In total, 53 percent of African migrants live in Africa and 47 percent live outside the continent.

Second, with the exception of forced migration movements, the majority of migration within Africa is developmental in nature, motivated by the search for better economic opportunity and building sustainable livelihoods at home (often at the microscale of households and communities). Migrants are driven by the desire to obtain the resources (financial and otherwise) to reduce poverty and to ensure a better standard of living for their dependents, including children. They also generally maintain much stronger social and economic ties with home than those who have left the continent. Circular migration is fast becoming a new "development mantra" in the North (Newland, Rannveig Agunias, and Terrazas 2008; Vertovec 2007).[2] Within Africa, however, circular migration has been the dominant form of migration for decades. If diaspora engagement is defined by actual or potential involvement in the development of countries of origin, then most African migrants in Africa are already fully engaged.

Third, another new "mantra" in the migration-development debate is the idea of "codevelopment." African diasporas within Africa are clear agents of "codevelopment," contributing to the development of origin *and* destination countries. Their contribution to countries of destination is often downplayed or minimized; migrants are rarely seen as a development resource in African countries of destination. More often they are viewed as a threat to the interests of citizens, as takers of jobs, bringers of crime, consumers of scarce resources, and drainers of wealth. Across the global South, the activities of migrants are increasingly and often misleadingly viewed as antithetical to development (Crush and Ramachandran 2009, 2010). The xenophobic violence that rocked South Africa in May 2008 and left 64 people dead and scores injured was accompanied by a bellicose antiforeign rhetoric that blamed migrants for many of South Africa's social and economic ills and ignored the contribution of migrants to South Africa's own development (SAMP 2008).

Fourth, members of the African diaspora in Africa are often closely networked personally and economically with the diaspora outside Africa. These economic linkages are particularly intense in the case of globalized trading networks such as those run by Senegalese and Somalians. Zimbabweans living in the United Kingdom are often referred to as a "diaspora" while those in South Africa are generally not (Crush and Tevera 2010). Yet both send large sums in remittances back to Zimbabwe, sometimes to the same household. There is no logic to why remittances from Zimbabweans in Europe are designated a "diaspora" contribution while those from South Africa are not. More generally, to ignore the African diaspora in Africa is to exclude over half of all African migrants as potential participants in, and beneficiaries of, diaspora policy initiatives.

Fifth, "elitist" definitions of the African diaspora tend to focus on the development contributions of the highly skilled, educated, and networked members of diasporas in the North. This is highly problematic since it excludes many ordinary development actors who have migrated out of Africa. It has the added disadvantage of excluding African migrants in Africa on the grounds that most are supposedly unskilled and have low earning power. This is a dangerous assumption since it excludes, by definition, the development contribution of such migrants and many highly skilled, educated, and networked Africans who do live and work in other countries in Africa.

The next section considers these arguments in the context of South Africa, one of Africa's major countries of migrant origin and destination.

South Africa's Two Diasporas

South Africa is a country of significant in-migration and out-migration. Prior to 1994, immigration easily exceeded emigration.[3] After 1994, legal immigration fell while emigration continued to grow. Since 2000, both have increased sharply (figure 1.1). Official statistics significantly under-count both immigration and emigration, but the trends shown are generally illustrative of postapartheid migration movements. Together, these flows have created a growing African diaspora within South Africa, a sizable South African diaspora outside the continent, and a smaller South African diaspora within Africa. This chapter focuses on the first two of these diasporas: the African diaspora within South Africa and the South African diaspora outside Africa.

The African Diaspora Within South Africa

South Africa's migrant stock was just over 1 million in 2001 (table 1.3).[4] Of these, 23 percent were from Europe (a legacy of apartheid-era immigration) and 72 percent were from Africa (Peberdy 2009). The 2001 South

FIGURE 1.1
Official Levels of Migration, South Africa, 1990–2002

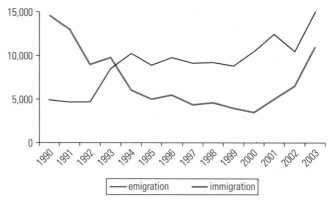

Source: Unpublished data from Statistics South Africa.

TABLE 1.3
Migrant Stock in South Africa, 2001

Region of Origin	Number	Percent
NORTH		
Europe	236,000	23.0
North America	9,000	1.0
Australasia	4,000	0.5
Subtotal	249,000	24.5
SOUTH		
Africa	729,498	71.5
Asia	27,000	3.0
Middle East	6,000	0.5
Latin America	13,000	1.0
Subtotal	776,000	76.0
TOTAL	10,25,000	100.0

Sources: Unpublished data from Statistics South Africa; 2001 Census.

African Census recorded 730,000 foreign-born African migrants from 54 African countries. However, the vast majority were from other states within the Southern African Development Community (95 percent). Of these, 39 percent were from Mozambique, 19 percent were from Zimbabwe, 17 percent were from Lesotho, 5 percent were from Namibia, and 4 percent were from Swaziland (table 1.4). Around 20,000 migrants were from East Africa, 16,000 were from West Africa, and 4,500 were from North

TABLE 1.4
SADC Countries of Origin of Migrants to South Africa, 2001

Country of Migrant Origin	Number	Percent
Mozambique	269,669	39.2
Zimbabwe	131,887	19.2
Lesotho	114,941	16.7
Namibia	38,148	5.5
Swaziland	28,278	4.1
Zambia	20,770	3.0
Malawi	19,673	2.9
Botswana	14,955	2.2
Angola	9,937	1.4
Congo, Dem. Rep.	3,772	0.5
Tanzania	3,330	0.5
Mauritius	2,577	0.4
Other	191	<0.1
TOTAL	687,899	100.0

Sources: Unpublished data from Statistics South Africa; 2001 Census.

Africa. Since 2001, the number of migrants from Zimbabwe, in particular, has increased markedly (Makina 2010).

There is actually considerable uncertainty about the current number of African migrants in South Africa. The 2001 South African Census recorded 690,000 other Southern African Development Community–born migrants. The latest iteration of the Sussex University Global Migrant Origin Database v4[5] has an almost identical total but a totally different distribution by country of origin (with Angola and the Democratic Republic of Congo combined increasing from 16,000 to 300,000), and Mozambique falling by 120,000, Lesotho by 107,000, and Zimbabwe by 73,000 (table 1.5).

The latest World Bank estimates confuse the situation still further, increasing Lesotho by 200,000, Mozambique by 120,000, and Zimbabwe by 451,000. The World Bank total is 1.1 million but records no migrants at all from key sending countries such as Angola, the Democratic Republic of Congo, Tanzania, and Namibia. Official estimates of the number of irregular migrants in South Africa bear no relationship to any of these estimates, varying between 4 million and 10 million (with the number of Zimbabweans usually put at 2 million to 3 million). None of these estimates have any basis in fact and are likely highly exaggerated. One study used 2001

TABLE 1.5
Variable Estimates of Southern African Development Community Migrant Stock in South Africa

Country of Origin	2001 South Africa Census	Global Migrant Origin Database (Version 4)	World Bank
Angola	11,806	152,057	0
Botswana	17,819	2,989	24,849
Congo, Dem. Rep.	4,541	149,462	0
Lesotho	114,941	8,246	208,226
Madagascar	220	316	0
Malawi	25,090	26,568	10,662
Mauritius	3,500	32,149	0
Mozambique	269,669	150,369	269,918
Namibia	46,225	4,215	0
Seychelles	257	3,144	0
Swaziland	34,471	2,007	80,593
Tanzania	3,923	52,554	0
Zambia	23,550	44,809	0
Zimbabwe	131,887	59,109	510,084
TOTAL	687,899	687,994	1,104,331

Source: Statistics South Africa, Global Migrant Origin Database v4, World Bank.

South Africa Census data and projections from date of entry by a large migrant sample in Johannesburg, and estimated that there were 900,000 Zimbabweans in South Africa in 2007 (Makina 2010).

Unpublished data from Statistics South Africa for the 2001 Census allow the construction of a general profile of the African diaspora in South Africa at that time (table 1.6). The Census showed that 80 percent of the African-born migrant stock was black and 20 percent was white (primarily immigrants from ex-settler colonies such as Mozambique, Namibia, Zambia, and Zimbabwe). The migrant stock is also male dominated, although the feminization of migration is proceeding rapidly (Dodson 2008). In 2001, approximately 64 percent of the migrant stock was male and 36 percent was female. The Census also reveals that far from being an undifferentiated, unskilled, and marginalized group of migrants, there is considerable variety in the skill levels and earnings of African migrants in South Africa. For example, only a quarter of the migrants were in unskilled ("elementary") occupations. Just as many were in skilled and professional positions, and 45 percent were doing semiskilled jobs.

TABLE 1.6
Demographic Profile of African Diaspora in South Africa, 2001

	Number	Percent
Race/Sex		
Black male	380,866	53.5
Black female	188,484	26.5
Subtotal	569,350	80.0
White male	68,144	9.6
White female	74,265	10.4
Subtotal	142,409	20.0
TOTAL	711,759	100.0
Occupation		
Skilled		
Senior managers/officials	21,991	6.6
Professionals	28,021	8.4
Technical	21,582	6.5
Farmers	12,087	3.6
SUBTOTAL	83,681	25.1
Semiskilled		
Plant/machine operators	26,625	8.0
Crafts and trades	66,638	20.0
Clerical	21,824	6.5
Services	33,682	10.1
SUBTOTAL	148,769	44.6
Unskilled		
Elementary occupations	82,244	24.6
Other	19,167	5.8
TOTAL	333,861	100.0

Income bracket	Number	Percent	Cumulative %
R1–R400	81,412	19.6	19.6
R401–R800	70,375	17.0	36.6
R801–R1,600	94,996	22.9	59.5
R1,601–R3,200	70,447	17.0	76.5
R3,201–R6,400	39,734	9.5	86.0
R6,401–R12,800	31,079	7.5	93.5
R12,801–R25,600	16,923	4.1	97.6
R25,601–R51,200	6,227	1.5	99.1
R51,201–R100,240	1,979	0.5	99.6
R100,241–R200,480	1,097	0.3	99.9
>R200,480	595	0.1	100.0
TOTAL	413,874	100.0	

Source: Unpublished Data from Statistics South Africa.
Note: R = Rands.

The income range of migrants was also considerable. Of those earning an income, 60 percent earned less than R18,000 a year in 2001 and 86 percent less than R72,000 a year. Less than 1 percent earned more than R250,000 a year. In part, the low overall earnings are a function of the low rates of remuneration for most unskilled and semiskilled positions in South Africa. Rates of pay for skilled and professional migrants are higher but still do not compare with those in Europe or North America. Many poorer households, however, supplement their income through informal sector activity, which is generally not reflected in the Census data. Also, many migrants are unable to get jobs commensurate with their qualifications and experience and end up working in lower-paid jobs.

The South African Diaspora Outside Africa

The collection of systematic comparative data for the South African diaspora outside Africa is in progress by the Southern African Migration Programme. The precise number of South African emigrants is unknown because official South African emigration statistics are known to undercount the flow by as much as two-thirds (Stern and Szalontai 2006). Destination-country immigration statistics are more reliable, but they do not always record departures, so census data need to be used to provide a more accurate picture of cumulative migration. The Global Migrant Origin Database V4 suggests that Europe is the major location of South African migrant stocks (at 244,000, or 40 percent of the total) (table 1.7). The main countries of destination are the United Kingdom, the Netherlands, and Germany. Other important regions of destination include North America (18 percent of the total) and Australasia (each at 18 percent). In other words, three-quarters of South Africans abroad live in the North. The large number of South Africans recorded as living in other African countries (especially Mozambique and Zimbabwe) is almost certainly incorrect.

The South African diaspora outside Africa is therefore located mainly in countries with historical immigration ties to South Africa (Germany, the Netherlands, Portugal, and the United Kingdom) and newer destinations (Australia, Canada, New Zealand, and the United States) (table 1.8). Migration to all of these destinations continues in considerable numbers. In the case of Australia, for example, the 2006 Census shows that 4,000 to 6,000 migrants entered from South Africa each year from 2001 to 2006,

TABLE 1.7
Regional Distribution of South African Diaspora

Region	Number	Percent
NORTH		
Europe	243,716	40.0
North America	108,221	18.0
Australasia	105,721	18.0
Subtotal	457,658	76.0
SOUTH		
Africa	302,764	20.0
Asia	14,042	2.0
Middle East	9,500	1.5
Latin America	2,305	0.5
Subtotal	328,613	24.0
TOTAL	786,721	100.0

Source: Calculated from Global Migrant Origin Database v4, updated March 2007; http://www.migrationdrc.org/research/typesofmigration/Global_Migrant_Origin_Database_Version_4.xls.

TABLE 1.8
Major Countries of South African Diaspora

	Numbers
United Kingdom	142,416
Australia*	104,120
United States	70,465
Canada	37,681
Germany	34,674
New Zealand*	26,069
Netherlands	11,286
Portugal	11,197

Source: Calculated from Global Migrant Origin Database v4, updated March 2007; http://www.migrationdrc.org/research/typesofmigration/Global_Migrant_Origin_Database_Version_4.xls.
Note: *Updated for 2006 Census.

adding to the 22,000 who arrived in the immediate postapartheid period (between 1995 and 2000) and the 40,000 who moved there during the apartheid period. The 2006 New Zealand Census shows that 3,000 to 4,000 migrants arrive from South Africa each year. In this country, too, there was a postapartheid surge (14,000 between 1996 and 2001) of migration from South Africa.

Out-migration from South Africa occurred in three distinct phases:

- *Pre-1990 (primarily migrants, exiles, and refugees of all races leaving apartheid South Africa):* Emigration spiked during periods of political unrest (such as in the 1960s after the Sharpeville massacre, in the 1970s after the Soweto Uprising, and during the state of emergency in the 1980s). Australia, Canada, and the United Kingdom were primary destinations during this period.
- *1990–2000:* Departure of many conservative whites who were not prepared to live under a democratic African National Congress government and objected to the loss of historical white privileges. Most of these migrants went to Australia and the United Kingdom, but the numbers moving to New Zealand increased sharply.
- *Post-2000:* Growing migration of skilled people and professionals of all races pushed by concerns about crime and safety and attracted by the more open immigration policies of skills-seeking Organisation for Economic Co-operation and Development countries.

As table 1.9 shows, annual immigration to Canada has remained reasonably constant, but there has been a major increase in the rate of migration to Australia and New Zealand.

The emigration potential of skilled South Africans still in the country remains extremely high. In a survey of health professionals in South Africa, the Southern African Migration Program found that 50 percent of all health professionals had given a "great deal" of consideration to leaving

TABLE 1.9

Phases of South African Immigration to Australia, Canada, and New Zealand

	Australia		Canada		New Zealand	
	Number	Average per year	Number	Average per year	Number	Average per year
Pre-1990	38,860	—	19,505	—	2,877*	—
1991–2000	29,202	2,920	12,790	1,297	19,668**	1,311
2001–2006	32,723	6,544	6,795	1,160	18,273	3,655

Source: 2006 Census.
Note: — = not available.
* Pre-1986.
**1986–2000.

the country and 30 percent expected to be gone in five years (Pendleton, Crush, and Lefko-Everett 2007). According to every social and economic measure (except collegiality), there were more dissatisfied than satisfied professionals, and the "Most Likely Destination" rated more highly than South Africa. The Most Likely Destinations were Australia and New Zealand (33 percent), the United Kingdom (25 percent), the United States (10 percent), Europe (9 percent), and Canada (7 percent). Nearly 40 percent of professionals had "often" been contacted by a recruitment agency in South Africa and 25 percent were "personally approached" about working abroad (Rogerson and Crush 2008).

Most South African emigration consists of families rather than individuals and the gender split is very even in the diaspora. In Australia, for example, there were 51,037 male and 53,095 female South African migrants at the time of the 2006 Census. The age profile of South Africans in New Zealand shows that a quarter of South African migrants were under age 20 in 2006, again an indication of extensive and recent family unit migration. The largest adult group (40 percent) was people in their 30s and 40s, presumably their economically active parents.

A precise occupational breakdown of the South African diaspora has yet to be compiled, but it is known that many migrants enter countries of destination under skilled immigration categories (Bhorat, Meyer, and Mlatsheni 2002). Rates of unemployment are also extremely low in the diaspora. In Australia, for example, 35,115 male South Africans and 29,663 females were employed in 2006 (and only 1,329 working-age males and 1,424 working-age females were unemployed.) Health profession data suggest that this is one of the major professions for migrants in destination countries, where South African medical school qualifications are generally recognized (table 1.10). The United Kingdom (27.5 percent of the total) has been the major destination for South African physicians followed by the United States (27 percent) and Canada (21 percent). Nurse migration is also dominated by the United Kingdom (49 percent), followed by Australia (19 percent) and the United States (14 percent). The United Kingdom is even more important as a destination for South African dentists (68 percent) and pharmacists (42 percent).

In summary, the African diaspora in South Africa and the South African diaspora outside Africa display distinctive and different characteristics. Table 1.11 summarizes the major differences in terms of overall sociodemographic profile, migration type, spatial distribution, behavior, degree of

TABLE 1.10

Health Professionals in the South African Diaspora, Circa 2000

OECD Country	Doctors		Nurses		Dentists		Pharmacists	
Australia	1,111	15.1	1,083	18.6	152	12.0	23	15.9
Austria	13	0.2	16	0.3	2	0.1	0	0.0
Canada	1,545	21.0	280	4.8	60	4.7	15	10.3
Denmark	2	<0.1	16	0.3	1	0.1	0	0.0
France	16	0.2	4	0.1	0	0.0	0	0.0
Germany	12	0.2	22	0.4	3	0.2	0	0.0
Ireland	45	0.6	105	1.8	3	0.2	0	0.0
Mexico	3	<0.1	0	0	0	0.0	0	0.0
New Zealand	555	7.5	432	7.4	24	1.9	6	4.1
Norway	0	0.0	49	0.8	0	0.0	0	0.0
Portugal	44	0.6	58	1.0	0	0.0	0	0.0
Spain	4	0.1	3	0.1	0	0.0	0	0.0
Sweden	11	0.1	10	0.2	0	0.0	0	0.0
Switzerland	22	0.3	55	0.9	8	0.6	0	0.0
United Kingdom	2,022	27.5	2,844	49.0	862	68.3	61	42.1
United States	1,950	26.6	829	14.3	150	11.9	40	27.6
TOTAL	7,355	100.0	5,806	100.0	1,265	100.0	145	100.0

Source: Compiled from Organisation for Economic Co-operation and Development, Health Workforce and Migration Data; http://www.oecd.org/document/47/0,3746,en_2649_37407_36506543_1_1_1_37407,00.html.

integration in destination countries, and remitting behavior (the subject of the next section). This comparative typology is a useful precursor to a discussion of diaspora engagement since different types of diasporas have different potentials and propensities for involvement in development activities that benefit their countries of origin.

Forms of Diaspora Engagement

The division into distinct periods of South Africa's global diasporic dispersal in the previous section is important because the character of actual and potential diaspora engagement differs for each group of immigrants. Engagement interest is relatively high among many pre-1990 emigrants who have risen to positions of professional prominence and economic power and maintain a strong interest in the development of a democratic South Africa. The second group (the migrants of the 1990s) are the least likely to engage, since they left precisely because they objected to the transformation in South Africa and are extremely critical of and negative

TABLE 1.11
Comparing the Diasporas

	South African diaspora outside Africa	African diaspora in South Africa
Sociodemographic profile	White (> 80%), family, skilled, tertiary educated, professional	Black (> 80%), individual (75% male), all skill levels and all education levels
Main migration type	Permanent	Temporary, circular, transnational
Spatial distribution	Concentrated in 6 countries	From 50 African countries but majority (90%) from the Southern African Development Community
Integration	High economic and social integration	Low integration and high barriers to permanent residence and citizenship
	High rates of permanent residence and citizenship	High levels of discrimination and xenophobia
	Qualifications recognized	Deskilling common
Remittances	Low in comparison to income	High in comparison to income

Source: Author's compilation.

about their country of origin. The third group, the post-2000 migrants, retain the strongest personal ties with South Africa and are generally less enamored with their countries of destination. They are aware of the enormous social and economic challenges that South Africa faces, have a modicum of guilt about their personal reasons for leaving, and retain an interest in events there. This group displays high use of social networking sites and organizes cultural nostalgia events.

As a country of migrant origin and destination, South Africa both sends and receives remittances. World Bank calculations suggest that both flows have been increasing in recent years, although the outflow is larger than the inflow. There have been no studies of the remitting behavior of the South African diaspora abroad. Little is known about who remits, how the remittances are sent, who they are sent to, and how they are spent. Anecdotal evidence suggests that a main motivation for personal remitting is to support elderly parents and relatives who remain in South Africa (Robertson 2008). There also appears to be a considerable amount of investment in real estate, but how much of the country's sizable inward flows of foreign investment is motivated or catalyzed by diaspora individuals or companies is unclear.

The most common form of engagement by the diaspora abroad appears to be tourism and the nostalgia trade. Many South Africans in all of the major destination countries make regular return trips to visit the country, family, and friends. The nostalgia trade is partly responsible for the world-wide diffusion and adoption of products such as South African wine and the ubiquitous rooibos tea. Diaspora-owned companies in all the major destination countries import South African products and African crafts for sale to the diaspora and more broadly. Other common forms of diaspora engagement include support for charities and nongovernmental organizations, involvement in aid programs, and political activities (such as voting in elections).

Much more is known about the remitting behavior of the African diaspora in South Africa (Crush and Pendleton 2009). The Southern African Migration Programme's study of five sending countries found that 84 percent of migrant-sending households receive regular remittances from South Africa (compared with only 7 percent that receive income from agriculture). Remittances (cash plus goods) are the most important source of household income. Around 60 percent of remitting migrants remit at least monthly and 95 percent remit annually while 80 percent use informal channels. The amount remitted varies with marital status, age, gender, occupation, and skill level.

Remittances are spent primarily on household needs—food, clothing, school fees, and transportation (table 1.12). Over 80 percent of household expenditures in most livelihood categories are met from remittances. The "development impact" of remittances is therefore primarily related to securing household food security and educating children. The expenditure of remittances does benefit informal sector traders and small, medium, and micro enterprises, but the primary beneficiaries of food purchase are increasingly South African–owned supermarket chains in origin countries. Levels of investment, savings, and business development from remittances are generally low. Little is invested in agricultural production. The question of how to enhance the development uses and impacts of sizable remittance flows has received little attention.

Both diasporas are involved in various forms of associational activity with a focus on their home countries. In South Africa, these range from forms of political organization and activism (in the case of Zimbabweans in South Africa), to home cultural associations (particularly common among migrants from West and Francophone Africa in South Africa), and informal migrant mutual help groups such as burial associations and savings and credit groups. Migrant social networks are particularly strong in helping new migrants find accommodations and employment and, given the

TABLE 1.12
Use of Remittances in Countries of Origin*

Expenditure category	Number of households	Percent
Food	3,297	81.9
School fees	2,106	52.3
Clothing	2,101	52.2
Fares (bus, taxi)	1,361	33.8
Seed	968	24.0
Fertilizer	613	15.2
Tractor	549	13.6
Savings	503	12.5
Cement	448	11.1
Funeral	434	10.8
Funeral and burial policies	393	9.8
Roofing	301	7.5
Doors and windows	284	7.1
Bricks	279	6.9
Cooking fuel	240	6.0
Labor	221	5.5
Cattle purchase	187	4.6
Repay loans	168	4.2
Marriage	150	3.7
Purchase goods for sale	147	3.7
Small stock purchase	146	3.6
Feast	139	3.5
Walls	142	3.5
Other building material	121	3.0
Paint	108	2.7
Dipping/veterinary costs	106	2.6
Oxen for ploughing	97	2.4
Vehicle purchase/maintenance	98	2.4
Poultry purchase	92	2.3
Insurance policies	87	2.2
Wood	89	2.2
Vehicle/transport costs	73	1.8
Other special events	45	1.1
Equipment	39	1.0
Labor costs	40	1.0
Other business expenses	24	0.6
Other farm input	23	0.6
Other personal investment	25	0.6
Machinery/equipment	18	0.4
Other transport expenses	17	0.4

Source: Southern African Migration Programme 2005; http://www.queensu.ca/samp.
Note: *Botswana, Lesotho, Mozambique, Swaziland, Zimbabwe.

general xenophobic atmosphere in South Africa, provide migrants with solidarity and physical protection.

The South African diaspora abroad is considerably more dispersed, and associational life generally takes the form of cultural associations with only limited development engagement with South Africa. However, there are important diaspora development-oriented organizations and networks— such as the African Diaspora Network and the Nelson Mandela Children's Foundation in Canada—in which South Africans play a prominent role. Elite knowledge networks have also begun to emerge in the diaspora. The first and potentially most innovative of these, the South African Network of Skills Abroad, has received much positive attention in the literature but failed to deliver on its promise to mobilize the diaspora to address South Africa's skills shortages. A more recent initiative is the Global South Africans network (which describes itself as a "brain bank of the 1,000 or so best and brightest minds"), which aims to mobilize South Africans in positions of power and influence for investment and skills development in South Africa (Barber 2007).

Conclusion

A strong case can be made for expanding the definition of the "African diaspora" to include migrants within Africa itself. However, as this chapter has shown with regard to South Africa, there are significant differences between the diasporas within and outside of Africa. This means that the nature of their contribution to the development of their home countries also varies. The argument has often been made that the "creation" of a South African diaspora abroad has been driven by the labor needs of major Western countries and has had very negative development consequences for South Africa itself. In recognition of this, the South African Government developed a new skills-based immigration policy in the form of the Immigration Act of 2002. Growing African migration to South Africa has undoubtedly mitigated some of the negative impacts of the South African brain drain.

The contribution of the diaspora in South Africa to the development of their countries of origin is clearly sizable. The Lesotho and Mozambique economies would be hard-pressed to even exist without migration and remittances (Crush et al. 2010; de Vletter 2010). Households with migrants have much better development outcomes in both countries than those that do not. Zimbabwe's economic collapse would have happened much sooner and would have been far more devastating but for the massive flow of remittances across the border from South Africa (Crush and Tevera 2010; Mupedziswa 2009; Tevera and Chikanda 2009). Remittances and return migration will continue to play a key role in the reconstruction and rebuilding of the country. The potential contributions of diaspora engagement to South African development need further research. Indeed, the new research agenda identified in this chapter should provide invaluable evidence on how the contributions of both diasporas can be maximized in the interest of those who cannot or choose not to move but to remain.

Notes

1. The author would like to thank the International Development Research Centre for its support of the Southern African Migration Programme's ongoing program of research on the African diaspora and development.
2. Circular migration, as defined by Newland (2009:2), consists of movement back and forth between home countries and destinations abroad. Through circular migration, people can "avoid making a definitive choice between origin and destination countries (or locations within a country) but, rather, can maintain significant ties in both."
3. The term "immigration" describes the process by which a person moves into a country for the purpose of becoming a permanent resident. In such a case, the individual is not a native of the country which he or she immigrates to. "Emigration" refers to the process whereby a person leaves his or her place or country of residency to live elsewhere.
4. Migrant stock is the number of people born in a country other than the one in which they live.
5. See http://www.migrationdrc.org/research/typesofmigration/Global_Migrant _Origin_Database_Version_4.xls.

References

African Union. 2005. "Report of the Meeting of Experts from Member States on the Definition of the African Diaspora." Addis Ababa, April 11–12.

Bakewell, O. 2008a. "In Search of the Diasporas Within Africa." *African Diasporas* 1: 5–27.

————. 2008b. "Keeping Them in Their Place: The Ambivalent Relationship between Development and Migration in Africa." *Third World Quarterly* 29 (7): 1341–58.

————. 2009a. "Which Diaspora for Whose Development? Some Critical Questions about Roles of African Diaspora Organizations as Development Actors." Danish Institute for International Studies Brief, Danish Institute for International Studies, Copenhagen.

————. 2009b. "South-South Migration and Human Development: Reflections on African Development." Human Development Research Paper 2009/07, United Nations Development Programme, New York.

Barber, S. 2007. "A 'Brain Bank' of Expats." *Mail & Guardian*, November 5. http://www.mg.co.za/article/2007-11-05-a-brain-bank-of-expats.

Bhargava, K., and J. Sharma. 2008. "Building Bridges: A Case Study on the Role of the Indian Diaspora in Canada." School of Policy Studies, Queen's University, Kingston, Canada.

Bhorat, H., J.-B. Meyer, and C. Mlatsheni. 2002. "Skilled Labour Migration from Developing Countries: Study on South and Southern Africa." International Migration Papers No 52, International Labour Organization, Geneva.

Clemens, M. 2007 "Do Visas Kill? Health Effects of African Health Professional Emigration." Working Paper Number 114, Center for Global Development, Washington, DC.

Crush, J. 2006. "The International Migration and Development Debate: The Implications for Canada." Report for Citizenship and Immigration Canada and Canadian International Development Agency, Ottawa.

Crush, J., B. Dodson, J. Gay, and C. Leduka. 2010. "Migration, Remittances and Gender-Responsive Local Development: The Case of Lesotho." Report for /UN-INSTRAW, Santo Domingo, the Dominican Republic.

Crush, J., and W. Pendleton, 2009. "Remitting for Survival: Rethinking the Development Potential of Remittances in Southern Africa." *Global Development Studies* 5 (3–4): 53–84.

Crush, J., and S. Ramachandran. 2009. "Xenophobia, International Migration and Human Development." Research Paper 2009/47, United Nations Development Programme, New York.

————. 2010. "Xenophobia, International Migration and Development." *Journal of Human Development and Capabilities* 11 (2): 209–28.

Crush, J., and D. Tevera, eds. 2010. *Zimbabwe's Exodus: Crisis, Migration, Survival.* Cape Town: Southern African Migration Programme and Ottawa: International Development Research Centre.

de Haas, H. 2006a. "Engaging Diasporas: How Governments and Development Agencies Can Support Diaspora Involvement in the Development of Origin Countries." Report for Oxfam Novib, International Migration Institute, Oxford University, Oxford, England.

———. 2006b. "Turning the Tide? Why 'Development Instead of Migration' Policies are Bound to Fail." IMI Working Paper No. 2. International Migration Institute, University of Oxford, Oxford, England.

de Vletter, F. 2010. "Migration and Development in Mozambique: Poverty,
Inequality and Survival." In *Surviving on the Move: Migration, Poverty and Development in Southern Africa*, ed. J. Crush and B. Frayne. Cape Town: Idasa Publishing
and Midrand: Development Bank of Southern Africa.

Dodson, B. 2008. "Gender, Migration and Remittances in Southern Africa." Southern African Migration Programme Migration Policy Series No. 49, Cape Town,
South Africa.

Geithner, P. Johnson, and L. Chen, eds. 2004. *Diaspora Philanthropy and Equitable
Development in China and India*. Cambridge, MA: Harvard University Press.

Makina, D. 2010. "Zimbabwe in Johannesburg." In *Zimbabwe's Exodus: Crisis, Migration, Survival*, ed. J. Crush and D. Tevera. Cape Town: Southern African Migration Programme and Ottawa: International Development Research Centre.

Mbeki, T. 2007. "Address at the AU-African Diaspora Ministerial Conference."
Gallagher Estate, Midrand, South Africa, November 16. http://www.polity
.org.za/article/sa-mbeki-african-unionafrican-diaspora-ministerial-conference-
16112007-2007-11-16.

Mupedziswa, R. 2009. "Diaspora Dollars and Social Development: Remittance
Patterns of Zimbabwean Nationals Based in South Africa." *Global Development
Studies* 5 (3–4): 229–72.

Newland, K. 2009. "Circular Migration and Human Development." Research Paper
2009/42, United Nations Development Programme, New York.

Newland, K., D. Rannveig Agunias, and A. Terrazas. 2008. "Learning by Doing:
Experiences of Circular Migration." Migration Policy Institute, Washington, DC.

Nyberg-Sørensen, N., ed. 2007. *Living Across Worlds: Diaspora, Development and
Transnational Engagement*. Geneva: International Organisation for Migration.

Peberdy, S. 2009. *Selecting Immigrants: National Identity and South Africa's Immigration
Policies, 1910–2008*. Johannesburg: Wits University Press.

Pendleton, W., J. Crush, and K. Lefko-Everett. 2007. "The Haemorrhage of Health
Professionals From South Africa: Medical Opinions." Southern African Migration Programme Migration Policy Series No. 47, Cape Town, South Africa.

Ratha, D., and W. Shaw. 2007. "South-South Migration and Remittances." World
Bank Working Paper No. 102, World Bank, Washington, DC.

Robertson, G. 2008. *South Africans in London*. Wandsbeck: Reach Publishers.

Rogerson, C., and J. Crush. 2008. "South Africa and the Global Recruitment of
Health Professionals." *Africa Insight* 37 (4): 1–15.

SAMP (Southern African Migration Programme). 2008. "The Perfect Storm: The
Realities of Xenophobia in Contemporary South Africa." Southern African
Migration Programme Migration Policy Series No. 50, Cape Town, South Africa.

Stern, M., and G. Szalontai. 2006. "Immigration Policy in South Africa: Does it Make Economic Sense?" *Development Southern Africa* 23 (1): 123–45.

Tevera, D. and A. Chikanda. 2009. "Development Impact of International Remittances: Some Evidence from Origin Households in Zimbabwe." *Global Development Studies* 5 (3–4): 273–302.

Van Hear, N., F. Pieke, and S. Vertovec. 2004. "The Contribution of U.K.-Based Diasporas to Development and Poverty Reduction." Report for the U.K. Department for International Development, Centre on Migration, Policy and Society, Oxford University, Oxford, England.

Vertovec, S. 2007. "Circular Migration: The Way Forward in Global Policy?" Working Paper No. 4, International Migration Institute, Oxford University, Oxford, England.

World Bank. 2008. "The African Union and World Bank: Mobilizing the African Diaspora." World Bank, Washington, DC. http://web.worldbank.org/WBSITE/EXTERNAL/COUNTRIES/AFRICAEXT/0,,contentMDK:21936148~pagePK:146736~piPK:226340~theSitePK:258644,00.html.

CHAPTER 2

Another Link in the Chain: Migrant Networks and International Investment

David Leblang

While it is generally recognized that we live in an increasingly globalized world, it is also evident that the effects of globalization are unequal. Despite the enormous size of global capital markets, peoples, states, and economies have varying degrees of access to international financial markets. The ability of public and private entities to attract global investment has dramatic consequences for growth, development, and equality. That is why scholars have devoted significant energy to understanding the factors that lead capital to flow from one country to another. A dominant line of thinking holds that institutional differences across countries explain why some countries are able to borrow internationally while others are not. Countries with institutions that enable policy makers to demonstrate a credible commitment to stable and liberal economic policies, so the argument goes, are able to attract investment because investors envision a lower risk of expropriation (Alfaro, Kelemli-Ozcan, and Volosovych 2006; Buthe and Milner 2006; Jensen 2003; Pevehouse 2002).

It is difficult to overstate the importance of credible commitments. The institutional story, however, only goes so far in helping us understand the pattern of international investment. While not dismissing the importance of institutions, we argue that investors are faced with tremendous asymmetries of information when considering alternative investment environments. Investors may not know about investment opportunities within various countries. This chapter argues that migrant networks—connections between migrant communities in the investing country and the migrant's country of origin—facilitate cross-border investment by decreasing information asymmetries. Because migrants have specific information about language, customs, culture, and regulations in potential markets, they help resolve informational hurdles associated with cross-border investment. Further, because migrants are dispersed across a wide range of countries, they can act as an enforcement mechanism, steering investment toward stable markets and directing it away from others. Finally, migrant networks can help separate relevant information from noise—something especially important in an environment in which investors are bombarded with massive amounts of information on a daily basis.

This chapter examines the effect of migrant networks on cross-national investment patterns using a dyadic data set composed of investment from 58 source countries into 120 destination countries for 2002. Empirically, we ask how migrant networks influence both portfolio and foreign direct investment.[1] Looking at both portfolio and foreign direct investment allows us to evaluate the generality of our argument, because these two types of investment are fundamentally different. While portfolio investors purchase stocks and bonds in open markets, foreign direct investors own a fixed stake in a plant or machinery. In addition, portfolio and foreign direct investment differ in terms of their heterogeneity; while portfolio investment opportunities are bounded by the offerings of private and public entities, foreign direct investment (FDI) represents a seemingly endless set of options. In spite of broad similarities to some investors, both the ownership structure and heterogeneity of these investments mean that investors are faced with investment opportunities that differ in terms of both risk and expected return.

Following a brief literature review, this chapter

- Develops the argument linking migrant networks to cross-national investment and derives hypotheses
- Discusses the sample, data, and measures used to test our hypotheses
- Reviews empirical results
- Offers conclusions.

Determinants of International Investment

Consider an investor in country j deciding whether to purchase stocks, bonds, or both in foreign country i_1. The investor compares the expected return on an investment in country i_1 to the expected return in country j and the expected return in country i_2. How does an investor decide where to invest? One set of scholarship assumes that investors are risk averse and use the International Capital Asset Pricing Model (ICAPM) to understand international portfolio diversification. ICAPM models conclude that in the absence of information asymmetries and transaction costs, investors should hold domestic assets in their portfolio in proportion to their country's share of global market capitalization.[2] The rationale behind this result is that the risk of an individual's entire portfolio can be reduced by holding foreign assets that are negatively correlated with returns in the home country, allowing at least average returns while minimizing the overall variance of the portfolio.

Empirical work, however, finds little support for the result of the ICAPM and documents the existence of a "home bias"—a situation where investors prefer to invest at home rather than abroad.[3] The "home bias" is puzzling because it means that investors are not only foregoing higher returns from investing abroad, but they are also holding a portfolio that is not sufficiently diversified. Scholars have argued that a large measure of the home bias can be explained in terms of information asymmetries.[4]

A set of empirical studies asks whether different institutional structures help solve the commitment problem and provide borrowing countries with better access to international capital markets. One set of scholarly contributions argues that domestic political institutions can signal a commitment to the protection of property rights (for example, Heinsz 2000; Jensen 2003). Another related literature explores aggregate measures related to institutional quality and good governance (Alfaro, Kelemli-Ozcan, and Volosovych 2006). Studies in this tradition view governance and institutional quality as a cluster of characteristics including the protection of private property rights, the existence of an independent judiciary, the provision of constitutional rights, and low levels of public corruption. Countries that have these institutional characteristics are favored by international investors who value transparency, the rule of law, and low corruption (Wei 2000).

Migrant Networks as a Conduit for Capital

Scholars have long recognized the importance of social networks for fostering economic exchange either when formal institutions are absent or when they are incomplete (for example, North 2005).[5] We argue that migrant networks help facilitate cross-national investment by helping reduce asymmetries of information between source (j) and destination (i) countries and by mitigating transaction costs that may otherwise prevent economic exchange.

A migrant community from India residing in the United States, for example, can provide U.S. investors with a signal of the work ethic, labor quality, and business culture that exists in India. These signals enhance the quality of information that U.S. investors have about India, allowing them to make forecasts about their ability to invest in potentially profitable assets offered on the Indian market. In his study of the Indian community residing in the United States, Kapur (2001) explains how the mere presence of that community enhances investment opportunities in India: "Companies like Yahoo, Hewlett Packard and General Electric have opened R&D centers in India largely because of the confidence engendered by the presence of many Indians working in their U.S. operations. This points to the cognitive effects arising from the projection of a coherent, appealing, and progressive identity on the part of the diaspora which signals an image of prosperity and progress to potential investors and consumers."[6]

Along with the provision of an image of their home country, migrant networks can provide business opportunities through formal (for example, business) or information (for example, familial) contacts in their home country. These linkages have been extensively documented in studies of specific industries and migrant communities, although they are likely best documented in studies of the overseas Chinese (Rauch and Casella 2001). In their study, the *Bamboo Network*, Weidenbaum and Hughes (1996) detail the comparative advantage overseas Chinese have when it comes to investing in China and argue that it goes well beyond commonality of language, knowledge of cultural, legal barriers, and preexisting familial connections. Wang's study shows how ethnic Chinese residing abroad provide a "linkage between China and the rest of the world [in that they] facilitate the understanding of and access to *guanxi* [business relationship] networks by other foreign investors. Without the agency of ethnic Chinese, it would have been much more difficult for foreign companies to use informal personal networks to complement and compensate for the weak formal legal institutions in China" (Wang 2000).

These familiarity effects are important because they help investors overcome general problems associated with information asymmetries. Migrant communities can also play a more direct role in facilitating cross-national portfolio investment by helping reduce barriers to entry—through knowledge of language, institutional rules, and/or regulatory hurdles—that may otherwise prevent a foreign investor from purchasing equities or bonds. This knowledge of on-the-ground conditions is costly (and not necessarily private) and provides investors with the ability to "match" investments with investment opportunities as they exist. This "matching" function of migrant networks has been observed in studies of international trade where Rauch and Trindade (2002) find that migrant-generated information helps match buyers with sellers, a function that becomes more important as goods become increasingly heterogeneous.[7]

Migrant networks provide investors with an informational advantage because they are in a position to have information regarding investment opportunities in their home country. Bandelj (2002) provides some evidence concerning the investment behavior of Western European and North American investors after the opening of markets in Eastern Europe. Investment in Eastern European countries was "often based on ethnic ties between sizable and relatively affluent expatriate communities and their home countries" (Bandelj 2002:421), and there was an informational advantage because "firms amassed information about investment opportunities through their business or personal ties" (Bandelj 2002:412). This informational advantage can translate into higher-than-average expected returns if the migrant herself or himself has a higher level of human capital. In his assessment of the Armenian diaspora, Freinkman notes that "when compared to the average economic agent, diaspora businessmen and professionals face a lower risk of becoming the first movers, that is, the first one to make an investment. They benefit from a specific informational advantage: common cultural background and established social links between diaspora and local entrepreneurs help them to reduce transaction costs of new entry and building new partnerships" (Freinkman 2002:6).

Because larger migrant networks provide costly and private information, we hypothesize that they will exert a positive influence on cross-border investment. The effect of migrant networks should increase when the migrants themselves are the entrepreneurs, because there will be lower barriers to entry and even smaller asymmetries of information. Not all information is positive, however. Migrant networks may pass on information that the regime in their home country is corrupt or that the potential for expropriation is high. Migrant communities that carry negative information about their home country could actually decrease invest-ment in their country of origin.

The positive effect of migrant networks on cross-national investment is predicated not only on the transmission of information, in general, but on the provision of information that allows the investor to make a higher-than-expected return. In efficient markets, investors can profit by exploit-ing costly or private information—information that is not (yet) available to all market participants. We argue that migrant networks facilitate cross-border investment by providing private information—either directly or through the familiarity channel—to investors. The aggregate nature of our data makes it difficult to directly test the effect of private information, so we follow Rauch and Trindade (2002) and argue that migrant networks should play a larger role in the trade of heterogeneous assets than in the trade in homogenous assets. This is because the information asymmetries associated with heterogeneous assets are significantly larger than those associated with homogenous assets. FDI opportunities vary by commodity class and by ownership stake and constitute a more heterogeneous class of investment opportunities than portfolio investment opportunities, which are defined by the issuing agency. Because FDI faces higher risks of expro-priation, information about the investment environment is more valuable. We hypothesize, therefore, that the effect of migrant networks on FDI will be larger than the effect of migrant networks on portfolio investment, all else being equal.

In the next section we discuss the empirical model, data, and variables used to test these hypotheses. Empirical results follow.

Empirical Model, Sample, Data, and Variables

We embed our hypothesis tests within a gravity model of trade in financial assets. While traditionally used to study trade in commodities, the gravity model has recently been used to examine bilateral trade in financial assets. When applied to trade in financial assets, studies have also found that cross-national investment is a positive function of economic size, common language, shared colonial history, and a negative function of distance (for example, Eichengreen and Luengnaruemitchai 2006; Portes and Rey 2005). We take this augmented gravity model as our point of departure and use it to investigate the effect of migrant networks.

To examine the link between migrant networks and bilateral portfolio investment, we use data from the International Monetary Fund's Coordinated Portfolio Investment Survey (CPIS). The CPIS collects information on the stock of cross-border investments in equities and in short and long-term bonds broken down by issuer's country of residence. For the 2002 CPIS, 62 countries participated and reported holdings for over 150 destination countries.[8] Because of data constraints, we are able to use data on the investment portfolio of only 58 origin (reporting) countries and 120 destination countries.

Our data on FDI come from the Organisation for Economic Co-operation and Development's (OECD's) International Direct Investment Statistics, which reports aggregate annual measures. This source is limited in that it only provides data for outflows from OECD countries. Therefore, our sample is restricted to 26 origin countries and 120 destination countries.

Our key independent variable—migrant networks—measures the stock (or total number) of migrants from country i residing in country j. These data come from a World Bank project on South-South migration and remittances and are based on data from national statistical bureaus (censuses and population registers) and secondary sources (OECD, the International Labour Organization, and the United Nations). A 162×162 matrix of the migrant stock in country j from country i classified according to the migrant's country of birth is constructed from these national sources (Ratha and Shaw 2007). While some of the underlying data are from the late 1990s, the majority corresponds to migrant stock for 2000 or 2001. We assume that population does not change dramatically over time and treat it as measuring migrant stock in 2001.

Following the gravity approach to trade, we measure the size of the origin and destination economies in terms of their total gross national product using data from the Penn World Tables (the Mark 6.2 database) augmented with data from the World Bank's *World Development Indicators*. We also account for the distance between the origin and destination countries and whether they have a common colonial heritage and if, by law, they have the same official language. These three variables are from the Centre d'Études Prospectives et d'Informations Internationales bilateral distance data set.

Taking our cue from earlier work applying the gravity model to trade in financial assets, we add measures of the destination country's capital account policy and capital stock. Specifically, we include a variable from the International Monetary Fund's *Annual Report on Exchange Arrangements and Exchange Restrictions* (2003) that is coded 1 if the destination country has controls on capital market securities and 0 if the destination country does not have controls on capital market securities. We proxy for the capital stock by including a variable that measures the average years of education obtained by the population in the destination. The use of a human capital measure has two advantages over using indicators of financial capital. First, the stock of financial capital—even lagged—is likely correlated with the stock of portfolio investment in the destination. Second, since we are interested in the influence of migrant networks, controlling for the stock of human capital in country i should decrease the effect of these networks if it is only the highly educated who emigrate.

We include a variable measuring the correlation in growth rates between the source and destination country as a means of accounting for risk diversification: ICAPM models hold that source countries should invest in destinations with dissimilar business cycles to diversify their portfolios. To minimize the risk of reverse causality—running from investment to correlated growth rates—we calculate the correlation in growth rates using a five-year moving average.

Countries are, all things being equal, more likely to invest where risks of exchange rate depreciation are smaller and where there are minimal transactions costs associated with converting foreign to domestic currency. We therefore include a variable that is coded 1 if the source and destination countries either share the same currency (for example, dollarization) or they both peg to the same currency. Along these lines, we also control for the existence of a dual tax treaty—a bilateral agreement that prevents double taxation.

Following our discussion of the existing literature, we use two different variables to measure domestic institutional constraints, one that taps political stability and one that captures institutional transparency. The first is a measure of institutional democracy, which, all things being equal, should proxy for the stability of the political environment in the destination country. We use the Polity measure of democracy, which is a 21-point scale running from -10 to $+10$, with higher values indicating more democratic institutions. We also measure the quality of domestic institutions using measures from the World Bank's Worldwide Governance Indicators.[9] For our measure of governance, we sum the indicators corresponding to voice and accountability, political stability, regulatory quality, rule of law, and control of corruption. Destination countries with higher values on this index have better and more transparent political institutions.

We use three measures to account for international institutional constraints. We include a dichotomous measure that is coded 1 if both countries i and j are members of the World Trade Organization. We measure membership in Preferential Trade Agreements (PTAs) in two ways. First, we include a variable indicating that both the source and destination have a bilateral PTA. Second, in an effort to see if credibility can be imported from other countries, we include a measure of the total number of PTAs that the destination country has, less a PTA with the source country.

Finally, we include the logged value (in U.S. dollars) of bilateral trade between the source and destination countries. Inclusion of this variable serves several purposes. First, preexisting trading between the source and destination is an indicator of a level of information flow between the two countries, something we claim is captured by the measure of migrant networks. Second, the measures of PTAs and membership in the World Trade Organization could simply be proxying for bilateral trade. Explicitly including trade means that the aforementioned institutional measures will more accurately capture institutional solutions to the credibility problem. Finally, the inclusion of bilateral trade allows us to see how three factors—trade, investment, and migrants—are related to one another.

We estimate the effect of migrant networks on bilateral investment for 2002. To decrease the potential for reverse causality, all independent variables are lagged one year with the exception of governance, which is lagged two years, because the World Bank did not compile it for 2001. Because the dependent variable (and most of the independent variables) corresponds to country pairs—source to destination—we report robust standard errors.

Results

Table 2.1, column 1, contains results from estimating a gravity model of country j's portfolio investment in country i for 2002. Variables used in other gravity-based models of portfolio investment enter with the expected sign and significance: investment is greater between economically larger countries and between countries that (a) have a common colonial history, (b) share a common official language, (c) peg their exchange

TABLE 2.1
Effect of Organizations, Institutions, and Information on Cross-Border Investment

	Effect of immigration		Educated immigrants		"Bad" information	
	Portfolio	FDI	Portfolio	FDI	Portfolio	FDI
Log (migrant stock)	0.19**	0.48**	0.16**	0.45**	0.19**	0.48**
	(0.01)	(0.03)	(0.03)	(0.04)	(0.01)	(0.03)
% with tertiary education			1.21**	0.97**		
			(0.35)	(0.41)		
Log (refugee stock)					−0.30**	−0.31**
					(0.08)	(0.10)
GDP(i)xGDP(j)	0.32**	0.23**	0.43**	0.26**	0.32**	0.23**
	(0.03)	(0.06)	(0.05)	(0.07)	(0.03)	(0.05)
Log (distance)	−0.30**	−0.18**	−0.30**	−0.31**	−0.30**	−0.18**
	(0.06)	(0.09)	(0.09)	(0.10)	(0.06)	(0.09)
Shared colonial origin	0.99**				0.99**	
	(0.28)				(0.28)	
Common official language	0.49**	0.22	0.54**	0.27	0.50**	0.21
	(0.12)	(0.16)	(0.16)	(0.18)	(0.12)	(0.16)
Human capital (D)	0.05**	−0.16**	0.10**	−0.14**	0.05**	−0.16**
	(0.02)	(0.03)	(0.03)	(0.03)	(0.02)	(0.03)
Capital controls (D)	0.13	−0.27**	0.20	−0.25*	0.13	−0.29**
	(0.09)	(0.13)	(0.13)	(0.15)	(0.09)	(0.13)
Log (bilateral trade)	0.02	0.23**	0.05	0.22**	0.02	0.22**
	(0.02)	(0.05)	(0.04)	(0.05)	(0.02)	(0.05)
Correlation of growth rates	0.52**	0.62**	0.91**	0.86**	0.52**	0.63**
	(0.07)	(0.11)	(0.11)	(0.12)	(0.07)	(0.11)
Common currency peg	1.20**	0.80**	1.65**	0.94**	1.21**	0.78**
	(0.16)	(0.21)	(0.21)	(0.22)	(0.15)	(0.21)

Both in World Trade Organization	0.16	−0.08	−0.25	−0.11	0.14	−0.10
	(0.12)	(0.24)	(0.23)	(0.28)	(0.12)	(0.24)
Dual Taxation Treaty	0.71**	0.40**	0.25*	0.36**	0.71**	0.41**
	(0.11)	(0.14)	(0.14)	(0.16)	(0.11)	(0.14)
Polity Score (D)	0.05**	0.01	0.08**	0.01	0.05**	0.01
	(0.01)	(0.01)	(0.01)	(0.01)	(0.01)	(0.01)
Governance (D)	0.16**	0.15**	0.19**	0.15**	0.16**	0.15**
	(0.01)	(0.02)	(0.02)	(0.02)	(0.01)	(0.02)
Bilateral Preferential Trade Agreement	0.15	−0.38**	0.09	−0.51**	0.17	−0.35*
	(0.11)	(0.19)	(0.20)	(0.22)	(0.11)	(0.19)
Total Preferential Trade Agreements (D)	0.00**	−0.00**	0.00**	−0.00**	0.00**	−0.00**
	(0.00)	(0.00)	(0.00)	(0.00)	(0.00)	(0.00)
Constant	−14.49**	−13.12**	−20.64**	−13.65**	−14.65**	−13.27**
	(1.26)	(2.03)	(2.14)	(2.49)	(1.26)	(2.02)
Adjusted R-squared	0.570	0.673	0.670	0.675	0.573	0.675
F-Statistics	276.223	281.419	275.937	224.624	265.095	265.619
Observations	3,462	1,508	1,726	1,207	3,462	1,508

Source: Author's calculations.

Note: Cell entries are ordinary least squares estimates with robust standard errors in parentheses.

FDI = foreign direct investment. GDP = gross domestic product.

* $p < 0.10$. ** $p < 0.05$.

rates to a common currency, (d) have signed a dual taxation treaty, and (e) have similar growth cycles. Countries with higher average levels of education—our measure of human capital—receive more portfolio investment while those with capital account restrictions receive less.

Our results also reinforce the odd finding from prior research that distance has a statistically significant and negative effect on bilateral portfolio investment. Recall that the standard ICAPM model would suggest a positive relationship because countries farther away from one another would be less likely to experience similar economic shocks. The negative finding, however, is consistent with earlier findings and may reflect what Portes, Rey, and Oh (2001) refer to generically as "informational frictions."[10]

The indicators of domestic political commitments are also as expected: countries with credible domestic institutions (higher values of governance and the Polity score) receive larger amounts of portfolio investment, a result that is consistent with aggregate studies of foreign investment (for example, Alfaro, Kelemli-Ozcan, and Volosovych 2006; Jensen 2003).[11] The results for international commitment mechanisms are mixed: membership in the World Trade Organization or having a bilateral PTA has no statistically significant effect on investment—likely as a result of its significant bivariate correlation with bilateral trade—but the total number of PTAs does, which indicates that the sheer number of PTAs is a signal that politicians in country i are committed to the protection of property rights.[12]

Turning to our variable of interest—that of total migrant stock—we find the estimated parameter is positive and statistically significant. An advantage of using a logarithmic transformation for both migrant stock and investment is that the point estimate can be interpreted as an elasticity. Our results, then, show that increasing the migrant stock from country i in country j by 1 percent increases portfolio investment by .15 percent.

Table 2.1, column 2, repeats this analysis substituting FDI for portfolio investment as the dependent variable. While there are some differences in terms of the parameter estimates on trade and trade institutions, differences we discuss in greater detail below, the effect of migrant networks remains strong (an elasticity of almost .5) and statistically significant.

The results thus far support the hypothesis that migrant networks encourage cross-border investment because they provide investors with information about investment opportunities across particular destinations.

We expect that this effect will be more pronounced when the migrants themselves are involved in the investment process. Unfortunately, we cannot directly measure migrant-based investment, so we proxy for it using the percentage of migrants from country i living in country j that have higher (tertiary) education.[13] We also include the log of the total number of migrants so that the former variable is not capturing the effect of the latter variable.

The results in table 2.1, columns 3 and 4, support the role of highly educated immigrants in the investment process. Highly skilled immigrants increase both portfolio and foreign direct investment to their home country, a conclusion consistent with the anecdotal evidence from Saxenian (2002, 2006), Kleiman (1996), and Kapur (2001). Inclusion of a variable measuring the human capital of migrants does not render our measure of migrant stock statistically insignificant, a result that would occur if only entrepreneurial migrants were the ones investing.

In table 2.1, columns 5 and 6, we attempt to account for the fact that migrants can often provide "bad" information—that is, information that would lead investors away from their country of origin. Again, we cannot measure this concept directly, so we proxy for it using the number of refugees (asylum seekers) in country j that originate in country i. Refugees, by definition, are designated as such, because of the adverse conditions that exist within their country of origin, conditions that likely are not conducive to investment.

Inclusion of the size of the refugee stock (logged) along with the size of the migrant population provides substantively and statistically compelling results. Countries that are the source of large refugee populations received smaller amounts of investment (both portfolio and foreign direct).[14] And inclusion of this variable does little to change the effect of the migrant stock, our primary measure of information networks.

We check the robustness of our central findings in a number of ways. First, we include a set of dummy variables for source countries, for destination countries, and for both source and destination countries. Second, to check whether investment and migrants both move in the same direction, we also include the stock of migrants from country j residing in country i. Both robustness tests do not alter our central findings—that migrant networks exert a positive and statistically significant effect on cross-border investment.[15]

Endogeneity

It is plausible that the results we report are spurious. We investigate this possibility in two ways.

First, in results not reported, we use data on the stock of migrants from country i residing in country j in 1991, that is, migrant stock lagged 10 years. This alteration does not change our fundamental finding that migrant networks increase investment activity.

Second, we instrument the migrant stock from country i residing in country j. Finding valid instruments is no easy task because most plausible instruments for cross-national migration are also determinants of cross-national investment.[16] Prior research (Leblang, Fitzgerald, and Teets 2007) has found that migrants are drawn to countries that grant citizenship based on birth (jus solis) rather than on blood (jus sanguinis). The determination of jus solis versus jus sanguinis is based on legal tradition and country norms, and we are confident that it does not have an independent effect on a country's decision to invest abroad. Our instrument for the migrant stock from country i living in country j is citizenship policy, which is coded 1 if country j provides for citizenship by birth.

The results from our instrumental variables model are contained in table 2.2. The effect of our instrumented measure of migrants from country i residing in country j is positive and statistically significant at conventional levels. The instrument is strong in both the portfolio and the FDI models, with F-statistics far exceeding the rule-of-thumb cutoff of 10, and the substantive results are consistent with our expectations.

Migrant Networks and Heterogeneous Investments

Our next hypothesis suggests that migrant networks facilitate cross-border investment through the provision of private information. Following Rauch and Trindade (2002), we argue that the informational role of migrant networks should be more important for trade in heterogeneous commodities—commodities where private information has greater value. As mentioned, we believe that FDI opportunities are significantly more heterogeneous than portfolio investment opportunities. Not only are there an infinite number of FDI opportunities—ranging from joint ownership to greenfield investments—they also differ in that they are risky because the possibility of expropriation is higher. Portfolio investment, on the other hand, can only be made in assets that are publicly issued by either governmental or corporate interests, entities that provide relatively

TABLE 2.2
Endogeneity

	Portfolio		Foreign Direct Investment	
	2nd stage	1st stage	2nd stage	1st stage
Log (migrant stock)	0.11**		0.75**	
	(0.04)		(0.09)	
GDP(i)xGDP(j)	0.36**	0.45**	0.10	0.44**
	(0.04)	(0.04)	(0.06)	(0.04)
Human capital (D)	0.05**	0.08**	−0.16**	0.05**
	(0.02)	(0.02)	(0.03)	(0.02)
Log (distance)	−0.40**	−1.33**	−0.07	−0.59**
	(0.08)	(0.08)	(0.09)	(0.07)
Shared colonial origin	0.93**	−0.60*		
	(0.27)	(0.36)		
Common official language	0.62**	1.00**	−0.40	1.79**
	(0.13)	(0.15)	(0.25)	(0.15)
Capital controls (D)	0.12	−0.12	−0.27**	0.16
	(0.09)	(0.12)	(0.13)	(0.10)
Log (bilateral trade)	0.05*	0.32**	0.13**	0.29**
	(0.03)	(0.03)	(0.05)	(0.027)
Correlation of growth rates	0.52**	0.09	0.60**	0.15*
	(0.07)	(0.10)	(0.12)	(0.09)
Common currency peg	1.24**	0.48**	0.88**	−0.41**
	(0.16)	(0.20)	(0.22)	(0.18)
Both in World Trade Organization	0.33**	1.78**	−0.06	0.01
	(0.14)	(0.16)	(0.25)	(0.19)
Dual Taxation Treaty	0.75**	0.51**	0.28*	0.41**
	(0.11)	(0.14)	(0.15)	(0.11)
Polity score (D)	0.05**	0.02**	0.00	0.04**
	(0.01)	(0.01)	(0.01)	(0.10)
Governance (D)	0.14**	−0.21**	0.18**	−0.10**
	(0.02)	(0.012)	(0.02)	(0.01)
Bilateral Preferential Trade Agreement	0.09	−0.73**	−0.36*	−0.17
	(0.11)	(0.15)	(0.19)	(0.15)
Total Preferential Trade Agreements (D)	0.00**	−0.01**	−0.00**	0.001
	(0.00)	(0.001)	(0.00)	(0.001)
Jus solis (D)		1.77**		1.36**
		(0.11)		(0.09)
Constant	−16.09**	−14.77**	−7.43**	−17.58**
	(1.50)	(1.57)	(2.61)	(1.45)
Adjusted R-squared	0.565	0.46	0.655	0.70
F-statistic	251.040	192.17	225.007	244.66
F-statistic for excluded instrument		290.00		223.22
Observations	3,462	3,462	1,508	1,508

Source: Author's calculations.
Note: Cell entries are instrumental variables estimates with robust standard errors in parentheses.
GDP = gross domestic product.
* $p < 0.10$.
** $p < 0.05$.

more information to markets. And because portfolio investment is more liquid, it can more easily be moved from market to market and from asset to asset, something that requires relatively less information than FDI. We therefore expect that migrant networks should be substantively more important for FDI than for portfolio investment.

We examine this hypothesis in table 2.3, where we estimate a seemingly unrelated regression of the determinants of both portfolio investment and bilateral trade in commodities. Rather than report standard errors, we provide bootstraped 95 percent confidence intervals, which permits us to test the null hypothesis that the effect of migrant networks on portfolio investment is equal to its effect on trade in commodities.[17]

Table 2.3 presents the results of this analysis. We find that larger migrant networks increase both portfolio investment and foreign direct investment but that the effect on FDI is substantively larger, and statistically different, from the effect on portfolio investment. In fact, the substantive effect for FDI is almost twice that for portfolio investment. This is consistent with our expectations: because portfolio investment represents a more homogenous opportunity set, private information provided by migrant networks becomes increasingly valuable for investors evaluating more heterogeneous options.

Conclusion: Harnessing the Diaspora

Access to international capital markets is a perennial problem confronted by all countries. Students of international political economy have invested considerable time trying to understand the theoretical and empirical connections across countries and markets. One general conclusion from these efforts is that information asymmetries represent a large cost to cross-border economic transactions. We have demonstrated that migrant networks—connections between immigrants and their homeland—play an important role in decreasing asymmetries and in promoting portfolio investment. In addition, we have presented evidence that migrant networks do this by providing information about investment opportunities that exist across countries.

Given that migrant networks are a conduit for international investment flows, how can governments harness their diaspora in the face of the continuing competition for capital? One mechanism that governments use to demonstrate their commitment to their external populations is through

TABLE 2.3

Information and Heterogeneous Investments

	Portfolio	FDI
Log (migrant stock)	0.23**	0.45**
	[0.15, 0.31]	[0.36, 0.54]
GDP(i)xGDP(j)	0.56**	0.14*
	[0.40, 0.72]	[−0.01, 0.29]
Human capital (D)	0.07*	−0.14**
	[−0.01, 0.16]	[−0.23, −0.06]
Log (distance)	−0.25**	−0.29**
	[−0.46, −0.03]	[−0.48, −0.10]
Log (bilateral trade)	0.04	0.35**
	[−0.11, 0.19]	[0.17, 0.53]
Common official language	0.99**	0.16
	[0.53, 1.44]	[−0.15, 0.47]
Capital controls (D)	−0.24	−0.18
	[−0.54, 0.07]	[−0.45, 0.09]
Correlation of growth rates	0.85**	0.78**
	[0.62, 1.09]	[0.54, 1.01]
Common currency peg	1.54**	0.69**
	[0.98, 2.10]	[0.22, 1.17]
Both in World Trade Organization	−0.18	−0.18
	[−0.86, 0.50]	[−0.89, 0.52]
Dual Taxation Treaty	0.02	0.25
	[−0.30, 0.33]	[−0.16, 0.65]
Polity score (D)	0.07**	0.00
	[0.04, 0.11]	[−0.02, 0.03]
Governance (D)	0.20**	0.14**
	[0.14, 0.26]	[0.09, 0.20]
Bilateral Preferential Trade Agreement	−0.29	−0.73**
	[−0.71, 0.12]	[−1.09, −0.37]
Total Preferential Trade Agreements (D)	0.00	−0.00
	[−0.00, 0.01]	[−0.01, 0.00]
Constant	−27.06**	−9.30**
	[−32.77, −21.34]	[−14.29, −4.32]
Observations	1,080	

Source: Author's calculations.
Note: Cell entries are seemingly unrelated regression estimates with bootstrapped 95 percent confidence intervals in square brackets.
GDP = gross domestic product.
* $p < 0.10$. ** $p < 0.05$.

the provision of voting rights to expatriates. Table 2.4 offers suggestive evidence of the importance of these rights. In columns 1 and 3 we include a dummy variable that is coded "1" for emigration countries (country i) that allow their expatriates to vote in national elections. Countries that allow expatriate voting generate larger portfolio investment; we find no statistically significant effect on FDI. Countries, however, differ in how they allow their expatriates to vote. Countries such as Mexico require that expatriates go to embassies or consulates to vote in person, while others, such as Brazil, allow voting by mail. In columns 2 and 4, we break down these policies and find, unsurprisingly, that postal voting has a substantively larger and statistically significant effect on generating bilateral investment. It is indeed a signal of the emigration country's desire to maintain contact with its overseas population.

How do these findings square with the literature on immigration and capital flows? Studies have already documented that migrant laborers remit a substantial amount of capital (Leuth and Ruiz-Arranz 2006; Ratha and Shaw 2007). Our findings suggest that migrant-driven investment is yet another way in which diaspora communities influence developments in their home countries. And these two flows of capital likely have different effects on inequality and poverty, providing an interesting avenue for future work connecting diasporas to development.

TABLE 2.4
External Voting Rights

	Portfolio		FDI	
Log (migrant stock)	0.19**	0.19**	0.48**	0.48**
	(0.01)	(0.01)	(0.03)	(0.03)
External voting	0.20**		0.16	
	(0.08)		(0.11)	
Voting via post		0.36**		0.29**
		(0.09)		(0.14)
Voting in person		0.00		−0.01
		(0.10)		(0.15)
GDP(i)xGDP(j)	0.32**	0.32**	0.23**	0.23**
	(0.03)	(0.03)	(0.06)	(0.05)
Human capital (D)	0.04**	0.05**	−0.16**	−0.15**
	(0.02)	(0.02)	(0.03)	(0.03)
Log (Distance)	−0.30**	−0.30**	−0.18**	−0.17**
	(0.06)	(0.06)	(0.09)	(0.09)

(continued next page)

TABLE 2.4 (continued)

External Voting Rights

	Portfolio		FDI	
Shared colonial origin	1.02**	1.00**		
	(0.28)	(0.28)		
Common official language	0.49**	0.48**	0.21	0.18
	(0.12)	(0.12)	(0.16)	(0.16)
Capital controls (D)	0.10	0.17*	−0.29**	−0.21
	(0.09)	(0.09)	(0.13)	(0.13)
Log (bilateral trade)	0.03	0.02	0.22**	0.22**
	(0.02)	(0.02)	(0.05)	(0.05)
Correlation of growth rates	0.50**	0.52**	0.60**	0.62**
	(0.07)	(0.07)	(0.11)	(0.11)
Common currency peg	1.21**	1.21**	0.81**	0.81**
	(0.16)	(0.16)	(0.21)	(0.21)
Both in World Trade Organization	0.19	0.18	−0.04	−0.07
	(0.12)	(0.12)	(0.24)	(0.24)
Dual Taxation Treaty	0.69**	0.68**	0.38**	0.39**
	(0.11)	(0.11)	(0.14)	(0.14)
Polity score (D)	0.05**	0.05**	0.01	0.01
	(0.01)	(0.01)	(0.01)	(0.01)
Governance (D)	0.16**	0.14**	0.15**	0.14**
	(0.01)	(0.01)	(0.02)	(0.02)
Bilateral Preferential Trade Agreement	0.14	0.16	−0.39**	−0.35*
	(0.11)	(0.11)	(0.19)	(0.19)
Total Preferential Trade Agreement (D)	0.00**	0.00**	−0.00**	−0.00**
	(0.00)	(0.00)	(0.00)	(0.00)
Constant	−14.53**	−14.58**	−13.20**	−13.31**
	(1.26)	(1.26)	(2.03)	(2.02)
Adjusted R-squared	0.571	0.572	0.674	0.674
F-statistic	260.982	249.160	267.294	252.848
Observations	3,462	3,462	1,508	1,508

Source: Author's calculations.
Note: Cell entries are ordinary least squares estimates with robust standard errors in parentheses.
GDP = gross domestic product.
* $p < 0.10$.
** $p < 0.05$.

Notes

1. Javorcik et al. (2006) explore the link between migrant networks in the United States and U.S. FDI.
2. See Lane (2005) and Lane and Milesi-Ferretti (2004) for studies of bilateral investment that are explicitly derived from the ICAPM model. Elton et al. (2003) present a textbook exposition of capital asset pricing models.

3. See French and Poterba (1991) and Tesar and Werner (1995). Lewis (1999) contains a review of the relevant literature.

4. Kang and Stulz (1997), for example, document that foreign investors in Japan disproportionally own more shares of those firms whose information is more readily available. More generally, Tesar and Werner (1995:479) argue that factors such as "language, institutional and regulatory difference" explain the propensity of investors to invest at home rather than abroad. French and Poterba (1991) also account for home bias with reference to a set of factors they broadly categorize as "familiarity" effects.

5. The relational approach to economic sociology focuses on relations between parties to a transaction rather than on the transaction itself. This view—that economic processes are "embedded" in social relations—has been used to study labor markets (Granovetter 1973), business transactions (Uzzi 1996), and FDI (Bandelj 2002).

6. Kapur and McHale (2006) refer to this as "branding" and argue that the Indian diaspora has created a brand name by signaling the potential productivity and trustworthiness of their countrymen.

7. The role of migrant networks in facilitating bilateral trade has been studied by Gould (1994) for the United States and by Head and Reis (1998) for Canada.

8. Lane and Milesi-Ferretti (2004), and Eichengreen and Luengnaruemitchai (2006), point out some advantages and disadvantages of the CPIS data. In designing the survey, the International Monetary Fund has attempted to ensure comparability across countries; to that end, the surveys are structured to prevent double counting. That said, the CPIS does not report the domestic holdings of investors, which makes testing theories of portfolio allocation and home bias difficult with these data, and it is possible that there is some under-reporting. Most significantly for our purposes, it does not have data on the foreign holdings of a few large origin countries, including China and Saudi Arabia (though it does have these countries as destinations).

9. http://info.worldbank.org/governance/wgi/index.asp.

10. Coval and Moskowitz (1999) also find that distance has a negative effect on investment decisions because U.S. investors and portfolio managers have a preference for geographically proximate investments because they have better information about them. In a study of stockholdings in Finland, Grinblatt and Keloharju (2001) find that distance—their proxy for dissimilarity in language and culture—influences portfolio choice. Hau (2001) reaches a similar conclusion with regard to German traders who consistently earn higher average returns compared with foreign investors trading on the same exchange.

11. Adding these two variables separately does little to alter their parameter estimates and does not decrease their level of statistical significance.

12. This is a confirmation of the finding regarding the importance of PTAs for aggregate FDI reported in Buthe and Milner (2006).

13. We use data from the OECD's Immigration and Expatriate Database. This database only has information on immigrants into OECD countries; consequently, the sample size is greatly reduced.

14. This could be the result of the fact that countries that generate large numbers of refugees are generally environments that are inhospitable to foreign investment. To disentangle whether the estimated effect is a function of poor investment environments or due to the provision of information, we include a measure of the total number of refugees generated by a particular destination country. Both this variable and the one measuring the bilateral stock of refugees are statistically significant, making us unable to disentangle these two explanations. We are grateful to an anonymous referee for pointing out this possibility.

15. We do not include the results due to space constraints; full results are available from the author on request.

16. A discussion of push and pull factors influencing cross-national migration is contained in Leblang, Fitzgerald, and Teets (2009). Javorcik et al. (2006) use instrumental variables in their study of the effect of migrants on U.S. FDI and use passport costs in country i as their instrument for migrant stock. While theoretically reasonable, this variable is highly correlated with governance structures in country i (countries with worse governance charge more for passports than countries with better governance), so we remain skeptical about whether it satisfies the exclusion restriction (McKenzie 2005).

17. Hypothesis testing using seemingly unrelated regressions assumes that the errors from both equations are distributed normally. In the case of trade, the residuals are not due to a large number of zeros. We therefore calculate standard errors and associated confidence intervals using bootstrap resampling with 50 replications. Varying the number of replications up to 500 only increases the strength of our conclusions.

References

Alfaro, L., S. Kelemli-Ozcan, and V. Volosovych. 2006. "Why Doesn't Capital Flow from Rich to Poor Countries? An Empirical Investigation." Harvard Business School, Cambridge, MA.

Bandelj, N. 2002. "Embedded Economies: Social Relations as Determinants of Foreign Direct Investment in Central and Eastern Europe." *Social Forces* 81 (2): 411–44.

Buthe, T., and H. Milner. 2006. "The Politics of Foreign Direct Investment in Developing Countries: Increasing FDI through International Trade Agreements?" Department of Political Science, Duke University, Durham, North Carolina.

Coval, J., and T. Moskowitz. 1999. "Home Bias at Home: Local Equity Preference in Domestic Portfolios." *Journal of Finance* 54: 2045–73.

Eichengreen, B., and P. Luengnaruemitchai. 2006. "Bond Markets as Conduits for Capital Flows: How Does Asia Compare?" National Bureau of Economic Research, Cambridge, MA.

Elton, E., M. Gruber, S. Brown, and W. Goetzmann. 2003. *Modern Portfolio Theory and Investment Analysis*. New York: John Wiley and Sons.

Freinkman, L. 2002. "Role of the Diasporas in Transition Economies: Lessons from Armenia." World Bank, Washington, DC.

French, K., and J. Poterba. 1991. "Investor Diversification and International Equity Markets." *American Economic Review* 81: 222–26.

Gould, D. M. 1994. "Immigrant Links to the Home Country: Empirical Implications for U.S. Bilateral Trade Flows." *Review of Economics and Statistics* 76 (2): 302–16.

Granovetter, Mark. 1973. "The Strength of Weak Ties." *American Journal of Sociology* 78 (6): 1360–80.

Grinblatt, M., and M. Keloharju. 2001. "How Distance, Language, and Culture Influence Stockholdings and Trades." *The Journal of Finance* 56 (3): 1053–74.

Hau, H. 2001. "Location Matters: An Examination of Trading Profits." *Journal of Finance* 56: 1959–83.

Head, K., and J. Reis. 1998. "Immigration and Trade Creation: Econometric Evidence from Canada." *Canadian Journal of Economics* 31 (1): 47–62.

Heinsz, W. J. 2000. "The Institutional Environment for Multinational Investment." *Journal of Law, Economics and Organization* 16 (2): 334–64.

IMF (International Monetary Fund). 2003. *Annual Report on Exchange Arrangements and Exchange Restrictions*. Washington, DC: IMF.

Javorcik, B., C. Ozden, M. Spatareanu, and C. Neagu. 2006. *Migrant Networks and Foreign Direct Investment*. Washington, DC: World Bank.

Jensen, N. 2003. "Democratic Governance and Multinational Corporations: Political Regimes and Inflows of Foreign Direct Investment." *International Organization* 57 (3): 587–616.

Kang, J., and R. Stulz. 1997. "Why Is There a Home Bias? An Analysis of Foreign Portfolio Equity Ownership in Japan." *Journal of Financial Economics* 46: 3–28.

Kapur, D. 2001. "Diasporas and Technology Transfer." *Journal of Human Development* 2 (2): 265–86.

Kapur, D., and J. McHale. 2006. *Give Us Your Best and Brightest: The Global Hunt for Talent and Its Impact on the Developing World*. Washington, DC: Center for Global Development.

Kleiman, E. 1996. *Jewish and Palestinian Diaspora Attitudes to Philanthropy and Investment*. Tel Aviv: Hebrew University Press.

Lane, P. R. 2005. *Global Bond Portfolios and EMU*. Dublin: University of Dublin.

Lane, P. R., and G. M. Milesi-Ferretti. 2004. *International Investment Patterns*. Washington, DC: International Monetary Fund.

Leblang, D., J. Fitzgerald, and J. Teets. 2009. "Defying the Law of Gravity: The Political Economy of International Migration." Department of Political Science, University of Virginia, Charlottesville, VA.

Leuth, E., and M. Ruiz-Arranz. 2006. *A Gravity Model of Workers' Remittances*. Washington, DC: International Monetary Fund.

Lewis, K. 1999. "Trying to Explain Home Bias in Equities and Consumption." *Journal of Economic Literature* 37: 571–608.

McKenzie, D. 2005. "Paper Walls are Easier to Tear Down: Passport Costs and Legal Barriers to Emigration." World Bank, Washington, DC. http://go.worldbank.org/2B0K1Q64S0.

North, D. C. 2005. *Understanding the Process of Economic Change*. Princeton, New Jersey: Princeton University Press.

Pevehouse, Jon C. 2002. "Democracy from the Outside-In? International Organizations and Democratization." *International Organization* 56 (3): 515–49.

Portes, R., and H. Rey. 2005. "The Determinants of Cross-Border Equity Flows." *Journal of International Economics* 65: 269–96.

Portes, R., H. Rey, and Y. Oh. 2001. "Information and Capital Flows: The Determinants of Transactions in Financial Assets." *European Economic Review* 45: 783–96.

Ratha, D., and W. Shaw. 2007. *South-South Migration and Remittances*. Washington, DC: World Bank.

Rauch, J. E., and A. Casella. 2001. *Networks and Markets*. New York: Russell Sage Foundation.

Rauch, J. E., and V. Trindade. 2002. "Ethnic Chinese Networks in International Trade." *Review of Economics and Statistics* 84 (1): 116–30. http://www.catchword.com/rpsv/catchword/mitpress/00346535/contp1-1.htm.

Saxenian, A. 2002. *Local and Global Networks of Immigrant Professionals in Silicon Valley*. San Francisco, CA: Public Policy Institute of California.

Saxenian, A. 2006. *The New Argonauts: Regional Advantage in a Global Economy*. Cambridge, MA: Harvard University Press.

Tesar, L., and I. Werner. 1995. "Home Bias and High Turnover." *Journal of International Money and Finance* 14 (4): 467–92.

Uzzi, B. 1996. "The Sources and Consequences of Embeddedness for the Economic Performance of Organizations: The Network Effect." *American Sociological Review* 61: 674–98.

Wang, H. 2000. "Information Institutions and Foreign Investment in China." *The Pacific Review* 13 (4): 525–56.

Wei, S. 2000. "How Taxing is Corruption on International Investors?" *Review of Economics and Statistics* 82 (1): 1–11.

Weidenbaum, M., and S. Hughes. 1996. *The Bamboo Network*. New York: The Free Press.

CHAPTER 3

Return Migration and Small Enterprise Development in the Maghreb

Flore Gubert and Christophe J. Nordman

The Middle East and North Africa region is one of the most remarkable regions in the world in terms of international migration, with several coexisting "migration systems" (labor-exporting countries in the Maghreb and Mashreq, labor-importing Gulf Cooperation Council states, both labor-exporting and transit countries, and so forth). Within the Grand Maghreb, Algeria, Morocco, and Tunisia have been experiencing massive labor emigration to Europe since the 1960s. This is particularly true for Morocco, where emigration has always been considered an export that should be promoted for the benefit of the country. Algeria and Tunisia initially followed a similar policy, but in the 1970s, both encouraged their emigrants to return (Baldwin-Edwards 2005).

The impact of return migration is central to a discussion on the benefits and costs associated with migration. While remittances fill a central role in providing foreign exchange and lowering poverty, it is increasingly acknowledged that migration can lead to other forms of beneficial transfers

This study was commissioned by the World Bank and is part of the MIREM project financed by the European Union and the European University Institute (www.mirem.eu). The authors would like to thank Jean-Pierre Cassarino, Antonella Guarneri, Oleksiy Ivaschenko, Sara Johansson de Silva, and the participants of the Second Meeting of the MIREM Project in April 2008 for very helpful suggestions and comments on first drafts of this study.

back to home countries, in the form of technological, managerial, and entrepreneurial know-how. Some migrants who return home may have acquired the financial resources, but also the work experience abroad, to provide an impetus to the local economy and become engines of innovation, employment, and economic growth. However, while there is now a sizable literature on the welfare implications of migration and on the use and impact of remittances, the determinants and impact of return migration have so far been comparatively underresearched.

This paucity of research on the subject of return migration is mainly due to a lack of good-quality data. In the case of Algeria, Morocco, and Tunisia, in particular, existing statistical sources do not provide a comprehensive and precise view on the sociodemographic characteristics of the returnees. Nor do they allow the return migration phenomenon and the link between return migration and development in migrants' countries of origin to be properly understood and analyzed.

The "Collective Action to Support the Reintegration of Return Migrants in their Country of Origin"—the MIREM project[1]—aims at filling this knowledge gap (Cassarino 2008). Launched in 2005 and financially supported by the European Union and the European University Institute, the project intends to better take into consideration the challenges linked to return migration and its impact on development. To this end, field surveys were conducted by the project team among a sample of return migrants from Algeria, Morocco, and Tunisia, between September 2006 and January 2007. Based on a common questionnaire in all three countries, the survey collected detailed information on the returnees' conditions before migration, the returnees' experience abroad, and the returnees' postreturn conditions in the country of origin.

This study takes advantage of this original database to analyze returnees' entrepreneurial behavior in Algeria, Morocco, and Tunisia. It aims to understand whether and to what extent the interviewees' situation prior to migration and their experience of migration have impacted their propensity to engage in entrepreneurial activity. The point is to shed light on the following questions:

- Are financial capital and new skills acquired abroad used productively back home?
- What are the characteristics of the returnees' investment projects upon return?

- How is entrepreneurial behavior related to migrant characteristics and overseas experience?
- Is there a link between migration duration and after-return activity?

To answer these questions, this chapter:

- Describes the database and provides summary statistics on returnees' migration experience and sociodemographic characteristics
- Explores the link between return migration and entrepreneurship by describing entrepreneurial behavior among returnees of the MIREM survey and discussing the characteristics of the returnees' investment projects in their home country
- Disentangles, using a probit econometric model, the determinants of becoming an entrepreneur after migration
- Discusses estimation results and compares them to results found in the empirical literature
- Investigates what determines optimal migration duration and how this decision interacts with activity choice after return
- Offers conclusions.

Data and Descriptive Statistics

The data used in this study are drawn from three surveys on returned migrants simultaneously conducted in Algeria, Morocco, and Tunisia in 2006 as part of the MIREM project. About 330 returned migrants were interviewed in each country using a common questionnaire. In each country, the sampling procedure was based on a geographic stratification process. A few specific regions were selected using official statistics on return flows, so the survey data should not be viewed as reflecting national trends. For the MIREM project, a returnee is defined as "any person returning to his/her country of origin, in the course of the last ten years, after having been an international migrant (whether short-term or long-term) in another country. Return may be permanent or temporary. It may be independently decided by the migrant or forced by unexpected circumstances." This definition draws on the one recommended by the United Nations. It refers specifically to migrants who returned to their country of origin during the past 10 years, because this time limit allows for assessment of the impact of the experience of migration on the interviewee's pattern of reintegration. It also allows the respondents to recount their migratory experiences more precisely.

The questionnaire is structured around three modules relating to the different migratory stages:

- The returnees' conditions before they left for abroad
- The returnees' experience of migration lived abroad
- The returnees' postreturn conditions in the country of origin.

Because the data focus on returnees only, they are perfectly suited to identify the various factors that motivated and shaped the migratory stages, to analyze why and how the human, social, and financial capital of the interviewees has changed over time; and to identify why and how patterns of reintegration differ between returnees and countries. These questions are generally not addressed in the literature and as such are original to the MIREM project. Other questions, however, cannot be addressed.

First, since there are no nonmigrant individuals in the sample, the questions of whether the entrepreneurial behavior of return migrants differs from that of nonmigrants or whether experience abroad affects the characteristics of businesses established by the returnees cannot be explored. For interested readers, these questions have been investigated elsewhere (see, for example, Kilic et al. [2007] for Albania and Wahba [2004] for Egypt).

Second, the data set focuses on returnees and as such is not a representative sample of migrants in general. Since migrants from Maghreb countries are not mandated to return (even though some of them are sometimes "encouraged" to do so), returnees are unlikely to constitute a random sample of the migrant population. It may be the case that those who have failed economically or socially in host countries, or those who are retired, are overrepresented in the return migrant population. Controlling for this would require having data on migrants who still reside in immigration countries. Since such data could not be collected for obvious logistic and financial reasons, the conclusions that are derived from the analyses that follow apply only to the surveyed returnees and cannot be generalized to the whole population of migrants.

Returnees' Migration Experience

Within the sample, most international migrants went to a European country (85 percent), mainly to France, with a mean overseas stay of 15.2 years. Return migrants who left before the end of the 1970s were predominantly from rural areas, but after the 1970s migrants were predominantly from urban areas. However, sharp differences exist among the Algerian, Moroccan, and Tunisian samples:

- The Algerian sample is mainly composed of return migrants who went to France, while destinations are much more diversified in the Moroccan and the Tunisian samples (table 3.1).
- The sample of Tunisian migrants suggests that the Middle East and North Africa region is one of the main destinations of urban migrants, together with Italy and, to a lesser extent, Germany.
- The distribution of returnees by date of first departure strongly differs between the Algerian sample and the Moroccan and Tunisian samples. The share of Algerian returnees who left their country in the 1950s and 1960s is much higher than in the two other samples.

TABLE 3.1
Overseas Destination and Mean Duration of Stay of Returnees

	Algeria			Morocco			Tunisia		
	Rural origin	Urban origin	Total	Rural origin	Urban origin	Total	Rural origin	Urban origin	Total
Country of destination (%)									
France	85.2	70.5	75.6	25.8	30.1	28.5	65.1	40.3	47.9
Germany	2.6	3.7	3.3	2.3	4.6	3.6	7.8	8.4	8.2
Italy	1.7	3.7	3.0	45.5	41.8	43.0	8.7	15.0	13.3
Middle East and North Africa	4.4	5.1	4.8	0.8	0.0	0.3	13.6	21.7	19.1
North America	3.5	3.7	3.6	0.8	2.0	1.5	1.0	3.1	2.4
Spain	0.0	3.2	2.1	11.4	5.6	7.9	0.0	0.0	0.0
Other Europe	1.7	9.7	6.9	5.3	7.1	6.4	1.0	8.0	5.8
Other countries	0.9	0.5	0.6	0.8	0.0	0.3	1.0	2.2	1.8
No reply	—	—	—	7.6	8.7	8.5	1.9	1.3	1.5
Mean duration of stay (in years)									
France	27.4	14.8	19.7	24.8	12.0	16.7	26.0	18.3	21.6
Germany	16.0	12.0	13.1	13.3	10.6	11.3	24.5	18.1	20.0
Italy	11.0	7.1	8.0	13.6	8.2	10.5	12.9	8.8	9.6
Middle East and North Africa	2.4	6.9	5.5	30.0	—	30.0	12.4	7.1	8.3
North America	20.5	8.6	12.6	11.0	9.8	10.0	2.0	10.3	9.3
Spain	—	8.3	8.3	3.2	7.5	5.0	—	—	—
Other Europe	26.0	7.7	9.3	22.4	9.4	13.7	6.0	13.4	13.0
Other countries	6.0	4.0	5.0	17.0	—	17.0	19.0	5.6	7.8
No reply	—	—	—	9.5	15.7	12.9	16.5	7.3	11.0
Number of observations	115.0	217.0	332.0	132.0	196.0	330.0	103.0	226.0	330.0

Sources: Authors' calculations; MIREM@EUI; http://cadmus.eui.eu/bitstream/handle/1814/7720/ MIREM_RAPPORT_GENERAL _2007 _10.pdf;jsessionid=49704E1E0ED849713E863539C37C6ABA?sequence=1.
Note: — = no data.
EUI = European University Institute.

Returnees' Characteristics

Table 3.2 describes the characteristics of all returnees by country of origin. Several salient features emerge.

First, a large majority of the returnees are male and aged between 41 and 49. Since, on average, four years have passed since they have returned from overseas, their mean age on return was between 36 and 45. Overall, returnees were quite young when they migrated, with a mean age at departure between 17 and 22. Due to the life-cycle effect, the share of married individuals is higher after migration than before migration.

Second, international migrants returning to Maghreb countries were drawn from a wide spectrum of educational backgrounds. In Algeria, for example, 34 percent were university graduates, but 23 percent had no education. As clearly suggested by table 7.2, a significant proportion of migrants took advantage of their overseas stay to get higher education: in all three countries, the percentage of university graduates increased between the pre- and postmigration periods.

Third, an examination of the status of employment before and after migration reveals noticeable changes. In particular, the proportion of employers rose from 1 percent to 15 percent of the whole sample between the premigration and postreturn periods. This increase arises largely because some of those individuals who were waged workers prior to migration (31 percent of the whole sample prior to migration) became employers. This shift in employment status is particularly pronounced in the case of Tunisia, where the percentage of employers rose from 1 percent to 23 percent between the premigration and postreturn periods.[2]

There are three explanations for this apparent link between experience abroad and small business development:

- Accumulated savings abroad might contribute to alleviating domestic capital imperfections
- Overseas work experience might generate new skills and new ideas. The econometric analyses that follows will try to evaluate the respective influence of these two factors. Table 3.2 also suggests that at the outset, these returnees were not predominantly unemployed or inactive people, but also employed people seeking better living and/or working conditions abroad. In accordance with statistics on education, a significant proportion of migrants also left as students

TABLE 3.2

Characteristics of Return Migrants

	Algeria			Morocco			Tunisia			All		
	Before	After	Today	Before	After	Today	Before	After	Today	Before	After	Today
Individual characteristics												
Female (%)	13.6			12.7			11.5			12.6		
Born in rural areas (%)	34.6			40.0			31.2			35.3		
Mean age (in years)	21.6	45.2	49.1	17.3	36.4	40.9	21.5	42.3	46.9	20.2	41.3	45.7
Marital status (%)												
Single	62.3	—	41.3	67.9	—	44.6	67.0	—	43.1	65.7	—	43.0
Married	37.0	—	50.9	27.0	—	44.3	32.1	—	50.8	32.1	—	48.7
Divorced	0.3	—	5.4	1.8	—	8.0	0.6	—	4.9	0.9	—	6.1
Widow	0.3	—	2.4	0.0	—	0.9	0.3	—	1.2	0.2	—	1.5
Unknown	0.0	—	0.0	3.3	—	2.2	0.0	—	0.0	1.1	—	0.7
Education (%)												
None	23.2	22.0	22.0	11.5	10.1	10.1	9.4	9.8	9.8	14.7	14.1	14.1
Preschool	3.9	4.2	4.2	5.8	4.1	4.1	3.0	3.1	3.1	4.2	3.8	3.8
Primary school	10.8	10.8	10.8	17.6	15.5	15.5	20.9	19.9	19.9	16.4	15.4	15.4
Secondary I	10.5	11.1	11.1	13.3	10.4	10.4	5.8	4.9	4.9	9.9	8.8	8.8
Secondary II	16.6	13.9	13.9	25.2	17.7	17.7	39.4	30.4	30.4	27.0	20.6	20.6
Higher I (DEUG and Maîtrise)	22.3	15.7	15.7	20.0	16.8	16.8	19.4	19.3	19.3	20.6	17.2	17.2
Higher II (3rd cycle)	11.7	16.3	16.3	2.7	13.9	13.9	1.8	7.1	7.1	5.4	12.4	12.4
Other	0.9	5.7	5.7	0.9	11.1	11.1	0.3	4.3	4.3	0.7	7.0	7.0
Unknown	0.0	0.3	0.3	3.0	0.3	0.3	0.0	1.2	1.2	1.0	0.6	0.6

(continued next page)

TABLE 3.2 (continued)
Characteristics of Return Migrants

	Algeria			Morocco			Tunisia			All		
	Before	After	Today	Before	After	Today	Before	After	Today	Before	After	Today
Employment status (%)												
Waged	37.5	25.3	25.9	19.0	21.3	21.6	36.6	25.8	26.7	31.3	24.2	24.8
Employer	1.8	9.3	11.1	0.7	11.9	15.9	1.2	23.4	28.2	1.3	14.9	18.4
Self-employed	15.1	14.2	15.4	15.1	16.6	17.5	14.6	12.0	13.8	14.9	14.2	15.5
Seasonal worker	12.4	0.9	0.3	9.8	7.5	8.6	15.8	3.7	1.8	12.7	4.0	3.5
Family worker	2.1	0.0	0.0	5.6	0.6	0.6	3.4	1.8	2.1	3.7	0.8	0.9
Unemployed	17.2	13.0	11.1	9.8	18.8	14.9	9.9	10.5	6.4	12.4	14.0	10.8
Retired	0.3	31.3	31.3	0.3	5.3	5.7	0.0	15.4	16.9	0.2	17.5	18.2
Student	10.3	2.1	0.9	28.9	2.2	0.6	12.7	1.5	0.3	17.0	1.9	0.6
Inactive	3.3	3.9	3.9	1.0	3.4	3.2	4.3	2.8	2.1	2.9	3.4	3.1
Other	0.0	0.0	0.0	9.8	12.2	11.4	1.2	3.1	1.5	3.5	5.0	4.2

Sources: MIREM@EUI; authors' calculation.

Note: — = Not applicable.

DEUG = Diplôme d'Etude Universitaire Générale and corresponds to two years of university. Maîtrise corresponds to four years of university.

• In terms of industry of employment, figures suggest that migrants returned to broadly similar industrial patterns of employment. Within the whole sample, about 9 percent fewer worked in agriculture and 4 percent fewer worked in construction, and about 3, 4, and 6 percent more worked in hotels and restaurants, services, and trade, respectively.

Return Migration and Entrepreneurship

This section focuses on returnees who became entrepreneurs after returning to their home countries. In the discussion that follows, two definitions of "entrepreneur" are used. In the restricted definition, an entrepreneur is defined as any individual who is either an employer, a regular self-employed, or an irregular self-employed with at least one employee. In the extended definition, an entrepreneur is defined as any individual who is either an employer, a regular self-employed, an irregular self-employed with at least one employee, or anyone who invested in a project hiring at least one employee.

Table 3.3 presents an overview of the characteristics of those returnees who became entrepreneurs (either employers or self-employed) and those returnees who did not after returning to their home countries, using the restricted definition. As the table suggests, there are sharp differences between nonentrepreneurs and entrepreneurs and, within entrepreneurs, between employers and self-employed. Entrepreneurs among returnees are more likely to be male in all countries and are on average younger than nonentrepreneurs in Algeria and Tunisia.

With regard to education, those returnees with high education levels are clearly overrepresented among employers in Algeria and Morocco: 51 percent and 47 percent of Algerian and Moroccan entrepreneurs, respectively, have a tertiary diploma. In contrast, self-employed workers are found neither among the least nor among the most educated returnees, except in Morocco, where a significant share of the self-employed (56 percent) is found to have a very low level of education. Employers and self-employed workers also differ in terms of their location of residence after return, the former being much less likely to reside in rural areas than the latter in Algeria and Morocco.

Entrepreneurs and nonentrepreneurs also differ according to their employment status while overseas. In particular, it appears that those

TABLE 3.3

Characteristics of Return Migrants by Employment Status

	Algeria				Morocco				Tunisia			
	Non-entrepreneurs	Self-employed	Employers	All	Non-entrepreneurs	Self-employed	Employers	All	Non-entrepreneurs	Self-employed	Employers	All
Female (%)	15.9	2.7	8.1	13.6	16.4	4.2	4.0	12.7	16.0	3.1	4.3	11.5
Age after return (in years)	47.0	38.0	39.7	45.2	35.7	40.6	35.7	36.4	44.3	35.6	40.2	42.3
Education after migration (%)												
None	26.8	2.7	8.1	22.1	9.5	20.8	0.0	9.7	14.7	0.0	2.2	9.8
Preschool	4.7	2.7	2.7	4.2	4.7	4.2	0.0	4.0	4.9	0.0	0.0	3.1
Primary	11.3	16.2	2.7	10.9	12.1	31.3	12.2	14.9	18.6	22.6	22.0	19.9
Secondary I	9.7	13.5	18.9	11.2	13.4	2.1	2.0	10.0	2.5	3.2	11.0	4.9
Secondary II	11.3	32.4	13.5	13.9	16.8	12.5	22.4	17.0	25.0	48.4	36.3	30.4
Higher I (DEUG & maitrise)	12.8	18.9	32.4	15.7	14.2	20.8	20.4	16.1	21.1	9.7	18.7	19.3
Higher II (3eme cycle)	16.3	13.5	18.9	16.3	13.4	0.0	26.5	13.4	8.3	3.2	5.5	7.1
Other	7.0	0.0	2.7	5.7	11.2	8.3	10.2	10.6	3.9	9.7	3.3	4.3
Unknown	0.4	0.0	0.0	0.3	0.0	0.0	2.0	0.3	1.0	3.1	1.1	1.2
Location (%)												
Rural resident after migration	17.1	21.6	13.5	17.2	15.9	22.9	8.0	15.8	12.6	9.4	8.7	11.2
Back to birth location	18.2	21.6	27.0	19.6	36.6	41.7	32.7	36.7	33.0	34.4	48.9	37.6
Back to location before migration	43.4	59.5	54.1	46.4	26.9	16.7	22.4	24.7	37.9	34.4	20.7	32.7
Marital status after migration (%)												
Single	44.2	32.4	29.7	41.3	44.4	35.4	54.0	44.6	41.2	31.3	51.6	43.1
Married	46.5	64.9	67.6	50.9	44.9	60.4	26.0	44.3	52.9	59.4	42.9	50.8
Divorced	6.2	2.7	2.7	5.4	8.0	4.2	12.0	8.0	4.4	9.4	4.4	4.9
Widowed	3.1	0.0	0.0	2.4	0.9	0.0	2.0	0.9	1.5	0.0	1.1	1.2
Unknown	0.0	0.0	0.0	0.0	1.8	0.0	6.0	2.2	0.0	0.0	0.0	0.0

112

Employment status overseas (%)

Employer	0.8	0.0	10.8	1.8	1.3	4.2	10.6	3.1	0.0	0.0	25.0	7.0
Waged	59.7	56.8	59.5	59.3	41.4	27.1	48.9	40.4	62.3	46.9	48.9	57.0
Self-employed	4.7	21.6	2.7	6.3	9.3	54.2	14.9	16.8	6.9	34.4	13.0	11.3
Seasonal worker	4.3	8.1	2.7	4.5	17.2	10.4	8.5	14.9	4.9	9.4	3.3	4.9
Family worker	0.0	0.0	2.7	0.3	2.6	0.0	0.0	1.9	0.0	0.0	0.0	0.0
Unemployed	6.2	2.7	5.4	5.7	4.8	2.1	2.1	4.0	5.9	3.1	2.2	4.6
Student	10.9	8.1	10.8	10.5	5.7	2.1	2.1	4.7	3.9	3.1	3.3	3.7
Retired	6.6	2.7	0.0	5.4	1.3	0.0	· 0.0	0.9	9.8	0.0	2.2	6.7
Inactive	5.0	0.0	5.4	4.5	1.8	0.0	0.0	1.2	4.4	3.1	0.0	3.0
Other	1.9	0.0	0.0	1.5	14.5	0.0	12.8	12.1	2.0	0.0	2.2	1.8

Industry overseas (%)

Agriculture	2.7	8.1	0.0	3.0	12.9	10.4	4.0	11.2	2.4	6.3	5.4	3.6
Manufacturing and mining	12.8	5.4	10.8	11.7	8.2	10.4	8.0	8.5	5.8	6.3	10.9	7.3
Construction	18.6	16.2	13.5	17.8	10.3	6.3	8.0	9.4	16.5	18.8	12.0	15.5
Utilities	0.8	0.0	5.4	1.2	1.3	0.0	4.0	1.5	1.5	0.0	4.3	2.1
Trade	6.2	24.3	13.5	9.0	20.7	45.8	14.0	23.3	4.9	21.9	13.0	8.8
Public administration	2.3	0.0	0.0	1.8	1.3	0.0	4.0	1.5	1.9	0.0	1.1	1.5
Education	4.3	0.0	2.7	3.6	3.4	0.0	4.0	3.0	14.6	6.3	2.2	10.3
Finance	0.8	2.7	0.0	0.9	2.6	0.0	4.0	2.4	0.5	0.0	1.1	0.6
Hotels and restaurants	9.3	10.8	18.9	10.5	6.9	2.1	16.0	7.6	7.3	18.8	28.3	14.2
Services	8.1	10.8	10.8	8.7	5.6	6.3	16.0	7.3	7.8	6.3	8.7	7.9
Transport	4.7	8.1	2.7	4.8	5.2	8.3	2.0	5.2	5.8	6.3	1.1	4.5
Unknown	0.8	0.0	0.0	0.6	8.2	6.3	12.0	8.5	7.3	0.0	4.3	5.8
Out of labor market	28.7	13.5	21.6	26.2	13.4	4.2	4.0	10.6	23.8	9.4	7.6	17.9

Last immigration country (%)

France	78.3	64.9	67.6	75.6	29.7	14.6	36.0	28.5	47.6	53.1	46.7	47.9
Italy	1.9	10.8	2.7	3.0	40.5	64.6	34.0	43.0	11.2	21.9	15.2	13.3

(continued next page)

TABLE 3.3 (continued)

Characteristics of Return Migrants by Employment Status

	Algeria				Morocco				Tunisia			
	Non-entrepreneurs	Self-employed	Employers	All	Non-entrepreneurs	Self-employed	Employers	All	Non-entrepreneurs	Self-employed	Employers	All
Spain	2.3	0.0	2.7	2.1	9.9	4.2	2.0	7.9	0.0	0.0	0.0	0.0
Germany	2.3	8.1	5.4	3.3	4.3	2.1	2.0	3.6	4.4	9.4	16.3	8.2
Other Europe	6.2	8.1	10.8	6.9	6.0	6.3	8.0	6.4	5.3	0.0	8.7	5.8
Middle East and North Africa	4.7	5.4	5.4	4.8	0.4	0.0	0.0	0.3	23.8	15.6	9.8	19.1
North America	3.5	2.7	5.4	3.6	0.9	0.0	6.0	1.5	2.9	0.0	2.2	2.4
Other	0.8	0.0	0.0	0.6	0.0	2.1	0.0	0.3	2.9	0.0	0.0	1.8
Unknown	0.0	0.0	0.0	0.0	8.2	6.3	12.0	8.5	1.9	0.0	1.1	1.5
Characteristics of overseas stay												
Migration duration (in years)	19.4	11.3	11.6	17.7	11.7	16.0	13.7	12.6	17.2	12.4	17.7	16.9
Vocational training received abroad (%)	12.8	24.3	29.7	16.0	12.9	12.5	34.0	16.1	14.6	21.9	33.7	20.6
Was alone when overseas (%)	45.3	62.2	40.5	46.7	46.6	37.5	44.0	44.8	46.6	62.5	67.4	53.9
Conditions of return (%)												
Returned for administrative reasons	11.6	21.6	5.4	12.0	28.4	12.5	6.0	22.7	13.6	28.1	5.4	12.7
Thinks return is permanent	22.5	35.1	35.1	25.3	15.5	25.0	20.0	17.6	26.7	21.9	30.4	27.3
Thinks of migrating again	36.8	24.3	29.7	34.6	46.6	16.7	38.0	40.9	44.7	40.6	34.8	41.5
Returned with family members	10.9	10.8	16.2	11.4	15.3	17.4	14.0	15.4	21.5	15.6	30.4	23.4
Number of observations	258	37	37	332	232	48	50	330	206	32	92	330

Sources: MIREM@EUI; author's calculations.

114

returnees who were employers abroad are more likely to be employers after return.

Interestingly, the entrepreneurial behavior of returnees appears to differ according to the last immigration country. In particular, returnees who went to Italy are overrepresented among entrepreneurs in all three countries and, within entrepreneurs, among the self-employed. Whether these differences hold when controlling for the returnees' individual characteristics remains to be investigated. But one possible explanation could be the kind of jobs obtained by migrants from Maghreb countries in Italy compared to the other countries. As shown in table 3.4, there are marked differences in the distribution of migrants by employment status among European countries. While more than 57 percent of the migrants who went to France were salaried workers, only 33 percent were salaried workers in Italy. However, in Italy, the share of migrants who were entrepreneurs at the time of migration was comparatively much higher than in France. Those migrants who went to France could thus be less well prepared to become entrepreneurs.

Interesting features also emerge with regard to the characteristics of overseas stay and conditions of return. While time overseas does not seem to play a role in the probability of a returnee becoming an entrepreneur, the reverse holds true for vocational training received abroad: trained migrants are clearly overrepresented among those migrants who became entrepreneurs after migration, especially among those who became employers. This correlation could be spurious, however, and could reflect some unobserved characteristics. For example, those migrants who chose to get trained may be more dynamic or have stronger unobserved ability and skills, and thus may be more able to benefit from entrepreneurial activity on return than those who did not choose to get trained. Whether there is a causal link between vocational training and entrepreneurship remains to be investigated.

Turning to conditions of return, figures suggest that those migrants who returned for administrative reasons (that is, those migrants who did not freely choose to return) are underrepresented among employers. The same holds true for those returnees who plan to remigrate. These two results lend support to the idea that those migrants who are "ill-prepared" for return are unlikely to be actors of change in their home country. Interestingly, "forced" returnees are overrepresented among the self-employed.

TABLE 3.4
Employment Status during Migration, by Last Country of Immigration[a] (pooled sample)

	France	Germany	Italy	Spain	Other Europe
Waged	57.1	46.9	**33.0**	**27.3**	52.4
Employer	2.2	**8.2**	4.1	**0.0**	**12.7**
Self-employed	9.4	8.2	**23.2**	**0.0**	11.1
Seasonal	4.8	10.2	**16.5**	**42.4**	1.6
Family worker	0.2	0.0	1.6	**6.1**	0.0
Unemployed	4.0	4.1	6.7	**9.1**	6.4
Retired	7.6	**8.2**	0.5	0.0	0.0
Student	7.4	**12.2**	0.5	3.0	6.4
Inactive	4.2	0.0	1.0	6.1	3.2
Other	3.0	2.0	**12.9**	6.1	6.4
Number of observations	499.0	49.0	194.0	33.0	63.0

Sources: MIREM © EUI; authors' calculations.
Note: a. Statistics for non-European countries are not presented in the table.

Determinants of Becoming an Entrepreneur After Migration

As suggested by the statistics, entrepreneurs among returnees are on average different in some ways from nonentrepreneurs; for example, they are more likely to be male, younger, and have neither low nor high education levels. In addition, the probability of becoming an entrepreneur after return seems to be higher for returnees with a first experience as employers or self-employed, for those who received vocational training while abroad, and for those who independently and freely chose to return.

This section constructs an econometric model of the probability of a returnee becoming an entrepreneur in order to examine whether these correlations hold in a multivariate analysis. To fuel the discussion, estimation results will be compared to those found in other studies focusing on the same issue but in other countries (Ammassari 2003; Black, King, and Tiemoko 2003; Ilahi 1999; McCormick and Wahba 2001).

Econometric Model

We estimate the probit version of a discrete choice econometric model where the dependent variable is a dummy variable taking the value *1* if the returnee has become an entrepreneur since return, and *0* otherwise, using the restricted definition for an entrepreneur.

Formally, the model may be written as follows:

$$\begin{cases} E = 1 \;\; if \;\; E^* > 0 \\ E = 0 \;\; if \;\; E^* \leq 0 \end{cases}$$

where E^* is a latent variable measuring the payoff from becoming an entrepreneur after return. We assume that, $E^* = bX + \varepsilon$, where X is a vector of independent variables and ε a normally distributed error term.

Six blocks of independent variables are introduced in this model.

The first block includes *demographic characteristics of the migrants* such as sex, age, region of origin (the reference being rural), and being binational.

The second block contains five *education* dummies reflecting schooling attainment at the time of the survey, namely primary cycle, secondary cycles (I and II), university level (until the fourth year of higher education), and higher degrees above the fourth year of university (the reference being no schooling).

The third block comprises controls for the *occupational situation of the migrant prior to migration*. More precisely, a dummy for being an entrepreneur prior to migration (the reference being any other occupation) is included. The idea is to find out whether being an entrepreneur before migration affects the probability of being one upon return once sociodemographic characteristics of the returnees and conditions of their return are accounted for.

A fourth block of determinants includes *characteristics of the migrants' overseas stay*. These are important covariates deemed to influence the probability of professional success or failure after return. Among them, we include proxies of human capital accumulated abroad such as whether the migrant worked when he or she was abroad or whether he or she received vocational training. We also include one variable measuring migration duration as a proxy for professional experience in the labor market of the receiving country and for skill acquisition. Three dummies scaling the amount of remittances the migrants used to send before returning to their home countries are included as well (the reference being no remittances). Indeed, migrants may face capital market imperfections in the origin country so that overseas savings and remittances are subsequently able to fuel productive investments (McCormick and Wahba 2001). For this reason, this information may affect migrants' professional trajectories. Since there is no direct measure of overseas savings in the MIREM survey, we use these remittances dummies to control for the effect of savings.

A fifth block of independent variables is included to control for *conditions and timing of return*. Time elapsed since return controls for labor market experience in the home country, while conditions of return are captured by a dummy variable indicating whether the migrant deliberately chose to return or was forced to do so. A dummy variable indicating whether the returnees plan to remigrate is also introduced. This variable is indeed likely to affect entrepreneurial behavior if return migrants consider their return transitory. Three dummies controlling for the potential effect of location after return are used: one dummy for being back in the birthplace and two dummies for the size of the city (capital and secondary city, the reference being a small city).

Finally, a set of *destination country dummies* is considered. These variables may capture environmental, institutional, or network effects in the last immigration country that may affect the migrants' success or failure after return.

Estimation Results

Estimation results are reported in annex 3.1. To facilitate their interpretation, only marginal effects of the covariates are shown. The following features emerge.

In line with what was suggested by descriptive statistics, female migrants are significantly less likely to become entrepreneurs after return, all else being equal. The effect is particularly strong for Tunisian migrants (with a marginal effect of −0.34 compared to −0.14 for Algeria).

Turning to the age variable, its expected effect on entrepreneurial behavior is unclear. As argued by Ilahi (1999), if age is synonymous with labor market experience, and wages rise with experience, then age should be negatively associated with the probability for self-employment or, turning it the other way around, age should be positively associated with waged work. Age, however, might have a positive influence on managerial talent and hence on the likelihood of becoming an entrepreneur. Estimation results suggest that the latter effect dominates for Algerians and Moroccans, while the opposite is true in the Tunisian sample, where age appears to be detrimental to becoming an entrepreneur.

With regard to the returnees' other characteristics, originating from an urban area is positively associated with the probability of taking up an entrepreneurial job in Tunisia. In the case of Algerian migrants, having double nationality is also strongly linked to engagement in entrepreneurial activities.

Strong positive impacts of education are found for all countries. For Algerians, for instance, the education dummies are all significant at the 10 percent level and disclose an increasing marginal effect from the primary to the university level: Algerian returnees holding a university degree are indeed 47 percent more likely to become entrepreneurs after returning compared with the reference category of "no education," compared to only 20 percent for Algerian returnees who dropped out after primary school.

The reverse holds true for Tunisian returnees. Those with high university degrees do not have an entrepreneurial behavior significantly different from those with no schooling. For Moroccans, the impact of education is less pronounced, especially at intermediate levels of schooling. Holding a high university degree actually exerts a positive and significant impact on entrepreneurial behavior in the Algerian case only. These differences in the relationship between education and entrepreneurship among countries are likely to result from particular national characteristics of the structure and functioning of the labor market. In Algeria, for example, highly educated people have long had access to relatively high-paid jobs in the public sector. However, the sharp contraction of public employment through downsizing and restructuring in the 1990s, together with the lack of job opportunities in the private sector, may have encouraged skilled workers to establish their own businesses.

As expected, the positive effect of being an entrepreneur before migration is found for all countries. The impact is more significant and of a greater magnitude for Algerian returnees: previous Algerian entrepreneurs are about 27 percent more likely to become entrepreneurs after returning compared to 19 and 18 percent, respectively, for Moroccans and Tunisians. This result corroborates the idea according to which, all else being equal, entrepreneurial engagement upon return is conditioned by previous experience in related activities. A similar result is found by McCormick and Wahba (2001) and by Ilahi (1999) in the case of Egyptian and Pakistani returnees, respectively.

Among the characteristics of overseas stay that are considered, vocational training overseas is positively and significantly associated with entrepreneurship for Moroccan and Tunisian returnees. As mentioned, however, any causal relationship between these two variables is risky to ascertain, because training may be endogenously determined in this type of model. With regard to migration duration, the usual assumption is that the longer the time spent overseas, the greater the opportunity for skill acquisition. As a result, migration duration is expected to positively influence entrepreneurship. Regression results suggest, however, that migration duration discloses a positive impact only in the case of Tunisia. The influence of migration duration is not found to be significantly different from zero in the cases of Algeria and Morocco.

These results are in sharp contrast with those found by McCormick and Wahba (2001). Using a sample of Egyptian returnees, they find that time spent overseas has a positive and highly significant effect on being an entrepreneur. However, after interacting the variable with a dummy taking value 1 for illiterates, they find no significant influence from longer periods overseas on the likelihood of becoming an entrepreneur among illiterates. Following this approach, similar interacted terms were computed and introduced in the regressions, but they were ultimately dropped for lack of significance. It could be argued, of course, that migration duration and activity choice after return are jointly chosen and hence that the regression results presented so far suffer from an endogeneity bias. This issue raised by Dustmann (2003) and Dustmann and Kirchkamp (2002) is investigated more thoroughly in a companion paper by Gubert and Nordman (2008).

Turning to the other regressors relating to characteristics of overseas stay, past remittance behavior is found to have a positive effect on the probability of becoming an entrepreneur for Moroccans and Tunisians. This is an expected result because this information accounts for savings, which are clearly an important asset for being able to open a business.

Conditions of return appear to be strong determinants of the probability of engaging in entrepreneurial activities upon return.

First, time elapsed since return is always positively correlated to entrepreneurship. This finding probably reflects the positive effect of returnees' human capital accumulation after return, namely, experience and knowledge gained of the local market conditions and rules for running a business. The finding might also reveal the existence of a required time for gathering financial resources once back.

Second, a "forced return" is negatively associated with the probability of setting up entrepreneurial activities, especially for Moroccan and Tunisian returnees. Also, planning to remigrate is negatively correlated to entrepreneurship, for all countries. This is a somewhat expected result because remigration is not compatible with a desire to engage time and financial resources in the home country's labor market.

Third, migrants' location after return appears to be a significant determinant of entrepreneurial activities, especially for the sample of Moroccan returnees. Unlike their Algerian and Tunisian counterparts, Moroccan migrants engage more in businesses when they go back to their birthplace, all else being equal, and when they return to relatively large cities. By contrast, as far as entrepreneurship is concerned, Algerians and Tunisians do not seem to benefit from returning to the capital city. As suggested by Ilahi (1999), this may be due to the fact that urban areas offer better access to waged employment and raise the opportunity cost of self-employment.

Finally, turning to the role of the last immigration country, we find little evidence of a decisive impact of the last destination country on the probability of becoming an entrepreneur after return. Wald tests of joint significance show that we cannot reject the null hypothesis of destination-country coefficients being equal to zero in the Algerian and Moroccan cases (with P-values 0.76 and 0.13, respectively). The test hardly rejects the joint nullity for Tunisia only (P-value 0.10). For Moroccan and Tunisian returnees, however, having migrated to Italy and Germany, respectively, plays a significant role in the probability of entrepreneurship after return. This result somewhat conforms to previous statistical findings on the overrepresentation of entrepreneurs among migrants who went to Italy and Germany in our returnee samples. We now find that these effects persist once sociodemographics and conditions of overseas stay and return are accounted for.

As a robustness check, we run the same probit regressions using the extended definition of being an entrepreneur after return as the dependent variable. We observe that the pattern of the determinants of entrepreneurship is very similar with this extended definition, indicating that the main previous findings are robust to the changing definition of entrepreneurship. The few noticeable changes concern the fact that being an entrepreneur before leaving is no more significant for Moroccan returnees, that planning to remigrate becomes insignificant for Tunisian migrants, and that returning to birthplace is no more significant for Moroccans. Also, the impact of migration to Italy becomes insignificant for Moroccan returnees, as it was for their Algerian and Tunisian counterparts.

Conclusion

Using an original database, this study analyzed the entrepreneurial behavior of returnees in Algeria, Morocco, and Tunisia. Several interesting features have emerged from both the descriptive and econometric analyses.

First, one-third of returnees did invest in projects and businesses after return, although this share widely varies among countries. Algeria clearly stands apart, with both a lower share of returnees being either employers or self-employed and a lower share of returnees being investors. This lower propensity to invest partly results from the fact that a significant share of Algerians within the sample went to France as early as the 1960s and occupied low-qualified positions that did not allow them to acquire entrepreneurial skill. In addition, Algerian sample returnees are older, on average, and most of them are now retired. More generally, the lower propensity of Algerian returnees to invest may also be due to Algeria's business environment. Characterized by poor infrastructure, red tape, a lack of transparency, and unstable regulations, it may indeed keep potential entrepreneurs from engaging in large and innovative investments.[3]

Second, entrepreneurs among returnees are, on average, different in some ways from nonentrepreneurs: they are more likely to be male, younger, and have medium education levels. In addition, the probability of becoming an entrepreneur after return seems to be higher for returnees with a first experience as employers or self-employed, for those who received vocational training while abroad, and for those who independently and freely chose to return. There is no clear correlation, however, between migration duration and entrepreneurship, even after controlling for the potential endogeneity of migration duration. Entrepreneurs do not form a homogenous group, though, and sharp differences emerge when employers and self-employed are considered separately. Compared to their self-employed counterparts, employers appear much more educated on average, are more likely to reside in urban areas after return, have received more training during their migration stay, and the vast majority have chosen to return.

To conclude, returnees show a high ability to create small or medium businesses and to generate jobs. But, as suggested by the returnees themselves, some improvements could be explored. When asked about the constraints they faced when setting up their businesses, half of the interviewees cited administrative and institutional constraints, 40 percent cited excessive competition, and 27 percent cited lack of capital. The percentage of investors who suffered from administrative constraints is, however, much higher in the Algerian sample (77 percent) than in the Moroccan (55 percent) or Tunisian (34 percent) samples. Moroccan investors, on the other hand, seem to face particularly high competition.

Those returnees who did not invest upon return (but wished to do so) perceived lack of capital as the major obstacle in all three countries, especially in Morocco, followed by lack of experience and training, and administrative and institutional constraints. This suggests that small business start-up programs with market studies, microcredit, and training components could be tried to ease constraints on entrepreneurship that arise from capital market imperfections or other market failures. For those programs to be effective, however, local governments should also create better conditions for returnees to integrate and stay in their home countries.

ANNEX 3.1: ESTIMATION RESULTS
Probit of Becoming an Entrepreneur after Migration (marginal effects)

	Algeria	Morocco	Tunisia
Demographic characteristics			
Female	−0.138***	−0.254***	−0.341***
	(2.67)	(3.47)	(4.24)
Age	−0.002	−0.003	−0.032***
	(0.60)	(0.61)	(4.73)
Region of origin: urban	0.050	0.035	0.182**
	(1.00)	(0.50)	(2.42)
Binational	0.271**	0.116	0.160
	(2.48)	(1.00)	(1.58)
Education [ref. is none]			
Primary	0.203*	0.225**	0.445***
	(1.85)	(1.99)	(3.45)
Preparatory	0.291**	−0.170	0.519***
	(2.36)	(1.48)	(2.81)
Secondary	0.298***	0.186*	0.370***
	(2.66)	(1.70)	(2.87)
University	0.468***	0.252**	0.297**
	(3.58)	(2.19)	(2.02)
Higher diplomas	0.255**	−0.034	−0.049
	(2.24)	(0.30)	(0.30)
Was an entrepreneur before leaving	0.266***	0.186**	0.176*
	(3.77)	(2.07)	(1.74)
Characteristics of overseas stay			
Trained during migration	0.087	0.209**	0.179**
	(1.35)	(2.41)	(2.09)
Duration of the last migration (in years)	−0.001	0.008	0.019***
	(0.30)	(1.45)	(2.89)
Sent less than €500 per year	0.108	0.048	−0.025
	(1.14)	(0.51)	(0.22)
Sent between €501 and €1,000 per year	0.071	0.006	0.153
	(0.98)	(0.08)	(1.39)
Sent more than €1,000 per year	0.065	0.266***	0.253***
	(0.95)	(2.98)	(2.86)
Conditions of return			
Time elapsed since return (in years)	0.021***	0.016*	0.053***
	(2.58)	(1.94)	(4.24)
Forced return (expulsion or illegal conditions)	−0.077	−0.195***	−0.168*
	(1.31)	(2.65)	(1.91)
Plans to remigrate	−0.108**	−0.102*	−0.113*
	(2.37)	(1.67)	(1.72)
Back to birth place	0.017	0.116*	0.056
	(0.31)	(1.71)	(0.80)

(continued next page)

Probit of Becoming an Entrepreneur after Migration (marginal effects)

	Algeria	Morocco	Tunisia
Back to capital city [ref. is small city]	−0.132**	0.234***	−0.171**
	(2.41)	(2.60)	(2.06)
Back to secondary city [ref. is small city]	−0.071	0.189*	−0.016
	(1.34)	(1.77)	(0.16)
Destination country [ref. is France]			
Germany	0.131	0.032	0.317**
	(1.01)	(0.18)	(2.30)
North America	0.081	0.194	−0.228
	(0.63)	(0.76)	(1.40)
Other Europe	0.108	0.032	−0.064
	(1.15)	(0.24)	(0.46)
Spain	−0.014	0.063	—
	(0.10)	(0.41)	
Italy	0.164	0.229**	−0.080
	(1.15)	(2.33)	(0.79)
Middle East and North Africa	0.011	—	−0.040
	(0.12)		(0.40)
Unknown	—	0.323**	−0.251
		(2.20)	(1.26)
Observations	331	294	312
Pseudo R-squared	0.29	0.30	0.35

Source: MIREM@EUI; authors' calculations.
Note: Absolute values of z statistics are in parentheses.
* = significant at 10 percent; ** = significant at 5 percent; *** significant at 1 percent.
— = Not applicable.

Notes

1. For further details on the project, see http://www.mirem.eu.
2. This might result from the labor market policies implemented by the Government of Tunisia, which aim at easing entry into entrepreneurship among job seekers by extending loans under preferential conditions and providing state guarantee and other fiscal incentives (Achy 2010).
3. The World Bank's 2010 *Doing Business* report ranks Algeria 136th of 183 countries; it lags behind Tunisia (69th) and Morocco (128th).

References

Achy, L. 2010. "Trading High Unemployment for Bad Jobs. Employment Challenges in the Maghreb." Carnegie Paper No. 23, Carnegie Middle East Center, Washington, DC.

Ammassari, S. 2003. "From Nation-building to Entrepreneurship: The Impact of Elite Return Migrants in Côte d'Ivoire and Ghana." Sussex Centre for Migration Research, Brighton, U.K.

Baldwin-Edwards, M. 2005. "Migration in the Middle East and Mediterranean." Regional Study prepared for the Global Commission on International Migration, Mediterranean Migration Observatory, University Research Institute for Urban Environment and Human Resources, Panteion University, Athens.

Black R., R. King, and R. Tiemoko. 2003. "Migration, Return and Small Enterprise Development in Ghana: A Route Out of Poverty?" Sussex Migration Working Paper No. 9, Sussex Centre for Migration Research, Brighton, U.K.

Cassarino, J.-P., ed. 2008. "Return Migrants to the Maghreb: Reintegration and Development Challenges." MIREM Global Report, Robert Schuman Centre for Advanced Studies, European University Institute, San Domenico di Fiesole, Italy.

Dustmann, C. 2003. "Return Migration, Wage Differentials, and the Optimal Migration Duration." *European Economic Review* 47 (2): 353–69.

Dustmann, C., and O. Kirchkamp. 2002. "The Optimal Migration Duration and Activity Choice After Re-migration." *Journal of Development Economics* 67: 351–72.

Gubert, F., and C. J. Nordman. 2008. "Return Migration and Small Enterprise Development in the Maghreb." Background Paper for the Middle East and North Africa Department, World Bank, Washington, DC. World Bank; MIREM Analytical Report, MIREM AR2008-02, RSCAS/EUI, Florence, 2008.

Ilahi, N. 1999. "Return Migration and Occupational Change." *Review of Development Economics* 3: 170–86.

Kilic, T., G. Carletto, B. Davis, and A. Zezza. 2007. "Investing Back Home: Return Migration and Business Ownership in Albania." Policy Research Working Paper 4366, World Bank, Washington, DC.

McCormick, B., and J. Wahba. 2001. "Overseas Work Experience, Savings and Entrepreneurship Amongst Return Migrants to LDCs." *Scottish Journal of Political Economy* 48 (2): 164–78.

Wahba, J. 2004. "Does International Migration Matter? A Study of Egyptian Return Migrants." In *Arab Migration in a Globalised World.* Geneva: International Organisation for Migration.

World Bank. 2010. *Doing Business.* Washington, DC: World Bank.

CHAPTER 4

Diaspora Bonds: Tapping the Diaspora during Difficult Times

Suhas L. Ketkar and Dilip Ratha

In the current environment of a crisis of confidence in debt markets, many countries are encountering difficulty obtaining private financing using traditional financial instruments. The scarcity of capital threatens to jeopardize long-term growth and employment generation in developing countries, which tend to have limited access to capital even in the best of times. Official aid alone will not be adequate to bridge near- or long-term financing gaps. Ultimately, it will be necessary to adopt innovative financing approaches to target previously untapped investors. Diaspora bonds are one such mechanism that can enable developing countries to borrow from their expatriate (diaspora) communities.[1]

A diaspora bond is a debt instrument issued by a country—or, potentially, a subsovereign entity or even a private corporation—to raise financing from its overseas diaspora. Israel, annually since 1951, and India, on three occasions since 1991, have raised nearly US$44 billion using these bonds. The rationale behind the Government of Israel's issuance of diaspora bonds has been different from that of the Government of India. The Government of Israel has offered a flexible menu of diaspora bonds since 1951 to keep the Jewish diaspora engaged. Furthermore, the Jewish diaspora has often paid a large price premium, thereby providing a significant "patriotic" discount in borrowing costs. The Indian authorities, in contrast, have used this instrument for balance-of-payments support, to raise financing during times when they had difficulty in accessing international capital markets. Members of the Indian and Israeli diasporas have found such bonds attractive because of the opportunities they provide for effective risk management. Furthermore, diaspora communities may have a "home bias" toward their country of origin and may be willing to purchase diaspora bonds.

While India and Israel have been at the forefront in issuing diaspora bonds, many other nations also have large diaspora communities in the world and could benefit from issuing such bonds. These bonds could be a potentially important and innovative source of financing for development and are worthy of more detailed examination. As a vehicle for such examination, this chapter:

- Briefly discusses the rationale for countries of origin to issue, and for diaspora communities to purchase, diaspora bonds
- Compares the Israeli and Indian approaches to the issuance of diaspora bonds and draws lessons for potential issuers of these bonds (while several countries have declared their intention to tap diaspora wealth, the actual issuance of diaspora bonds has been rather limited)
- Explores the reasons for the limited issuance of diaspora bonds and presents ideas on how to alleviate constraints
- Highlights the potential role diapora bonds can play in providing financial help to earthquake-ravaged Haiti (beyond Haiti, many countries in the developing world could also place bonds with their sizable diaspora communities in developed and emerging economies)
- Summarizes the findings and discusses the direction of future research.

Rationale for Diaspora Bonds

Diaspora bonds can be an attractive vehicle for countries to secure a stable and cheap source of external finance. Since patriotism is the principal motivation for purchasing diaspora bonds, they are likely to be in demand in fair and foul weather. Indeed, the purchase of bonds issued by Israel rose during the Six-Day War in 1967. Similarly, India was able to raise funds from its diaspora in the wake of the balance-of-payments crisis in 1991 and again following the nuclear explosion in 1998 when the country faced sanctions from the international community. Also, as discussed further below, the diaspora may provide a "patriotic" discount in pricing these bonds. The Israeli experience, and to a lesser extent the Indian experience, are in keeping with this hypothesis.

Another factor that might play into the calculus of the diaspora bond-issuing nation is the favorable impact it would have on the country's sovereign credit rating. By making available a reliable source of funding that can be called upon in good and bad times, the nurturing of the diaspora bond market improves a country's sovereign credit rating. Credit rating agencies believe that Israel's ability to access the worldwide Jewish diaspora for funding has undoubtedly supported its sovereign credit rating.[2] But the rating agencies do not view this source of funding as decisive in determining Israel's credit rating. Standard and Poor's, for example, cites Israel's inability to escape painful adjustment programs in the 1980s in reaching this conclusion.[3] In other words, the availability of financing from the Jewish diaspora did not allow Israel to avoid a crisis rooted in domestic mismanagement. While Jewish diaspora investors have stood by Israel whenever the country has come under attack from outside, they have not been as supportive when the problems were homegrown.

While concurring with the above assessment, Moody's analysts also point out that the mid-1980s economic adjustment that brought down inflationary expectations and the 2002/03 structural reforms that improved Israel's economic fundamentals have sharply reduced country's dependence on foreign financing. Furthermore, diaspora bonds and the U.S.-Government-guaranteed debt make up the bulk of Israel's total external indebtedness. As a result, Israel's ability to issue diaspora bonds is now much more important in underpinning Israel's sovereign credit rating than it was in the 1980s, when the country had a much larger financing requirement.

India's access to funding from its diaspora did not prevent the rating agencies from downgrading the country's sovereign credit rating in 1998 following the imposition of international sanctions in the wake of the nuclear explosions. Moody's downgraded India from Baa3 to Ba2 in June 1998 (*Indian Express* 1998a), and Standard and Poor's cut the rating from BB+ to BB four months later in October 1998 (*Indian Express* 1998b). But the excellent reception that Resurgent India Bonds in 1998 and India Millennium Deposits in 2000 received in difficult circumstances has raised the relevance of diaspora funding to India's creditworthiness. Unlike Israel, however, India has not made diaspora bonds a regular feature of its foreign financing. Instead, diaspora bonds are used as a source of emergency finance. While not explicitly stated, India has tapped this funding source during times of balance-of-payments difficulties. India's ability to do so is now perceived as a plus.

Why would investors find diaspora bonds attractive? Patriotism is one reason. The discount from market price at which India, Israel, and Lebanon have managed to sell such bonds to their respective diasporas is a reflection of the charity implicit in these transactions. Until the end of the 1980s, Israel sold bonds with 10- to 15-year maturities to members of the Jewish diaspora in the United States (and, to a lesser extent, in Canada) at a fixed rate of roughly 4 percent, without any reference to changes in U.S. interest rates. U.S. 10-year yields over the same period averaged 6.8 percent, implying a significant discount to market. It was only in the 1990s that the interest rates paid by Israel started to rise toward market interest rates. While members of the Indian diaspora offered little patriotic discount, they provided funding when the ordinary sources of finance had disappeared following the balance-of-payments crisis in 1991 and the nuclear testing in 1998.

Beyond patriotism, however, several other factors may also help explain diaspora interest in bonds issued by their country of origin. Principal among these is the opportunity such bonds provide for risk management. A significant risk associated with diaspora bonds is that the issuing country may be unable to make debt service payments in hard currency. Its ability to pay interest and principal in local currency, however, is perceived to be much stronger. This is an attractive feature of such bonds for diaspora investors. Typically, diaspora investors have current or contingent liabilities in their home country and hence may not be averse to accumulating assets in local currency. Consequently, they view the risk of receiving debt service in local currency with much less trepidation than purely dollar-based investors. They are also likely to be much less concerned about the risk of currency devaluation.[4]

Furthermore, the well-documented home bias, which keeps investors' portfolios heavily concentrated in their home-country assets (Ahearne, Griever, and Warnock 2004; French and Poterba 1991; Tesar and Werner 1998), is likely to apply to the case of diaspora investors. Since restrictions on international capital flows driving home bias have lost much of their relevance in recent years, analysts have focused on alternative hypotheses. One such hypothesis contends that home investors have superior access to information about domestic firms or economic conditions (Brennan and

Cao 1997; Pastor 2000; Portes, Rey, and Oh 2001). For members of the diaspora, such informational asymmetry may actually imply superior knowledge of firms and economic conditions in their countries of origin. In addition, diaspora members may have a comparative advantage in acquiring information about their countries of origin, as Van Nieuwerburgh and Veldkamp (2009) have argued. All this may lead to a country-of-origin as opposed to country-of-destination bias in the portfolios of diaspora investors and may provide yet another reason for their willingness to purchase diaspora bonds.

Other factors supporting purchases of diaspora bonds include the satisfaction that diaspora investors gain from contributing to the economic development of their home country. Diaspora bonds offer investors a vehicle to express their desire to do "good" in their country of origin through investment. Furthermore, diaspora bonds allow investors the opportunity to diversify their assets away from their adopted country. Finally, diaspora investors may also believe that they have some influence on policies at home, especially on bond repayments. Whether such influence is real or imaginary is irrelevant. Diaspora members will be motivated to purchase diaspora bonds as long as they believe they have influence on policies.

Israeli Compared to Indian Issuance of Diaspora Bonds

Israel's diaspora bonds differ from India's in several ways (table 4.1). Israel views its diaspora as a reliable source of external capital and has tapped their wealth and goodwill year after year on a regular basis. India, however, has used diaspora funding only opportunistically.

While the Government of Israel established the Development Corporation for Israel (DCI) to issue diaspora bonds, India relied on the government-owned State Bank of India (SBI). Israel has always viewed DCI's diaspora bond issuance as a catalyst for economic development and growth. Over US$32 billion in proceeds from such issuance has been used in energy, telecommunications, transportation, water resources, and other essential infrastructure projects. In contrast, India has turned to the SBI to raise funding from members of the Indian diaspora in times of balance-of-payments weaknesses. Thus, the SBI has tapped members of the diaspora for funding on three separate occasions—India Development Bonds following the balance-of-payments crisis in 1991 (US$1.6 billion), Resurgent

TABLE 4.1
Comparison of Israeli and Indian Diaspora Bonds

Israel	India
Annual issuance since 1951	Opportunistic issuance in 1991, 1998, and 2000
Development-oriented borrowings	Balance-of-payments support
Large though declining patriotic discount	Small patriotic discount, if any
Fixed-, floating-rate bonds and notes	Fixed-rate bonds
1- to 20-year maturities with single repayment at maturity	Five-year with bullet maturity
Targeted toward but not limited to diaspora	Limited to diaspora
Direct distribution by Development Corporation for Israel	State Bank of India distribution in conjunction with international banks
Registered with U.S. Securities and Exchange Commission	Not registered with U.S. Securities and Exchange Commission

Source: Authors' compilation.

India Bonds following the imposition of sanctions in the wake of nuclear testing in 1998 (US$4.2 billion), and India Millennium Deposits in 2000 (US$5.5 billion).

The 4 percent coupon and the yield on the DCI's fixed-rate bonds from 1951 to 1989 was often far below the yields on 10-year U.S. Treasury notes. Thus, the Jewish diaspora initially provided a large patriotic discount to the DCI. But the patriotic discount has dwindled in recent years. This is perhaps due to the fact that younger Jewish investors are seeking market-based returns. More important, the decline in patriotic discount is also due to the availability of other Israeli bonds that trade in the secondary market and provide alternative avenues for acquiring exposure to Israel (Rehavi and Asher 2004). In contrast to the Jewish diaspora, Indian investors provided little overt discount—interest rates and yields on the SBI-issued bonds were about the same as comparably rated U.S. corporate bonds. But the fact that members of the Indian diaspora purchased these bonds when India had lost its access to international capital markets suggests that the Indian diaspora in reality offered a large discount.

Another noteworthy difference between the Indian and Israeli approaches to diaspora bonds is the variety of instruments that were made available to the respective diasporas. The SBI's diaspora bonds were nonnegotiable, fixed-rate bonds with a five-year maturity. The minimum investment amount was US$2,000. While the DCI also offered nonnegotiable bonds, it provided a large menu of options—fixed- and floating-rate bonds and notes in denominations ranging from a low of US$100 to a high of US$1 million with maturities ranging from 1 year to 20 years. This is due in large measure to Israel's desire to build ties with members of the Jewish diaspora that go beyond raising development finance.

Another difference also stands out. The DCI marketing efforts were targeted toward but not limited to the Jewish diaspora. The SBI, in contrast, restricted access to Resurgent India Bonds and India Millennium Deposits to investors of Indian origin. There are several possible explanations for limiting the size of this market:

- Restricting Resurgent India Bonds and India Millennium Deposits sales to the Indian diaspora may have been a marketing strategy introduced in the belief that Indian investors would be more eager to invest in instruments that are available exclusively to them
- The SBI perhaps believed that the Indian diaspora investors would show more understanding and forbearance than other investors if India encountered a financial crisis; having local-currency-denominated current or contingent liabilities, the Indian diaspora investors might be content to receive debt service in rupees
- The SBI concluded, based on the know-your-customer argument, that it knew its Indian diaspora investor base well enough to feel comfortable that the invested funds did not involve money laundering.

A final difference between the Israeli and Indian approaches to diaspora bonds has to do with U.S. Securities and Exchange Commission (SEC) registration. The DCI decided to seek SEC registration. But India went out of its way to avoid SEC registration, even though it meant losing access to the retail U.S. investor base. Generally, high costs, stringent disclosure requirements, and lengthy lead times are cited as the principal deterrents to SEC registration. These were probably not insurmountable obstacles for the SBI, however. Indeed, SBI officials pointed to the plaintiff-friendly U.S. court system in relation to other jurisdictions as the principal reason for eschewing SEC registration. Perhaps an argument can be sustained, as in Chander (2001), to make the U.S. SEC registration optional. Investors who value such registration highly will then be prepared to pay a price premium while unregistered bonds will fetch lower prices (higher yields). In other words, the law and forum would then become another attribute of the security, which will influence its market price.

Giving investors the choice of law and forum can be supported on efficiency grounds. Proposals giving such a choice to investors were floated toward the end of the 1990s (Choi and Guzman 1998; Romano 1998).

However, markets were roiled since then by the collapse of Enron and MCI, and more recently by the Madoff scandal, signaling that markets do not always work in the best interest of investors. In view of this, it is highly unlikely that the U.S. SEC or the U.S. Congress would in the near future relax regulations and permit international investors to opt out of U.S. laws and courts. The inability to register with the SEC may selectively limit the ability of some developing countries in placing diaspora bonds.

While the DCI's and SBI's diaspora bonds were quite different, one common thread in their success was the in-house marketing capability. The DCI sold its bonds directly to the Jewish diaspora. Currently, there are about 200 DCI employees in the United States who maintain close contacts with Jewish communities in various regions of the country to understand investor profiles and preferences.[5] They host investor events in Jewish communities with the express purpose of maintaining ties and selling bonds. The SBI's presence in the United States helped marketing of Resurgent India Bonds. Furthermore, where the Indian diaspora was known to favor specific foreign banks, such as Citibank and HSBC in the Gulf region, the SBI outsourced the marketing of Resurgent India Bonds and India Millennium Deposits to them. Not having their own marketing and distribution channels may, however, hamper the efforts of other countries in issuing diaspora bonds.

Potential for Diaspora Bonds

Highly skilled migrants in the rich countries are likely to be the principal purchasers of diaspora bonds. Table 4.2 lists 25 developing countries ranked by the presence of their diasporas in the Organisation for Economic Co-operation and Development countries. Column 3 of the table also presents the total stock of migrants from these countries in the world at large. The presence of millions of Mexican nationals in the United States is quite well known. China, India, the Philippines, the Republic of Korea, and Vietnam from Asia; Colombia, the Dominican Republic, El Salvador, Guatemala, Haiti, and Jamaica from Latin America and the Caribbean; and Poland from Eastern Europe have a significant diaspora presence in the United States. Diaspora presence is also significant in other parts of the world, such as the Chinese and Korean diasporas in Japan; the Indian and Pakistani diasporas in the United Kingdom; the Croatian, Serbian, and

TABLE 4.2
Countries with Large Diasporas Abroad
(sorted by high-skilled migrants)

		High-skilled emigrant stock (thousand)	Total emigrant stock (thousand)
1	Philippines	1,126	3,631
2	India	1,038	9,987
3	Mexico	923	11,503
4	China	817	7,258
5	Vietnam	506	2,225
6	Poland	449	2,316
7	Iran, Islamic Rep.	309	970
8	Jamaica	291	1,038
9	Russian Federation	289	11,480
10	Ukraine	246	6,082
11	Colombia	234	1,969
12	Pakistan	222	3,416
13	Romania	176	1,244
14	Turkey	174	4,403
15	Brazil	168	1,135
16	South Africa	168	713
17	Peru	164	899
18	Dominican Republic	155	1,069
19	Haiti	153	834
20	Nigeria	149	837
21	Egypt, Arab Rep.	149	2,399
22	Serbia	148	2,298
23	Morocco	141	2,719
24	Lebanon	138	622
25	El Salvador	128	1,129

Sources: Docquier and Marfouk 2004 for high-skilled migrants abroad in high-income Organisation for Economic Co-operation and Development countries as of 2000; Ratha and Shaw 2007 for total migrants abroad in 2005.

Turkish diasporas in Germany; the Algerian and Moroccan diasporas in France; and large pools of migrants from Bangladesh, India, Indonesia, Pakistan, the Philippines, and Africa in the oil-rich Gulf countries.

But for diaspora investors to purchase hard currency bonds issued by their countries of origin, there has to be a minimum level of governability. Absence of governability, as reflected in civil strife, is clearly a big negative for diaspora bonds. While this requirement would not disqualify most countries in the Far East and many countries in Eastern Europe, countries such as Cuba, Haiti, and Nigeria (and several others in Africa) that have large diasporas abroad but low levels of governance may be found wanting.

Indian and Israeli experience also shows that countries will have to register their diaspora bonds with the U.S. SEC if they want to tap into the retail U.S. market.

The customary disclosure requirements of U.S. SEC registration may prove daunting for some countries. Some of the African and East European countries and Turkey with a significant diaspora presence in Europe, however, will be able to raise funds on the continent, where the regulatory requirements are relatively less stringent than in the United States. Arguably, diaspora bonds could also be issued in the major destination countries in the Gulf region and in Hong Kong SAR, China; Malaysia; the Russian Federation; Singapore; and South Africa. Thus, the potential for developing countries to issue diaspora bonds is large.[6] As many as 11 countries—Ethiopia, Ghana, Grenada, Jamaica, Liberia, Morocco, Nepal, the Philippines, Rwanda, Sierra Leone, and Sri Lanka—are believed to be thinking about this financing vehicle.

The actual issuance of diaspora bonds, however, remains meager to date, for the following reasons.

First, there is limited awareness about this financing vehicle. Governments and other entities are often deterred by the complexities of bond instruments. Lacking the capacity to undertake bond issuance, they take the easy way out of depending upon national banks to generate local and foreign currency deposits from diaspora investors. While foreign currency deposits attract foreign currency inflows, these can be withdrawn at any time. This is certainly true of demand and savings deposits. But even time deposits can be withdrawn at any time by forgoing a portion of accrued interest. Therefore, foreign currency deposits are likely to be much more volatile, requiring banks to hold much larger reserves against their foreign currency deposit liabilities, thereby reducing their ability to fund investments. All bonds, including those targeted at the diaspora, in contrast, are long term (until maturity) in nature. Hence, the proceeds from such bonds can be used to finance investment with some predictability.

In view of this, many developing country policy makers would benefit from technical assistance aimed at improving their understanding of structuring bond offerings, registering them with regulatory agencies such as the U.S. SEC, and whether or not such instruments need to be rated by rating agencies. Not only are potential issuers uninformed about diaspora bonds, market players and regulators in the developed destination countries are also unfamiliar with them.

Second, many countries still have little concrete appreciation of the capabilities and resources of their respective diasporas. As a 2009 World Bank survey (Plaza 2009) pointed out, few governments have a complete mapping of their diaspora. Data on diasporas are mainly based on those who register with embassies. But such registration is incomplete, at best. Furthermore, there is little coordination at the embassy or consular level when dealing with diasporas. As a result, many governments do not know where their diasporas are located. They also have little knowledge of how much members of their diaspora earn, save, and invest. This is now beginning to change, however. With remittances becoming an increasingly important source of development finance, countries are now becoming more and more interested in tracking their diasporas. Countries are also moving toward giving their diasporas dual citizenship.

Third, many potential issuers fail to plan ahead. Indeed, many potential issuers resort to whatever instruments are at hand at the last minute of need. Furthermore, many abandon their plans for using new financing mechanisms as soon as the financing gap is resolved. This seems to have happened in the Philippines and Sri Lanka, for example. The Central Bank of Sri Lanka was contemplating issuing diaspora bonds until recently. But the possibility of raising US$1 billion by selling plain vanilla bonds persuaded the authorities to abandon diaspora bonds.

As mentioned, diaspora investors must have confidence in the government of their country of origin if they are to purchase bonds issued by those governments. Thus, countries that have a hostile diaspora are unlikely to succeed in raising financing through diaspora bonds. Also, countries with political insecurity and weak institutional capacity would find it hard to market diaspora bonds unless credit enhancements are provided by more creditworthy institutions. While patriotism motivates members of diasporas to provide funding at discounted rates, they must have confidence that the funds would be used productively.

Such confidence can be generated by creating appropriate structures for the productive use of the proceeds from diaspora bonds. For example, proceeds from diaspora bonds can be earmarked for specific projects favored by members of the diaspora. A number of examples come to mind such as community infrastructure, housing, medical facilities, modernization of airports and railways, extension of transport infrastructure to smaller cities, and tourism development. On a smaller scale, diaspora investors may also find it attractive to purchase bonds whose proceeds are to be used to fund microfinance institutions. Of course, it is not enough to simply earmark proceeds from diaspora bonds to specific projects; it is also paramount to establish appropriate transparency, accountability, and governance necessary to enforce contracts.

Diaspora Bonds for Haiti

This section explores the constraints on Haiti's ability to issue diaspora bonds and offers ideas on overcoming these constraints.

Given Haiti's massive financing requirements in the wake of the January 2010 earthquake, one crucial question is: where will the money come from? Obviously, support needs to be made available in the immediate future. Also, the level of funding has to be predictable over time in order to maintain what will be a long and expensive rebuilding process. International assistance from governments, multilateral institutions, and private foundations is essential, but tapping the wealth and goodwill of the people of the nation living abroad can also be very effective. In the near term, the Haitian diaspora is likely to contribute to both humanitarian relief and development through increased remittances to families. It can also contribute to the country's rebuilding effort through investment in reconstruction diaspora bonds.

According to official statistics (Ratha 2010), about 1 million Haitians are currently living overseas, and about half of them are in the United States. Newspapers often report that a million Haitians live in the neighboring Dominican Republic. Haiti receives US$1.5 billion to US$1.8 billion in remittances each year, over one-half of the country's national income (Ratha 2010). In a laudable measure that will benefit Haitians more than any other aid and assistance, announced just three days after the devastating earthquake in Haiti, the United States granted temporary protected status for 18 months to Haitians already in the United States. The temporary protected status would allow 100,000 to 200,000 Haitians residing in the United States without proper documentation to live and work in the United States legally, without fear of deportation (U.S. DHS 2010). It would also allow them to send money home quickly and efficiently through formal remittance channels.

Remittances to Haiti in 2010 will surge, as they have done whenever and wherever there has been a crisis or natural disaster. If the temporary protected status results in a 20 percent increase in the average remittance per migrant, an additional US$360 million in remittances could be expected to flow to Haiti in 2010. If the temporary protected status were extended once beyond the currently stipulated 18 months (an extension is almost certain to happen, judging by the history of temporary protected status extensions for immigrants from El Salvador, Honduras, Nicaragua, Somalia, and Sudan), additional flows to Haiti would exceed US$1 billion over three years. Beyond remittances, the temporary protected status will also enhance the ranks of members of the Haitian diaspora in the United States, facilitating the issuance of diaspora bonds.

If members of the million-plus Haitian diaspora invested US$500 each in diaspora bonds, it would add up to millions of dollars. The incentive for such investments by Haitians would come partly from patriotism and partly from higher returns. A 5 percent tax-free dollar interest rate, for example, could attract a large number of Haitian investors who are getting close to a zero interest rate on their deposits. Regarding the question of whether Haitian immigrants are too poor to invest in diaspora bonds, consider this fact from the Current Population Survey of the United States[7]: nearly one-third of legal Haitian immigrants in the United States earned more than US$60,000 in 2009. In comparison, less than 15 percent of immigrants from the Dominican Republic, El Salvador, and Mexico in the United States had this level of household income. A quarter of Haitian immigrants, especially women, are reportedly in the relatively higher-paying health care and education sectors, and only a small number are in the construction sector. Not only Haitians, but also foreign individuals interested in helping Haiti, even charitable institutions, are likely to be interested in these bonds. That would further expand the pool of potential investors in Haiti's diaspora bonds.

Lack of trust in public institutions, including the government, is likely to be one major obstacle to Haitians and others purchasing diaspora bonds issued by the Haitian government. Haiti was a weakly governed state even before the January 2010 earthquake further eroded confidence in its ability to deliver. Such concerns can, in part, be overcome by establishing a Haiti Reconstruction Authority in partnership with the United Nations or other internationally reputable organizations.[8] The Haiti Reconstruction Authority could then raise funds by issuing diaspora bonds. That alone may not suffice to overcome the lack of investor confidence in Haiti. In all likelihood, these bonds would require credit enhancement from multilateral or bilateral donor agencies. Our preliminary calculations suggest that a US$100 million grant from official or private donors to guarantee such bonds (say, for 10 years, on an annual rolling basis) could generate US$600 million of additional funding for Haiti.[9] Such a guarantee structure could also raise the rating on these bonds to investment grade, reducing interest rates from over 15 percent to potentially 5 percent. Marketing of such diaspora bonds in the United States would, however, require a temporary exemption from U.S. SEC regulations.

Conclusion

This chapter discussed the rationale and potential for issuing diaspora bonds as instruments for raising external development finance, mostly drawing on the experiences of India and Israel. The Government of Israel has nurtured this asset class since 1951 by offering a flexible menu of investment options to keep the Jewish diaspora engaged. Indian authorities, in contrast, have used this instrument opportunistically to raise financing during times when they had difficulty accessing international capital markets (for example, in the aftermath of their nuclear testing in 1998).

Although, thus far, only state-owned entities have issued diaspora bonds, there is no reason why private sector companies cannot tap this source of funding. While India's SBI succeeded on one occasion in the past in bypassing U.S. SEC registration, that is unlikely to happen again in the near future. U.S. investors are unlikely to be allowed to choose the law and forum governing bond contracts.

Finally, factors that facilitate the issuance of diaspora bonds include having a sizable and wealthy diaspora abroad and a strong and transparent legal system for contract enforcement at home. Absence of civil strife is a plus. In addition, earmarking proceeds from diaspora bonds for specific projects should also help improve their marketability. While not a prerequisite, the presence of national banks and other institutions in destination countries would facilitate the marketing of bonds to the diaspora.

In the specific context of Haiti, diaspora bonds could be a useful source of funding to rebuild the country's earthquake-ravaged economy. Given the Haitian Government's poor track record in governance, however, overseas Haitian investors' willingness to purchase diaspora bonds will hinge critically on the endorsement and involvement of more trustworthy partners. The United Nations or other international organizations can lend credibility to the agency in charge of issuing diaspora bonds for reconstruction activities. That may have to be complemented with explicit credit enhancement of these bonds by multilateral or bilateral donors.

There is also a need for clarity on regulations in the host countries that allow diaspora members to invest or that constrain them from investing in these bonds. A pertinent question in this context is: should these bonds be nonnegotiable or should there be efforts to develop a secondary market for these bonds? An argument can be made for the latter on the grounds that tradability in the secondary market would improve the liquidity and pricing of these bonds.

Notes

1. See, in particular, chapter 3 in Ketkar and Ratha (2009a); and Ketkar and Ratha (2009b) for a broader discussion of innovative market-based financing mechanisms.
2. In a report dated March 13, 2009, Standard & Poor's said, "We do not...expect Israel to face significant or sustained difficulties in securing external financing." Among the reasons: "We...expect Israel to make use of its additional borrowing flexibility provided by the loan guarantee program with the U.S. and the Israel Bonds Corporations (sic)." Similarly, in an overview issued March 18, 2009, Fitch cited Israel Bonds as "a reliable source of external financing." In January 2009, Moody's stated, "the (Israeli) government has a critical resource for external liquidity—the Israel Bonds program" (Moody's Investor Services 2009).
3. Conversation with Standard and Poor's credit analyst David Beers in early 2007.
4. Pratima Das of the State Bank of India (SBI) and V. Gopinathan of SBICAP Securities were quite explicit in telling us, in early 2007, that members of the Indian diaspora knew SBI to be rupee-rich and, hence, never questioned its ability to meet all debt service obligations in rupees.
5. Conversation with Shirley Strifler of the Israeli Ministry of Finance and Tamar Roth-Drach of the Israeli Mission to the United Nations in early 2007.
6. Ratha, Mohapatra, and Plaza (2008) estimate that countries in Sub-Saharan Africa could potentially raise US$5 billion to US$10 billion annually by issuing diaspora bonds to tap into the wealth of the diaspora abroad and the flight capital held by its residents.
7. http://www.bls.gov/cps/.

8. Gros (2010) has proposed the creation of such a Haiti Reconstruction Authority (HRA) with a much broader mandate to govern Haiti over the next few
   years. What we have in mind is an HRA, much like Israel's DCI, with a limited
   responsibility for reconstruction. Unlike DCI, which works closely with Israel's
   Ministry of Finance, the HRA would be accountable to the United Nations.
9. This calculation draws on Gelb and Ratha (2009).

References

Ahearne, A., W. Griever, and F. Warnock. 2004. "Information Costs and Home
Bias: An Analysis of U.S. Holding of Foreign Equities." *Journal of International
Economics* 62 (2): 313–36.

Brennan, M., and H. Cao. 1997. "International Portfolio Investment Flows." *Journal of Finance* 52 (5): 1851–80.

Chander, A. 2001. "Diaspora Bonds." *New York University Law Review* 76 (4) (October): 1005–99.

Choi, S. J., and A. T. Guzman. 1998. "Portable Reciprocity: Rethinking the International Reach of Securities Regulation." *Southern California Law Review* 71 (5)
(July): 903–53.

Fitch Ratings. 2009. Fitch Rates State of Israel's USD Soverign Bond "A", March.
www.fitchratings.com.

French, K., and J. Poterba. 1991. "International Diversification and International
Equity Markets." *American Economic Review* 81 (2): 222–26.

Gelb, A., and D. Ratha. 2009. "Catalyzing Private Flows—Thoughts on a Pilot
Structured Guarantee." World Bank, Washington, DC.

Gros, J. G. 2010. "Propositions Pour La Reconstruction d'Haiti." http://groups
.google.com/group/soc.culture.haiti/browse_thread/thread/86dbb8132e6487ec.

Indian Express. 1998a. "Moody's Downgrades India by Two Notches." June 20.

———. 1998b. "Standard and Poor's Downgrades India's Sovereign Rating by One
Notch to BB." October 23.

Ketkar, S., and D. Ratha, eds. 2009a. *Innovative Financing for Development.* Washington, DC: World Bank.

———. 2009b. "New Paths to Funding." *Finance and Development* 46 (2) (June):
43–45. International Monetary Fund, Washington DC.

Moody's Investor Services. 2009. Credit Crunch and Gaza Conflict: New Challenges to Israel's Credit Rating, January. http://www.moodys.com.

Pastor, L. 2000. "Portfolio Selection and Asset Pricing Models." *Journal of Finance*
55 (1): 179–223.

Plaza, S. 2009. "Promoting Diaspora Linkages: The Role of Embassies." Paper presented at the International Conference on Diaspora for Development at the World Bank, Washington, DC. July 14–15.

Portes, R., H. Rey, and Y. Oh. 2001. "Information and Capital Flows: The Determinants of Transactions in Financial Assets." *European Economic Review* 45 (4–6): 783–96.

Ratha, D. 2010. "Mobilizing the Diaspora for Reconstruction of Haiti." Social Science Research Council Publication. February. http://www.ssrc.org/features/pages/haiti-now-and-next/1338/1438/.

Ratha, D., S. Mohapatra, and S. Plaza. 2008. "Beyond Aid: New Sources and Innovative Mechanisms for Financing Development in Sub-Saharan Africa." Policy Research Working Paper WPS4609, World Bank, Washington, DC. April.

Ratha, D., and W. Shaw. 2007. "South-South Migration and Remittances." World Bank Working Paper 102, World Bank, Washington, DC. May.

Rehavi, Y., and W. Asher. 2004. "Fifty Years of External Finance via State of Israel Non-negotiable Bonds." Foreign Exchange Activity Department, Assets and Liabilities Unit, Bank of Israel, Jerusalem. September 6.

Romano, R. 1998. "Empowering Investors: A Market Approach to Securities Regulation." *Yale Law Journal* 107 (8) (June): 2359–2430.

Standard and Poor's. 2009. Foreign Currency Credit Rating AA-/Stable/A-1+/Stable A-Rationale, March. www.standardandpoors.com

Tesar, L., and I. Werner. 1998. "The Internationalization of Securities Markets Since the 1987 Crash." Brookings-Wharton Papers on Financial Services, The Brookings Institution, Washington, DC.

U.S. DHS (U.S. Department of Homeland Security). 2010. "Statement from Homeland Security Secretary Janet Napolitano on Temporary Protected Status (TPS) for Haitian Nationals." Press release, January 15. http://www.dhs.gov/ynews/releases/pr_126.

Van Nieuwerburgh, S., and L. Veldkamp. 2009. "Information Immobility and the Home Bias Puzzle." *Journal of Finance* 64 (3) (June): 1187–1215.

CHAPTER 5

African Diaspora Associations in Denmark: A Study of Their Development Activities and Potentials

Lars Ove Trans and Ida Marie Vammen

Since the early 1990s, an increasing number of African migrants have come to Denmark, where they have formed a large number of migrant associations. This chapter presents selected findings from a comprehensive survey of African diaspora associations in Denmark conducted in spring 2008. The survey includes 123 associations representing 22 countries and three pan-regions in Africa.

This chapter:

- Presents a brief overview of the African association landscape with a specific focus on the associations that carry out development activities in their countries of origin[1]
- Examines how the Danish institutional framework shapes the activities of these associations and explores some of the limitations and potentials of this framework.

Research on Migrant Associations in Denmark

There has been relatively little research on migrant associations in Denmark, and the studies have generally tended to focus on the associations' potential for aiding integration into Danish society (Hjære and Balslev

2001) or their influence on the Danish political scene (Gundelach and Torpe 1999; Hammer and Bruun 2000; Hussain 2002; Togeby 2003).

The perspective used in these studies, however, typically neglects the transnational field that many of these associations are also a part of, and they thereby exclude an important component of the associational life of migrant groups in Denmark. Only a smaller number of research projects have included the role of the associations' transnational engagement (Kleist 2007; Mikkelsen 2003a, 2003b; Østergaard-Nielsen 2002).

Definition of Migrant Associations and Methodology

The aim of the survey is to locate a broad range of associations involving African migrants in order to gain a comprehensive understanding of their activities and engagement with their countries of origin. Thus, the present study has used a broad definition of what constitutes migrant and diaspora associations, and we have therefore also included 11 free churches with congregations of African immigrants. The main criterion for including an association in the survey is that immigrants from Africa (North as well as Sub-Sahara) or, in a few cases, their descendants (regardless of their status as Danish or foreign citizens),[2] are actively involved, for instance, as members of the board, and that the association has some form of expressed affiliation with Africa. Of the associations included in the survey, about half (53.6 percent) stated that all their members are of African origin, 36 (29.3 percent) reported that a majority of their members are of African origin, and 21 (17.1 percent) said that a majority of their members are of Danish origin. The latter associations would probably more accurately describe themselves as "friendship associations" rather than as "migrant" or "diaspora" associations. However, it is difficult to separate these associations into neat categories that can be labeled as either "migrant" or "friendship" associations. A migrant association may, for instance, evolve into a friendship association as it reaches out and seeks to attract members of Danish origin who have an interest in the relevant country. Or, vice versa, a friendship association may be unsuccessful in attracting Danish members and eventually end up having only migrants as members.[3]

We have not used strict criteria regarding the degree of formalization needed for an association to be included in the study, but the vast majority (85.4 percent) of the associations are formal in the sense that they have written bylaws and an elected board. The high degree of formalization among the associations may not be surprising, as Hjære and Balslev (2001:20) point out, since this is often a prerequisite for receiving financial support from the Danish state. The remaining 18 associations merely function as loosely organized networks, but they are nevertheless all characterized by being, to some degree, "recognized" as associations in the sense that representatives from other associations have referred us to them and that all of them have an "official" name.

Most of the associations in the survey were located through various publically available databases and sources found on the Internet. In addition, we used the snowball-sampling technique by asking respondents to give us information on other African migrant associations that they knew of. We learned of 159 associations. However, 36 could either not be located or did not respond to our calls and e-mails, which left us with a response rate of 77.4 percent. All the survey interviews were conducted via telephone with either the chairperson or a representative from the board and lasted from 20 minutes to an hour.[4]

African Migrants and Diaspora Associations in Denmark

Since the 1960s, immigration to Denmark has changed in volume and areas of origin. Until the 1950s, Denmark was a country of net emigration—and the majority of the immigrants came from the neighboring Nordic countries and other Western countries. However, following the economic upturn during the 1960s and the increased demand for labor, immigration shifted toward developing countries as Denmark officially began to invite "guest workers," as they were then called, to come from Morocco, Pakistan, Turkey, and Yugoslavia. With the economic decline and the rising unemployment in the early 1970s, labor immigration was halted, although people from developing countries still came to Denmark as part of family reunification and—particularly in the 1980s and 1990s—as refugees (Pedersen 1999:233ff.).

Even though there has been a significant increase in the number of African migrants in Denmark due to the intake of refugees, the total number of African immigrants and descendants was only 45,562 in 2008, equal to 9.1 percent of the total number of immigrants and descendants in Denmark and less than 1 percent of the total population.[5] One of the main factors behind the growth in the number of African migrants is the arrival of the Somalis during the 1990s. While only a few Somalis had come prior to the 1990s as refugees from the Barre regime, the spread of civil war in 1991 caused Somalis to begin to flee in great numbers and to come to Denmark, first as asylum seekers and later through family reunification regulations (Fink-Nielsen, Hansen, and Kleist 2002). Today, Somalis are by far the largest group of Africans in Denmark, numbering 16,550, and constitute 36.3 percent of the total group of African immigrants and descendants.

These migration trends are also reflected in the formation of associations among the African migrants, where there has been a significant increase since the 1990s.[6] Thus, the associations are generally young, and most (79 percent) have existed less than 13 years. In particular, the Somalis have been active in forming associations (Kleist 2007), and they are also the most represented group in the survey, with 50 associations. Another notable feature of the associations is that they are relatively small. Almost three-quarters (74 percent) have fewer than 99 members. However, this is comparable to other types of local associations in Denmark (Torpe and Kjeldgaard 2003).

Primary Activities and Focus of the Associations

The associations typically engage in a wide range of activities. The most frequently mentioned activity in the survey is "social activities," cited by 87 associations (70.7 percent). In fact, many of the associations stated that their primary purpose was to create a meeting place and strengthen networks among their compatriots. Other significant types of activities hosted by the associations include informational (59.3 percent), cultural (48.8 percent), sports (39.8 percent), and youth-related (31.7 percent) activities. Only to a much lesser degree do they engage in religious (22 percent) and politically oriented (18.7 percent) activities (both in relation to Denmark and country of origin).

Based on the main activities and primary focus of the associations in the survey, three types of associations can be identified:

- *Ethnonational associations,* which focus mostly on the lives and situations of the migrant group and their children in Denmark and seek to provide a space for social and cultural activities, often coupled with the aim of promoting integration into Danish society

- *Religious associations,* which center on religious worship but frequently also host other types of social activities
- *Development-oriented associations,* which are organized around development projects.

While development-oriented associations focus mainly on development projects, ethnonational and religious associations might also have development components. In the following sections we examine in more detail all the associations that engage in development activities.

Funding Possibilities for Development Initiatives

Seventy associations (56.9 percent) in the survey reported that they have been involved in some kind of development activities. Significantly, almost three-quarters (71.4 percent) reported that they have received financial support from public funds for their development projects and activities. It is therefore worth exploring the funding opportunities available in Denmark for migrant associations to carry out development projects.

The most commonly used programs for applying for financial support for development projects are administered by MS ActionAid Denmark (Mellemfolkeligt Samvirke) and the Project Advice and Training Centre (PATC).[7] Generally, a migrant association can apply for these funds on equal terms with other Danish associations. Both programs require that the association have contact with a partner nongovernmental organization (NGO) in the receiving country.

By far, the most frequently used program is "Recycling for the South," which is a government fund administered by MS ActionAid Denmark. The program grants financial support to individuals and associations for renovation and shipment of collected recycled equipment to partner associations or state-run projects in countries with a 2008 per capita gross domestic product below US$2,397. MS ActionAid Denmark also supports a number of renovation workshops around the country that can assist associations with collecting and refurbishing equipment. However, most migrant associations use their personal contacts, for instance with the municipality, local schools, or hospitals, to collect the used equipment. Box 5.1 provides an example of how support provided by MS ActionAid Denmark can aid the work of an association.

BOX 5.1

Danish Senior Citizens

A group of Danish senior citizens had regularly sent used equipment to Lithuania and Poland with the support of the MS ActionAid Denmark program. However, when the two countries entered the European Union in 2004, they no longer qualified for MS ActionAid Denmark support. At the same time, the senior citizens were contacted by a Somali man who presented his ideas about sending computers and school and hospital equipment to Somaliland.

Since then, the group has sent 20 containers to Gabiley and Hargeisa in Somaliland. The Danish-Somali collaboration has benefited from having access to the Somali migrant's personal network in Somaliland and from the senior citizens' networking with a municipality in Denmark, which has helped them collect the needed equipment.

Two years ago the group visited the projects in Somaliland together with the Somali, who also functioned as interpreter. The senior citizens described the trip as a great experience, one in which they also met with government ministers.

Currently, the group is planning to build a fire station in Hargeisa.

Source: Interview with the Somaliland Committee.

The second program, known as the "Mini-Project Fund," supports development projects up to DKr 3 million (€400,000) and is one of the most important sources of financial support for small and medium-size NGOs involved in development work.[8] The fund is administered by PATC—an organizational network consisting of approximately 220 NGOs engaged in development work—on behalf of the Danish International Development Agency.

Since 2005, the PATC has put special emphasis on involving immigrants and refugees as an active part and resource of Danish aid to developing countries. Nevertheless, because the PATC works within the Danish International Development Agency's Civil Society Strategy, which emphasizes support for capacity building rather than traditional reconstruction projects, many of the projects suggested by the migrant associations do not qualify for support. This is particularly the case for projects that focus on countries involved in present or past conflicts and therefore often concentrate on the provision of basic necessities, such as potable water or other types of reconstruction projects. The limitations set by the Civil Society Strategy help explain why, of the 19 associations formed entirely by migrants or refugees who applied for financial support from the Mini-Project Fund from 2005 to 2007, only four associations (of which three consist entirely of African migrants) received grants, which were all less than DKr 400,000 (Frederiksen 2007).

Types of Development Activities

Except for Nigeria and Sudan, all of the countries represented by migrant associations in the survey have benefited from development activities carried out by one or more of the associations. The types of development activities and projects are illustrated in figure 5.1.

The activity most frequently performed by the associations is the shipment of used equipment in containers—typically destined for schools, universities, orphanages, and hospitals—which 41 of the associations have done, often a number of times. In almost all of the cases, the transportation has been facilitated by MS ActionAid Denmark.

The second-most-frequent activity is the sending of collective remittances, which 27 associations have done. Typically, the money is generated from parties or collected among the migrants and is sent to finance specific projects in the country of origin or for humanitarian relief in the wake of natural or human disasters. The sending of collective remittances can also take a more institutionalized form as, for example, in the case of several Eritrean associations that send regular donations to the Eritrean state to support development projects.

The third-most-frequent activity is informational campaigns and education. These activities cover, for instance, campaigns to promote HIV/AIDS awareness or the prevention of female circumcision, but they may also seek to advance civil rights, more generally. In other cases, they can be more narrowly focused on providing capacity training to local NGO staff or teaching vocational skills to a group of adolescents. Most of the associations

FIGURE 5.1
Types of Development Activities

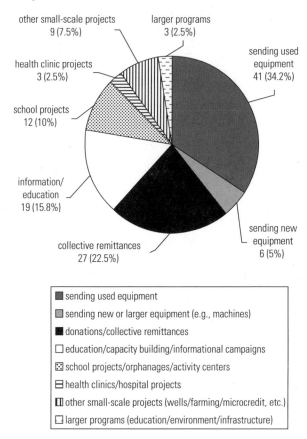

other small-scale projects
9 (7.5%)

larger programs
3 (2.5%)

health clinic projects
3 (2.5%)

sending used
equipment
41 (34.2%)

school projects
12 (10%)

information/
education
19 (15.8%)

sending new
equipment
6 (5%)

collective remittances
27 (22.5%)

- sending used equipment
- sending new or larger equipment (e.g., machines)
- donations/collective remittances
- education/capacity building/informational campaigns
- school projects/orphanages/activity centers
- health clinics/hospital projects
- other small-scale projects (wells/farming/microcredit, etc.)
- larger programs (education/environment/infrastructure)

Source: Authors' calculations based on survey.
Note: Since some associations are (or have been) involved in several different types of development activities, the activities total 120. This figure, however, does not indicate the volume of the activities undertaken by the associations.

that have received funds from the PATC to carry out larger development projects typically also engage in some kind of capacity building, as required by the Danish International Development Agency's Civil Society Strategy.

Among the remaining categories, 12 associations are involved in projects that focus on constructing schools, orphanages, or activity centers, or on sustaining existing schools and centers by financing staff salaries. Nine associations carry out "other small-scale projects," such as the construction of wells, implementation of farming or smaller business projects, and provision of microcredit loans. Six associations have sent new or larger equipment, which is sometimes used for these types of small-scale projects. Three associations are engaged in constructing health clinics or hospitals and two of these associations have received funding through the PATC. Finally, the "larger programs" involve three associations that have received larger grants from the PATC to carry out projects related to education, health, and the environment.

Which Types of Associations Become Involved in Development?

To examine what typically characterizes the associations that engage in development activities, we have, based on cross tabulations, sought to isolate a number of organizational characteristics and their relation to development. For instance, the length of existence of the association does not seem to influence whether it becomes involved in development activities, nor does length of existence seem to be related to the size of the development projects the association is able to carry out. Rather, the ability of the association to undertake larger projects is more likely to be related to the experience and networks of the individuals in the association. Similarly, there is no clear indication that the size of the association in terms of members is related to its involvement in development activities.

Membership composition in terms of origin, however, does seem to be an important indicator for engagement in development activities. As table 5.1 shows, about half of the associations whose members are all of African origin (47.7 percent) or have a majority of members of African origin (50 percent) are involved in development activities. However, if the majority of the members are of Danish origin, the association is much more likely to carry out development activities. Thus, of the 22 associations that have a majority of Danish members, 21 (95.5 percent) carry out development activities.

Two of the reasons for the higher involvement in development activities of associations with a majority of members of Danish origin could be that the Danish members bring knowledge about available funding opportunities and that they can facilitate the process of applying for funds for development projects. For example, language barriers and lack of familiarity with Danish application procedures can hinder migrants' ability to access external sources of funding. The main sources used for financing development activities in relation to the membership composition of the associations are listed in table 5.2.

TABLE 5.1
Development Activities in Relation to Membership Composition (n = 123)

Composition of members	No development activities	Development activities	Percent with development activities
All members of African origin	34	31	47.7
Majority of members of African origin	18	18	50.0
Majority of members of Danish origin	1	21	95.5
Total	53	70	56.9

Source: Authors' calculations based on survey.

TABLE 5.2
Funding Sources in Relation to Membership Composition (n = 70)

Composition of members	Self-financed	MS	Larger funds (PATC)
All members of African origin (n = 31)	16	15	2
Majority of members of African origin (n = 18)	10	8	0
Majority of members of Danish origin (n = 21)	0	18	7
Total	26	41	9

Source: Authors' calculations based on survey.
Note: More than one answer is possible for the associations that have received financial support depending on whether they have received funds from "MS" and/or "larger funds (PATC)." Thus, six associations have received both types of funding (two associations with all members of African origin and four with a majority of members of Danish origin).
MS = MS ActionAid Denmark.
PATC = Project Advice and Training Centre.

Among the associations in which all the members are of African origin, 16 (51.6 percent) are self-financed and 15 (48.4 percent) have received support from MS ActionAid Denmark, two of which (6.5 percent) have also been able to access larger funds. The associations with a majority of members of African origin largely follow the same pattern, although they tend to be slightly more self-financed, and none of them have been able to obtain support from the larger funds.[9] In contrast, the associations in which a majority of the members are of Danish origin have all received some kind of financial support from external funds to carry out their development activities. In this category, 18 associations (85.7 percent) have received support from MS ActionAid Denmark and seven (33.3 percent) have been able to access larger funds (four associations received both types of funds).

Institutional Barriers

One explanation for the relatively large numbers of self-financed development activities among the associations in which all or a majority of the members are of African origin could be, as a number of the chairmen expressed, that they are unaware of the existing funding opportunities. However, a lack of knowledge of the available sources is only part of the answer. Among those associations that aspire to initiate larger projects with financial support from PATC's Mini-Project Fund, many complained about the complex application procedures, which require not only a high level of writing skills but also knowledge about how a project should be formulated in a Danish context. For example, the chairman of a relatively newly formed Somali association explained that they wanted to apply for PATC funds for a project in Somalia, but that it is impossible for them to write the application because of the language barrier, and so far they have been unable to find any Danes who could assist them.

Similarly, a report on PATC's experiences working with migrant associations concludes that it is crucial for these associations to have a Danish resource person or a second-generation immigrant involved in the application process in order to tackle linguistic challenges and aid with knowledge about Danish bureaucratic procedures (Frederiksen 2007). The need for this type of knowledge was also stressed by a representative of an association with members of both Danish and African origin who had successfully applied for PATC funds: "It has been a process of bridging the two cultures, and we have deliberately tried to 'Danicize' the methods in the application so they fit the demands of the funding authorities."

Nevertheless, even when Danes are involved in the association, the application process is still perceived as being difficult. For instance, a member of Danish origin of an association explained: "There is too much emphasis on the form [of the application]. Just because you do not use the prevalent matrix, it doesn't mean that you can't conduct a good project. There are too many 'holy cows' that have to be mentioned and therefore it is most of all an academic, stylistic exercise to apply for funding." In one case, an association sought to address the complex application procedures by hiring a professional consultant to formulate the project description and write the final application for the Mini-Project Fund. Even so, the application process often takes a great toll on the time and resources of the associations and it can therefore be difficult for them to handle a rejection after having invested months of work on it.

In the case of the two associations in which all the members are of African origin and which have been able to receive PATC funds, they also work on issues related to integration into Danish society and have received funding from the municipality. They have, therefore, been able to build up networks of Danes and Danish NGOs, which in both cases have facilitated the process of applying for PATC funds. For instance, in one of the associations, formed by women from Somalia, the members did not themselves have the capacity to write the application even though many are well integrated and speak Danish. Instead, they received help from a group of Danish women who volunteered to write the application for them.

Typology of the Development Associations

One finding that emerges from the survey is that the institutional context described above to a large degree shapes the characteristics of the associations and the development activities they carry out. Table 5.3 presents four types of associations that have been identified in the survey based on their involvement in development activities.

The kitchen-table grassroots associations are characterized by having only a few (less than 10) members, although most of them aspire to get more members. The majority of members of most of the 11 associations included in this category are of African origin. Their development activities center on collecting and sending used equipment to schools and hospitals, for which all of the associations have received support from MS ActionAid Denmark. Some of the associations also do vocational training for women or informational activities related to AIDS and health in the project countries.

The ethnonational associations with development activities are generally characterized by not having development as a main objective. Instead, they tend to be organized around social, cultural, informational, and youth-related activities, and their members are predominantly of African origin. When it comes to development activities, the ethnonational associations can be divided into two groups: Those that give donations and those that send used equipment or are directly involved in smaller projects. The former group includes 16 associations that collect money from their members for emergency relief or to support various projects, such as schools or

TABLE 5.3

Typology of the Associations Involved in Development Activities (n = 70)

	The kitchen-table grass roots (n = 11)	The ethnational associations with development activities (n = 27)	The development-oriented project associations (n = 23)	Semiprofessional NGOs (n = 9)
Development activities	Send used equipment for schools and hospitals	Half send donations for projects or emergency relief; the other half send used equipment	Most send used equipment; some are involved in smaller projects	Larger projects (education, health, and environment) and capacity training
Size	Small (1 to 9 members)	Medium to large	Small to medium	Medium
Organization structure	Loosely organized	Formally organized	Formally organized	Formally organized
Origin of members	Primarily members of African origin	The majority have only members of African origin	Half have a majority of Danish members and the other half have a majority of African members	Most have a majority of Danish members; two have only African members
Active members	All members are active	Most are active	About half of the members are active	A smaller group
Funding sources	All use the MS; a few also contribute with funds themselves	Most are self-financed; those that send equipment have received MS support	All have received MS support and half have received other sources of funds	All have received funding from PATC and/or other larger funds; most also receive MS support
Other activities	No other activities	All have social activities; most also have cultural, informational, and sports activities	Most have informational activities and some have social and cultural activities	Most have informational activities about projects; about half have cultural and social activities
Activity level	Most meet 1 to 3 times per year to organize and send equipment	Most have weekly activities related to life in Denmark	Most have monthly or bimonthly activities	Most have monthly or bimonthly activities

Source: Survey conducted by authors.

Note: MS = MS ActionAid Denmark.

PATC = Project Advice and Training Centre.

orphanages, undertaken by others in the country of origin. Most of these associations also expressed an interest in becoming more directly involved in development projects in the future. The second group, which includes 11 associations, is engaged in various, smaller types of development activities, such as sending used equipment destined for schools and hospitals in their countries of origin.

The development-oriented project associations all have development as their main objective. Most (87 percent) of the 23 associations send used equipment for schools and hospitals, for which all of them have received support from MS ActionAid Denmark. About half of the associations have informational activities about the relevant project country. Only to a lesser extent do they host social (39 percent) or cultural (17.4 percent) activities. Generally, the size of the associations varies from small to medium (10 to 100 members), and on average about half of the members are active. However, apart from these shared characteristics, the development-oriented associations differ in the composition of the members: In half of the associations the majority of members are of African origin, while in the other half the majority are of Danish origin. In terms of other sources of funding besides MS ActionAid Denmark, it is notable that the associations with a majority of African members tend to rely more on self-financing and generally have a much higher membership fee—in four associations the fee is above DKr 1,000 per year. In contrast, the associations with a majority of members of Danish origin have lower fees, but they are more often able to access other kinds of smaller funds to support their work. They are, therefore, often able to supplement the sending of equipment with other kinds of support, and they are more likely to be involved in other small-scale projects.

The semiprofessional NGOs include nine associations that have all received PATC funding to plan and carry out larger projects related to health, education, and the environment. Like the development-oriented project associations, the activities of the semiprofessional NGOs are mainly focused on their development projects. Thus, most of the associations have informational activities about the relevant project country, but many also have cultural and social activities. The semiprofessional NGOs are generally medium size (50 to 100 members) but only a smaller group of the members are actively involved. In seven of the associations the majority of members are of Danish origin. Indeed, some of these associations have only a few African migrants among their active members. In the remaining two associations, however, all the members are of African origin.

The Importance of Networks

The associations with a majority of members of Danish origin range from small associations, where an African migrant has managed to get a group of Danes interested in a project in his or her country of origin, to the larger and more established friendship associations often formed by Danes who have lived in the particular country. Compared to the associations where all or a majority of the members are of African origin, these associations are more often involved in larger projects and, as mentioned above, generally are more successful at obtaining funds. Nevertheless, the associations also typically benefit from having members of African origin, not only because they bring knowledge about local conditions and needs, but also because they can provide access to networks in the relevant country of origin. As the case provided in box 5.2 illustrates, having access to

BOX 5.2

The Ghanaian Female Chief

When Anna Ekua Saakwa, a Ghanaian woman living in Denmark, was nominated as the chief of two remote villages in Ghana in 2004, she decided to form an association that could help create schooling possibilities and reduce poverty for the people living in the area. She has a lot of experience working with both Danish and migrant associations and had been a member of the Copenhagen City Council. By mobilizing her Danish networks from Seniors Without Borders and Rotary, her association collected money for a well and is now planning to build schools and implement a project with a focus on "infrastructure, the village inhabitants, parents' influence and local ownership in the two villages."

In Ghana, Anna works in partnership with a local NGO that she located through her personal network. She explained that the title of chief gives her authority and power to create changes in the area while also opening doors to important people in high positions. She hopes that the association will grow and become a model for projects in other villages.

Source: Interview with Anna Ekua Saakwa.

networks in Denmark and in the country of the project can greatly facilitate implementation of the project.

In the Danish context, the networks can provide sources of financial and material support, and in the project country, they can give access to local partner NGOs and facilitate political and popular support for the implementation of the projects. With regard to implementation, the social capital that the migrants add to the development projects can potentially help to bridge some of the donor-recipient gaps often confronted by Western development agencies and NGOs without access to these networks. Furthermore, by involving their personal networks, migrants might reach segments of the population in conflict or postconflict countries not necessarily reached by the development NGOs.

Potentials and Limitations

Based on the findings of the survey, there are a number of measures that could be taken to strengthen the development potential of African migrant associations in Denmark.

First, help applying for funds could be offered to ethnonational associations interested in carrying out development activities but that lack the knowledge of available funding opportunities. In the survey, of the 53 associations that are not engaged in development activities, almost two-thirds (64.2 percent) stated that they would like to conduct projects in the future, if they had the financial means or if they could get help applying for funds.

Second, capacity training could be offered to key members from the associations with few or no members of Danish origin that are already involved in some type of development activity. This training should focus on developing competences that could facilitate applications for larger funds but also assist them in the planning and implementation of relevant projects. In this context, the above typology provides a tool for identifying the associations that could be "lifted" into the categories of associations that are able to carry out larger projects.

Third, programs could be established that seek to initiate collaboration between groups of Danes and "ethnonational" associations so that they get access to Danish networks and resources. This point is also illustrated in the two cases described in boxes 5.1 and 5.2, in which local groups of Danish senior citizens (other potential groups could be sports and youth associations) have become actively involved in development projects initiated by migrants.

Fourth, alternative application procedures and funding programs could be created aimed at the intermediate level of associations. These programs should take into account that most of the associations have few organizational resources to put into the application process. This problem could be addressed by having alternative application procedures, which depend less on formal and written applications and allow for a more personal evaluation of the association and the potential of the proposed project. The study shows that many of the associations with a majority of members of African origin are willing to self-finance their projects. The alternative application procedures could therefore be implemented in connection with a matching funds program, where the amount donated by the association is matched by an equal or larger amount from a relevant funding agency.

In spite of these potentials, there can also be certain limitations in working with diaspora groups. For instance, migrant associations tend to support mainly their hometown or region, leaving other areas without the benefit of this type of support (Kleist 2009). Furthermore, diasporas are often likely to have an elite position vis-à-vis the local communities in the homeland—particularly because they control resources and have power to decide how they should be allocated—and they might sometimes use this position to impose their view of development or undertake inappropriate, status-oriented projects (Bakewell 2009:3).

Concluding Remarks

This study of African migrant associations in Denmark reveals that a majority of the associations are currently (or have been) involved in development activities. Furthermore, the study shows that most of these associations have received some kind of financial support—primarily from MS ActionAid Denmark and only to a lesser degree from PATC—to undertake the projects. Thus, external funding and support play an important role for the type and scope of involvement of the African migrant associations in their countries of origin. With the aid of the funding programs, the possibilities of implementing a development project or providing material resources for a school or a hospital become a realistic goal. An important conclusion that can be drawn from the study is, therefore, that the engagement of migrant associations in development activities is not only a relation shaped by the diaspora and the country of origin, but also, to a large extent, a result of the institutional framework and the opportunity structures in the receiving country.

The study also shows, nevertheless, that the way the institutional framework is currently set up not only creates possibilities, but also poses a number of challenges for many of the migrant associations that want to become involved in larger projects. This is particularly the case for the associations with none or only a minority of members of Danish origin (found among the ethnonational associations with development activities and the development-oriented project associations), which often lack the organizational resources and the required knowledge about how a project should be formulated in a Danish context. Furthermore, the emphasis put on capacity building by the Danish International Development Agency's Civil Society Strategy, within which the PATC operates, also limits the possibilities of obtaining funds for the types of projects that focus on implementing basic infrastructure.

There are, however, as argued in the study, a number of reasons why it can be beneficial to involve diaspora groups and associations in development projects in their countries of origin and to seek to create funding programs that take the above factors into account. For example, migrants typically have intimate knowledge about local conditions and needs, and by using their social networks in the countries of origin, they can often obtain the support and goodwill of local authorities and help to mobilize popular support and involvement.

Nevertheless, it is also necessary to take into account that migrants often tend to focus only on their particular home regions and that the projects initiated by the migrants might sometimes seem to reflect more their own wishes and aspirations than the most pressing needs of the local population.

Notes

1. The word "development" is used in this chapter to refer to the projects and activities that the associations carry out in their countries of origin. However, by referring to the activities and projects in this way, we do not intend to say anything about their actual impact in the local context.

2. To avoid confusion on the issues of citizenship and ethnic belonging, the African immigrants and their descendants are also referred to as "of African origin," while Danes (born of Danish parents) are referred to as "of Danish origin."

3. Some of the migrant associations with all members of African origin did in fact express that they would like to attract members of Danish origin. The vast majority (85.5 percent) of the associations stated that they do not have any official membership criteria, such as that a member should come from a specific country of origin.

4. The questionnaire contained a mix of closed and open-ended questions that allowed the respondent to give more detailed information on issues of relevance for the particular association. In this chapter, the quotes cited from the interviews are kept anonymous to protect the confidentiality of our informants.

5. According to Statistics Denmark, a "descendant" is defined as "a person born in Denmark whose parents (or one of them if there is no information on the other parent) are either immigrants or descendants with foreign citizenship." When one or both of the parents who were born in Denmark acquire Danish citizenship, their children will no longer be counted as descendants. See Statistics Denmark, http://www.statistikbanken.dk

6. Associations from most of the traditional migrant-sending states from the Maghreb region in Northern Africa (Algeria, Morocco, and Tunisia) and Egypt are either underrepresented according to their number of immigrants in Denmark or, more often, nonexistent in the survey.

7. Only a few of the more experienced associations have received funding through the larger pools of funds, such as the Danish International Development Agency's framework grant.

8. The total grant in 2007 was DKr 51,533,244 (approximately €6.9 million). The budget for 2008 will be close to €8.5 million (see http://www.prngo.dk/Default.aspx?ID=15991).

9. This may seem contrary to the above-stated assumption that involvement of members of Danish origin makes it more likely that the association is engaged in development activities. However, one explanation could be that the members of Danish origin tend to be "passive" members in these associations.

References

Bakewell, Oliver. 2009. "Which Diaspora for Whose Development? Some Critical Questions about the Roles of African Diaspora Organizations as Development Actors." Danish Institute for International Studies Brief, Danish Institute for International Studies, Copenhagen.

Fink-Nielsen, Mette, Peter Hansen, and Nauja Kleist. 2002. "Repatriering – Afsluttet eller fortsat mobilitet." Den Ny Verden 32 (3): 52–65.

Frederiksen, Marianne. 2007. "Erfaringer fra flygtninge og indvandrerindsatsen i Projektrådgivningen 2006." Internal report, The Project Advice and Training Centre, Aarhus. http://www.prngo.dk/Admin/Public/DWSDownload.aspx? File=%2FFiles%2FFiler%2FPRNGOdokumenter%2FEgne+dokumenter% 2FRapporter+mv%2FF-I_Rapport_2006.doc.

Gundelach, Peter, and Lars Torpe. 1999. "Befolkningens fornemmelse for demokrati: foreninger, politisk engagement og demokratisk kultur." In Den demokratiske udfordring, ed. Jørgen Goul Andersen, Peter Munk Christiansen, Torben Beck Jørgensen, Lise Togeby, and Signild Vallgårda, 70–91. Copenhagen: Hans Reitzels Forlag.

Hammer, Ole, and Inger Bruun. 2000. Etniske minoriteters indflydelseskanaler. Århus: Aarhus Universitet.

Hjære, Mette, and Mille Balslev. 2001. Frivillighed blandt etniske minoritetsforeninger. Center for frivilligt socialt arbejde, Odense.

Hussain, Mustafa. 2002. "Etniske minoriteters organisering i Danmark." In Bevægelser i demokrati. Foreninger og kollektive aktioner i Danmark, ed. Flemming Mikkelsen, 160–76. Aarhus: Aarhus Universitets Forlag.

Kleist, Nauja. 2007. "Spaces of Recognition: An Analysis of Somali-Danish Associational Engagement and Diasporic Mobilization." PhD dissertation, Department of Sociology, University of Copenhagen, Copenhagen.

———. 2009. "African Diaspora Organizations and Homeland Development: The Case of Somali and Ghanaian Associations in Denmark." Danish Institute for International Studies Brief, Danish Institute for International Studies, Copenhagen.

Mikkelsen, Flemming, ed. 2003a. Indvandrerorganisationer i Norden. Copenhagen: Nordisk Ministerråd.

———. 2003b.Integrationsstatus 1999–2003. 5 år i et integrationsperspektiv. Catinét Research, Copenhagen.

Østergaard-Nielsen, Eva. 2002. Politik over grænser: Tyrkeres og kurderes engagement i det politiske liv i hjemlandet. Magtudredningens Sekretariat, Institut for Statskundskab, Århus.

Pedersen, Søren. 1999. "Vandringen til og fra Danmark i perioden 1960–1997." In Indvandringen til Danmark: internationale og nationale perspektiver, ed. David Coleman and Eskil Wadensjö, 233–284. Rockwool Fondens Forskningsenhed. Copenhagen: Spektrum.

Togeby, Lise. 2003. Fra fremmedarbejdere til etniske minoriteter. Aarhus: Aarhus Universitets forlag.

Torpe, Lars, and Torben Kjeldgaard. 2003. Foreningssamfundets sociale kapital. Danske foreninger i et europæisk perspektiv. Aarhus: Aarhus Universitets forlag.

CHAPTER 6

The Financial Consequences of High-Skill Emigration: Lessons from African Doctors Abroad

Michael A. Clemens[1]

Views of the Financial Effects of High-Skill Emigration

A common view in the social science literature is that the emigration of publicly trained professionals from developing countries causes the country of origin to lose the amount invested in their training. In this view, having a skilled diaspora can carry enormous public costs for the country of origin, and a variety of proposals have been advanced to offset those costs. These proposals include measures to limit skilled emigration, such as restrictions on international recruitment, taxes on highly trained emigrants, and systems of compensation from destination-country governments to origin-country governments.

Kirigia et al. (2006), for example, show that the Kenyan public invests the equivalent of US$48,169 in the medical training of each physician—an astronomical sum in a country where the average person earns about US$1.30 per day—and that the emigration of such a physician causes the country to lose this amount in medical training costs. This comports with other estimates of the cost of training a physician in several other African countries, typically US$5,000 to US$10,000 per year of medical schooling (Hagopian et al. 2005), normally taken to represent the public loss arising from the emigration of physicians thus trained. Clearly, the departure of a skilled worker is the proximate cause of a change in the amount and distribution of the returns to that investment. It is also the proximate cause of a reduction in revenues from taxes that person would have paid at home.

Thus, many observers have concluded that the departure of a skilled person constitutes a massive loss of public finance to the country of origin. Desai et al. (2009) claim that the emigration of skilled Indians causes India to lose 2.5 percent of fiscal revenue. Some have gone further and suggest that the value of the loss should be set far above any direct cost of public training, such as the value of what that training cost would have earned if invested in a bank account instead (for example, Kirigia et al. 2006), or what the cost of training that person in the destination country would have been (Bhargava 2005). Bhagwati (1976) has advocated an emigration tax on high-skill workers who retain citizenship in the country of origin—though it is not limited to publicly trained workers—a proposal that has evolved somewhat since (Wilson 2008). Many policy makers have urged that developing countries that publicly train skilled professionals who emigrate be given a compensation payment of some kind by the destination countries. Advocates of this approach include former Irish president Mary Robinson (McColl 2008) and a committee convened by the U.K. parliament (Select Committee on Science and Technology 2004:para. 144).

New Data on African Physicians in North America

Before exploring these commonly held views, it would be useful to establish a series of facts about the behavior of one skilled emigrant population that has been of interest to policy makers—African physicians in North America. Those facts will then be used as a tool to question many of the common suppositions about the financial effects of high-skill worker emigration, using African physicians as a suitable group with which to test the assumptions underlying mainstream views of the financial impacts of these movements. This chapter discusses only the financial impacts of the emigration of African physicians. Impacts of their emigration on morbidity and mortality can be found elsewhere (Clemens 2007).

Clemens (2011) reports the results of a new mail survey asking African doctors abroad about their remittances, year of arrival, country of training, and other migration-related traits. The survey was sent to all 6,775

African-born members of the American Medical Association, and all 3,117 African-trained members of the Canadian Medical Association.[2] "Africa" here is defined as all 54 countries of the African continent. This includes Sub-Saharan Africa (as defined by the World Bank, which includes Madagascar, Mauritius, and other nearby island nations) plus all of North Africa (Algeria, Djibouti, Egypt, Libya, Morocco, and Tunisia).

A total of 1,759 African physicians answered the survey, giving a response rate of 17.78 percent. This is strikingly high for a "one-off" mail survey with no participation incentive. But it is low enough that great care must be taken in assessing whether the respondent's characteristics are representative of the population that was sampled. Clemens (2011) describes multiple methods used to correct the estimates described here for potential sources of bias due to nonresponse.

The first of these corrections is post-stratification. When the distribution of potential respondents' traits in the whole population is known, the answers can be adjusted for any factors causing nonresponse that are correlated with those traits. In this survey, the American Medical Association and Canadian Medical Association records indicate the country of birth or training, age, gender, medical specialty, and state or province of residence. For example, if remittances by Ghanaian physicians are higher than those by South African physicians, and South Africans are more likely to respond than Ghanaians, the raw survey data would tend to underestimate remittances in the population. But if we know how many Ghanaians and South Africans are in the population that received the questionnaire, we can reweight the remittance estimates to account for different response rates by Ghanaians and South Africans. The post-stratified average remittance estimate in this example would assign greater weight to each Ghanaian because Ghanaians were less likely to respond. Post-stratification produces a moderate adjustment to the findings of the survey reported below.

A second correction is a randomized survey design. Perhaps the most important unknown trait of African physicians that might influence their response to a survey about remittances is the level of remittances themselves. People who send large remittances might fear reporting this fact; conversely, people who send no remittances might see a survey about remittances arrive in the mail and discard it as irrelevant to them. For this reason, a version of the mail survey questionnaire without any questions about remittances was sent to a randomly chosen subset of the population. Any difference between response rates for the different questionnaires must be caused by the presence of a remittance question. This allows bounds to be placed, as reported below, on the degree to which remittance behavior itself could produce bias by directly causing nonresponse.

A third correction is response time analysis. People who have a greater degree of interest in answering the survey might plausibly be expected to return it quickly; people with less interest might return it with a greater delay. If nonresponders differ substantially from responders on a particular characteristic, then we might expect late responders to differ substantially from early responders on that characteristic. For example, it was found that reported remittances do not decline as the response time increases, as would be expected if nonresponders remit more than responders. Responders who took several months to return the survey form reported no lower remittances than those who responded within a week. This is suggestive evidence that reported remittances are not biased upward by nonresponse.

A fourth correction is conservative bounding. Many survey respondents, for example, returned the survey but left blank the answer to the question about remittances. Does this constitute a refusal to answer, or does it mean that the respondent sent no money? The most conservative approach, to establish a lower bound on remittances, is to assume that "item nonresponse" of this kind means that no remittances were sent.

Readers with interest in these and other methodological details of the survey are referred to Clemens (2011). For the present purpose, the estimates discussed below are adjusted for nonresponse bias by all of these methods, and in all cases they are assumed to represent conservative estimates of the traits of the underlying population.

Country of Training

The first useful fact from the survey is that about 51 percent of the African-born physicians residing in the United States received their doctor of medicine degrees in their country of birth. Thus, about half received their medical training in the United States or in a third country prior to arriving in the United States, not in the countries they come from.

Figure 6.1 shows the post-stratified estimates of the percentage of African-born physicians in the United States trained in the country of birth.[3] The dark gray column shows this figure for all countries of birth. The light gray columns show it for selected countries of birth with a

FIGURE 6.1

Percentage of African-Born Doctors in the United States Who Received Their Medical Doctor Degrees in Their Countries of Birth (selected countries)

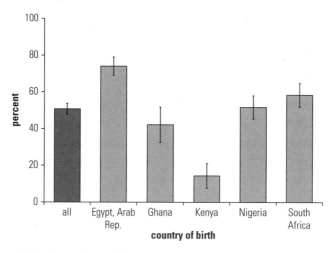

Source: Author's calculations based on Clemens 2011.
Note: Includes only those doctors residing in the United States; there are no data for Canada. Ninety-five percent confidence intervals shown with black error bars. All are post-stratified averages: Post-stratification is by all possible combinations of two gender strata; five age strata (quintiles); four medical specialty strata (grouped by average income); and six strata combining country of residence, country of birth or country of training, or both (three categories for U.S. residents born in Northern Africa, South Africa, and all others; and three more categories for Canada residents trained in Northern Africa, South Africa, and all others).

sufficient sample size to achieve a reasonably precise estimate of the mean. There is great heterogeneity across countries of birth: less than a fifth of Kenyan-born physicians in the United States became doctors in Kenya, whereas about three-quarters of Egyptian doctors in the United States became doctors in Egypt.

Timing of Departure

The second useful fact from the survey is that the typical African-born, African-trained physician who is living and working in Canada and the United States spent at least five years working as a physician in his or her country of birth before emigrating, and probably substantially more.

The survey questionnaire asked each physician his or her country of birth, country of medical training, year of receiving their doctor of medicine degree, and year of arrival in Canada or the United States. This allows calculation, for those trained in their countries of birth, of the amount of time that elapsed between receipt of their doctor of medicine degree and arrival in Canada or the United States. Figure 6.2 shows a density plot of this elapsed time for the African-trained physicians only. While the figure makes clear that many arrived quickly after graduating, the average elapsed time among survey respondents is 8.5 years. When post-stratified to adjust for nonresponse bias, this average falls to 7.2 years.

It is not obvious that all of this time was spent in the country of birth for all physicians, but there is strong evidence that most of these physicians spent most of that time in their country of birth. Clemens (2011) shows that around 75 percent of African-born physicians who received U.S. permanent residency between 1980 and 2000 listed their previous country of residence as their country of birth. Even those who did not state this might have spent a substantial portion of their postgraduation time in their countries of birth,

FIGURE 6.2

Time Elapsed between Receipt of Doctor of Medicine Degree and Arrival in Canada or the United States, for Those Who Received Their Doctor of Medicine Degree in Their African Country of Birth

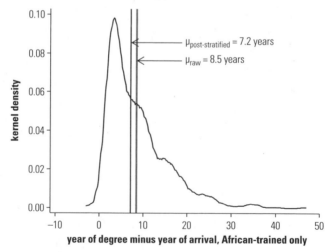

Source: Author's calculations based on Clemens 2011.
Note: Kernel density plot with Epanechnikov kernel, bandwidth 1. Vertical axis shows fraction of total density. Sample of 1,149 African-born physicians who received a doctor of medicine degree in their countries of birth, who were residing in the United States and Canada in 2006. Post-stratification is by all possible combinations of two gender strata; five age strata (quintiles); four medical specialty strata (grouped by average income); and six strata combining country of residence and country of birth, country of training, or both (three categories for U.S. residents born in Northern Africa, South Africa, and all others; and three more categories for Canada residents trained in Northern Africa, South Africa, and all others).

but to be conservative, let us assume that all of those who were African trained and did not list their country of birth as their country of previous residence left their country of birth immediately after graduation to depart to some third country from which they arrived in the United States.

Suppose we assume that (a) the tendency for African physicians arriving in the United States to remain for a time in their country of birth postgraduation is roughly similar to that of those who arrive in Canada; and that (b) the behavior of those with permanent residency is roughly similar to those in the sample, either because the sample largely includes those with permanent residency or because those without permanent residency in the United States did not have a greatly different tendency to remain in their country of birth postgraduation than those with permanent residency. Both of these assumptions are plausible. Under these assumptions, a conservative lower bound on the number of years spent postgraduation in their countries of birth by African-trained physicians is 0.75×7.2 years, or 5.4 years, which we conservatively round down to 5.

One reason this is quite conservative is that a large majority of medical students work in a patient-care capacity closely mimicking that of a graduated physician even while they are still in medical school. Thus, the number of years of patient care provided in the home country by these physicians prior to emigration is very likely to be higher than five.

Remittances

The third useful fact from the survey is that African physicians in Canada and the United States send an average of more than US\$4,500 per year to their countries of birth, including nonremitters. Average remittances of the subset of those who received their medical degree in their African country of birth are more than US\$6,500 per year.

Figure 6.3 shows these estimates. The light gray columns show averages for all African-born physicians; the dark gray columns show the average for those who are both African born and received a doctor of medicine degree in their country of birth. The black error bars show 95 percent confidence intervals for the mean remittance in each population. The leftmost pair of columns shows the average reported by those who answered the survey. The second pair of columns adjusts that mean, as described above, by simultaneously post-stratifying by country of birth or training, age, sex, medical specialty, and Canadian province or U.S. state of residence.[4] The

FIGURE 6.3

Annual Remittances to Country of Birth for Physicians Born in Africa, Residing in Canada and the United States in 2006, Including Nonremitters

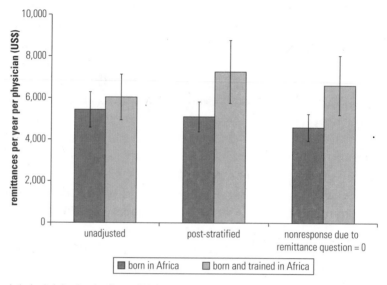

Source: Author's calculations based on Clemens 2011.

Note: Post-stratification is by all possible combinations of two gender strata, five age strata (quintiles), four medical specialty strata (grouped by average income), and six strata combining country of residence and country of birth or country of training (three categories for U.S. residents born in Northern Africa, South Africa, and all others; and three more categories for Canada residents trained in Northern Africa, South Africa, and all others).

estimate for all physicians' remittances modestly declines and that for African-trained physicians modestly rises, though neither of these changes is statistically significant.

The final pair of columns makes two very conservative assumptions about the relationship between nonresponse and remittances: first, that all respondents who left the remittance question unanswered sent zero remittances, and second, that all respondents who were caused not to return the survey by the presence of a remittance question (that is, 4 percent of nonresponders, as revealed by the aforementioned randomized survey design) also sent zero remittances. This final pair of columns, therefore, represent a conservative lower bound on remittances sent by the population sampled. It is plausible, for example, that many of those who chose not to answer the remittance question specifically, or chose not to answer the entire survey because of the remittance question, were sending large amounts and chose not to answer for that reason.

Lessons of the Financial Cost of High-Skill Emigration

These facts shine light on how we might think about the financial consequences of high-skill emigration in the particular context of African doctors working in a rich country. All of them suggest, in different ways, that it is simply wrong to count up the number of African physicians abroad to calculate the financial loss to their countries in the amount of the full public cost of their training.

Lesson 1: Large percentages of skilled professionals from developing countries were trained outside of the countries they come from.

Most obviously, we must account for the fact that important percentages of emigrant skilled professionals from developing countries became skilled professionals abroad. Only about half of the African-born physicians in the United States became physicians in their countries of birth.

This suggests that very little public money from their countries of origin was spent on their medical training. Some countries do offer scholarships for overseas study and it is possible that a small number of those physicians were funded by their countries of birth to train as doctors abroad. The enormous costs of medical school in rich countries suggest that this number is likely to be very small, indeed.

It is true that even African doctors who received their medical training abroad are likely to have received public subsidies for lower-level education such as primary school. But the idea that all 200 million international migrants on earth owe money to their countries of primary education in the amount of their primary schooling costs has not been (nor should be) proposed in credible policy research. Few would argue that the expenditure of money by the French state on the primary education of French citizens creates a property right to those citizens' brains that must be paid in full upon emigration to avoid charges of embezzling public funds. And, anyway, the other costs of education are much smaller than medical costs. Kirigia et al. (2006), for example, show that the cost of medical education is 73 percent of the total public cost of all education (including primary and secondary) typically received by physicians in Kenya.

The experience of African doctors abroad also suggests that it is simply not accurate or meaningful to count the number of tertiary-educated people born in a developing country who live abroad and describe this as a generalized measure of "brain drain." Docquier and Marfouk (2006) provide groundbreaking counts of the number of tertiary-educated people born in each developing country residing in a rich destination country and refer to this number as a measurement of "brain drain." Docquier and Marfouk do not in any way claim that their numbers are directly informative about the financial effects of emigration, but common usage of the term "brain drain" does tend to include the presumption of negative financial effects. Yet, the stock of tertiary-educated people born in Cape Verde who live in the United States may be enormously different from the number of tertiary-educated people who left Cape Verde, if many of them acquired tertiary education in the United States, and it is not at all clear that many or even most of them would have acquired tertiary education had they been unable to leave Cape Verde. One lesson from African physicians is that the stock of skilled workers abroad can be very different from the number of skilled workers who left.

Lesson 2: A substantial portion of the public's financial investment in training emigrants is recouped before they depart, even for those who never return.

Even those African physicians who were trained in their countries of birth—the vast majority with substantial public subsidy—spent an average of more than five years in their countries of birth prior to emigrating. Even those physicians who depart, never return, never send any money home, and never interact in any way with their country of birth are therefore typically giving their country of training a substantial return on its public investment. This bears directly on the financial cost of their departure: They are not taking the entire training investment with them, because the country has already typically realized a substantial return on that investment.

What portion of the public investment is recouped by receiving (conservatively) five years of service? Many states do permit limited contractual relationships that limit movement in exchange for public funding of higher education, but these limits rarely amount to five years of movement restrictions. Brazil's National Council for Scientific and Technological Development, for example, awards scholarships for a few years of postgraduate study abroad that require the same number of years of residence in Brazil thereafter. The Turkish government's Scientific and Technological Research Council also publicly sponsors doctoral research abroad in exchange for an obligation to live thereafter in Turkey, usually for no more than two years. The United States government pays for much of the training cost of physicians who agree to two years of work in certain facilities on Native American reservations.

The fact that in all of these cases the public debt is considered repaid with a few years of residence is suggestive. Where governments have explicitly spelled out the amount of time it takes for publicly trained professionals to repay their debt to society through service provision, the amount of time does not typically extend beyond five years; nowhere does it appear to be measured in decades. Because the typical experience of publicly trained African emigrant doctors is to remain longer than five years after graduation, it might be reasonable to think that the typical African-trained doctor who emigrates has already paid back most or all of their debt through service.

Lesson 3: The emigration of publicly trained doctors from Africa typically results in the transfer of money within the African countries they come from, not a transfer of money out of those countries.

The emigration of African-trained physicians in Canada and the United States produces financial flows that are tremendously at odds with conventional wisdom. Rather than representing a transfer of money *out* of the country of origin, the departure of a publicly trained African physician to Canada and the United States causes a transfer of money *within* the country of origin, from the state to private hands—with much more money entering private hands than leaves public coffers.

The reason for this is that the remittances typically sent by African-trained physicians in North America are substantially greater than the amount spent to train those physicians. As discussed above, the publicly borne medical training cost of a physician in Sub-Saharan Africa is typically about US$10,000 per year of school, usually for around six years. The average African physician in Canada or the United States who was trained in his or her country of birth—including those who send no money—sends upward of US$6,500 per year to family, friends, or charitable organizations in that country. In the same sample in Clemens (2011), the average number of years since arrival in Canada or the United States is 21.1 years, and remittances start out slightly higher than average in the first year since arrival, declining very slowly over time. All of this means that the typical African-trained physician in Canada or the United States has cumulatively sent home much more than the public cost of his or her medical training. A back-of-the-envelope estimate would suggest that this cost was about US$70,000 or less, and that the average cumulative amount sent home for those remaining long term in Canada or the United States is US$130,000 or more.

To be sure, the source and destination of these financial flows within the home country are very different: The cost of training might come from the budget of the Ministry of Education or Ministry of Health, and the immediate destination of remittances is most often the hands of the physicians' family members. Of course, this does not rule out a substantial positive fiscal impact, since very little of remittances would tend to be spirited away to foreign bank accounts; the vast majority is spent in the African country to which it is sent. Indeed, spending is typically the purpose for which it is sent. Such spending would be expected to have a Keynesian multiplier effect: people building new houses pay construction workers, who buy food from farmers, and so on. To the extent that any such activity is taxed, there could well be positive fiscal effects.

But even setting aside any such knock-on positive fiscal effects, at the very least the evidence from African doctors abroad suggests that we adopt a fundamentally different conception of the nature of financial flows caused by the departure of publicly educated skilled professionals from developing countries. It is common to look upon a dollar spent on the public medical training of an African emigrant physician as a dollar lost to the country of origin. In rough terms, it is more like a one dollar net *gain* to the country of origin—with a dollar being thereby lost to public coffers, and two dollars being thereby gained by consumers in the country of origin. Again, this ignores the possibility of positive fiscal effects from taxed expenditure of the two dollars in private hands and its multiplier effects on other spending.

How Much Compensation Is Enough?

As discussed, there are various proposals for payments from migration destination countries to compensate countries for the financial loss occasioned by the emigration of publicly trained professionals. Let us assume for a moment that such payments are justified and inquire only about the amount. For publicly trained African physicians who have departed for North America, how much would be the proper compensation payment?

Many Sub-Saharan African countries typically spend about US$70,000 on the medical training of each emigrant physician, most of which typically comes from public coffers. Assuming that this is the financial cost to be off-set by a compensation payment, the following facts bear on the proper amount of the payment:

- Large fractions of the African doctors abroad were not publicly trained in their home countries, so any calculation of the payment must focus on those who are trained and leave, not simply the number who are abroad.
- Those who are publicly trained in their home countries typically serve in that country for at least five years before departing—not counting care they provide while in medical school. Certainly this diminishes the fiscal loss caused by their departure, since it represents the realization of a substantial portion of the public investment prior to their departure.
- The same doctor, if bound for a rich destination country like Canada or the United States, can be expected to send home roughly double his or her training cost in unrequited financial transfers—unless of course he or she returns home, in which case the question of compensation becomes moot.

The size of the compensation payment would depend on these and other factors. At the least, it would depend on the value placed on a year of service in the country of origin. The revealed preference of many governments, as discussed above, is that a few years of work con-stitutes full compensation for the public's investment, and the typical publicly trained African emigrant physician is already doing this. Fur-thermore, it would depend on the relative social value of a dollar in public hands and two dollars in private hands—with the complication that some portion of the two dollars in private hands would eventually reach public coffers.

Whatever the social value of the cumulative US$130,000 sent home by the average, African-trained, long-term emigrant physician living in Canada or the United States, it is surely not zero, because its expendi-ture in the origin country must create some degree of employment and economic activity beyond any effects on the public coffers. Both of these suggest that whatever the proper compensation payment might be, even if we were strictly interested in offsetting the financial loss to the country, it is substantially less than the full training cost of the physician, and it is not obvious that the proper compensation payment is greater than zero.

Additional Questions About Policies to Remedy Financial Impacts

The preceding discussion has assumed that the policy goal is to offset the strictly financial loss of having a publicly subsidized mind depart the country. There are additional reasons to question the propriety and amount of compensation payments, presented in detail in Clemens (2011)—reasons that arise separately from the magnitude of the financial flows considered so far.

First, the question of compensation for training costs cannot be divorced from measurement of the social benefit provided by those workers. (An extreme example to make this point is that the proper compensation payment for the emigration of publicly trained astrologers is zero, because they have little social benefit, regardless of their training cost.) And it is unclear that the *social* benefit of each and every physician trained by an African country exceeds their training cost. The majority of publicly trained physicians in South Africa, for example, do not work in public clinics or hospitals and do not work in poor areas of the country. A donor that chooses to compensate the training cost of one of these physicians who departs South Africa is choosing to subsidize physician education—rather than, say, the education of community health workers or water sanitation workers, whose training expense might have a much higher social return. A donor whose objective is not simply to offset strictly financial costs of public training, but to generate improved health, might wish to target subsidies elsewhere than strictly physician training. The optimal payment by such a donor in compensation for publicly subsidized training of emigrant physicians would be something less than the full training cost of the physician.

Second, even if all African physicians were fully publicly educated at home, departed their countries of birth immediately upon graduation, never sent any money home, and would have enormous social benefits if they stayed in their home countries—even in this extreme counterfactual case—would it be correct to say that exactly 100 percent of their training cost has been wasted if they leave the country that trained them, requiring a payment of compensation in the amount of 100 percent of their training cost to pay the public debt they owe? That is, does *absolutely all* of the social value of educating a skilled professional arise from the provision of services in their country of training? To believe that, we would need to believe that there is *zero* social value per se in creating a country where a person who wishes to become a doctor can become a doctor, regardless of their social background.

The constitutions of many African countries state that their citizens have a right to higher education if they are qualified for it, a statement that is meaningless if the only and exclusive social value of training skilled workers arises from the services those people provide. We would also need to believe that public subsidies for individuals' education create an unlimited state property right to those people, valued at the full value of the training cost. As discussed, some states do consider public education subsidies to create a *limited* public property right to people who receive them—and therefore require a few years of residence or public service following graduation—but no state recognizes the creation of an unlimited public property right to the brains of those publicly educated, for example, by requiring *permanent* residence or *lifelong* public service after graduation. These states already accept, then, that the degree of public property right to publicly educated individuals does not extend to the full cost of training them.

Third, there are ethical complexities involved in requiring any amount of compensation from emigrants. Bhagwati and Dellalfar (1973) propose a tax on skilled émigré citizens of developing countries, to be collected under United Nations auspices in rich destination countries and sent back to the countries of origin. Part of the justification for this tax is that it would only be levied on those who choose to retain citizenship in the country of origin—a provision intended to lessen the degree of coercion embodied in the tax. But the decision to accept public training subsidies, the decision to depart one's country of birth, and the decision to retain citizenship in the country of origin are not frequently free of coercion. If the tax were levied only on those publicly trained (which many support but Bhagwati and Dellalfar do not suggest), it would be ethically complex to require compensation payments from people who were born in countries that do not have quality private universities and were forced to rely on publicly subsidized education, but not to require such payments from those born in other countries with viable private options.

Beyond this, it may be unethical to require a Zimbabwean physician to pay money to a government that, by provoking economic collapse in Zimbabwe, obliged him or her to emigrate. And it is not clearly ethical to require people "choosing" to retain citizenship in their countries of birth to pay a tax when many migrants who would prefer to be citizens of their destination cannot be; in 2008, the waiting list for legal permanent residency in the United States was 2.5 million people, many of whom have been waiting several years. Highly skilled emigrants among them would be forced to choose between paying a tax to their only country of citizenship or to become stateless. At the very least, such a tax involves ethical complexities that often go unaddressed.

Conclusion

This chapter is not an attempt to categorically state that the financial impacts of medical or any other high-skill emigration are positive or negative, that compensation payments for training costs are always or never justified, or what the precise amount of compensation should be in any particular case. Rather, the goal has been to argue that the assumptions we would need to make to believe that skilled emigrants should make compensation payments to their countries of origin for the full amount of their skilled training costs are clearly violated by the behavior of one important group of skilled emigrants: African physicians abroad.

Many of those physicians are trained abroad, and even those trained at home typically spend substantial periods in their country of training prior to departure and send amounts of money home that greatly exceed their training costs. Rather than caricature public training subsidies as "lost" to the country of origin when skilled emigrants leave, it would be better to recognize that they are often recouped to a substantial degree before the trained professionals leave, and that they generate enormous flows of money into the private sector of the origin countries that must also help to recoup the loss in some nonzero measure. Building on facts like these might lead to a more constructive discussion about the financial effects of high-skill migration and policies associated with it.

Notes

1. The author would like to thank Nathan Converse, Jenny Kenney, Fitzhugh Mullan, Çağlar Özden, Peter Timmer, and Doug Wissoker for their helpful comments. Gunilla Pettersson impeccably managed the survey administration,

and Paolo Abarcar and Sami Bazzi provided additional research assistance. The author gratefully acknowledges financial support from the William and Flora Hewlett Foundation and the John D. and Catherine T. MacArthur Foundation. The views expressed herein are those of the author and do not necessarily represent those of the Center for Global Development, its board, or its funders.

2. The American Medical Association has no record on the country where its members received their degrees, and the Canadian Medical Association has no record of its members' country of birth. The American sample thus includes African-born physicians, trained both in Africa and abroad, while the Canadian sample includes physicians trained exclusively in Africa (the large majority of whom are African born). African-born, Canadian-trained physicians were not sampled.

3. There are no corresponding estimates for those resident in Canada because the survey sample for Canada only included African-trained physicians.

4. There are two gender strata, five age strata (quintiles), four medical specialty strata (grouped by average income), and six strata combining country of residence and country of birth and country of training (three categories for U.S. residents born in Northern Africa, South Africa, and all others; and three more categories for Canada residents trained in Northern Africa, South Africa, and all others). Clemens (2011) reports estimates post-stratified by individual countries of birth or training, and other choices of strata.

References

Bhagwati, J. N., ed. 1976. *Taxing the Brain Drain, Vol. 1: A Proposal.* Amsterdam: North Holland.

Bhagwati, J. N., and W. Dellalfar. 1973. "The Brain Drain and Income Taxation." *World Development* 1 (1–2): 94–101.

Bhargava, A. 2005. "The AIDS Epidemic and Health Care Infrastructure Inadequacies in Africa: A Socioeconomic Perspective." *Journal of Acquired Immune Deficiency Syndromes* 40 (2): 241–42.

Clemens, M. A. 2007. "Do Visas Kill? Health Effects of African Health Professional Emigration." CGD Working Paper 114, Center for Global Development, Washington, DC.

———. 2011. "The Financial Effects of High-Skill Emigration: New Data on African Physicians Abroad." CGD Working Paper, Center for Global Development, Washington, DC.

Desai, M. A., D. Kapur, J. McHale, and K. Rogers. 2009. "The Fiscal Impact of High-Skilled Emigration: Flows of Indians to the U.S." *Journal of Development Economics* 88 (1): 32–44.

Docquier, F., and A. Marfouk. 2006. "International Migration by Education Attainment, 1990–2000." In *International Migration, Remittances and the Brain Drain*, ed. C. Özden and M. Schiff. New York: Palgrave Macmillan.

Hagopian, A., A. Ofosu, A. Fatusi, R. Biritwum, A. Essel, L. G. Hart, and C. Watts. 2005. "The Flight of Physicians from West Africa: Views of African Physicians and Implications for Policy." *Social Science and Medicine* 61 (8): 1750–60.

Kirigia, J. M., A. R. Gbary, L. K. Muthuri, J. Nyoni, and A. Seddoh. 2006. "The Cost of Health Professionals' Brain Drain in Kenya." *BMC Health Services Research* 6: 89. http://www.biomedcentral.com/1472-6963/6/89.

McColl, K. 2008. "Robinson's Crusade." *British Medical Journal* 337 (October 25): 960–61.

Select Committee on Science and Technology. 2004. "Science and Technology – Thirteenth Report." United Kingdom House of Commons, London. http://www.publications.parliament.uk/pa/cm200304/cmselect/cmsctech/133/13302.htm.

Wilson, J. D. 2008. "Taxing the Brain Drain: A Reassessment of the Bhagwati Proposal." In *Trade, Globalization, and Poverty*, ed. Elias Dinopoulos, Pravin Krishna, Arvind Panagariya, and Kar-Yiu Wong. New York: Routledge.

CHAPTER 7

France's Codevelopment Program: Financial and Fiscal Incentives to Promote Diaspora Entrepreneurship and Transfers

Marion Panizzon

Codevelopment is the process through which immigrants contribute to the socioeconomic development of their country of origin while assimilating into the country to which they have immigrated, to the mutual benefit of both countries. France was one of the first countries to officially recognize the value of codevelopment and of the key transnational role the diaspora has played in source country development (Daum 2007/2008; de Haas 2006; Katseli 2008; Levitt 2009). France, which ranks fifth among the top migrant-receiving countries after the United States, Russia, Germany, and Ukraine (World Bank 2008:1) and is the fourth-largest donor of official development assistance to Africa, at US$4.9 billion, is one of the first countries to incorporate codevelopment strategies into overseas development assistance policy (Bräutigam 2010:12).[1]

Codevelopment embodies an "integrated development" model that links a community of origin to its counterpart in the migrant's destination country (GCIM 2005:8,64,73,77), but adds the destination country as a "partner" to such preexisting transnational networks. In doing so, codevelopment

The author would like to thank Ndioro Ndiaye, former Deputy Director General, International Organization for Migration; and Türkan Karakurt, Director, the Friedrich Ebert Foundation, Geneva, for critiquing an earlier draft of this chapter; and Lisa Salcedo, PhD candidate at the World Bank Institute, Bern, for editorial assistance.

introduces a type of mutual collaboration that goes beyond the state-centric, classic North-South transfers of development aid disbursed within the strict confines of intergovernmental cooperation (Ndione and Bröekhuis 2006: 14–15). Codevelopment overcomes the bipolar model of migration, which separates sending from receiving areas, and push factors of out-migration from pull factors of in-migration. Instead, codevelopment operationalizes the theory of migrant transnationalism, which conceptualizes the migrant as a "go-between" between identities, cultures, societies, spaces, and markets (Brettell 2008: 120). Pursuant to this model, the migrant is conceived as an "agent of change" and the process of migration is viewed as "deterritorialized" from nation states. Thus codevelopment policy relies on and promotes circular migration, but clashes with the more "classic" assimilation/integration policies of migration (Schmitter-Heisler 2008).

Under the term "codevelopment," France includes all development aid involving the participation of immigrants living in France, whatever their contribution, pursuant to the so-called "whole of government approach."[2] Through codevelopment, France seeks to remove incoherence in migration policy formulation among its different government branches, so as to adopt a more unified negotiating position vis-à-vis migrant source countries.[3] And, like most migrant host countries, France is searching for innovative ways to draw on the financial resources and human capital of migrants in order to decrease public spending on official development assistance. Among countries in Europe, France has been particularly innovative in identifying policies to empower migrants—both individually and collectively—to contribute to the development of their countries of origin.

Over time, France has oscillated between encouraging and discouraging the mainstreaming of development into migration policies, which the concept of codevelopment seeks to achieve. The various levels of funding allocated to codevelopment were not only politically motivated but were also driven by inconclusive research results. Some had found that development in the source country would decrease migration pressure, while others found that once the country of origin attains higher levels of development, emigration will increase rather than slow down. This was shown to be the case with Tunisia, where a higher level of development, not least a free trade agreement with the European Union (EU), contributed to much higher numbers of emigration than in the Sub-Saharan African context, particularly compared to Congolese or Senegalese arrivals in France (Stark and Wang, 2002; Tasca 2008:13). In addition, the amount of trust that French codevelopment policies had invested in immigrant associations, source-country governments, and migrants themselves, varied over time.

Such variances more broadly reflect the way global migration trends respond to the desirability of a migration development linkage in the first place (Sørensen and Van Haer 2003). This ambivalence was responsible for the limited practical success of the concept (de Haas 2006:69 with reference to Lacroix 2003:299–300).

First, the codevelopment agenda has always been determined by official and less officially stated policy goals, and this duality affected the overall credibility of France's development aid (de Haas 2008:1314). Despite being officially driven by "a desire to address the internal and external aspects of these policies within a systematic and coherent manner" (OECD 2008a:34), reality shows that not all migrants can be treated equally; some have managerial and entrepreneurial abilities that others may not have.

Second, the welfare effects of migrants' intangible contributions, such as transmissions of skills and knowledge acquired or improved and networks established abroad, but also their tangible contributions, such as remittances, have a different impact on their home country economy than their physical return. Whereas the latter is the stated priority of France's immigration policy, physical return is not necessarily the goal of France's codevelopment policy. Codevelopment encourages development-at-a-distance, and thus tangible and intangible transfers by those migrants who more permanently remain abroad.

Third, France failed to factor in the long- and short-term effects of development aid. For a long time, it was also not receptive to the fact that return migration is anathema to the positive attitude that source countries harbor toward emigration and the negative attitude they display toward return migrants, even their own citizens (Olesen 2002:127,137). In sum, French migration policy was often guided by the idea that stimulating return migration would increase source-country development and reduce the push factors of migration. Together these factors accounted for a certain measure of inconsistency in French migration and development policy formulation and for the varying degrees of intensity with which

France aligned development to migration policies. Reflecting such inconsistencies, the concept of codevelopment over time acquired and shed again a variety of facets.

While criticism voiced by the diaspora eventually led France to decouple development aid from return migration in the 1980s, another major shift in the concept of codevelopment came about with France's 2006–07 immigration law reform, which considerably changed France's codevelopment strategy, ministerial responsibilities, and funding schemes. Two French laws are at the forefront of the reform—Law No. 2006-911 of July 24, 2006, relating to immigration and integration, which modifies the French code on entry and admission of foreigners and the right to asylum; and Law No. 2007-1613 of November 20, 2007, relating to the management of immigration, integration, and asylum, which creates the codevelopment savings account.

Both laws move France's immigration policy away from migration based on family reunification to a system of selective labor migration ("immigration choice"). In addition, during the reform, France designed migration pacts to coordinate migration management. The pacts are currently in the process of being concluded with francophone migrant-sending countries, primarily in West and North Africa. These efforts have renewed the concept of codevelopment, a pillar of French migration policy since the 1970s. Codevelopment was, for the first time, firmly positioned in legally binding laws, a fact that contributes to the concept's visibility and enhances its predictability, transparency, and responsibility. Another main change is to formally bind the migrant-sending countries to the concept of codevelopment. An additional paradigm shift is to move away from funding migrants' collective investments and instead to reward individual migrants in France for productively investing savings in their country of origin.

The Evolution of Codevelopment Policy

As a multistakeholder strategy, the concept of codevelopment relies on "preferential" partners for its implementation[4]—so-called "development actors" (Connan 2005:1)—which can be decentralized government entities (municipalities, districts, cities, departments, and regions), international or nongovernmental organizations (NGOs), other nonstate actors and, most important, migrants themselves. In doing so, codevelopment reaffirms a phenomenon that is as old as migration itself: immigrants, foremost those leaving for work abroad, have always supported, individually or collectively, their communities of origin (Ndione and Bröekhuis 2006:14–15).

This section identifies four phases of French codevelopment policies by describing how French codevelopment policies evolved:

- From assisting with the integration of migrants
- To encouraging migrants to leave
- To providing aid with the goal of reducing migratory pressures, or, possibly
- To cofinancing diaspora contributions to public goods in countries of origin.

The First Stages of Codevelopment: From Integration to a Return Strategy 1970–93

Initially, the concept of codevelopment included initiatives to facilitate the *integration* of migrants in France. Later, the Ministry of the Interior used codevelopment to mobilize migrants nearing the end of their lawful stay in France to return home voluntarily (1970–86). In 1977, France, following the example of Germany (1972) and the Netherlands (1975), started experimenting with granting financial "bonuses" to migrants returning to their countries of origin with a business plan (Wihtol de Wenden 2008:2; Terrot 2009:17). Eligibility for codevelopment financing was then expanded to those diaspora organizations in France that agreed to identify their compatriots staying in France unlawfully (Wihtol de Wenden 2008:2). Codevelopment thus became a sort of "compensation" offered by France to those diaspora organizations that agreed to identify their nationals on illegal stays in France. The diaspora thus was tasked with acting on behalf of its uncooperative government, which most often refused to identify its citizens. Codevelopment's policy objective was to delegate governmental functions to a nongovernmental entity, the diasporas in France, which were then rewarded for cooperating with France, the host country government, in combating irregular migration.

Not surprisingly, this use of codevelopment funds was severely criticized by members of the diaspora. Between 1983 and 1993, the "political discourse abandoned the explicit link to return policies and emphasized development aid as a factor to reduce migratory pressure" (de Haas

2006:67). France began consultations to seek input from development-oriented actors, even if diaspora associations were not yet systematically interviewed. Around this time, France also experimented with projects of decentralized government cooperation, the Local Migration Development Programme (Programme d'aide à la reinstallation) in the region of Kayes (Mali), which was a main point of departure for France (Lacroix 2009:9). Migrants planning to return to a job; those engaged in a creative project; or those ready to establish small-scale economic activity in the fields of agriculture, commerce, or handicrafts, could receive financial assistance in addition to the return and reintegration funds, which the various National Agencies for the Admission of Migrants (Agence Nationale de l'Accueil des Etrangers et des Migrations) operating in francophone migrant source countries, like Mali, Senegal, and Tunisia,[5] were disbursing to help pay for their return to their country of origin.[6]

For the project to be eligible for cofinancing, the French Government would carry out a feasibility study to assess the merits of the project. Once the project is up and running, it is closely monitored for a year.[7] Even if, officially, codevelopment financing was no longer conditional upon voluntary return, indirectly the linkage remained, because only those migrants were eligible who also qualified for assisted and voluntary return and reintegration funding. During that time, France multiplied its efforts to negotiate agreements on the vocational and professional training for Algerian and Senegalese migrants wishing to return to a job in their home countries.[8] These agreements were not officially concluded as part of the French codevelopment policies. A certain level of incoherence thus emerged between migrants receiving training for return and those qualifying as recipients of codevelopment. For example, most Senegalese applying for French codevelopment funding have completed tertiary education but then often lacked the entrepreneurial, managerial, and marketing skills and tools to succeed with their export/import enterprises or consultancy projects, which codevelopment was funding (CICI 2009:195–6).

The Pasqua Laws of 1993 and the Tightening of French Migration Policies

As a result of the right-wing Pasqua laws of 1993, the Interministerial Mission for Codevelopment and International Migrations (Mission interministerielle au co-développement et aux migrations internationals) was created and was tasked with tightening return policies. Stricter surveillance of return aid and reintegration support was instituted because of the infamously "lost" 1 million French francs of Lionel Stoléru, the State Secretary of Immigration and Manual Work in France in 1977, who initiated return policies under the motto of "Leaving to stay" ("partir pour rester") by providing migrants willing to go home with the cash to do so (Wihtol de Wenden 2008:2). The Mission on Migration and Co-development in 1998 devised a broad-based financial aid and reintegration support system to create incentives for undocumented migrants from Mali, Morocco, and Senegal who were not eligible for amnesties, to voluntarily return home (OECD 2008a:30).

What came to be known as Contracts of Reinsertion in the Country of Origin (Contrats de Réinsertion dans le Pays d'Origine, CRPO) was initiated, whereby a migrant signs a contract with France that requires him or her to return to the home country. In return, the migrant obtains financial aid, the so-called return and reintegration support, and often training to prepare for his or her return to a job in Senegal, particularly in the catering, food, and transport industries (Ndione and Bröekhuis 2006:17). CRPO funding targets migrants who either had entered France with falsified entry visas and identities or who had overstayed their residency permit and were thus in unauthorized stays in France and who, pursuant to French immigration law, were being mobilized to return home voluntarily. Unrealistic goals and a credibility gap left the CRPO, like previous financial reward schemes of the 1970s and 1980s, with unsatisfactory results. In addition, the financial resources allocated to codevelopment projects were modest (compared to remittances transfers), and the training programs for employment upon return were inadequately tailored to the employment prospects in the home countries. The result was a low number of applicants for these schemes. The credibility of codevelopment further suffered because return and reintegration funds were often used by the migrants for other purposes, such as purchasing luxury goods (Terrot 2009:17).

In the late 1990s, France reorganized diaspora associations and sought to integrate them under an umbrella organization called the Organizations of International Solidarity for Migration (Organisations de Solidarité International Issues des Migrations, OSIM) (Lacroix 2009:10). In 2001, Charles Josselin, then-Minister of Cooperation and Francophone Countries, established the Forum of Organizations of International Solidarity Issued from

Migration (Forum des Organisations de Solidarité Internationale Issues des Migrations),[9] which is a platform reuniting the different OSIMs.

The Forum is the result of the second series of consultations that the French Government conducted with members of the diaspora and other nonstate actors engaged in migration in light of the limited success of return and reintegration support schemes (Lacroix 2009:10). Unlike the OSIMs, which are for the most part regionally organized, the Forum of Organizations of International Solidarity Issued from Migration brings together not only the various OSIMs, but also links them up with government representatives and associations working on development assistance.

The OSIMs' mandate is to report on the development actions in home countries and in France, and to initiate programs to foster better integration in France. They also play an important role in managing diaspora-led development initiatives outside the formal cofunding schemes. By officially entering into dialogue with members of the disapora, France had pioneered a new type of migration-development nexus, which still qualifies as an innovative move in migration policy formulation in Europe today (de Haas 2006:68).

In response to OSIM's request, France added cofunding of diaspora projects to the menu of codevelopment. France would cofund diaspora-led investments in local development projects in home countries and conduct feasibility studies to find project partners. In-kind support included mentoring programs with French business for return migrants wanting to create small and medium enterprises in countries of origin.[10] De Haas (2006:79–80) and Lacroix (2009:14–15) argue that involving diaspora members in return strategies was the only way France could ensure that its immigration laws would be upheld.

When France concluded a codevelopment convention with Senegal on May 25, 2000, which was updated by a complementary cofunding convention of February 3, 2005 (Tasca 2008:36), the link between codevelopment and migration control and return policies again resurfaced in French migration policies. For example, Article 1 of France's codevelopment convention with Senegal, which lists the "purposes" of codevelopment, omits to mention assisted and voluntary return and reintegration support. Only Article 4 on the "joint control of migration flows," mentions return and reintegration support, thus associating the latter type of aid with migration control and the fight against irregular migration. The existence of this "hidden" return and forced repatriation agenda in a codevelopment convention, the primary purpose of which was to strengthen source country development, was heavily criticized. Critics, among which were the OSIM and the source country governments, claimed that codevelopment, which is a means of ex-ante migration management, should be kept separate from measures of ex-post migration control, such as return and reintegration support. By mixing the two policies, the purpose of codevelopment was being diverted or at worst abused to achieve restrictive immigration policies (Courtin 2007:393–408).

Unsurprisingly, source countries, like Mali and Senegal, stiffly resisted efforts to condition codevelopment aid on taking back citizens who had been on irregular stays in France but who did not wish to return home (de Haas 2006:70). Thus, France did not succeed in negotiating codevelopment conventions with other African countries beyond Senegal, as it had hoped to do. On the other hand, Mali and Senegal left France with no other choice than to use codevelopment funds to get their governments, which otherwise refused to take back their citizens in unlawful stays in France (Aleinikoff 2003:1–27; Noll 2003:S.61–74,67), to comply with this customary international obligation (Groff 2005:2).

Shifting Ministerial Competencies and the Redesign of Codevelopment, 2002–06

In reaction to criticism by members of the diaspora, migration control and prevention were officially kept separate from codevelopment strategies. Thus, in 2002, the Interministerial Mission for Codevelopment and International Migrations was dissolved because it was widely held that the CRPO had failed. It was replaced by a Minister-delegate for Cooperation and Francophony, who was tasked with implementing the codevelopment programs and reporting directly to the Ministry of the Interior (de Haas 2006:70). First, the CRPO was reformed so that it no longer offered only financial sponsorship but also EU Schengen visas to reward migrants who signed those contracts, which required the migrant to leave for his or her home country by the end of his or her legal stay. France had implemented these measures under pressure from EU neighboring countries, which were opposed to France engaging in mass regularizations the purpose of which would have been to give resident status to all migrants in unlawful stays in France (Ndione and Bröekhuis 2006:17).

In 2003, the responsibilities for codevelopment shifted to the Ministry of Foreign Affairs, which alone became entrusted with the codevelopment portfolio. The Ministry of Foreign Affairs redefined codevelopment as assisting migrants who, individually or collectively, act as agents of development of their home countries (Adebusoye 2006:16–19). Primarily, codevelopment funding seeks collective investments by migrants. It also relies on matching funds from NGOs, international organizations, immigration associations, local (source country) communities, the private sector, and other governments, as long as a project is related to migration. Institutionally, the Ministry of Foreign Affairs "formalized" codevelopment funding, by establishing transparent selection criteria and embedding codevelopment into France's Framework Partnership Documents, which centrally disbursed the funds as one part of Priority Solidarity Funding (PSF). PSF is development assistance granted over renewable two-year periods[11] and is a prioritized credit line in France's Framework Partnership Documents, which France signs with countries of the priority solidarity zone.[12]

These memorandums of understanding, which France signs with countries of its priority solidarity zone, determine whether a country qualifies for the disbursement of development assistance. The Framework Partnership Documents, which embed the PSF development aid programs, are signed with countries in the so-called priority solidarity zone encompassing former French colonies. Despite its seeming complexity, this setup allows maximum flexibility to directly involve the diaspora community by circumventing the source-country government; the Framework Partnership Document earmarks the funding, and there is no need for France to conclude an additional agreement or convention on codevelopment projects with the source-country government.[13] PSF development assistance matches up to 25 percent of any public or private investment or transfer made by the diaspora community collectively or by an NGO in a country of origin.

Under the Ministry of Foreign Affairs and until the immigration law reform of 2006–07, France's codevelopment policy was mainly applied to Mali and Senegal, with a few select actions and smaller-scale codevelopment projects targeting the Comoros (Martin, Martin, and Weil 2002:236). Between 2002 and 2008, all 28 countries forming part of France's priority solidarity zone became eligible for multilateral codevelopment funding, just as they also qualified for higher levels of return and reintegration support than countries outside that zone.

Cofunding is not unique to France. At least one migrant-sending country, Mexico, also operates a cofunding scheme. Whereas in the case of France it is the host country that provides the matching funds, in the case of Mexico's 3x1 Program, Mexico provides the funds. The Mexican State of Zacatecas, and other Mexican States, match migrants' investments in their home countries (de la Garza and Hazan 2003; Hazan 2009). France's concept of codevelopment not only relies on the diaspora, but also on other partners to contribute. In France's codevelopment programs with Mali (2001) and with Senegal (2005), 29 percent of the codevelopment funds were financed by migrants, 63 percent by France, and 8 percent by other partners (AFD 2006). For 2009, the diaspora in France financed up to €3.3 million worth of projects in Senegal. In the spirit of the Mexican 3x1 program, Senegal is one of the few African governments to match the French funding (of €9 million for three years starting in 2009) with €0.57 million (CICI 2009:195–96). Unlike other African governments, Senegalese authorities have taken an active role in policy formulation in the field of migration and development by establishing a joint Franco-Senegalese review committee to monitor the actions funded and to sketch out the strategic direction of the projects.

Despite encouraging signs, codevelopment funding in France turned out to be a mixed success because it was too tightly conditioned on the migrant's voluntary return (Courtin 2007:393). Most collective investments by members of the diaspora were found to fund infrastructure of public buildings, such as schools, hospitals, dams (for retaining water to produce electricity), and renovation of water distribution systems. Of the 123 projects established between 2003 and 2005 in the framework of codevelopment with Mali, 60 percent have achieved sustainability, 20 percent were unsustainable, and 20 percent were droped. On average, each enterprise generated two jobs (de Haas 2006:76). In terms of numbers of migrants taking advantage of the program, PSF project cofunding proved to be not very effective (OECD 2008b:192). In 2002, only 46 migrants returning from France to Mali applied for codevelopment project funding (Diatta 2008:129).

In 2004, a program was launched to channel migrant remittances flows into productive investments and awareness-raising cultural programs for linking second-generation migrants to their country of origin (de Haas 2006:70). In the case of Senegal, reintegration support was stepped up with more tailored programs such as the "Programme for Assisting Migrant

Projects in Senegal "(Articles 3 and 4 of the France-Senegal Codevelopment Convention of 2001.[14] In this context, France and Senegal jointly established an Office of Reception, Orientation and Follow-up of Actions for the Reinsertion of Emigrants (Bureau d'Accueil, d'Orientation et de Suivi des Actions de Réinsertion des Émigrés), to provide institutional capacity for managing the reintegration of migrants. Because of "administrative deficiencies, insufficient funding and migrants' lack of confidence in the organization," the bureau has not been used very much (Gerdes 2007:3–4).

Training-for-return and socioeconomic reintegration in the agriculture and health sectors was also provided for. The first multiple-entry visas were issued; in contrast with the current circular visas, these early schemes were limited to return migrants employed under the auspices of a local migration development program.[15] Whereas codevelopment during that time never lost its underlying goal of migration control, it had improved the balance between source- and host-country interests with respect to migration. However, the concept of codevelopment despite new trends still enjoyed only limited visibility.[16]

From Codevelopment to Solidarity Development in Sarkozy's Immigration Law Reform of 2006–07

Codevelopment experienced yet another turnaround under France's Immigration and Integration Law of 2006, proposed by Nicolas Sarkozy when he was Minister of the Interior. When Sarkozy acceded to the French presidency, he created a special ministry in 2007, the Ministry of Immigration, Integration, National Identity and Solidarity Development (Ministère de l'immigration, de l'intégration, de l'identité national et du développement solidaire, MIIINDS). By decree of March 18, 2008, a new tool labeled "solidarity development" was designed to remedy some of the shortcomings of the traditional cofunding facility (de Haas 2206:80). Solidarity development financially supports educational, vocational, and professional training for specific sectors in the source country, such as agriculture, fishery, and health (Tasca 2008:19). It is government-to-government funding of development initiatives with an emphasis on reducing migratory root causes, like unemployment. Unlike codevelopment funding, which is directly disbursed to private parties, that is, to diaspora members, solidarity development qualifies as structural aid, meaning the type of development aid that is directly granted to a government in a long-term effort, as opposed to short-term disaster relief or humanitarian aid. Structural aid is also different from individualized return and reintegration support and cofunding of diaspora projects, since the latter two types of aid circumvent the partner country's government by being directly disbursed to either an individual or a collectivity. Much of solidarity development aid is disbursed as "decentralized government cooperation" with the goal of retaining and upgrading skills in regions with heavy out-migration. It requires the "twinning" of local governments in France and in the migrant source country. Cities, provinces, but also universities, education and research institutes, and migrant source countries could be twinned. Such decentralized development cooperation complements France's codevelopment assistance to diaspora projects.

Institutionally, responsibilities for development aid for migration are split between the MIIINDS, which funds solidarity development, that is, structural development aid, and the Ministry of Foreign Affairs, which remains responsible for codevelopment assistance to the diaspora.[17] According to Wihtol de Wenden (2008:8), there are three reasons for this split:

- The failure of codevelopment to stimulate more entrepreneurial activity by the diaspora community
- The shallow volume of funds reserved for codevelopment (roughly €3 million)
- The low number of countries to which codevelopment was applied.

Some concern over the split responsibilities has been voiced because the interministerial tug-of-war over the proper allocation of migration and development issues institutionally undermined the concept of codevelopment and the overall coherence of migration policy. For example, as of November 2010, the French Development Agency (Agence Française de Développement) is under the shared management of the Ministry of Immigration, the Ministry of the Interior, the Ministry of Foreign Affairs, and the Ministry of the Economy. To avoid the risk of the Ministry of Immigration taking some of the development responsibilities away from the Ministry of Foreign Affairs, a report issued by the French National Assembly has called on the new Ministry to avoid acting in an isolated manner and to ensure that the new pacts on concerted migration management expressly refer to the Framework Partnership Documents, which the Ministry of Foreign Affairs concludes with those same countries (Terrot 2009:33).

One positive effect of the split ministerial responsibility over codevelopment, however, is that the French Ministry of Foreign Affairs freed additional resources for sectoral funding schemes in health, education, and banking. Financial return and reintegration assistance to low-skilled or nonformally skilled migrants who return to a job or to small-scale economic activity in agriculture, commerce, or handicrafts was retained.[18] Even if never stated explicitly, the implicit goal of codevelopment remains a security-driven one of controlling migration flows (de Haas 2008:1314). Nonetheless, with the ministerial reallocation, codevelopment gained visibility, not least because the concept was integrated into France's new bilateral agreements on migration, which the MIIINDS had designed as a by-product of the immigration law reform it had undertaken in 2006–07, as discussed below.

Together, solidarity and codevelopment have twin goals: (a) channeling individual migrants' savings to productive investments, and (b) mobilizing the diaspora community to contribute financially and through the transfer of know-how to the socioeconomic development of their countries of origin.

Five actions are designed to achieve these goals (Tosca 2008:33):

- *Supporting local development in zones of high out-migration* (decentralized development). Such support can occur directly via development aid or indirectly via matching, by government funding, the contributions of the diaspora community in terms of the tangible and intangible transfer of resources to local development in their countries of origin to mobilize migrants settled in France (targeting mostly the diaspora elite).
- *Contributing to the human capital development of their countries of origin by virtual or physical return of competencies, skills, and expertise.* Circular migration for professional education and expert missions to their home countries by highly skilled members of the diaspora community is facilitated.
- *Encouraging productive investments by migrants in their home communities* (education, infrastructure, and essential services) and their entrepreneurship, whether or not the migrant returns.
- *Decreasing the costs of transferring remittances and offering tax breaks for productive savings.*

- *Improving the integration of young persons with a migratory background* to find work either in the host country or in their home country. This is a more recent goal, included since 2006, with the advent of the new migration pacts.[19]

Furthermore, in 2009, eligibility for multilateral codevelopment funding and reintegration support was narrowed to only those priority solidarity zone countries that have "large communities living in France and the degree of organization of these communities in France, as well as the willingness shown by the governments of those countries to associate their communities living abroad with their own development policies" (EMN 2010:26). Thus, priority countries benefiting from support today are Algeria, Benin, Burkina Faso, Burundi, Cameroon, Cape Verde, the Central African Republic, Chad, the Comoros, the Democratic Republic of Congo, Côte d'Ivoire, Gabon, Guinea, Haiti, Madagascar, Mali, Mauritania, Morocco, Niger, Nigeria, the Republic of Congo, Rwanda, Senegal, Somalia, Surinam, Togo, Tunisia, and Vietnam.

As regards reintegration support, the tightening occurred because reintegration aid often had the opposite effect from the one desired. Instead of mobilizing migrants to return and open a business, the reintegration support, which in Mali was up to €4,000 per migrant, triggered "me-too" actions whereby Malian citizens would follow the example of their fellow citizens and attempt to migrate to France simply to become eligible for this type of aid. Thus, individualized return and reintegration support has been found to increase, rather than decrease, migratory pressure (Martinez 2009:50–51). However, the amounts of reintegration support available for the individual migrant (€4,000 to €7,000 per project in 2009) are not higher if a country has signed a pact with France (Martinez 2009:50). Inversely, eligibility for additional, bilateral codevelopment funding (not reintegration aid), was now limited to countries that sign a bilateral migration pact with France (see section below).

Solidarity development and codevelopment were also incorporated into France's migration pacts, where they form the third component of such a pact. In a migration pact, the Ministry of Foreign Affairs will fund the diaspora initiatives incorporated into a pact, such as evidenced by Articles 22:6 and 22:7 of France's pact with Benin (Terrot 2009:33), even if the overall responsibility for the pact falls under the responsibility of the Immigration Ministry (which, since November 2010, has been downsized to a government agency operating within the Ministry of the Interior).

In 2008, the French Parliament authorized €30 million for codevelopment activities.[20] In the same year, Sub-Saharan and North African migrants in France sent €8 billion to their home countries (Martinez 2009:57). First results of bilateral cofinancing obtained for Senegal on December 31, 2008, show that of the 197 projects supported by 15 development operators (agencies, NGOs, public-private partnerships), 52 percent remain in an active phase of implementation and have generated investments of up to €130 million, with employment created for up to 800 individuals; yet up to 56 percent of the projects remain centered in the urban zone of Dakar (CICI 2009:196).

In 2009, the MIIINDS devoted €69 million to subsidize solidarity development initiatives (MIIINDS 2009). PSF contributed up to €2.5 million in matching funds for 182 projects in Mali during 2006–08. In comparison, Malians in France in 2005 sent €295 million in officially and unofficially recorded remittances (AfDB 2007:12).

NGOs like the Water Solidarity Network (Programme solidarité eau, pS-Eau), jointly run by the Ministry of Foreign Affairs, Euroresources, and France's PSF, offer technical support to migrant communities that wish to apply for codevelopment funding. To be eligible, migrants must carry at least 30 percent of the project costs, the project must be in line with the local development plan, and a feasibility study has to be conducted. Projects can expect to receive between €7,500 and €45,700.[21] The pS-Eau in Senegal has been somewhat successful at channeling investments into the country, and today it runs all codevelopment projects there.[22]

Financial Repackaging: Codevelopment in France's 2006–07 Immigration Law

Collective cofunding generated limited economic impact, because participation remained shallow. In reaction, Sarkozy's immigration law reform (2006–07) designed new codevelopment tools that financially repositioned the concept. Tax breaks and a codevelopment prize created in 2008 (see "Codevelopment Prize" subsection below) equip codevelopment with real-time enforcement mechanisms. Sarkozy's tools focused much more on mobilizing the individual migrant. For the first time in its 30-year history, the immigration law reform translated codevelopment into legal text and thus strengthened its visibility, since previously the government was carrying out a policy that had no legal sanction. Two French ministerial decrees have added flexibility to the codevelopment strategy. The MIIINDS, together with other relevant ministries, is empowered to conclude public-private partnerships with a bank, which then offers tax breaks through a special "codevelopment savings account" or "bank passbook" to the individual migrant in France, who invests his or her savings profitably in his or her source country. By defiscalizing those migrants' savings, which are invested profitably in the migrants' countries of origin, France individualized and "bancarized" codevelopment aid. The advantage of development aid being disbursed not in kind but in the form of tax breaks on migrants' individual savings is that it costs less for the French Government in terms of administration, all while increasing the revenue for commercial banks in the form of interest rates (Crayen, Hainz, and Ströh de Martínez 2010:3).

Defiscalization of Migrants' Productive Investments

France has broken new ground for European migration policies by *defiscalizing* migrants' savings. "Defiscalization" is a term French codevelopment policies use to label tax exemptions provided with the purpose of stimulating investments in the country of origin. Today, there are two initiatives for encouraging migrants in France to put their savings into the formal banking system: the codevelopment savings account and the codevelopment bank passbook. Both of these initiatives, if well managed, could result in a threefold gain: (a) migrants obtain a tax break, (b) French banks obtain the migrants' funds as fresh capital, and (c) the French Government, which concludes agreements with retail banks in the country of origin, encourages these banks to cooperate with French banks, while saving itself the cost of transferring development aid. The bancarization strategy, whereby commercial banks are authorized by the French Government to grant tax breaks on migrant savings, also stimulates retail banking as a source of employment in developing countries.

Defiscalization encourages migrants to use formal channels for transferring funds, thereby encourages the "bancarization" of savings and transfers. This, in turn, discourages the use of money transfer companies, which in West Africa handle 70 percent of official payments (IFAD 2008), or reliance on the informal "Fax" system, predominant in the Comoros, Mali, and Senegal, where it is based on the Hawala "banking" tradition of mutual trust (AfDB 2007:30).[23]

French Law No. 1631 of November 20, 2007, on controlling immigration, integration, and asylum (Article L 221-33), laid the foundation for the Prime Minister to decree on February 19, 2007, the establishment of a codevelopment savings account. The codevelopment savings account receives savings destined to an economic investment in a migrant's country of origin from migrants who are from one of the 50 developing countries listed as eligible recipients in a decree jointly issued by the Minister of Foreign Affairs, the Minister of Economics, and the Minister of the Interior. Based on the decree of February 19, 2007, France would first sign public-private partnership agreements with banks, credit unions, and other financial establishments with the view of encouraging them to make available the codevelopment savings account. Based on that decree and its 2008 migration pact with Tunisia, France that year signed its first public-private partnership with the Union of Tunisian Banks (Terrot 2009:21).[24]

Eligibility for the codevelopment savings account is limited to migrants who hold a permit of stay valid for engaging in professional activity in France. These migrants may invest up to 25 percent of their savings, but not more than the annual ceiling of €20,000, into predefined projects, which then benefit from tax reductions of up to 40 percent of the total sum put into the savings account between January 1, 2009, and December 31, 2011. The minimum amount of the account is €50 and the maximum is capped at €50,000 per person. The duration of the account is limited to six years.[25]

To date, France's codevelopment savings account has not been used very much, because it is restricted to migrants engaging in a professional activity in France, a fact that reduces the scope of eligible persons to holders of the one-year temporary permit of stay. To make the savings scheme available to a wider circle of migrants in France, the Prime Minister, on June 28, 2008, decreed the creation of a codevelopment bank passbook.[26] Eligibility has been widened to any person lawfully entitled to stay in France, regardless of whether the migrant is gainfully employed or practices a profession in the country. Under the decree, foreigners with a residency limit (valid up to 10 years) became a new target group, but investments defiscalized through the bank passbook were limited to those made in countries with which France has concluded a new pact on migration management.[27] Only migrants keeping a certain level of savings in their account can get a loan, and only after a minimum savings period of three years.

Unlike the cofunding of collective investments, such fiscal incentives (and penalties) engage the personal responsibility of the migrant. That 96 percent of migrants in France have a bank account, which is close to the national median (of 98 percent), is evidence of this. Thus, of 4.9 million immigrants living in France (in 2006), only 200,000 fell outside the formal banking system due to scarcity of resources or to their recent arrival in the country (Milhaud 2006:7).

Roughly 40 percent (and for Sub-Saharan Africa, roughly 75 percent) of the immigrants in France send money back home. On a long-term basis, these transfers represent from 15 to 25 percent of the migrants' revenue and, depending on the recipient country, from 10 to 20 percent of the state budget (Martinez 2009:57). Yet, 75 percent of these transfers to migrant source countries flow to health expenditures and consumables instead of contributing to the development of the local economy. Even if French policies did not want to interfere with a migrant's freedom of choice, the codevelopment savings account and bank passbook are incentives to encourage more investments into collective equipment, infrastructure, and entrepreneurial projects (Milhaud 2006:9).

Reducing the Costs of Remittances Transfers

France is the world's 12th-highest remittances-sending country (World Bank 2008:14). Like other host countries, it aims to lower the transfer costs of remittances, since remittances can contribute to source-country development (Martin and Abella 2009:432). Remittances are often described as the "easiest" transmission mechanism between migration and development, yet only 40 to 60 percent of the North and West African Diaspora in France remit compared to 70 to 80 percent of migrants remitting from other corridors (Ndione and Bröekhuis 2006). Not only is there potential to increase the amount of remittances transferred to Africa, but also to reduce the costs, which can be up to 25 percent of the amount sent and are thus significantly higher compared to other regions (IFAD 2009:2).

To that end, the French Development Agency established in 2007 an online fee-comparison tool[28] that compares what various financial and informal institutes charge for sending remittances back home. Most new pacts refer to that fee-comparison tool.[29] On October 23, 2009, the MIIINDS,

together with the African Development Bank and the International Fund
for Agricultural Development, signed a convention to launch a "multilateral solidarity development fund" for Africa. Its primary objective is to
decrease the costs of migrants' transfers in accordance with the strategy of
the G-8 July 2009 meeting, to achieve a 50 percent reduction in the costs
of transfers by 2014. The Fund, toward which France contributes €6 million, will also design new financial tools, to encourage migrants' savings
and investments in their countries of origin. This multilateral fund will
also cofinance, in the spirit of codevelopment, investments in the development of entrepreneurship in countries of origin, prioritizing calls for microcredit loans and support to small and medium enterprises (MIIINDS 2009).

Codevelopment Prize

France's Minister of Immigration, Integration, National Identity and Solidarity Development, Brice Hortefeux, on June 16, 2008, created a €3,000
Integration and Codevelopment Prize to be awarded annually to individuals or immigrant associations that have contributed to codevelopment of
their countries of origin while they remain in France (de Haas 2006:70;
IOM 2005:41) citing the Adviser to the Ambassador in charge of codevelopment, France). The prize is given to:

- Migrants living in France or those who have benefited from return and
  reintegration support of the National Agencies for the Admission of
  Migrants[30] who have created an enterprise or engaged in activities generating resources and employment opportunities in their countries of
  origin
- An exemplary model of decentralized development cooperation in the
  region of origin that is being cofunded by an association of migrants,
  the OSIM.[31]

Besides the €3,000, which is granted to the individual migrant or the
collectivity, the codevelopment project itself is also honored and can be
awarded up to €12,000.[32] A committee comprising representatives from
the Ministry of Immigration and successful migrants, including sportsmen,
writers, and entrepreneurs,[33] (although limited so far to permanent
migrants residing in France), will disburse the prizes. In 2009, the prizes
were awarded to projects that created a textile industry in Dakar; a phar-
macy in Bamako, Mali; and a fish farm in Keur Momar Sarr in Senegal. All

the projects were established by return migrants. The diaspora organization in France of the township of Gambi Diaobé was honored for constructing a hydroelectric dam in their village in Senegal.[34]

To summarize, French migration policy provides five instruments to incentivize migrants to invest their savings in their home countries: (a) the savings account, (b) the bank passbook, (c) the cofinancing of collective investments, (d) access to microcredit facilities and support from the new multidonor (African Development Bank, International Fund for Agricultural Development, and MIIINDS) solidarity development facility, and (e) the codevelopment prize. The next section discusses which of these and other codevelopment programs are specific to the new French migration pacts and thus are conditional on a migrant source country concluding such a bilateral migration agreement with France.

Bilateral Codevelopment Strategy in the New French Migration Pacts

Since the conclusion of the French pacts on migration management (Tasca 2008:5; Terot 2009:5), the policy of involving the migrant as an "agent of development," but also other codevelopment actors, has gained new momentum. France's pacts were designed by Brice Hortefeux, the first minister of the newly created MIIINDS, in 2007, and are to be concluded with the 28 countries of France's priority solidarity zone, with priority being given to those migrant source countries that have a considerable number of citizens residing temporarily or permanently in France, primarily Western and Northern Africa.

Of its 15 migration pacts, France has signed nine comprehensive pacts on migration management, as seen in table 2.1. These nine "classic" templates have three chapters that cover (a) the fight against irregular migration, (b) labor migration, and (c) solidarity development. Five of the pacts entered into force between late 2008 and 2010 (Benin, Gabon, the Republic of Congo, Senegal, and Tunisia) (see table 7.1) (Tasca 2008: 5).[35] At the time of writing, the pacts with Burkina Faso, Cameroon, Cape Verde, and Lebanon had been adopted by the respective national assemblies, but the ratification process had not been finalized by France. Four of the pacts are what this study will label "light" versions, because their scope is limited to stay and circular migration of professionals and solidarity development,

TABLE 7.1
French Migration Pacts

	Negotiations	Signature	Ratification	Entry into force
Algeria	opened in 2008			
Benin	November 28, 2007			March 1, 2010
Brazil	March 12, 1997			September 1, 2007
Burkina Faso		January 10, 2009	by the French National Assembly and transmitted to the Senate 8 April 2010	
Cameroon		May 23, 2009	transmitted to the French National Assembly 28 July 2010	
Cape Verde		November 24, 2008	by the National Assembly and transmitted to the Senate 8 April 2010	
Egypt, Arab Rep.	since late 2008			
Gabon		July 5, 2007		September 1, 2008
Haiti	since late 2008			
Lebanon		June 26, 2010		
Macedonia		December 1, 2009		
Mali	since 2006			
Mauritius		September 23, 2008		September 1, 2010
Montenegro		December 1, 2009		
Philippines	since late 2007 or early 2008			
Republic of the Congo		October 25, 2007,		August 1, 2009
Russian Federation		November 27, 2009		
Senegal		September 23, 2006 and covenant February 25, 2008		August 1, 2009
Serbia		December 2, 2009		
Tunisia		April 28, 2008		July 1, 2009

Source: Author's own compilation using data from the MIIINDS "Accords bilatéraux" and, for the Spanish agreements, from IOM 2008.

but excludes readmission and border securitization measures to combat irregular migration. During 2008–09, France signed such "light" migration pacts with the former Yugoslav Republic of Macedonia, Mauritius, Montenegro, and Serbia. So far, only the pact with Mauritius has entered into force, in September 2010. The pacts with the Western Balkan countries are awaiting ratification by both parties. Two of the pacts—one with Brazil and one with the Russian Federation—could qualify as "super-light" versions, because without chapters on readmissions and solidarity development aid, their only purpose is to facilitate the migration of professionals. The pact with Brazil is a nonbinding administrative arrangement that reads like a declaration of intent to engage in jointly managing each other's migration and police and security policies (Terrot 2010).

Additional pacts—with Algeria, Egypt, and Equatorial Guinea—are under negotiation. Discussions have been held on agreements with Haiti, Mauritania, Morocco, and the Philippines, countries that have signaled an interest in signing such agreements (CIMADE 2009:3; Terrot 2009:5). Negotiations with the Democratic Republic of Congo and Guinea have been suspended due to political instability. The agreements under negotiation with non-African countries (Brazil and the Russian Federation, but also with Georgia, India, and Vietnam) are slightly different, because those countries have already signed EU-wide readmission agreements or have far-reaching association, stabilization, or partnership and cooperation agreements with the EU. This means that certain elements, such as readmission obligations or development cooperation, are not reiterated in the bilateral migration pact signed with France.[36] No agreement could be reached with Mali, which refused to sign a new pact due to a clash with France over the number of Malians in unlawful stays in France. Mali wanted to have 4,000 to 5,000 of its citizens regularized; France offered to regularize 1,500, despite Mali being the main recipient of French development aid for Africa (Diatta 2008).

The pacts complement the French immigration laws of July 24, 2006, and November 20, 2007, in three ways.

First, they were designed to dissipate tensions with former colonies in West Africa, which had been disproportionately affected by the high-skill orientation of France's new immigration law of July 24, 2006. The pacts are in essence bilateral framework agreements with a trilateral structure composed of three chapters: border security, labor migration and development cooperation, and codevelopment policies. The new pacts thus formally embed codevelopment into the legally binding structure of a bilateral agreement. Unlike in the past, when the French codevelopment funding mechanisms bypassed the host country government in the sense that the funding went directly to an immigrant association, the pacts now commit the country of origin to sharing responsibility for the costs and benefits of implementing codevelopment policies. As codevelopment has moved to the forefront of similar strategies in Europe, it has emerged as a field of research and policy of its own.

Second, in addition to acting as a corrective to the high-skill bias of the 2006 and 2007 immigration laws, the French pacts also keep the French Government from having to regularize through nationwide amnesties the status of migrants in irregular stays. The goal is achieved by incorporating a readmission clause in each pact, which requires the migrant-sending country to take back its citizens, and in some cases third-country nationals that have transited through the country, who are in irregular stays in France. This increased security and enforcing of border controls is meant to combat irregular migration by incentivizing the migrant source countries to enforce the customary international law obligation to take back their own citizens, whether they are in lawful or unlawful stays in France and whether or not they return home voluntarily or have to be deported. Pursuant to a majority of international law opinion, any country has, as a matter of territorial sovereignty over its borders, a customary duty to take back its own citizens. From this customary obligation flows the duty to respect another country's immigration laws, from which flows the duty to cooperate with that other country when it comes to taking back its own citizens who are in irregular stays in the host country, without the need for the host country to "reward" such an action.

Yet, from a strictly human-rights-based approach, which is the approach source countries have been taking, the duty to take back its own citizens only applies to those citizens who return voluntarily. Under this more narrow view, a migrant-sending country would thus have the right to refuse to cooperate in deportations of its own citizens, which the host country seeks to forcefully expel, deport, and repatriate because they have violated immigration laws of that host country. This legally unclear situation has made the conclusion of readmission agreements with source countries difficult. Therefore, many host countries of migrants in Europe have stepped up readmission agreements by offering considerable development aid packages in return for the source country cooperating in readmission procedures (Hailbronner 1996). This paradigm shift has led, since the late 1990s, to the reemergence of bilaterally managed migration relations, mostly at the incentive of EU countries like France, Italy, and Spain, bordering the Mediterranean and securing the "front door" of Europe exposed to Sub-Saharan transit and North African (irregular) migration (Alscher 2005).

For this reason, the French pacts seek to engage the migrant source country more intensely in cooperating on managing migratory flows, but also to make host country governments responsible for migratory root causes in their country, such as illiteracy, poverty, and unemployment. Thus, their third function is to establish partnerships with source countries to create a platform where the common interests of France and source countries with respect to the management of migratory flows are shared (OECD 2008a:31).

Whereas previous pacts had a one-dimensional focus, the French pacts streamline all policies related to migration into a single package. Thus, not only are the pacts multidimensional in terms of focus, but they are also broader in terms of actors, because they delegate to individual government ministries or agencies the power to conclude public-private partnerships with nonstate actors. Examples of such partnerships include those made with banks for reducing the costs of remittance transfers, with migrant collectivities for cofunding diaspora projects, and with industry associations to establish preemployment training centers. For example, bilateral solidarity development funding in the French pact with Tunisia amounts to €20 million, of which €18 million is dedicated to upgrading the education of the Tunisian workforce with the view of increasing employability in the global and national labor market. The remaining funds are reserved for bank loans, which the French Development Agency offers to young Tunisian entrepreneurs (CICI 2009:193).

The French pacts differentiate them from free trade agreements, which also liberalize, but fail to regulate, the temporary movement of natural persons as service providers. The World Trade Organization/General Agreement on Trade in Services is architecturally constrained from regulating migration in a multidimensional manner similar to that with which these bilateral migration agreements have been experimenting. Whereas bilateral migration agreements typically open labor markets to the low-to-medium-skilled workers (Panizzon 2010:10–11,37,40; Sauvé 2008:624), trade agreements, notably the multilateral General Agreement on Trade in Services, remain high-skill biased. In addition, the General Agreement on Trade in Services does not provide for a negotiating mandate for World Trade Organization members to agree on rules for regulating the temporary movement of service providers. For now, the General Agreement on Trade in Services multilaterally liberalizes the temporary movement only of natural persons through requesting World Trade Organization Members to open their services markets to foreign-service-supplying persons in what are called "mode 4" market access commitments.

Moreover, French migration pacts confirm the finding that bilateral migration agreements institutionalize and facilitate the processes for recruiting migrant labor (Chanda 2009:479; Stephenson and Delourme 2010:12). Such regulatory features are particularly necessary where lower-skilled labor is to be recruited, for which no private-sector-driven selection processes are in place. In such cases, the host- and source-country governments need to establish facilities, which for high-skilled labor are provided by the transnational networks of multinational corporations (Sassen 1998:47). Yet, most bilateral, nontrade agreements remain asymmetrically tilted toward host-country interests, which are those of immigration control and border security.

The innovative feature of France's bilateral migration pacts, compared to their precursors, such as the 2000 codevelopment convention between France and Senegal, is to add legal migration as a further element of conditionality to the established nexus between development aid and combating irregular migration. As originally conceived by Brice Hortefeux, the new French migration pacts are traditionally composed of three interlinked components: a chapter on labor migration, including student mobility; a chapter on control and prevention of irregular migration and border securitization; and a chapter on development cooperation. Official development assistance in the field of migration is one of three components of the new migration pacts and splits into three actions: (a) sectoral aid ("solidarity development"), (b) cofinancing migrants' investments in their countries of origin ("codevelopment"), and (c) decentralized development aid. The "tone and style" of how the three subactions are allocated vary with each pact (Tasca 2008: 33).

Countries that conclude such a migration pact with France are eligible for the largest amount of co- and solidarity development aid, which is bilateral aid. Whereas in 2010, €2 million was earmarked as multilateral aid to solidarity development and a little over €4 million went to reintegration support for individual return migration, the bulk of French official development assistance granted to immigration and integration—€29.5 million—went to bilateral actions under the umbrella of solidarity development (MOB 2009), which is reserved for countries with which France has a bilateral migration pact.

Bilateral solidarity funding tops the "multilateral" solidarity development aid programs (mostly initiatives to reduce the costs of remittances transfers and stimulating a sustainable use of remittances channeled toward projects of source-country development) and reintegration support disbursed to the individual return migrant by the Bureau for Immigration and Integration (Office Français de l'Immigration et de l'Intégration). Together, these three actions (multilateral aid, bilateral solidarity actions, and return/reintegration support) form the 301 programs of solidarity development relating to migration (CICI 2009:184). In the multilateral context, codevelopment and solidarity development programs remain separate and are also managed by two different ministries—the Ministry of Foreign Affairs for codevelopment and the MIIINDS for solidarity development. Because the MIIINDS has overall responsibility for the French pacts, codevelopment actions, which for the most part fall under the auspices of the Foreign Ministry in the pacts, also fall under the MIIINDS mandate (CIMADE 2009:5).

Some pacts, such as the one with the Democratic Republic of Congo, have not yet identified specific codevelopment actions and thus delegate this task to a committee established to implement the agreement (Article 5:1 and Article 6) (Tasca 2008:36). Other pacts, such as the one with Benin, solicit funding complementary to French codevelopment and solidarity development, such as from private sponsors, professional associations, employer unions, universities, or international organizations, in particular for vocational training (Article 22:7–10).

Can Solidarity Development Aid Facilitate Labor Migration?

Criticism that PSF project funding had failed to increase the level of entrepreneurial activities by the diaspora prompted the French Ministry on Immigration to design a "sister" concept for codevelopment, named "solidarity development." The choice of the term "solidarity" refers to the solidarity, which migrants, individually or collectively, naturally demonstrate toward those remaining behind by sending home remittances or engaging in other types of transfers. Moreover, the term alludes to the solidarity France shows toward migrant source countries, particularly its former colonies. Whereas the term "codevelopment" implied a joint responsibility, "solidarity development" points to one-way transfers typical of government-to-government development aid. Solidarity development is not simply a relabeling of codevelopment, but "adds value" to it by widening the financial toolkit, previously limited to cofunding under the Framework Partnership Documents (Tasca 2008:33).

Solidarity development's new focus on labor migration programs has two goals:

- To ensure that the migrant workforce admitted into France has the skill levels that respond to French labor market needs
- To contain emigration to France by encouraging skill retention and creating employment opportunities in the countries of origin.

The bilateral pact with Tunisia of April 28, 2008, is the first to reflect, by modified treaty structures, "solidarity development." Concluded as a framework agreement, the pact with Tunisia is implemented by two protocols (Article 5).

The first protocol addresses migration management and contains the modalities for implementing family reunification; circular migration; student mobility; and migration for professional reasons, return, and readmission. An annex contains a list of occupations in which there is a shortage of workers.

The second protocol defines which actions fall under the concept of solidarity development and which fall under development aid. This delineation reflects the internal divide of responsibilities among the different French Ministries. This structure delinks even more clearly than before development cooperation from migration control, in particular migrant returns. There are three annexes, which offer the flexibility necessary for the French and Tunisian Governments to conclude, on an ad-hoc basis, understandings with nonstate partners for codevelopment, such as industrial and professional associations, enterprises, and universities.

The first annex lists the various professional and vocational training centers France projects to establish and fund in Tunisia, relating to those occupations for which Tunisia has stated a development need. None of this funding is provided to match diaspora initiatives contributing to the development of the home country. Instead, it is direct government funding to create new training centers or to modernize Tunisia's preexisting training centers in specifically defined sectors, such as construction, fashion, maritime, metallurgy, and woodworking.

The second annex lists those projects funded by the MIIINDS. These projects relate to fishery and social integration and bank credits to support young entrepreneurs.

The third annex lists development cooperation projects undertaken by other French ministries, which are not financed by the solidarity development fund and which, for the most part, relate to microcredit and support for public health. Based on these annexes, the French Development Agency and the French Association for the Vocational Training for Adults concluded a memorandum with the Tunisian Ministry of Education and Formation and with the Mechanical and Electrical Industries Centre and the Mediterranean Institute of Metallic Technologies.[37]

Agriculture and fishery are two key sectors that obtain solidarity development funding. Under Article 6:2 of the new pact, France strengthens Senegal's government-run Retour vers l'agriculture plan, especially its program for reintegrating return migrants, cofunded by France, Spain, and the EU (at a combined total of €20 million). Support for the financial sector in source countries is another typical solidarity development initiative whereby the French Development Agency refinances source country microfinance institutions and those source country banks that give credit to small and medium enterprises (SMEs).

Health Worker Repatriation and Retention

In Africa, where the emigration of physicians can reach 11.5 percent to 36 percent (Docquier and Bhargava 2006), strategies to incentivize African doctors and health professionals in the diaspora to return to a job in their countries of origin is a key goal of France's new pacts on migration management. The exception is the pact with Tunisia, where levels of development in the health sector are higher. In terms of *health worker repatriation*, the pacts with Benin (Article 22:5), the Democratic Republic Congo (Article 5:5), and Senegal (Article 6:1 and Annex II), raise the attractiveness of employment conditions in the source country by establishing a framework for lending and borrowing medical and technical equipment and for professional training centers on maintaining such equipment. Joint degree programs and a rotation scheme for generalist and specialist doctors and health professionals are planned (Tasca 2008:33). Specific to Benin is the objective of replenishing within three years its health sector with the necessary numbers of health professionals from France.

Skill retention is another solidarity development concern in the health sector. To that end, the pacts establish distance learning programs for medical personnel, a pilot-test phase with micromedical insurance schemes, and decentralized government cooperation between the public hospitals and Brazzaville and Dakar with their counterparts in Lyon and other cities.

Enhancing the Employment and Employability of the Workforce

With the realization that remittances play a key role in the development of migrant source countries, French migration policies started shifting the *ratio* between family reunification and student migration and economic migration of highly skilled or talented professionals. France's Government, under then-Minister of Interior Nicolas Sarkozy, instigated the 2006–07 immigration law reform culminating in the French Immigration and Integration Law 2006-911 of July 24, 2006, and its follow-up Law 2007-1631 of November 20, 2007, relating to immigration, integration, and asylum. Both laws move away from migration, which was perceived as "inflicted" upon France ("immigration subie") toward attracting labor, preferably "professional" migrants under the new concept of "targeted immigration" ("immigration choisie") (Chou and Baygert 2007).[38]

The new policy declared that priority be given to professional migration. This was done through designing a new entry category, the "skills and talents" admission card, but also by limiting family reunification and by increasing the number of deportations, through stricter enforcement of readmission agreements. To step up these efforts at readmissions, the President of the Republic set an annual target number of repatriations that the Minister of Immigration had to attain. Both factors led to gradually increased expulsions—from 18,735 in 2006 to 19,885 in 2007 to 19,274 in 2008 (Van Eeckhout 2009).

France continues to emphasize encouraging voluntary returns, and it seems that its new pacts have resulted in a successful policy mix combining channels for lawful migration with strict enforcement of readmissions and codevelopment tools. In a reversal of a previously high-skill-biased recruitment policy, France now "actively solicits low qualified labour" which, as it officially states, "complements" the common interests France and source countries have with respect to the management of migratory flows (OECD 2008a:31).

Yet, France could not ignore the fact that many source countries of migrants, namely former colonies in West and North Africa, would be disadvantaged by the change in terms of migrants' skill levels and categories admitted. Thus, France did three things:

- By decree, on January 18, 2008, it loosened its high-skill recruitment policy ("immigration choisie") (OECD 2008a:31) by drawing up lists of occupations in France in which there was a shortage of workers (shortage lists), to fast-track the recruitment of foreign labor for jobs in high demand in the French labor market (Cholewinski 2008:296). Countries signing a bilateral pact with France may add occupations to the shortage list of 60 occupations. France relaxes the work authorization process for these listed occupations by eliminating the economic needs test.

- Solidarity development funds preemployment vocational training centers to increase the employability and competitiveness of potential migrants. Reflecting a global trend, development aid emphasized the creation of employment and training centers in source countries (Tasca 2008:19). The old PSF cofunding scheme had failed to stimulate more diaspora entrepreneurship precisely because emigrants entering France prior to the reforms had for the most part been economically inactive, given that most were children or women migrants issued from family reunification or those admitted on student or stagiaire visas. These categories of migrants often did not have entrepreneurial skills or enough funds to contribute to the development of their country of origin.

- Public-private partnerships are concluded by the French immigration authorities with French employers or employer unions with the view of facilitating "the recruitment of foreign workforce according to business needs" (EMN 2010:22). A primary goal of these public-private partnerships is to fast-track the work authorization process for certain economic sectors where there are recruitment difficulties and thus an acute need for foreign workers, such as for caregiving, logistics, and transport personnel. A subsidiary but no less important policy objective is to shorten the delays in accessing work for those foreign job seekers who have signed a Reception and Integration Contract with the French Government, and prevent them from remaining unemployed for too long, which often results in such job seekers "lapsing into informal or illegal work" (EMN 2010:22). So far, the following public-private partnerships have been concluded in a migration/ employment context:

- A tripartite understanding on vocational training links France's Ministry of Immigration to Tunisia's Ministry of Education and the Mediterranean Institute of Metallic Technologies Menzel Bourguiba.[39] These understandings establish the modalities for spending the 80 million Tunisian Dinars that France projected for supporting 17 projects listed in Annex I of the pact's Protocol on Development over three years rather than to seek out complementary funding.
- An understanding was signed by the MIIINDS and the Vinci Construction company on April 11, 2009, to encourage foreign nationals who have signed a Reception and Integration Contract to apply for jobs in that company.
- An agreement that directly facilitates recruitment of foreign nationals between the MIIINDS and the Casino Group whereby the Casino Group will give priority to the recruitment to those job seekers that the French Bureau for Immigration and Integration has recommended.
- A partnership agreement with the French National Agency for Lifestyle and Home Care Services of June 2008 is geared toward training (including language training) those job seekers who have signed a Reception and Integration Contract, who are interested in taking a job in the caregiving sector. The memorandum of understanding, which MIIINDS signed with the Council of French Enterprises in Africa (Conseil des Entreprises Françaises en Afrique) on June 16, 2010, has a similar purpose.
- A partnership agreement between the Director General of the French Bureau for Immigration and the car manufacturer, Renault Maroc, and the French Consulate in Casablanca on July 19, 2010, to support the professional training program of Renault Maroc's subsidiary, the Renault Tanger Exploitation (S.A.S.), for the categories of executives, managers, and specialists, and nonessential automobile manufacturing workers. The main goal of that convention is to establish a one-stop-shop application procedure for obtaining an entry visa and an admission card for those Moroccan trainees pursuing Renault's training program and having to dislocate for that purpose for a limited time to Renault's headquarters in France.

○ A tripartite agreement signed in June 2009 between Club Med and the Labor Union for occupations in the food, agriculture, hotel and restaurant, and tobacco sectors, and with the European Federation of Employers for the agriculture, food, and tourism sectors. The primary goal of that agreement is not so much the recruitment of foreign labor, but to ensure the fair labor conditions of foreign workers employed by Club Med in its Europe-African zone.[40]

Yet, the spill-over effect from labor mobility on job creation and source-country development overall depends on the preexisting level of education of the migrant (Broadman, Pouget, and Gatti 2010). Whereas codevelopment, in particular structural aid programs in the abovementioned sectors requiring skill upgrading of the workforce, such as health, agriculture, or construction, can contribute to improving the skill level of a source country's human capital, the effect also depends on the level of policy coherence among French labor recruitment strategy, the openness of its labor market, and the type of return policies funded (short-term skill transfer missions by highly skilled migrants, circular migration visa).

For example, the number of jobs actually created by return migrants in the context of a French codevelopment project aiming at reintegration varies. The numbers range, for example, from one to seven for Mali and Senegal to much lower numbers for similar occupations in Eastern Europe. The one to two jobs created for Armenia, Bosnia and Herzegovina, Georgia, Moldova, and Romania, for example, could imply that the initial skills levels of persons emigrating from those countries differ starkly from those of other countries and that their prospects of receiving skills upgrading in a French job are lower. However, the difference may also be explained by cultural factors; for example, in an African context it takes more persons to do one particular job than in an Eastern European context. In addition, regarding Senegal, the fact that it was not the lower-skilled or unemployed Senegalese migrants in France that were returning voluntarily to Senegal and using development funds to reintegrate by setting up sustainable enterprises led France to realize its codevelopment policies were draining skills from Senegal and not targeting the "right persons." Such considerations may have led France to open more lower-skilled occupations to lawful labor migration in its bilateral migration pacts (CICI 2009:211). For example, France's migration pacts with Senegal and Tunisia have opened the French labor market to seasonal migrant workers, which are capped at 2,500 entries annually for Tunisia (Guibal 2009:27).

Source-Country Replications of Codevelopment: The Case of Senegal

In the case of Senegal, France's codevelopment strategies have worked reasonably well in areas where the Senegalese Government replicated the general direction or objective of France's migration policies. The Senegalese Government has been successful in identifying its nationals abroad and launching information campaigns to mobilize the diaspora to take responsibility for the development of their local communities. For instance, the government-run Investment Promotion and Major Works Agency, founded in 2000 under the auspices of the President of the Senegalese Republic, was essential for enticing the diaspora in France to invest in Senegal's infrastructure development, by building villages and sanitizing the water supply.

The Senegalese Investment Promotion and Major Works Agency also uses the funds from loans made by foreign governments, such as those of France and Germany, to finance projects facilitating the economic reintegration of return migrants. The "Entrepreneurship Diaspora" initiative of the Investment Promotion and Major Works Agency of Senegal has been replicated by at least three other ministries (Exterior, Women Entrepreneurship, and Senegalese Abroad and Tourism), which compete against each other for diaspora funds. The Ministry of Senegalese Abroad and Tourism installed an Internet portal in June 2008 to keep in touch with emigrants.[41] The portal feeds into an International Organization for Migration-run census project of Senegalese living abroad, the purpose of which is to categorize migrants according to their professions.

In addition, the portal targets Senegalese abroad as brokers of foreign direct investment. Unfortunately, none of these ministerial information platforms makes available cofunding to match transfers of migrants to their home communities, unless they have obtained French Government funding to do so (Ndione and Bröekhuis 2006:16–18). Statistical information on their success in attracting private capital by migrants is difficult to find. Since 2008, France and Spain have been helping Senegal and West Africa build their own administrative ability to manage migration. For instance, Spain established the Foundation of Senegalese Emigrants (Fondation des émigrés sénégalais) to facilitate diaspora-led investments in Senegal. This competition may infuse new life into the deadlocked and inefficient institutions that France had been cofunding since the 1980s.[42]

Migrants as Facilitators of Foreign Direct Investment and Brokers of Joint Ventures

Senegal shares with France the longest experience with codevelopment funding of any African country. The Franco-Senegalese development program is also the one that is most participatory in terms of the multiplicity of actors involved. The diaspora in France finances up to €3.3 million worth of projects in Senegal, while Senegal is one of the few African governments to match French funding—of €9 million for three years, starting in 2009—with €0.57 million (CICI 2009:195–96). In addition to cofinancing migrants' collective capital investments, the Franco-Senegalese partnership developed newer strategies, which encourage migrants to act as pathbreakers of foreign direct investment into Senegal or to broker joint ventures between a host-country firm and a Senegalese counterpart. The "Caravane of SMEs in Italy," initiated by Senegal's Ministry of Family, Women's Entrepreneurship and Micro-finance, is such an initiative. It formalizes and facilitates the joint ventures, business contacts, and professional networks, which lower-skilled Senegalese workers in the Northern Italian towns of Brescia, Lecco, and Parma had been establishing between their employers, food processing SMEs in Northern Italy (dried tomatoes and biscuits), and Senegalese agricultural producers (Panizzon 2008). The "bridge-building" function of such migrant networks is valuable for European SMEs that do not have the funding for obtaining destination-specific information. As Leblang (2009) shows, migrants have the advantage of knowing the conditions in the field, which may decrease the information asymmetry of a foreign direct investor about the country where the foreign investment is projected. For example, prompted by the many Senegalese workers in the area, the city of Parma has proposed receiving charter flights by Air Sénégal International and making freezer storage space available for storing tomatoes flown in from Senegal to have them dried in Italy (Senegal Ministry of Small and Medium Enterprises 2006).

NGOs Issued from Migration

Until FRONTEX, the European Union's border management agency, tightened border controls on the West African coast and started to clamp down on clandestine out-migration, there were no Senegalese NGOs active in migration. It was mostly NGOs in Europe, such as the French Panos Institute and the French Catholic Committee against Hunger and for Development that had launched their own codevelopment projects investing in large part in Senegal's infrastructure (for example, public facilities and water sanitization) (de Haas 2006:74). The 140 founding members of Gie Tekki fi ci Sénégal ("to succeed here in Senegal"), the only Senegalese NGO engaged in migration so far, were coincidentally all return migrants from Spain, that is, people who had been repatriated in the course of their clandestine journey at sea or during an attempted unauthorized entry into Spain (Panizzon 2008). Hometown associations from Senegal in France, such as the Association Drôme Ouro Sougui, have been particularly active among West African communities in transferring skills and investing in their communities of origin (de Haas 2006:76–79); Ndione and Bröekhuis 2006:17–18). In view of codevelopment's multistakeholder strategy, it will be important to cooperate with NGOs issued from migration.

International Codevelopment: Complement or Competitor?

Various codevelopment initiatives exist at the international level, such as the United Nations Development Programme's Transfer of Knowledge through Expatriate Nationals, launched for Senegal in 2002 with US$200 million, and the United Nations Digital Diaspora Network, launched in 2003 for Africa, both of which complement France's codevelopment tools. The Migration for Development in Africa program, which promotes links between the immigrant communities in Italy and their hometowns in Ethiopia, Ghana, and Senegal, is perhaps the international program most tailored to facilitating migrant entrepreneurship, even if it has not yet been launched for France. One of its key components is a database where Senegalese residing abroad can register their interest in contributing to the development of their country of origin and list their skills (de Haas 2006:29).

On a more political level, the United Nations Development Fund for Women calls for mobilizing diaspora resources as an additional way to achieve the Millennium Development Goals (Kampala Declaration 2003). The majority of Malian and Senegalese populations, particularly the unemployed workforces, have not really benefited from codevelopment initiatives, which primarily have targeted elites in cities. Islamic tradition and French cultural values are similar in their view of the desirability and value of intellectual careers and academic exchanges.

Conclusions: Advantages and Limitations of France's Codevelopment Concept

This chapter has described the manifold facets of codevelopment. It has shown that France went through a "learning process" and reinvented the concept as it internalized feedback from the diaspora. Codevelopment never quite lost its close link to return migration, a fact summarized in the slogan that codevelopment was designed to give a human face to a security agenda ("visage humanitaire d'une politique sécuritaire") (Lacroix 2009:15). Yet, gradually, codevelopment was redefined as a long-term strategy of development cooperation, rather than a short-term disbursement of return and reintegration support. Today, France's codevelopment savings account and bank passbook offer a valuable incentive mix of tax breaks and penalties, which has pioneered for Europe a promising new path for government-subsidized diaspora engagement. Even if more research needs to be undertaken on the costs of defiscalizing migrants' savings, which are invested productively in the countries of origin, a first appraisal leaves no doubt that the French ministry in charge of migration and development no longer incurs the administrative costs of transferring development funds.

This chapter argues that these new fiscal instruments are promising, because migrants are encouraged to bancarize their savings, which in turn helps to develop the banking sector in migrants' countries or origin. More critical is the fact that the French Government identifies, often without consulting the country of origin, the type of products into which migrants must invest in order to obtain the tax break.

The new strategy of individualizing codevelopment aid by offering tax breaks to migrants' savings has shifted the paradigm by relying less on migrant communities and more on an individual migrant's responsibility. Because only a few migrants from West and North Africa would have the capacity to take advantage of the targeted labor migration system introduced by France's immigration law of July 24, 2006, France's new pacts on migration management introduced labor market admission quotas for occupations in which there was a shortage of lower-skilled workers and cofunded vocational and professional training centers.

The emphasis on labor migration as a development issue marks another important change of focus in France's codevelopment strategy. The new policy mix, known under the labels of codevelopment, solidarity development, and decentralized government cooperation, and framed by France's immigration laws and its new pacts, has the potential to create the right incentives for migrants to contribute to their source countries' development and to mobilize their governments to match their investments.

Codevelopment has, however, been criticized for the following reasons:

- Placing the migrants themselves "at the heart of the process" has been overly idealistic. Not every migrant has the capacity, potential, or resources to be a manager, entrepreneur, or broker of joint ventures.
- France has often failed to "verify if the capacity of home structures allow the 'productive' returns of migrants." Corrupt practices, pressure by family members, and administrative difficulties in countries of origin have been underestimated (Wihtol de Wenden 2008:5).
- A channel for disbursing direct government-to-government aid, solidarity development is a sobering reversal from the overly idealistic partnership approach where the high hopes held in associating immigrant associations and NGOs in fostering development were not met.
- Codevelopment—in its classic sense of cofunding diaspora projects— failed to distinguish between migrants in unauthorized stays and those lawfully in France. This led to the paradox effect of clandestine immigration being somewhat rewarded.

The codevelopment savings account alleviated such concerns, since it is only available to migrants with valid documentation of stay in France. Counterintuitive as it may seem, France's new pacts on migration management have increased the coherence of France's migration policies, because structurally, codevelopment and solidarity development are mainstreamed into France's migration policies toward that specific country, alongside securitization of borders, readmission, and police cooperation, but also labor migration and integration strategies. For the concept to be more effective in the future, France should seek to incorporate similar initiatives formulated by international organizations, such as the International Organization for Migration's Migration for Development in Africa program; the United Nations Development Programme's Transfer of Knowledge through Expatriate Nationals; and the United Nations Educational, Scientific and Cultural Organization's Vocational Training program. So far, references in France's new pact have been limited to Senegal's government-run Retour vers l'agriculture plan and the pact of the Democratic Republic of Congo with the World Health

Organization and the United Nations Educational, Scientific and Cultural Organization.

France's long-standing experience with interlinked migration and development policies is "highly instructive" for countries that have only recently developed initiatives in the field (de Haas 2006:67). While France's codevelopment evolved because of the intensity of cultural, scientific, economic, and linguistic ties or shared education systems that have facilitated Eurafrican exchanges, it will be challenging for other migrant host countries that lack such links to replicate France's incentives.

Notes

1. In 2007, France was the fourth-largest donor of official development assistance, after the United States, which provided US$7.6 billion; the World Bank, which provided US$6.9 billion; and the European Commission, which provided US$5.4 billion.
2. French Ministry of Immigration, Integration, National Identity and Solidarity Development (MIIINDS); http://www.immigration.gouv.fr/spip.php?page =dossiers_them_dev&numrubrique=327, accessed August 31, 2009.
3. The "whole-of-government approach" seeks to create synergies among the different departments and ministries within a government, so as to integrate all policies with a potential migratory impact. It was proposed by the guidelines of the International Agenda for Migration Management (IAMM) and the Global Commission on International Migration (GCIM) Final Report.
4. Article 2 of the France-Senegal Co-development Convention.
5. In 2009, the National Agencies for the Admission of Migrants (http://www .anaem.fr/article.php3?id_article=490) was replaced by the Bureau for Immigration and Integration (Office Français de l'Immigration et de l'Intégration) (www.ofii.fr), created by Decree No. 2009–331 in April 2009, to administer the requests for professional migration, family reunification, integration, return, and reintegration support. The OFII's head office is in Paris, but it has regional representations in France and abroad. Those abroad are in countries with close ties to France: Cameroon, Canada, Mali, Morocco, Romania, Senegal, Tunisia, and Turkey, but also territories such as Gayana, Guadeloupe, La Réunion, Martinique, and St. Martin.
6. Reintegration aid can be defined as "start-up assistance for business or economic activity with the purpose of supporting the economic initiatives of migrants in their countries of origin" (EMN 2010:36); see also Article 3, para. c) of the Convention on Co-Development between the Government of the French Republic and the Government of the Republic of Senegal, of May 25, 2000, United Nations Treaty Series Volume 2129, I-37100.

7. French Senate, "Experimenting with Codevelopment"; http://www.senat .fr/rap.

8. The "Agreement on Training for Workers Who Have Temporarily Emigrated to France with a View to Their Return to Senegal and Their Integration into the Senegalese Economy," signed at Dakar on December 1, 1980, came into force on August 1, 1982 (United Nations Treaty Series Volume 1306, I-21788). In 1980, France and Senegal had already concluded an agreement on what today would be called "voluntary return." It provided for French Government support to the professional development of Senegalese in France to prepare them for their return to Senegal.

9. Forum of Organisations of International Solidarity Issued from Migration; http://www.forim.net/.

10. Article 3, para. c) of the France-Senegal Co-development Convention.

11. France-Diplomatie; http://www.diplomatie.gouv.fr/fr/actions-france_830/ aide-au-developpement_1060/politique-francaise_3024/instruments-aide_ 2639/fonds-solidarite-prioritaire-fsp_2640/index.html.

12. Ibid.

13. France-Diplomatie; http://www.diplomatie.gouv.fr/en/country-files_156/ senegal_233/france-and-senegal_5382/framework-partnership-document-france-senegal-2006-2010_8619.html.

14. National Agencies for the Admission of Migrants; http://www.anaem.fr/ article.php3?id_article=532.

15. Article 4 of the France-Senegal Co-development Convention.

16. MIIINDS; http://www.immigration.gouv.fr/spip.php?page=dossiers_det_dev& numrubrique=216&numarticle=1357.

17. France-Diplomatie; http://www.diplomatie.gouv.fr/fr/actions-france_830/ aide-au-developpement_1060/politique-francaise_3024/instruments-aide_ 2639/fonds-solidarite-prioritaire-fsp_2640/index.html.

18. Article 3, para. b) of the France-Senegal Co-Development Convention.

19. Article 22:1 Agreement on Migration Management and Codevelopment between France and Benin, signed at Cotonou on November 28, 2007; entered into force on March 1, 2010; Law No. 2009–581 of May 25, 2009, *Official Journal of the French Republic*, May 26, 2009, p. 8705; and Decree No. 2010–230 of March 5, 2010 on the publication of the agreement.

20. MIIINDS; http://www.immigration.gouv.fr/spip.php?page=dossiers_det_dev& numrubrique=216&numarticle=1357.

21. Euroresources; http://www.euroresources.org/guide_to_population_assistance/ france/co_development_initiatives.html.

22. pS-Eau, http://www.pseau.org/index_fr.php.

23. For instance, Senegal's migrants are increasingly using formal methods (45 percent still rely on informal methods, but in 2003, the number was over 60 percent).

24. MIIINDS; http://www.immigration,gouv.fr/spip.php?page=dossiers_det_dev& numrubrique=216&numarticle=1360.

25. France, Decree No. 2007–218 of February 19, 2007, relating to the co-development savings account, *Official Journal* No. 44 of February 21, 2007, p. 3074.
26. Article R221-117 of the Monetary and Financial Code of France.
27. See Article 22:4 of the Benin-France pact, Article 5 of the Senegal-France pact, and Article 5:3 of the Congo-France pact.
28. http://www.envoidargent.fr.
29. Article 22:3 of the Benin-France pact, Article 6:3(2) of the Senegal-France pact, and Article 5:2 of the Congo-France pact.
30. Renamed in 2009 the Office of Immigration and Integration.
31. MIIINDS; http://www.immigration.gouv.fr/spip.php?page=dossiers_det_dev&numrubrique=216&numarticle=1361.
32. Ordinance of June 16, 2008, establishing a co-development prize, *Official Journal of the French Republic,* June 28, 2008; http://www.legifrance.gouv.fr/affichTexte.do?cidTexte=JORFTEXT000019078829&dateTexte=.
33. Brice Hortefeux annonce la création d'un "Prix de l'Intégration et du Codéveloppement"; http://www.premier-ministre.gouv.fr/iminidco/actualites_829/brice_hortefeux_annonce_creation_59220.html.
34. MIIINDS; http://www.immigration.gouv.fr/spip.php?page=dossiers_det_dev&numrubrique=216&numarticle=1361.
35. The pacts are publicly available on at least three different sources. Whereas the French Government posts them only once they have been ratified by the French Parliament (http://www.immigration-professionnelle.gouv.fr/textes-de-r%C3%A9f%C3%A9rence/accords-bilat%C3%A9raux/accord-france-b%C3%A9nin), two French NGOs, the Comité Inter-Mouvements Auprès Des Evacués (http://www.cimade.org/uploads/File/solidarites-internationales/Documents/accords%20bilateraux/accord_senegal_230906.pdf) and the-Groupe d'Information et de Soutien des Immigrés (http://www.gisti.org/spip.php?rubrique135) publish the texts once they have been signed, if and when the NGO has succeeded in accessing the texts.
36. France, Diplomacy, Official Declarations concerning Foreign Policy, "Seminaire Intergouvernemental Franco-Russe Partenariat Pour La Mobilité, Profession-nelle, Communiqué du Ministère de l'immigration, de l'intégration, de l'identité nationale et du développement solidaire" of November 27, 2009; https://pastel.diplomatie.gouv.fr/editorial/actual/ael2/bulletin.asp?liste=20091130.html&xtor=EPR-7#Chapitre12.
37. French Embassy in Tunisia, *Franco-Tunisian Relations "Co-développement"*; http://www.ambassadefrance-tn.org/france_tunisie/spip.php?article584.
38. In 2007, family reunification was already down to 85,800 (10.6 percent). Since 2007, migration for work has increased by 14 percent, and 33,000 new migrant workers entered France in 2008.
39. French Embassy in Tunisia, *Franco-Tunisian Relations "Co-développement"*; http://www.ambassadefrance-tn.org/france_tunisie/spip.php?article584.
40. http://www.etlc-network.eu/labor-specific_information/trade_union_information_on_the_travel_and_tourism_sector/club_med_-_agreement_on_minimum_

social_standards/data/social_actu14247_accord-club-mediterranee-uita-effat_
2009_1_.pdf.
41. www.senex.sn.
42. The Council of Senegalese Abroad and the Bureau of Integration, Information and Follow-up for Emigrants (Bureau d'Accueil, d'Orientation et des
Suivi des Actions de Réinsertion des Émigrés) had been mandated to provide support for the reintegration of migrants, but have had limited success
due to "administrative deficiencies, and migrants' lack of confidence in the
organization," despite obtaining up to 400 million West African CFA francs
(Gerdes 2007:3–4).

References

Adebusoye, Paulina. 2006. "Geographic Labour Mobility in Sub-Saharan Africa."
IDRC Working Papers on Globalization, Growth and Poverty, No. 1 (March).
International Development Research Centre, Ottawa.

AFD (French Development Agency). 2006. "Migrants, Actors of Development."
Synthesis Report, Paris. March 29.

AfDB (African Development Bank). 2007. "Remittances by Migrants, A Development Challenge: The Comores, Mali, Morocco and Senegal." Interim Report,
Tunis Bélvèdere. October.

Aleinikoff, T. Alexander. 2003. "International Legal Norms and Migration, A
Report." In *Migration and International Legal Norms*, ed. T. Alexander Aleinikoff
and Vincent Chetail. The Hague: TMC Asser Press.

Alscher, Stefan. 2005. "Knocking at the Doors of 'Fortress Europe,' Migration and
Border Control in Southern Spain and Eastern Poland." CCIS Working Paper 126.
The Center for Comparative Immigration Studies, the University of California,
San Diego.

Bräutigam, Deborah. 2010. "China, Africa and the International Aid Architecture."
African Development Bank Group Working Paper, No. 107 (April), Tunis, Tunisia.

Brettell, Caroline. 2008. "Theorizing Migration in Anthropology, The Social Con-
struction of Networks, Identities, Communities, and Globalscapes." In *Migration
Theory, Talking across Disciplines*, ed. Caroline Brettell and James F. Hollifield.
New York: Routledge.

Broadman, Stefanie, Yann Pouget, and Roberta Gatti. 2010. "Labor Mobility in
the Middle East and North Africa: Challenges and Opportunities." World
Bank Middle East and North Africa Knowledge and Learning Quick Notes
Series, No. 30 (September). Marseille Center for Mediterranean Integration,
Marseille, France.

Cassarino, Jean-Pierre. 2007. "Informalizing Readmission Agreements in the EU
Neighborhood." *The International Spectator* 42 (2): 179–96.

Chanda, Rupa. 2009. "Mobility of Less-skilled Workers under Bilateral Agreements: Lessons for the GATS." *Journal of World Trade* 43: 479–506.

Cholewinski, Ryszard. 2008. "Formulation and Management of Foreign Employment Policies in Countries of Destination." In *World Migration Report*. International Organization for Migration, Geneva.

Chou, Meng Hsuan, and Nicolas Baygert. 2007. "The 2006 French Immigration and Integration Law: Europeanisation of Nicolas Sarkozy's Presidential Keystone?" Center on Migration Policy and Society Working Paper No. 45. Oxford University, Oxford, England.

CICI (Interministerial Committee on Immigration Control). 2009. "Secretary General of the Interministerial Committee on Immigration Control Report to the French Parliament." Paris, December.

CIMADE (Comité Inter-Mouvements Auprès Des Evacués). 2009. "French Agreements Concerning the Concerted Management of Migration Flows and Co-Development." Briefing Paper, Comité Inter-Mouvements Auprès Des Evacués, Paris. May 10.

Connan, Christian. 2005. *The Co-development Newsletter* 1 (July). French Ministry of Foreign Affairs, Paris.

Courtin, Christophe. 2007. "Le codéveloppement: un alibi pour des politiques migratoires restrictives." *Revue française de science politique* 68 (4): 393–408.

Crayen, Elizabeth, Christina Hainz, and Christiane Ströh de Martínez. 2010. "Remittances, Banking Status and the Usage of Insurance Schemes." CESifo Working Paper No. 3117 (July), Center for Economic Studies, Munich.

Daum, Christoph. 2007/2008. "Le codéveloppement grandeur et decadence d'une aspiration généreuse." *Revue international et stratégique* 68: 49–59.

de Haas, Hein. 2006. "Engaging Diasporas, How Governments and Development Agencies Can Support Diaspora Involvement in the Development of Origin Countries." International Migration Institute, University of Oxford, Oxfam Novib Study.

———. 2008. "The Myth of Invasion: The Inconvenient Realities of African Migration to Europe." *Third World Quarterly* 29 (7): 1305–22.

de la Garza, Rodolfo, and Miryam Hazan. 2003. "Looking Backward, Moving Forward: Mexican Organizations in the U.S. as Agents of Incorporation and Dissociation." The Tomas Rivera Policy Institute, Claremont, CA.

Docquier, Frédéric. 2006. "Brain Drain and Inequality Across Nations." Institute for the Study of Labor Discussion Paper, Bonn. November.

Docquier, Frédéric, and Alok Bhargava. 2006. "Medical Brain Drain – A New Panel Data Set on Physicians' Emigration Rates (1991–2004)." World Bank, Washington, DC.

EMN (European Migration Network). 2010. "Satisfying Labor Demand through Migration Report." http://emn.sarenet.es/Downloads/prepareShowFiles.do;jsessionid

=818814269F5571EDCEE357D4D777F379?entryTitle=01_Satisfying LABOUR DEMAND through migration.

GCIM (Global Commission on International Migration). 2005. "Final Report." Geneva.

Gerdes, Felix. 2007. "Senegal Country Profile." *Focus Migration*, No. 10 (November). Hamburg Institute of International Economics, Hamburg, Germany.

GISTI (Groupe d'Information et de Soutien des Immigrés). "Accords bilatéraux." http://www.gisti.org/spip.php?rubrique135.

Groff, Alberto. 2005. "Migration Partnerships: New Tools in the International Migration Debate." *Global Migration Perspectives*, No. 21 (January). Global Commission on International Migration, Geneva.

Guibal, Jean-Claude. 2009. "Report by Jean-Claude Guibal, Deputy, on behalf of the Commission on Foreign Affairs on the draft law adopted by the Senate, authorizing the ratification of the agreement on concerted migration management, the protocol on managed migration and the protocol on solidarity development between the Government of the Republic of France and the Government of the Republic of Tunisia of 17 February 2009." French National Assembly, No. 1472. Paris.

Hailbronner, Kay. 1996. *Rückübernahme eigener und fremder Staatsangehöriger, völkerrechtliche Verpflichtungen der Staaten.* Heidelberg: C.F. Müller Verlag.

Hazan, Miryam. 2009. "Beyond 3x1: Linking Sending and Receiving Societies in the Development Process." Presentation to the World Bank International Conference on Diaspora for Development, Washington, DC. July 13–14.

IFAD (International Fund for Agricultural Development). 2008. "Migration, Remittances and Rural Development." Rome.

———. 2009. "Sending Money Home to Africa. Remittance Markets, Enabling Environment and Prospects." International Fund for Agricultural Development, Rome. November.

IOM (International Organization for Migration). 2005. "Mainstreaming Migration into Development Policy Agendas." International Dialogue on Migration No. 8. International Organization for Migration, Geneva.

———. 2008. "IOM Compendium of Good Practice Policy Elements in Bilateral Temporary Labour Arrangements." http://www.iom.int/jahia/webdav/shared/shared/mainsite/published_docs/studies_and_reports/compendium_version_2.pdf.

Kampala Declaration. 2003. "Africa Launch of the Digital Diaspora Initiative." 2003. Kampala, Uganda. May 5–7. http://www.unifem.org/campaigns/wsis/documents/KampalaDeclaration.pdf.

Katseli, Louka. 2008. "Managing the Labour Migration and Development Equation." In *World Migration 2008, Managing Labor Mobility in the Evolving Global Economy* 4: 327–50. International Organization for Migration *World Migration Report* Series, Geneva.

Lacroix, Thomas. 2003. "Espace transnational et territories: les réseaux Marocains du développement." Unpublished PhD thesis. Université de Poitiers.

———. 2009. "Migration, Développement, Codéveloppement : quels acteurs pour quels discours?" Rapport de synthèse européen informer sur les migrations et le développement, Institut Panos, Paris.

Leblang, David. 2009. "Another Link in the Chain: Migrant Networks and International Investment." Presentation to the World Bank International Conference on Diaspora for Development, World Bank, Washington, DC. July 13–14.

Levitt, Peggy. 2009. "Routes and Roots: Understanding the Lives of the Second Generation Transnationally." *Journal of Ethnic and Migration Studies* 35 (7): 1225–42.

Martin, Philipp, and Manolo Abella. 2009. "Migration and Development: The Elusive Link at the GFMD [Global Forum on Migration and Development]." *International Migration Review* 43 (2): 431–39.

Martin, Susan, Philip Martin, and Patrick Weil. 2002. "Fostering Cooperation between Source and Destination Countries." Migration Information Source, Feature Story, Migration Policy Institute, Washington, DC. October.

Martinez, Henriette. 2009. "Report, Presented by Henriette Martinez to the Commission on Foreign Affairs on the Draft Law of Finances for 2009 (No. 1127), Public Development Aid." French National Assembly, No. 1201, Paris.

MIIINDS (Ministry of Immigration, Integration, National Identity and Codevelopment). 2009. "Accords bilatéraux." http://immigration-professionnelle.gouv.fr/nouveaux-dispositifs/accords-bilat%C3%A9raux.

Milhaud, Charles. 2006. "L'intégration économique des migrants et la valorisation de leur épergne." Report on behalf of the French Ministry of the Interior, Paris. September.

MOB (Ministry of the Budget). 2009. "Analysis of Program Costs and Actions 2009." Paris.

Ndione, Babacar, and Annelet Bröekhuis. 2006. "Migration International et développement, Points de vue et initiatives au Sénégal." Migration and Development Series Working Papers, Report No. 8. Radboud University, Nijmegen, Netherlands.

Noll, Gerhard. 2003. "Return of Persons to States of Origin and Third States." In *Migration and International Legal Norms*, ed. T. Alexander Aleinikoff and Vincent Chetail. The Hague: T.M.C. Asser Press.

OECD (Organisation for Economic Co-operation and Development). 2008a. "West African Mobility and Migration Policies of OECD Countries." OECD West African Studies. OECD Publishing, Paris.

———. 2008b. "Migration Outlook" 2008. OECD Publishing, Paris.

———. 2009. "African Economic Outlook." Development Center and African Development Bank, OECD Publishing, Paris.

Olesen, Henrik. 2002. "Migration, Return and Development: An Institutional Perspective." *International Migration* 40 (5): 125–50.

Panizzon, Marion. 2008. "Labour Mobiilty: A Win-Win-Win Model for Trade and Development: The Case of Senegal." National Center for Competency in Research Working Paper No. 7, Bern.

———. 2010. "Trade and Labor Migration? GATS Mode 4 and Migration Agreements." Friedrich Ebert Stiftung, Dialogue on Globalization Occasional Paper, No. 47 (January), Geneva.

Sassen, Saskia. 1998. *Globalization and its Discontents, Essays on the New Mobility of People and Money.* New York: The New Press.

Sauvé, Pierre. 2008. "Been There, Not Yet Done That: Lessons and Challenges in Services Trade." In *GATS and the Regulation of International Trade in Services,* ed. M. Panizzon, N. Pohl, and P. Sauvé. Cambridge, UK: Cambridge University Press.

Schmitter-Heisler, Barbara. 2008. "The Sociology of Immigration." In *Migration Theory, Talking across Disciplines,* ed. C. Brettell and J. Hollifield, 2nd ed. New York: Routledge.

Senegal, Ministry of Small and Medium Enterprises, Women's Employment and Microfinance. 2006. "Caravane of SMEs in Italy." June. http://www.commerce.gouv.sn/caravanepme_italie.pdf.

Sørensen, N., and N. Van Haer, eds. 2003. *The Migration Development Nexus.* International Organization for Migration, Geneva.

Stark, Oded, and Yong Wang. 2002. "Inducing Human Capital Formation: Migration as a Substitute for Subsidies." *Journal of Public Economics* 86 (1): 29–46.

Stephenson, Sherry, and Thieryy Delourme. 2010. "Labour Mobility and Political Economy Models." Paper prepared for the conference on The Political Economy of Liberalising Trade in Services. The Leonard Davis Institute for International Relations, Hebrew University of Jerusalem. June 14–15.

Tasca, Catherine. 2008. "Report by Mrs Catherine Tasca, Senator to the Commission on Foreign Affairs, Defense and Armed Forces on the Projected Laws Requiring the Approbation of the Agreements on Concerted Migration Management between France and Benin, Congo, Senegal and Tunisia of 10 December 2008." French Senate, Ordinary Session of 2008–2009, Paris.

Terrot, Michel. 2009. "Report by Michel Terrot on behalf of the Commission on Foreign Affairs on the draft laws concerning the approbation by the Senate of the laws authorizing the ratification of the agreements on concerted migration management between the French Government and Benin, Congo and Senegal of 17 February 2009." French National Assembly, No. 1471, Paris.

———. 2010. "Report by Michel Terrot on behalf of the Commission on Foreign Affairs on the draft laws concerning the adoption by the Senate of the laws authorizing the ratification of the agreement between the French Government and the Republic of Mauritius on professionnals' stay and circular migration. French National Assembly, No. 2343, February 24, Paris.

Van Eeckhout, Laetitia. 2009. "Immigration 29796 reconduites à la frontier en 2008." *Le Monde*, Janvier 14.

Van Hear, Nicolas, and Ninna Nyberg Sørensen. 2003. "The Migration-Development Nexus." International Organization for Migration, Geneva.

Wihtol de Wenden, Catherine. 2008. "Co-development Policies in Europe: Objectives, Experiences and Limits." Working Paper, Centre National de la Recherche Scientifique, Paris. November.

World Bank. 2008. *Migration and Remittances Fact Book 2008*. Washington, DC: World Bank.

CHAPTER 8

The Migration for Development in Africa Experience and Beyond[1]

Ndioro Ndiaye, Susanne Melde, and Rougui Ndiaye-Coïc[2]

The Migration for Development in Africa (MIDA) program is a capacity-building initiative whose purpose is to promote development goals through the participation and contribution of members of the African diaspora.[3] The MIDA approach[4] builds on the experience of the International Organization for Migration (IOM) Return of Qualified Nationals (RQN) programs undertaken since 1974, and advocates for a comprehensive long-term strategy. This includes a broad range of actions and concepts, such as the transfer of financial and human capital, the transfer of technology and specific work skills, and migration for development (figure 8.1).[5]

MIDA and similar projects have been developed in response to the increasingly prominent role attributed to migration in national and regional development policies and programs worldwide. To assist in making migration and development policies operational around the world, the optimization of the contributions of members of the diaspora to the development of home countries needs to be further assessed and institutionalized. This gathering of information and resources will provide a broader base of practical references for future program and policy planning.

FIGURE 8.1
MIDA Framework

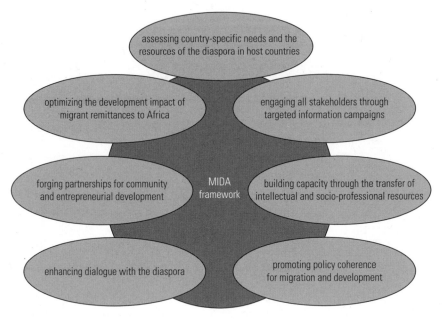

Source: Author.

This chapter describes the progress achieved in the implementation of MIDA projects, highlights essential lessons learned, and identifies elements of good practice that have emerged. Specifically, the chapter:

- Highlights the importance of trust-building mechanisms to develop links with members of the diaspora and of establishing diaspora rosters to "map" them (see subsection on diaspora rosters)
- Elaborates on opportunities and benefits of sharing human and techni- cal resources, especially the added value of involving members of the diaspora for development in MIDA projects
- Illustrates financial transfers on the basis of the MIDA model
- Explains the importance of integrating migration into the development plans of countries with large diasporas
- Presents key findings and recommendations.

Engaging Members of the Diaspora

Members of diasporas are the most important strategic stakeholders in the migration and development field. It is therefore essential that they be involved in policy discussions, since the practical implementation of any policy proposal requires migrants to play a leading role in the process. More important, migrants are the chief agents in the establishment of linkages between migration and development, and without their strategic interventions it is not likely that initiatives on development and migration can succeed or achieve the expected results. This reality makes it impossible to design appropriate policy instruments without creatively tapping into the input and intellectual resources of members of the diasporas, whose wealth of knowledge and practical experiences are largely undercapitalized. It is as simple as this: the best solutions are likely to be worked out when the primary stakeholders—in this case, the migrants—are involved from the outset (African Diaspora Policy Centre 2008).

To mobilize and engage diaspora members in development initiatives, actions are needed by governments and other stakeholders to develop linkages between the diaspora members and their countries of origin. Their level of participation in development initiatives depends to a large extent on the ability to reach and mobilize suitable and committed members. International agencies and representatives of the private sector and civil society can facilitate this process. Outreach and information campaigns are needed in countries of both origin and destination in order to raise awareness and interest on both sides. Formal cooperation and networks can also be established with diaspora (umbrella) associations.

One factor encouraging diaspora involvement is their degree of integration in the host country. The more integrated they are, the more they can concentrate their efforts on exploring opportunities of engagement for their country of origin and mobilizing their community contacts in both host and origin countries for the benefit of development initiatives. Integrated diasporas are more likely to have active partnerships with state actors at the regional, provincial, and municipal levels, and with local nonstate actors to implement projects through technical assistance and matching funds. The experience under the MIDA Italy projects confirms this finding.

In Italy, these partnerships, based on migrants' initiatives, supported 18 rural development programs and trained 40 migrants. Integrated diasporas also create associations and collectively remit for the purpose of investment (Stocchiero 2008). The integration of African migrants in the host countries was also found to be of indirect, albeit salient, significance to the development of Africa. Better integration of migrants in Europe stretches beyond the European context because there is a linear relationship between better integration into the host society and the active contribution to the society. Given this, being active agents in European societies, the diaspora would gain a space to shape policies, including policies that link Europe and Africa (African Diaspora Policy Centre 2008).

Building Trust: Diaspora Dialogues

Trust-building mechanisms are necessary for facilitating linkages with diaspora members. Diaspora members should be regarded and approached as partners and not as mere development resources,[6] especially when mistrust between members of the diaspora and their government might exist. This is important because the nexus between migration and development merits continued consultations and policy dialogue at different societal and policy levels. Furthermore, migration and development can be considerably more beneficial to all if they are effectively addressed as a permanent dialogue between diaspora and other stakeholders in the field. Dialogue mechanisms among diaspora members, host and origin governments, and other stakeholders can play an essential part in creating an environment conducive to the discussion of prodevelopment initiatives.[7]

Diaspora dialogues, which can be formal or informal, have thus become an integral part of many MIDA projects. They are intended to create communication channels and links, and to offer a friendly platform for mutually beneficial interactions among diaspora members, governments, and other stakeholders. One cost-effective approach that has been used with success is video conferencing. Since 2006, Diaspora Dialogue video conferences, each bringing together a range of interested interlocutors, have been conducted on topics as diverse as agriculture, health, human resource development, investment, and private sector development. Countries that have participated in these dialogues include Benin, Burundi, Cape Verde, the Democratic Republic of Congo, Ethiopia, Nigeria, Sudan, and Tanzania[8] (Diene 2007; IOM 2007a).

Research and evaluation are, however, still needed on how the Diaspora Dialogues can be improved and to explore what other confidence-building mechanisms could be implemented[9] in, for instance, postconflict and peace-building settings where the establishment of trust among different actors is seen as a prelude to reconciliation and eventual development activity (Kleist 2008).

Diaspora Rosters

Discussions among diaspora members and governments on how to best reach diaspora members and to ensure their participation in policies and programs have elicited broad agreement on the need for the development of registries, or databases. Once trust is established, these databases can be created. Database information should include the professional qualifications and skills of expatriates living in Europe and North America, and members of diasporas living in countries of the global South who are willing to contribute to migration for development projects. Such diaspora-mapping databases are now a part of most MIDA programs. (See figure 8.2 for an example of the kinds of information included in the MIDA Great Lakes database.)

FIGURE 8.2

Profiles of the 1,100 Candidates Registered in the MIDA Great Lakes Database

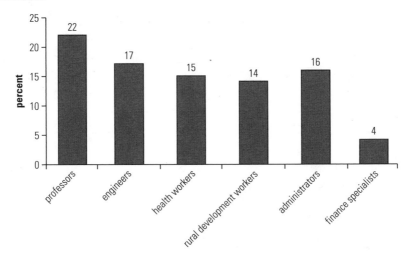

Source: Statistics December 2006—MIDA Great Lakes.

Two of the online databases[10] implemented by IOM are administered centrally in its headquarters in Geneva and gather information on the potential of African diaspora members, with a special focus on African women. Female expatriate experts of African origin, in particular, hold huge potential for contributions to the African development agenda. Indeed, the feminization of migration has led to an enormous untapped resource of highly educated and skilled African women diaspora members. These women can help women in their countries of origin break out of their traditional gender roles. Financial remittances can increase the active participation of all women in the development of their countries. Both migrant women and men send or take home "social remittances" in the form of new skills, attitudes, and knowledge that can lead to new gender norms. The social remittances of migrant women can boost socioeconomic development in their home countries, improve women's health, and promote human rights and gender equality. The social remittances men convey include adopting behavior they observed in other countries, such as choosing their own spouses and doing more of women's traditional work, including child care (UNFPA 2006).

Consequently, IOM, in partnership with the International Labour Organisation, is managing a database called "African Women at the Service of the Union" (ILO and IOM 2002), which has compiled more than 70 biographies[11] of skilled African women who can contribute to the realization of the goals of the African Union. The information resource is also a strategic tool for the promotion of gender equality. Indeed, this initiative may help with the current underrepresenation of women in decision-making positions in Africa. In fact, it might be argued that sustainable development policies will only be fully implemented when they take appropriate account of the principles of gender equality.[12]

Human and Technical Transfers

The MIDA framework model explores innovative possibilities to engage members of the diaspora in a range of actions aimed at harnessing migration for development. One important line of activity consists of opportunities for the temporary or virtual return of diaspora members for whom permanent return might not be a viable option (box 8.1).

BOX 8.1

Different Modalities of Transfer of Intellectual and Socioprofessional Resources

MIDA facilitates the virtual, sequenced or permanent transfer of intellectual and socio-professional resources of the diaspora to support the development of the countries of origin. In order to ensure sustainability, each transfer is brought into line with the national strategy of the respective countries and coordinated with different stakeholders who meet in national MIDA steering committees.

Sequenced/Repeat visits. In some cases, skills or competencies of the diaspora members are required in the country of origin to complement the efforts of colleagues on the job and to bring their international perspective to bear on a given assignment. The MIDA framework envisages that this type of assignment may require a limited number of round-trips, go-and-see visits, to encourage the circulation of skills.

Virtual/tele-work. The use of Information and Communications Technologies has significantly reduced costs, by eliminating—in many cases—the need for physical presence. Digital data broadcasting, distance business transactions (tele-conferencing) and e-learning are among the most cost-effective options for this type of resource transfer.

Permanent relocation. Permanent transfer to the country of origin is based on the voluntary decision of the diaspora member to physically return permanently and to contribute to the development of his or her country.

Source: IOM 2007b, 5.

The cultural and linguistic affinity of diaspora members and migrants with their society of origin and their ability to tackle legal barriers more easily (Devane 2006) are distinct advantages they have over more traditional development experts. Diaspora members and migrants tend to establish contact more quickly, can (re-)adapt more easily to the local context, and are more likely to invest in their country or community of origin than international investors (Kapur 2001).[13] Their high level of personal commitment also brings significant added value to MIDA programs, a fact underlined by their willingness to incur "sacrifices" in the form of unremunerated or annual leave taken or absorption of mortgage costs while away from their residence in the country of destination (IOM, forthcoming).

Transfer of Knowledge and Expertise

The temporary return of diaspora members to share skills and resources under IOM's MIDA programmatic framework aims to partially compensate for the brain drain of highly skilled professionals from developing countries. Ghana, for instance, is facing a high rate of emigration of its health professionals,[14] medical doctors and nurses, in particular. The MIDA Ghana Health Project aims to address this exodus of health workers, which negatively affects the quality of health care services in Ghana. This MIDA Project facilitates periodic and circular,[15] or temporary, returns of qualified health personnel among the Ghanaian diaspora living in the European Union to hospitals and medical training institutions. After an initial assessment of the interest and potential of the Ghanaian diaspora living in the Netherlands to engage in the development of their country of origin, during its second phase (2005–08), the MIDA Ghana Health Project enabled 65 temporary returns. During its current, third phase (2008–12), 150 temporary return assignments are envisaged.

In addition to these short-term missions of Ghanaian diaspora members, the project offers health care training opportunities in the Netherlands and the United Kingdom for capacity building of medical personnel who chose to remain in Ghana.[16] Besides financial support, IOM will provide assistance organizing the assignments and internships. IOM's services will include:

- Assistance with visa and work permit applications
- Organizing travel and lodgings

- Providing health and travel insurance
- Supervision and monitoring during assignments and internships.

The following groups can participate in the project:

- Ghanaians living and working in the Netherlands or other European Union (EU) countries with a relevant background in health care or a related field
- Health workers from Ghana
- Health institutions in Ghana (special attention is given to rural and deprived areas)
- Health institutions in the Netherlands.[17]

Transfer of Technology

A different strategic approach has been applied in the MIDA project implemented by IOM in Ethiopia. As part of this project, referred to as the MIDEth Health Project, technology in the form of medical equipment has been transferred to four hospitals in the country. Members of the Ethiopian diaspora and friends living in the United States donated the equipment, estimated to be worth US$1.8 million to US$2 million, and trained the staff of these hospitals, including in how to use the new technology.[18]

Virtual Transfers

A newer area of MIDA work focuses on the use of e-learning opportunities to enhance virtual transfers. Using new communication technology for the virtual transfer of knowledge has been found to be an innovative means of addressing the shortage and aging of university faculty in certain disciplines. The skills gaps in higher education institutions resulting from high levels of emigration can be reduced by highly skilled experts living abroad providing counseling and training via the Internet. This approach has been used in various MIDA projects, notably in the health sector. It is now clear that communication technology commonly used today enables qualified expatriates to share their expertise with colleagues in their country of origin without necessitating their physical presence in the country (IOM 2005b).[19] The experience in MIDA-type projects, such as MIDA Ghana and the Temporary Return of Qualified Nationals Project implemented by IOM in Afghanistan, Bosnia and Herzegovina, Ethiopia, Georgia,

Sierra Leone, and Sudan, highlighted the constraining lack of availability of this equipment in some host institutions.[20]

Opportunities Through Higher Education Institutions

Universities play a key role in the development of a country by contributing to the creation of a pool of knowledge and skills among those who provide vision and leadership in government, academic circles, business, and civil society.[21] Members of the diaspora can assist in this enterprise by sharing their expertise with their professional counterparts who have chosen to stay in their country of origin.

Sequential short-term assignments have been organized under the MIDA Great Lakes program covering Burundi, the Democratic Republic of Congo, and Rwanda to enable university lecturers to share their skills and assist in the development and teaching of courses (box 8.2). For instance, in 2004, a doctor of Congolese origin living in Belgium developed a distance course in anaesthesiology and intensive care at the University of Lubumbashi, Democratic Republic of Congo, with the MIDA program.[22] This diaspora engagement for development can lead to the establishment of long-term links between institutions and can support the reduction of education costs.

Higher education institutions can make an important contribution to the professional growth of these practitioners, especially by promoting study and research into the relationship between migration and development. To enhance the skills transfers by diaspora members, South-South and North-South twinning arrangements between universities are being explored by IOM. The offer of such migration study courses at universities and through university partnerships across regions can contribute not only to more effective policy formulation on migration management in general, but also to the elaboration of more effective policy linkages between migration and development.

To extend the potential of higher education as a development tool and to address long-term skills shortages, a core human resource planning strategy needs to be devised in crucial development sectors, including health care and education. This strategy should take account of the effects of migration on development in terms of service provision and human capital formation, and include the contribution through the transfer of

BOX 8.2

MIDA Great Lakes – Enhancing the Capacity of the University of Goma

The University of Goma hopes to ensure the autonomy of its "applied geology department" by 2011. Professor Wazi, a researcher at the University of Rouen in France, lends his knowledge and experience to help the University attain this objective. He undertook several MIDA missions to Goma between January 2006 and February 2007. While the MIDA programme had initiated the first steps (i.e., arranging the professor's missions, financing the syllabi, buying microscopes and geological maps, etc.), other partners have since joined in.

The University of Rouen's geology department in France contributes six scientific books to Goma on a weekly basis for a period of 18 months. The association "the friends of Goma" sent 100 books and scientific publications in a container to help researchers, students, and research assistants emerge from their scientific isolation.

Today, local academic personnel are trained to take over Professor Wazi's role in order to assure the independence of the geology department. Based on their personnel evaluation of these missions, both Professor Wazi and IOM are satisfied with the results and progress.

Source: IOM 2007b, 6.

skills and knowledge from migrant communities abroad to skilled workers in countries of origin (World Bank 2007).

Financial Transfers

Diaspora members are more likely to invest in their country or community of origin partly out of their personal affiliation to their home country, and partly because of their lower sensitivity to investment risks compared to international investors (Ratha, Mohapatra, and Plaza 2008). National experts living abroad also tend to be considered more trustworthy investors by government authorities and can pave the way for international investors (GFMD 2008).

Investments

While foreign direct investment can stimulate economic growth, facilitate the transfer of knowledge and technology, and generate employment, these financial transfers to developing countries remain relatively marginal compared to other financial flows.

According to the World Bank, in 2005, about US$167 billion in remittances to developing countries were sent through formal channels. Total remittances, including those sent through informal means, were estimated at over US$250 billion. For many developing countries, the amounts received through the diaspora and migrant remittances are greater than both foreign direct investment and Official Development Assistance. However, the bulk of remittances is spent on consumption rather than direct economic and income-generating activities.

Bringing recipient households into the formal financial sector is only the first step in using remittances more effectively. Country surveys undertaken by the International Monetary Fund indicate that, although households typically spend a large proportion of their remittances, their propensity to save can be as high as 40 percent (IMF 2007). For policy makers, the challenge is therefore to channel these savings into productive uses. This is one of the reasons many governments aim to mobilize the remittance flows received from abroad for investment purposes. According to the International Monetary Fund, banks located in Sub-Saharan Africa are a full part of this endeavor.

Sub-Saharan banks can indeed promote investment from remittances by bundling financial services like savings products and entrepreneurial loans for households that receive remittances. The market is currently dominated by specialized money transfer organizations like Western Union that are less likely to offer their clients ancillary financial products. Banks could also consider using the flow of remittances as collateral for small business loans (IMF 2007). The Government of Senegal, for instance, has identified several infrastructure projects as investment targets[23] (Panizzon 2008).

The MIDA model seeks, in various ways, to promote and facilitate the mobilization of remittances to achieve specific development objectives.

Private Sector Initiatives

The diaspora can act as a catalyst in private sector development. Several initiatives exist to promote diaspora engagement in the private sector with a view of tackling development challenges and opportunities (UNDP 2004). One promising initiative targets entrepreneurs of Sub-Saharan African origin who live in Europe and are willing to support the development efforts of their home countries. The Development Marketplace for African Diaspora in Europe, launched by the World Bank in 2007 with the support of several governments, provides access to funds for pioneering entrepreneurs from Sub-Saharan Africa living in Europe and North America[24] (World Bank 2009).

Financial Assets and Enterprise Creation

Although research on remittances has revealed much information, more analysis is needed on the effectiveness of transfer channels, remitting behavior, and the underlying social determinants guiding it. Different sending patterns between men and women,[25] and the investment climate and social relations determining the productive use of financial transfers, need to be analyzed in more detail. Household surveys, such as the one conducted by IOM (2008) Moldova, are useful means to explore opportunities and tools of achieving investment and development objectives of a country with the support of financial contributions received from members of the diaspora. Factors such as access to the formal banking sector and financial products will be examined in order to design income-generating programs involving diaspora communities and countries of origin.

Access to financial services and transfer services to remit money home can empower migrants and encourage socioeconomic development. The constraints to financial services often include:

- Mistrust on the part of immigrants, which may be related to cultural factors
- A general lack of information on the services available
- Migrants may lack a bank account in the country of origin to which to send the money.

Supply-side factors include:

- Access barriers to money transfer services at banks
- The absence of electronic transaction facilities such as automated teller machines for the direct transfer of remittances
- The possibility that the remittances market is considered a marginal sector in supplies to immigrants (Frigeri and Ferro 2006).

Innovative financial products could support the development and establishment of small and medium enterprises, which in turn create job opportunities and generate income and possibly trade. Access to these funds and related services must reflect the needs and constraints of diaspora members, their families, and the home community members (Frigeri and Ferro 2006).

The initiative implemented by the Netherlands-based Internationalisation of Entrepreneurship (IntEnt) aims to link migrant entrepreneurship and development by encouraging the creation of small and medium enterprises by migrants living in the Netherlands. Over the past 11 years, IntEnt has provided financial backing to enable approximately 2,500 migrants to invest 14.5 million euros, leading to the creation of over 200 businesses and generating employment for almost 1,100 people.[26] The principal lessons learned since the start of the program in 1996 include the relatively long time necessary to establish a business and to relocate to the country of origin, and the importance of social capital in the form of local business networks (IntEnt 2007).[27]

To address the lack of support in identifying, managing, or developing entrepreneurial activities, IOM's MIDA programs offer counseling and training to diaspora members, other interested business partners, and members of their communities of origin. As part of the efforts of the Government of Cape Verde to improve the investment climate in the country, the DIAS de Cabo Verde MIDA Project (DIASpora for DEvelopment of

Cape Verde),[28] implemented by the Institute of the Communities of the Cape Verdean Ministry of Foreign Affairs and IOM, engages the public Agency for Entrepreneurial Development and Innovation (Agência para o Desenvolvimento Empresarial e Inovação) in Cape Verde to offer advice to diaspora members and their business partners from host and origin countries in the area of small and medium enterprise creation and management, and investment opportunities in strategic sectors.

During the MIDA project undertaken in Guinea, prior assessment of the local context demonstrated that the methods used in Europe and North America to stimulate the creation of microenterprises were less applicable to the rural project locations in Guinea.[29] Based on these findings, qualified experts among the Guinean diaspora in the region of the Economic Community of West African States, instead of those living in Europe or North America, provided training to the women beneficiaries in the generation and management of microenterprises.[30] Furthermore, the MIDA Guinea project was built in partnership with the microfinance institution Rural Credit of Guinea,[31] which allowed participants to access small credits on more favorable terms than would be possible with other microcredit institutions. In November 2003, 56 microcredit loans were disbursed to the trainees to create or expand microenterprises. One year later, 55 microcredit loans had been reimbursed. At the end of the reimbursement period, three cooperatives were created by 50 initial beneficiaries. They were trained, in February 2005, to manage a revolving microcredit scheme. In July 2005, they welcomed 52 new members. This bank also offered support and counseling to the participants.

Tutoring and training in enterprise creation and management at specialized institutions in Ghana and Senegal are also a main feature of the MIDA Italy project.[32] Under this project, about 30 small and medium enterprises initiated by diaspora members in their countries of origin in Western Africa received support and cofunding. The empowerment of migrant associations was the goal of this project, because their role in mobilizing support in host and home communities and in promoting productive investments of remittances, as well as building of partnerships and joint ventures, has been acknowledged.[33] In terms of innovative practices concerning credit mechanisms for migrants and diaspora members, prepaid debit cards were developed under the Temporary Return of Qualified Nationals program, mentioned earlier. These cards function as secure money transfer facilities and thus improve financial services for migrants and their families.[34]

Trade Promotion

Compared to foreigners, members of the diaspora have the advantage of better access to information on the investment climate and overall conditions in their country of origin. Their network of business contacts and knowledge of the market places them in a better position to develop trade relations between origin and destination countries (IOM 2005a). In addition, migrants tend to foster the so-called "nostalgia trade" of typical products of the home country that were not available beforehand or whose sales volume might increase with the number of diaspora members buying them for patriotic reasons.

In 2005, Modena province (one of nine provinces in the Emilia-Romagna region of Ghana), together with other local actors, supported the creation of an import/export cooperative—the GhanaCoop—managed by a group of migrant workers living in Modena. Part of their profits has been invested in development projects implemented in the Gomoa Simbrofa village with the purpose of creating jobs and reducing the high poverty rates (Gallina 2007).

Thanks to these commercial relations between Modena and Ghana, an import/export cooperative named "GhanaItal" was later created in Modena, and the "Migrants for GhanaAfrica" cooperative was founded in Gomoa Simbrofo, producing pineapples and fresh vegetables. Besides these productive activities, the Ghanaian community in Italy has raised funds for the electrification of their rural villages. The project is cofunded by Modena Municipality; IOM, through a program financed by the Italian Ministry of Foreign Affairs; the Ghanaians Association of Modena; a local bank (Emilbanca); the Arcadia cooperative; and the Emilia-Romagna regional confederation of farmers' cooperatives.

A relevant economic aspect of the practice is the promotion of a low-cost remittance service offered to migrant workers by GhanaCoop. This service is also intended to raise contributions to cofund, together with other local actors, several social projects, such as Luce per il Ghana (Light for Ghana), completed in July 2006, with the construction of a solar plant in Gomoa Simbrofo to supply around 800 people with clean power (Ceschi and Stocchiero 2006). The economic impact of this project can be measured by the import/export flows, the remittances flows, and the number of jobs created locally (both in Gomoa Simbrofo and Modena). In addition, the project's focus on organic pineapple farming has a positive impact on the environment.

In Italy, the social impact of the project can also be measured in terms of the perception of the migrant workers in Modena by the Italian community and by the perception of the Ghanaian workers of the Italian society (Gallina 2007:20). The project introduces some innovative elements that benefit both Italy and Ghana. GhanaCoop succeeded in inserting its own products in the Transfair (Fair Trade) channels,[35] and in 2006 won the Ethics Award, given to the most innovative fair trade organizations. Since February 2006, typical Emilia-Romagna products have been introduced to the Ghanaian markets through the commercial links established with this project.

Integrating Migration into Development Plans

While the importance of migration for development is increasingly acknowledged, a structured, enabling policy environment is needed to ensure coherence and continuity of effort and, especially, the inclusion of a migration/diaspora platform in development and poverty alleviation strategies.

Opportunities and the Way Forward

Enhancing the positive linkages between migration and development requires coherence among potentially competing but cross-cutting policy agendas in the fields of development, health, labor, migration, security, and social welfare. Consistent and integrated policy approaches in the field of migration and development of national governments and regional and international organizations will increase the development potential of migration.

The MIDA framework aims to contribute to national, regional, and international coherence with regard to migration and development.

On a national level, the MIDA framework will:

- Ensure the integration of migration into government development policies, such as national Poverty Reduction Strategy Papers and national development plans[36]
- Encourage interministerial efforts in both host countries and countries of origin, bringing together relevant ministries whose fields of responsibility directly or indirectly involve migration and/or development.

On a regional level, the MIDA framework will:

- Enhance South-South cooperation by engaging diaspora members resident in other African countries in contributing to the development of their country of origin
- Promote the sharing of skills and expertise on a regional level.

Finally, on an international level, the MIDA framework will:

- Contribute to the establishment of strategies allowing for greater international cooperation, not only between countries of origin and host countries, but also among the diaspora communities as well
- Support the creation of policies for maintenance of the legal status of the African migrants in host countries
- Contribute to the achievement of the Millennium Development Goals.

The African Union recognized members of the African diaspora as key players in its Strategic Plan for 2004–07. African regional economic communities are also directing their work toward strengthening ties between migration and development in Africa. Donor communities and a large range of multilateral organizations have confirmed their interest in the MIDA program and are working closely to reinforce the positive impact and image of diaspora in both countries of origin and host communities. The African Union has adopted significant declarations and decisions targeting the involvement of the African diaspora, as follows:[37]

- In 2001, the African Union endorsed the MIDA program during its 74th ordinary session of the Council of Ministers
- In 2002, the 25th Ordinary Session of the Labour and Social Affairs Commission in Ouagadougou, Burkina Faso, called upon African countries to include MIDA in their national planning processes and in their respective National Indicative Programmes
- In 2003, the African Ministers of Health called upon governments to use African health workers in the diaspora in a range of interventions aimed at harnessing their skills for the benefit of their countries of origin
- 2004 was declared the "Year for Development of Human Resources in Africa"
- In 2006, a common African position on Migration and Development was adopted, as was a Migration Policy Framework and the Joint Africa-EU Declaration on Migration and Development

- In 2006, Article 21 of the African Youth Charter was adopted by the African Ministers of Youth, which states that all parties shall recognize the rights of young people to live anywhere in the world, and which generally encourages young people in the diaspora to engage themselves in development activities in their country of origin
- In 2007, the Executive Council endorsed the Decision on the Africa-EU Ministerial Conference on Migration and Development (Ex.Cl/Dec. 323 [X]) and called upon Member States to develop national plans of action, deploy resources, and report in 2008 on progress made.

All these decisions illustrate the good will and commitment of African governments to include the diaspora and migration in the continent's policies and action plans. (See box 8.3 for examples of plans in the Democratic Republic of Congo and Rwanda.) However, the various stakeholders now

---

BOX 8.3

How the Democratic Republic of Congo and Rwanda Include the Diaspora and Migration Communities in Country Policies and Action Plans

In 2006, the **Democratic Republic of Congo** included the positive contribution of the expertise, knowledge, and human and financial resources of African experts to development facilitated through the MIDA project under pillar 5 of its poverty reduction strategy. This pillar describes the support of a decentralized implementation structure of the poverty alleviation plan and thus envisages the initiation of a national migration for development program. Certain activities carried out in the framework of MIDA Great Lakes in the Democratic Republic of Congo have also been inserted into the Country Assistance Framework and the United Nations Development Assistance Framework (IOM 2008).

In the **Rwandan** Economic Development and Poverty Reduction Strategy (EDPRS), to be implemented during 2008–12 (Republic of Rwanda 2007), MIDA, together with the Transfer of Knowledge Through Expatriate Nationals Program of the United Nations Development Programme,

(continued next page)

BOX 8.3 (continued)

is mentioned as an ongoing activity under the umbrella of the "governance flagship programme."

In Rwanda, the Ministry of Finance, in charge of the coordination and elaboration of the EDPRS, consulted with ministries and local authorities and the private sector. As a civil servant of the Ministry of Labour, the local MIDA coordinator has played an active role in the insertion of MIDA into the strategic plan of the Ministry. Since the Ministry of Labour is taking the lead in the "Capacity Building and Employment Promotion" sector within the EDPRS, its strategic plan, and especially the role of the diaspora, has been included within the EDPRS.

The general political support that the Government of Rwanda has given to the role of its diaspora in recent years should be recognized as an important driving factor for the inclusion of migration into the Poverty Reduction Strategy Papers. Examples include the creation of a Directorate General within the Ministry of Foreign Affairs in charge of diaspora, annual diaspora conferences in Rwanda, and regular meetings between the President of Rwanda and the diaspora residing abroad.

Source: Information obtained via personal communication with Géraldine Ansart, Project Assistant, MIDA Great Lakes Programme, IOM Brussels, February 23, 2009.

need to work together to implement the decisions taken by policy makers in order for MIDA to achieve its objectives in a sustainable way. The way forward for MIDA consists of:

- Integrating MIDA into a broader development framework
- Strengthening partnerships with a large variety of interlocutors, notably, diaspora associations, the private sector, international agencies, research institutes, and recruitment agencies
- Systematically incorporating the gender dimension in all MIDA programs
- Reinforcing regional integration and cooperation for the mobilization of members of the diaspora.

Conclusions

Diaspora members of developing countries can make valuable contributions to the development efforts of their countries of origin. To fully tap that potential, links between origin countries and diaspora members need to be developed, strengthened, or both. Building trust and fostering dialogue among diaspora members, governments, and other actors is crucial in this endeavor. Based on interactive exchanges, an environment conducive to the discussion of development actions among the key stakeholders can be created.

The MIDA operational framework provides comprehensive strategic approaches to mobilize diasporas for development. Sharing of human and financial capital through temporary and virtual return and transferring technology offer opportunities to reverse brain drain in developing countries by building critical capacity. By addressing the skills gaps as a consequence of high levels of emigration among certain professionals from developing countries, MIDA projects can facilitate the process of using the expertise, knowledge, and skills diaspora members have acquired and are willing to share with their communities of origin.

The specific characteristics of each country and region need to be carefully factored into any practical and policy approach regarding migration for development. In addition, gender concerns should be assessed and addressed in policies and programs to harness the development potential of diasporas.

Despite being important development agents, involving diaspora members in development efforts should be complemented by other strategies. Their involvement should be part of an overall human resources planning strategy that addresses skills gaps in key development sectors. Universities have a key role to play in this regard. Diaspora members can contribute to human capital formation through transferring skills to lecturers at higher education institutions and training of trainers in areas that face a manpower shortage.

Including migration in the formulation of development policy can help ensure coherent and sustainable outcomes in the long term. Therefore, a policy environment is needed that fosters including the human mobility dimension in development and poverty reduction strategies and that acknowledges and facilitates the role of diasporas in development. Currently, however, only a few countries mention diasporas and migration in their development plans, and ways are needed to track this progress.

To assist in the process of using migration for development projects that foster diaspora contributions, governments can benefit from past experiences and insights gained from projects in various regions of the world, such as the MIDA programs and other projects based on this approach that are being implemented outside of Africa. Since these programs are linked to the priorities of the national development frameworks, their experiences can offer lessons learned and good practices on engaging diasporas in development initiatives of their countries of origin. The MIDA framework can also be extended to countries in other regions, such as Asia and Latin America, concerned with the emigration of professionals. The Migration for Development project in Latin America is one, for example, that is in its initial stages.

Notes

1. This chapter is based on *Operationalizing Migration for Development Across Regions—The MIDA Experience and Beyond*, International Organization for Migration 2009.
2. The authors would like to acknowledge the contribution of Meera Sethi, and to thank Gervais Appave, Christophe Franzetti, Paul Tacon, and Elizabeth Warn for their insightful comments on an earlier version of this chapter; and Ken Goenawan for his assistance.
3. In 2005, the following definition of African Diaspora was submitted to the Executive Council of the African Union for consideration by the African Union: "The African Diaspora consists of peoples of African origin living outside the continent, irrespective of their citizenship and nationality and who are willing to contribute to the development of the continent and the building of the African Union."
4. RQN programs have been conducted in Latin America since 1974, and were expanded to Africa in 1983 and to Asia in 1989. The RQN program in Africa started with three pilot countries, Kenya, Somalia, and Zimbabwe, in 1983, and was later extended to Ghana, Uganda, and Zambia. Funded by the European Community, the resulting return of 550 nationals slightly exceeded the expected number of participants. A similar program entailing returns from the United States was implemented until 1989 and facilitated the return of 150 African experts over a three-year period (Ducasse-Rogier 2001; ICM 1987; IOM 2001). Drawing on its experience with RQN programs in Africa, Asia, and Latin America, and informed by evaluations of previous models, IOM organized a workshop in Libreville in April 2001, which provided a forum

for African countries to discuss and contribute to the development of a new migration for development framework model (MIDA) adapted to changing realities. In July 2001, the MIDA program was endorsed by the Organization of African Unity (now the African Union) Council of Ministers in Lusaka in its Decision 614, requesting IOM to encourage African countries to give migration issues greater priority in their development policy making.

5. Understood as the concept revolving around the positive contribution of migration to development, in contradistinction to "migration and development," which includes the aspect of fostering economic and community development in areas of high emigration pressure.

6. Information obtained via interview with Peter Schatzer, IOM Rome, January 16, 2009.

7. The United States Institute of Peace hosted a series of workshops, "Trans-Atlantic Diaspora Dialogue," October 16, 2009; "Leveraging International Support to Build Peace in the Democratic Republic of Congo," March 18, 2010; and "Responsive and Accountable Leadership for a Peaceful and Prosperous Congo: Voices of the Diaspora," May 14, 2010, geared toward energizing members of the Congolese diaspora to contribute more effectively to conflict management and peace promotion in the Democratic Republic of Congo.

8. http://www.iom.int/jahia/webdav/site/myjahiasite/shared/shared/mainsite/published_docs/Diaspora%20Dialogue.pdf.

9. Based on information obtained by Elizabeth Warn, Migration and Development Focal Point, Labour and Facilitated Migration, IOM Headquarters Geneva, Switzerland, via communication dated May 12, 2009.

10. The Diaspora Database, http://www.iom.int/jahia/Jahia/pid/1810; and the African Women Database, http://www.iom.int/jahia/Jahia/pid/1904.

11. Each biography contains personal information and information on the educational background, professional experience, and the field in which each woman can potentially contribute.

12. According to Helen Clark, United Nations Development Programme Administrator, "Development cannot be achieved if 50% of the population is excluded from the opportunities it brings."

13. The factors that shape the role of diasporas in technology transfer are related to the broader set of factors that affect the forms and degree of engagement of the diaspora with the source country.

14. In 2000, over 500 nurses—more than double the number of graduates that year—left Ghana (Kingma 2007; Little and Buchan 2007). Thirteen percent of Ghanaian nurses and midwives live in seven Organisation for Economic Co-operation and Development countries (Canada, Denmark, Finland, Ireland, Portugal, the United Kingdom, and the United States) (WHO 2006b).

15. The Global Forum on Migration and Development defines circular migration as "the fluid movement of people between countries, including temporary or more permanent movement which, when it occurs voluntarily and is linked to the labor needs of countries of origin and destination, can be beneficial to all involved."

16. Information obtained via personal communication from Joost Van der Aalst, Chief of Mission, IOM the Netherlands; and Ralph Welcker, Manager, Migration and Development Department, IOM the Netherlands of May 14 and June 11, 2009.

17. For more information on the program, see http://www.iom-nederland .nl/dsresource?type=pdf&objectid=iom:1414&versionid=&subobjectname=.

18. Information obtained via personal communication from Charles Kwenin, Chief of Special Liaison Mission, IOM Addis Ababa, Ethiopia, of November 10, 2008.

19. In the framework of the MIDA Great Lakes program, a doctor and member of the Congolese diaspora in Belgium has taught two courses in anaesthesiology and intensive care to over 700 students at the University of Lubumbashi, the Democratic Republic of Congo. The courses were prepared in close collaboration with the Université Libre de Bruxelles in Belgium. (Information provided by Tamara Keating, Great Lakes program coordinator, IOM Brussels, was used in this section.)

20. Information obtained via communication with Ralph Welcker, Manager Migration & Development Department, IOM The Hague, the Netherlands, May 14, 2009.

21. As stated in 2000 by Kofi Annan, former United Nations Secretary General, "the university must become a primary tool for Africa's development in the new century. Universities can help develop African expertise; they can enhance the analysis of African problems; strengthen domestic institutions; serve as a model environment for the practice of good governance, conflict resolution and respect for human rights, and enable African academics to play an active part in the global community of scholars" (UNIS 2000). The New Partnership for Africa Development framework clearly specifies its "support of the immediate strengthening of the University system across Africa, including the creation of specialised universities where needed, building on available African teaching staff" (African Union 2001:30).

22. For more information, see: http://mida.belgium.iom.int/index.php?option= com_content&task=view&id=105&Itemid=111.

23. The construction of large houses for migrant workers in West Africa has spurred local economic activity through multiplier effects. In Mexico, the Sociedad Hipotecaria Federal, a government financial institution, provides long-term financing and partial mortgage insurance to Mexican mortgage providers that extend peso-denominated loans to emigrants for housing construction in Mexico. The scheme simultaneously encourages remittances and their productive use. Because of Africa's inadequate financial infrastructure, similar schemes can be more challenging to launch there, but they can spur a sustained housing boom with positive spillovers on the real and financial sectors of the economy.

24. For more information on this program, see: www.dmade.org. Sixteen winners from seven European countries were awarded approximately 600,000 euro

for the completion of projects to be implemented in 11 Sub-Saharan African countries.

25. According to a study by AfroNeth, remittances have a gender dimension, since women among the African Diaspora send a far greater proportion of money back home than men. This is mainly for two reasons. First, women tend to have limited socializing activities outside the home due to cultural reasons and thus tend to save more than men. Second, African women in the Netherlands use a rotating credit system whereby a group of women collects money from each other that is then given as a lump sum to a single member each month (Mohamoud 2003).

26. As of the end of 2007, most migrants invested in Suriname (over 800), Ghana (over 450), Morocco (320), and the Netherlands Antilles (215). Of enterprises created, 85 percent are still in business three years on. See: http://www .ondernemenoverdegrens.nl/indexuk.htm.

27. To this end, IntEnt has created so-called "business clubs" of migrant entrepreneurs linked to existing small and medium enterprise networks (IntEnt 2007).

28. DIAS de Cabo Verde is a project promoted by the Instituto das Comunidades de Cabo Verde and cofinanced by the European Commission and the Portuguese Government. IOM is the implementing partner in the project targeting Cape Verdeans residing in Italy, the Netherlands, and Portugal. IOM organizes networking missions to Cape Verde for interested entrepreneurs of the Cape Verdean diaspora to establish or foster contacts with local actors and to assess the feasibility of the business idea to facilitate transnational partnerships by linking interest and facilities. (Based on information received via personal communication with Monica Goracci, Chief of Mission, and Marta Bronzin, Project Assistant, IOM Lisbon, Portugal, June 22, 2009.)

29. For more information, please see the IOM's "Final Report to the Government of the United States, MIDA: Micro-enterprise Development for Guinean Women through the Provision of Micro-credits and Mobilization of Women from the Diaspora"; http://www.iom.int/jahia/webdav/site/myjahiasite/ shared/shared/mainsite/projects/documents/mida_final_report.pdf.

30. See IOM (2005a, 47) for more details. The MIDA Guinea project allows highly qualified expatriates from the Guinean diaspora to pass on the knowledge and know-how gained in destination countries to their fellow nationals at home.

31. Rural Credit of Guinea is present in remote and urban areas not covered by the classic banking system, enabling otherwise excluded rural and urban populations to access and benefit from their financial services. The reinforcement of the existing microfinance institutions was also in line with current Guinean national policies in this area.

32. Supported by the Italian Ministry of Foreign Affairs, one important outcome of the MIDA Italy project is the inclusion of the migration and development nexus in many local authorities' cooperation and development policies, such as the policy adopted by the Milan municipality.

33. Information obtained via personal communication from Tana Anglana and Elisa Piraccini, IOM Mission with Regional Functions, Rome, June 18, 2009.
34. Information obtained via communication with Ralph Welcker, Manager Migration & Development Department, IOM The Hague, Netherlands, May 14, 2009.
35. Personal communication with Tana Anglana, MIDA Project Manager, February 22, 2007.
36. Aspects of migration and the MIDA framework have been incorporated into the Poverty Reduction Strategy Papers of the Democratic Republic of Congo. The MIDA framework has been incorporated into the Strategy Document of the Ministry of Labour and Public Service of Rwanda. The Government of Burundi has adopted a "Strategic Framework of Growth and the Right Against Poverty" (Cadre stratÈgique de lutte contre la pauvreté), which includes the role and importance of the diaspora for the development of the country.
37. www.africa-union.org.

References

African Diaspora Policy Centre. 2008. "Engaging African Diaspora in Europe as Strategic Agents for Development in Africa." Seminar Report, June 25–26, Brussels.

African Union. 2001. "The New Partnership for Africa's Development," October. http://www.nepad.org/2005/files/documents/inbrief.pdf.

Ceschi, S., and A. Stocchiero. 2006. "Iniziative di partenariato per il co-sviluppo. La diaspora ghanese e senegalese e la ricerca azione CeSPI-OIM." Strategy Paper, Progetto MIDA Ghana Senegal, Rome, November.

Devane, R. 2006. "The Dynamics of Diaspora Networks: Lessons of Experience." In *Diaspora Networks and the International Migration of Skills*, ed. Y. Kuznetsov. World Bank Institute Development Studies. Washington, DC: World Bank.

Diene, M. 2007. "Dialogues with the Diasporas: Setting an Agenda for Development." *Migration*, Special Edition, July. International Organization for Migration, Geneva.

Ducasse-Rogier, M. 2001. *The International Organization for Migration 1951–2001*. Geneva: International Organization for Migration.

Frigeri, D., and A. Ferro. 2006. "Financial Instruments for the Optimization of the Role of Remittances in Development." Strategy Paper, MIDA Ghana/Senegal project. Centro Studi di Politica Internazionale and International Organization for Migration, Rome, November.

Gallina, A. 2007. "Migration & Development Linkage in Italy: A De-centralized Approach." Research Report Number 1/2007, Roskilde University, Roskilde, Denmark.

GFMD (Global Forum on Migration and Development). 2008. "Empowering Migrants and Diasporas to Contribute to Development." Roundtable 1.2 Working Paper. <http://government.gfmd2008.org/component/option,com_docman/Itemid,45/task,cat_view/gid,35/>.

ILO and IOM (International Labour Organisation and International Organization for Migration). 2002. *African Women at the Service of the Union.* ILO and IOM, Geneva, November. http://www.ilo.org/dyn/gender/docs/RES/300/F271144637/Directory%20African%20Women%20rev2.pdf.

IMF (International Monetary Fund). 2007. "Impact of Remittances on Poverty and Financial Development in Sub-Saharan Africa." IMF Working Paper No. 07/38. International Monetary Fund, Washington, DC.

IntEnt (International Entrepreneurship). 2007. "Migrant Entrepreneurs in the Driver's Seat." Presentation at European Conference Equal Opportunities For All, Citizenship and Human Capital in a Diverse Europe, November 28–29.

Intergovernmental Committee for Migration (ICM, later IOM). 1987. "Evaluation Report on the Implementation of the Project Expansion of ICM's Return of Talent Program to Africa from the USA." Intergovernmental Committee for Migration, Geneva, March.

IOM (International Organization for Migration). 2001. Report on the Technical Workshop on Migration for Development in Africa (MIDA), held in Libreville, Gabon, April 9–11, 2001, International Organization for Migration, Geneva.

———. 2005a. "Policy Approaches to Migration and Development." 2005. International Dialogue on Migration, IOM 90th Council Session, November 29–30. http://www.iom.int/jahia/webdav/shared/shared/mainsite/about_iom/en/council/90/MCinf281.pdf.

———. 2005b. *World Migration Report 2008. Costs and Benefits of International Migration*, Vol. 3, IOM World Migration Report Series, International Organization for Migration, Geneva.

———. 2007a. *Diaspora Dialogues.* Geneva: International Organization for Migration.

———. 2007b. *MIDA: Mobilizing the African Diasporas for the Development of Africa.* Geneva: International Organization for Migration.

———. 2008. "Programme de mobilisation des ressources de la communauté burundaise, congolaise et rwandaise de l'exterieur pour le developpement des pays des grands lacs." Programme MIDA Grands Lacs IV, Project document. International Organization for Migration, Brussels.

———. Forthcoming. *Operationalizing Migration for Development Across Regions – The MIDA Experience and Beyond.* Geneva: International Organization for Migration.

Kapur, Devesh. 2001. "Diasporas and Technology Transfer." *Journal of Human Development* 2 (2): 265–86.

Kingma, M. 2007. *Nurses on the Move: Migration and the Global Health Care Economy.* Ithaca, NY: Cornell University Press.

Kleist, N. 2008. "Mobilising 'The Diaspora': Somali Transnational Political Engagement." *Journal of Ethnic and Migration Studies* 34 (2) (March): 307–23.

Little, L., and J. Buchan. 2007. "Nursing Self-Sufficiency/Sustainability in the Global Context." International Centre on Nurse Migration, Geneva. http://www.ichrn.com/publications/policyresearch/SelfSufficiency.pdf.

Mohamoud, A. 2003. "African Diaspora and African Development." Background Paper for AfroNeth, presented December 5, Sahan Wetenschappelijk Adviesbureau, Amsterdam.

Panizzon, M. 2008. "Labour Mobility – A Win-Win-Win Model for Trade and Development. The Case of Senegal." Discussion paper, Geneva Trade and Development Forum, April.

Ratha, D., S. Mohapatra, and S. Plaza. 2008. "Beyond Aid: New Sources and Innovative Mechanisms for Financing Development in Sub-Saharan Africa." Policy Research Working Paper 4609, the World Bank Development Prospects Group, Migration and Remittances Team, Washington, DC, April. http://www-wds.worldbank.org/servlet/WDSContentServer/WDSP/IB/2008/04/28/000158349_20080428101826/Rendered/PDF/wps4609.pdf.

Republic of Rwanda. 2007. "Economic Development and Poverty Reduction Strategy, 2008–2012." Ministry of Finance and Economic Planning, September. http://siteresources.worldbank.org/INTPRS1/Resources/Rawanda_PRSP(March-2008).pdf.

Stocchiero, A. 2008. "Learning by Doing: Migrant Transnationalism for Local Development in MIDA Italy – Ghana/Senegal Programme." Working Papers 48/2008/EN, Centro Studi di Politica Internazionale, Rome, October. http://www.cespi.it/WP/WP-48-eng%20mida%20stocchiero.pdf.

UNDP (United Nations Development Programme). 2004. *Unleashing Entrepreneurship: Making Business Work for the Poor.* Commission on the Private Sector and Development, Report to the Secretary-General of the United Nations, United Nations Development Programme, New York, March 1.

UNFPA (United Nations Population Fund). 2006. *The UNFPA State of the World Population 2006.* New York: United Nations.

UNIS (United Nations Information Service). 2000. "Information Technology Should Be Used to Tap Knowledge from Greatest Universities to Bring Learning to All." Former UN Secretary General, speech upon receiving an honorary degree from the University of Ghana. UNIS/SG/2625, Ghana, August. http://www.unis.unvienna.org/unis/pressrels/2000/sg2625.html.

World Bank. 2007. *Mobilizing the African Diaspora for Development.* Washington, DC: World Bank. http://siteresources.worldbank.org/INTDIASPORA/General/21686696/conceptnote.pdf.

————. 2009. "Promoting Diaspora Investments and Innovative Entrepreneurial Activities in Africa." Development Marketplace for African Diaspora in Europe. http://www.dmade.org/.

Interviews/Communication

Anglana, Tana, IOM Mission with Regional Functions, Rome, Italy, via telephone interview on January 16, 2009 and via personal communication of June 18, 2009.

Ansart, Géraldine, Project Assistant, MIDA Great Lakes Programme, IOM Brussels, via communication of February 12 and 23, 2009.

Bronzin, Marta, Project Assistant, IOM Lisbon, Portugal, via personal communication of June 22, 2009.

Goracci, Monica, Chief of Mission, IOM Lisbon, Portugal, via personal communication of June 22, 2009.

Keating, Tamara, MIDA Great Lakes Programme Coordinator, IOM Brussels, Belgium, via telephone interview of January 13, 2009.

Kwenin, Charles, Chief of Special Liaison Mission, IOM Addis Ababa, Ethiopia, via personal communication of November 10, 2008.

Piraccini, Elisa, IOM Mission with Regional Functions, Rome, via personal communication of June 18, 2009.

Schatzer, Peter, Regional Representative, IOM Mission with Regional Functions, Rome, Italy, via interview of January 16, 2009.

Van der Aalst, Joost, Chief of Mission, IOM the Netherlands, via communication of May 14, 2009.

Warn, Elizabeth, Migration and Development Focal Point, Labour and Facilitated Migration, IOM Headquarters Geneva, Switzerland, via communication of May 12, 2009.

Welcker, Ralph, Manager Migration and Development Department, IOM Mission, The Hague, the Netherlands, via telephone interview of March 19, 2009 and communications of April 2, May 14, and June 11, 2009.

CHAPTER 9

Reinforcing the Contributions of African Diasporas to Development

Chukwu-Emeka Chikezie

Human beings have long used migration as a means of survival and renewal and in their search for new beginnings. Indeed, the term "diaspora," meaning "dispersed people," originally referred to Jewish people and their historically tragic condition of displacement and longing for their own homeland. The term diaspora is used here in its more generic sense to refer to any group of people with a shared sense of identity and a connection to a real or imagined place or sense of origin and "home" elsewhere. Given that Africa is the birthplace of humankind, without migration, today's world of continents with diverse peoples and cultures is unimaginable.

In the past 200 years of human history, we have clear instances in which the African diaspora has played a pivotal role in the affairs of Africa. One example is freed slaves, such as Olaudah Equiano,[1] who found their way to 18th century London and played a leading role in the abolition of the Atlantic Slave Trade and in setting the sail of the first ship of people hoping to resettle back in Africa, starting with what became known as Freetown, today the capital of Sierra Leone.

Similarly, in the aftermath of World War II, activists from various parts of the British Empire used the 1945 Fifth Pan-African Congress in Manchester, England to make a clarion call for independence. The struggle against apartheid in South Africa was another rallying point for the African diaspora, particularly among African-American students, whose campaigns for divestiture supported internal efforts to weaken the apartheid regime and bring about momentous change.

Today, if there is a big rallying point for the African diaspora, it is probably the fight against poverty. As early as the 1970s, Jamaican reggae singers such as Bob Marley and Dennis Brown were lamenting the replacement of the chains of slavery with the bonds of poverty.

These facts place today's development challenges in Africa in a historical context that might make sense to many Africans in the diaspora. They also remind African governments, especially, that while their quest to engage their own citizens abroad—the so-called neo-African diaspora—is understandable, African identities are complex, and that the challenges and opportunities of engaging the older, wider African diaspora are important and potentially rewarding, and the children and grandchildren of even contemporary African migrants represent an important resource to address and engage.

The purpose of this chapter is to help African governments identify ways to capitalize on the asset that the African diaspora represents and to better systematize the diaspora's contributions to Africa's development. The chapter:

- Outlines four key principles that underpin sound engagement with the African diaspora
- Focuses on enterprise development and the creation of jobs as one key outcome to which the African diaspora can contribute
- Provides an overview of a policy framework that might shape engagement with the diaspora
- Considers the different forms of capital that the diaspora brings to the table and specific policies and mechanisms that African governments can deploy to harness this "capital"
- Discusses the motivations that shape the African diaspora's engagement with Africa
- Presents an overall strategic framework that African governments might adapt to their specific needs and contexts
- Offers a number of recommendations for African governments and regional bodies such as the African Union

- Provides suggestions about what African governments can do on the proverbial "Monday morning," given the capacity constraints that hamper most of their efforts.

The chapter draws on the author's experience as cofounder and first executive director (1999–2009) of the London-based African Foundation for Development (formed in 1994), and as a consultant helping development agencies and governments devise engagement strategies with the African diaspora and harnessing the African diaspora's resources for private sector development in Africa. In its first 10 years of operation, the African Foundation for Development (a) helped raise awareness of the African diaspora's actual and potential contributions to Africa's development; (b) helped inform and shape policies aimed at tapping into the diaspora's resources in flexible ways that do not require permanent return; and (c) helped build the capacity of U.K.-based African diaspora organizations. More recently, the African Foundation for Development has focused on harnessing the African diaspora's resources to support entrepreneurs in creating and sustaining jobs in Africa and has developed innovative programs in several African countries to that end.

Principles of Engagement

African governments would be wise to pay attention to the following four principles when trying to engage the African diaspora to contribute to their home country development:

- Principle 1: Not only *be* inclusive but *be seen* as inclusive
- Principle 2: Orient engagement efforts around clearly defined development outcomes and results (as opposed to indulging in tokenism, propaganda, or public relations)
- Principle 3: Know and understand the diaspora and meet members half way
- Principle 4: Be strategic in focusing on needs and priorities; that is, insist on being demand driven, not supply led, and focus on both the country's and the diaspora's strengths while avoiding exacerbating the weaknesses and capacity constraints of both.

Inclusiveness

As mentioned, diasporic identities are complex and multifaceted. At the same time, for many African countries, nation building is a work in progress. A key difference between the old and new African diaspora is the unit of Africa with which members of the disapora relate. Africa's old diaspora, now to be found in the "New World" of the Americas, the Caribbean, and Europe, (through multiple waves of migration, for example, from Africa to the Caribbean and then onto the United Kingdom), tends to relate to Africa as a whole, because there is usually no known point of departure or reference (although recent trends in DNA testing demonstrate the demand that exists to know specific places of origin). In contrast, those who left Africa in more recent times have specific countries, regions, towns, villages, schools, and so forth with which they can and do relate. Given that patterns of migration often correlate with a country's political and economic turmoil in the postcolonial period, Africans in the diaspora often have complex and ambivalent relationships with their home countries.

African governments are caught between these two reference points. In theory, at least, they bear responsibility for national development, while segments of their diaspora may wish to engage in subnational development in ways that might even risk exacerbating patterns of internal regional inequality. Nonetheless, recent trends in democratic governance in Africa have greatly enhanced the legitimacy of regimes across the continent and the goodwill that the African diaspora feels toward them.

Postconflict countries face particular challenges and opportunities in engaging their diasporas in the task of rebuilding and developing the country. Identity and who really belongs is often a subtext of many contemporary conflicts in Africa. In such polarized contexts, diasporas can fuel divisions through their own intense experiences of identity. At the same time, populations that remained at home during the conflict often feel that, having borne its brunt, they should enjoy the lion's share of any peace dividend, such as jobs. Resentments often build up between returnees and "stayees" when, for example, the former, who often have more financial and other resources and more recognizable skill sets, land the plumb jobs and occupations in the postconflict rebuilding phase. Liberia, Sierra Leone, South Africa, and Southern Sudan all have examples of such tensions between returning exiles and those who remained at home.

In engaging their diasporas, African governments must be sensitive to these tensions. In many cases, it is the perception that only certain diaspora groups are being courted or are attractive that governments must counter. For instance, studies (Lubkemann 2008) point to the heterogeneity of the Liberian diaspora, many members of which have been returning since the conflict ended. Yet, the general perception among certain segments of the population has been that the Liberian government is paving the way for only a privileged elite wishing to return and reclaim lost assets, positions, and status. Similarly, the Government of Sierra Leone has proactively engaged the Sierra Leone diaspora (the president, elected in 2007, established an office for diaspora affairs within the presidency). However, years of diaspora citizen mistrust of their home government means that the government has an uphill task to reassure members of the diaspora that the engagement is intended to include everyone, not just the politically connected, and that efforts are not just propaganda aimed at maintaining the government's popularity.

African governments need to pay close attention to the retention of people at home while wooing those abroad. They need to couch the development challenge in ways that appeal to those who may feel most passionate about specific locations or subgroups while holding the whole nation together. At the same time, for historical reasons, some countries have special appeal to a wider African diaspora (Ghana, Liberia, and South Africa are examples), and those countries have the opportunity to reach out to these groups to include them in the pact for development.

Outcomes and Results Orientation

In the 1990s, some host country governments in the developed world (especially Europe) sought to engage migrants in development mainly to achieve the goal of immigration control (return of unwanted migrants). To achieve that goal, governments emphasized the potential role of immigrants to contribute to development in their countries of origin. These efforts were a dismal failure. Many of these same countries have recently "discovered" the diaspora (with less emphasis now on migrants) as a potential development resource. In the United Kingdom, for example, the first postdiscovery phase focused on diaspora engagement almost as an end in itself (not least because so little of development practice up to that point involved diaspora or ethnic minority input or involvement).

Now, however, the need to make clear distinctions between immigration and development policy is recognized, and it is understood that subjecting the latter to the demands of the former is counterproductive (Argunias Rannveig and Newland 2007) (although tensions remain because immigration and development concerns tend to pull in different directions). At the same time, there is a growing recognition that engaging members of diasporas as an end in itself is unhelpful. Many diaspora individuals and groups act precisely to achieve specific development outcomes, even if they do not necessarily frame their actions in terms of the Millennium Development Goals or other such purposes (Ndofor-Tah 2000).

Members of diasporas are, for example, typically interested in achieving poverty reduction goals through enterprise development and job creation, and in achieving socially oriented goals in the areas of health and education (although many diaspora actors are more likely to be inspired to engage around wealth creation and achieve more aspirational goals than are conventionally expressed by mainstream development actors). This chapter does not argue that African governments should limit their focus to development outcomes in these particular areas but that it is advisable for the goals of governments to be oriented toward developmental and results-oriented outcomes. There are three reasons:

- Africa faces clear and pressing development challenges
- Having measurable objectives and targets will help African governments undertake the necessary cost-benefit assessments to justify effort and resource expenditure in relation to returns on investment
- A results-oriented focus will help sustain and legitimize such efforts and thus create a virtuous cycle of development.

Knowing the Diaspora

It is a maxim of good marketing that you must know and understand your customers in order to win their business and serve them. The same principle applies for African governments reaching out to their diasporas. It is impossible to engage effectively or meaningfully with the African diaspora without first understanding what their strengths are and how to communicate with them, a subject that will be discussed in greater detail below.

Strategic Approach

African governments typically face certain capacity constraints within state structures and institutions, and these constraints frame the development challenge they face. African diaspora groups also face a number of organizational constraints. Most operate on a purely voluntary basis, so members must balance family and work obligations; organizations are not necessarily formally constituted as development organizations; and they often have multiple agendas. Yet, African governments and the diaspora have their respective strengths, needs, and priorities. It is important, therefore, as explained below, that African governments embark upon this venture in a sustained, systematic way that enhances capabilities and delivers tangible benefits.

Critics of previous development efforts have often complained that they have been too externally driven, overlooking or undermining Africa's own internally generated ideas and solutions to the continent's problems. It would be a mistake, therefore, not to take to heart this lesson in engaging with the African diaspora. In their enthusiasm to contribute, members of the African diaspora might imagine that they have all the solutions to Africa's problems. However, while fresh ideas and approaches are an essential ingredient in Africa's development, it is vital that countries focus on their needs and insist on being demand driven, not supply led. Moreover, it is now understood that solutions need to take firm root among the people they are meant to benefit, if they are not home grown, to secure wide ownership and legitimacy.

In keeping with these principles, the remainder of this chapter will focus on ways that African governments can harness the African diaspora's resources to enhance enterprise development outcomes in Africa.

Focus on Jobs

In October 2007, the United Nations General Assembly adopted a new target for the first Millennium Development Goal, which aims to halve the number of people living in poverty by 2015: "Achieve full and productive employment and decent work for all, including women and young people."

This presents a useful context for a discussion on the African diaspora's role in contributing to poverty reduction in Africa. Indeed, the Economic Commission for Africa has argued that Sub-Saharan Africa must create 8 million jobs a year every year to satisfy the growing number of job seekers (ECA 2006a). At the same time, focusing on the least developed countries (LDCs), the United Nations Conference on Trade and Development points out that:

> *[I]n almost all the LDCs there is an imbalance between the rate of growth of the labour force, which is very rapid owing to population growth, and the rate of capital accumulation and technological progress, which is generally slow. As a result, most workers have to earn their living using their raw labour, with rudimentary tools and equipment, little education and training, and poor infrastructure. Labour productivity is low and there is widespread underemployment. This is the basic cause of persistent mass poverty in the LDCs.* (UNCTAD 2006:x)

The quest for productivity improvements is relevant for both developed and developing countries. In the United Kingdom, the Department of the Treasury (finance ministry) has identified five drivers of productivity: (a) skills, (b) investment, (c) innovation, (d) enterprise, and (d) competition. In Africa, in addition to infrastructure, good governance might also be added, drawing on the way, for instance, postelection violence in Kenya in 2008 destroyed productivity and wealth creation prospects almost overnight.

In recognition of the pivotal role that the private sector must play in tackling poverty in Africa, many African governments have developed or are developing private sector development strategies at the core of their efforts to transform their countries. Most likely, any such strategy will incorporate some variation of the five drivers the United Kingdom has identified, tailored to the specific country's circumstances.

The key message is that this is the starting point for any discussion about tapping into the African diaspora's resources to develop the country—there has to be some sense of what the country needs, what its own framework is, what it is seeking to achieve, what its demands are, and so forth.[2] This is the necessary antidote to drifting into being supply-led and possibly pursuing a number of unfocused agendas that do not deliver useful results.

With this clear sense of purpose and direction, it then helps to understand what members of the diaspora bring to the table and what motivates them, which is the focus of the next section.

Understanding the Diaspora

Diasporas are most celebrated for the remittances they send "home" to their countries of origin. However, it is useful to think of multiple forms of diaspora capital with implications for development.

The 5Cs of Diaspora Capital

The 5Cs of diaspora capital are:

- *Financial capital:* As noted, remittances are probably the most tangible "currency" of the migration-development debate. Recipients put remittances to a variety of uses. Some studies indicate that the bulk of remittances are used for basics such as food, clothing, housing, health, and education (Boon 2006). Other studies also point to investment in entrepreneurship. For instance, a survey of small firms in Mexico found that remittances account for 20 percent of total capital invested in urban microenterprises (World Bank 2006). In this chapter, we also consider the consumer spending power of diasporas as a form of financial capital with relevance for development.
- *Intellectual capital:* Another topic that has generated significant interest in the migration-development debate is the so-called "brain drain" of skilled personnel from developing to developed regions and various strategies to mitigate the effects, given the purported skills deficits that now hamper development efforts. However, in more recent times, focus has shifted to prospects for circular migration[3] and tapping into the know-how and skills of members of the diaspora in more flexible ways that do not demand permanent return.
- *Political capital:* Members of diasporas also deploy political influence on a range of issues with a bearing on development. These might be local, domestic issues; issues of national import; or even global issues, as the struggle against apartheid became with the considerable engagement of African-American activists.
- *Cultural capital:* Often, members of diasporas acquire a set of values, norms, and perspectives while abroad that differ markedly from those dominant in their countries of origin. In some cases, members of diasporas blend two sets of values to produce a unique "insider-outsider" perspective. New ways of seeing, being, working, and doing are arguably

central to the quest for needed innovation. At the same time, imposition of completely alien values on people is counterproductive. To the extent that new ideas or norms are needed, somehow refracting them through already legitimated norms may be necessary. Members of diasporas are often well placed to serve as a bridge between old and new ways of seeing and being.

- *Social capital:* This is not a resource per se that members of diasporas deploy; rather, social capital includes "the ties that bind," the glue, rationale, obligations, feedback, satisfaction, and even the channels and networks.[4]

Table 9.1 illustrates the correlation of the drivers of productivity identified in the previous section with the diaspora's different forms of capital.

As we can see, there is a good potential fit between what the African diaspora can bring to the table and what is required to enhance productivity and create widespread wealth. Below, we will examine specific initiatives and policies that can help harness the African diaspora's resources to contribute to enterprise development in Africa. First, however, we consider what motivates the African diaspora.

The 3Ps of Diaspora Motivation

While some people engage in development activities for ideological reasons, it is neither helpful nor necessary to assume that members of diasporas do so for similar reasons. Experience suggests that diasporas are broadly motivated to engage in development-related activity by a mix of the "3Ps":

- *Pecuniary interests:* Many diaspora members intend to return to their countries of origin and are motivated by the desire to ensure that they

TABLE 9.1
Correlating Productivity Drivers with Forms of Diaspora Capital

Productivity driver	Diaspora capital
Skills	Intellectual
Innovation	Intellectual, financial
Investment	Financial
Enterprise	Financial, intellectual
Competition	Political

Source: Author's compilation.

have remunerative activities adequate to sustain themselves. This is especially true for temporary migrants or migrants whose status in the host country is irregular. Another reason for pecuniary interest may be to reduce, over the long term, the dependency of family and friends in the country of origin upon the finite resources of the sender.

- *Private interests:* Beyond immediate pecuniary or financial gain, diaspora members might also direct their resources to the private sphere of the immediate household or narrowly defined community.
- *Public philanthropic interests:* Diaspora members also engage in resource transfers and activities aimed at the public sphere for which there is no prospect of tangible personal gain or reward.

Thus, altruism is only one motivating factor explaining why some members of the African diaspora may choose actions that produce development outcomes. The key point is that the payback that members of the African diaspora may be seeking might be measured in financial, social, or emotional terms.[5] Efforts to mobilize the diaspora must take account of these different motivating factors and their interaction.

In the next section, we look at the specific ways African governments can translate African diaspora resources into development gains.

Strategic Framework

African governments have been proactive in recent years in reaching out to their diaspora communities. Both Ghana and Sierra Leone have organized homecoming summits. Ghana, Mali, and Senegal are just three examples of countries with ministers with portfolios that include diaspora affairs. The Government of Nigeria, under President Obasanjo, established a special presidential advisor for diaspora affairs. Indeed, President Obasanjo went one step further to encourage the formation of the Nigerians in Diaspora Organization. Sierra Leone has an Office for Diaspora Affairs located in the Office of the Presidency. Ruling and opposition parties actively fund raise in the diaspora, and few transnational politicians lack ambitions or reticence in claiming that they could do a better job of running their home countries. In the run-up to the 2007 Nigerian presidential elections, presidential hopeful Pat Utomi launched a "Contract with the Diaspora" tour of the United States and the United Kingdom.

In spite of these encouraging developments, African governments have largely failed to integrate their diaspora-mobilization efforts into their overall development strategies.[6] Even in cases where poverty reduction strategies do incorporate a diaspora element, they do not take account of the local, decentralized focus of most diaspora efforts. An example is Ghana, which operated on the premise that most Ghanaians will rally to the nation-state-building cause. In fact, the African Foundation for Development made an effort to connect the Ghanaian diaspora to development efforts in Ghana and highlighted some unfinished business of the decolonization era:

> Ghana's venerated chieftaincy institutions enjoy something of a comparative advantage in the diaspora mobilization business, given the appeal and hold of cultural identity, especially for a diasporic community. And yet, diaspora resource mobilization for development via the chieftaincy raises intriguing challenges around accountability, participation and civic rights. These are not necessarily new themes in modern day Africa but both migration and decentralization throw them into sharp relief. How can the expectations of citizenship be reconciled with the constraints of subject-hood? What are the lines of demarcation between the roles and responsibilities of Chiefs and District Assemblies? These are broad constitutional questions of which diaspora is but one part. (Zan 2004)

In this section, we examine several strands of what a strategy that incorporates a component of mobilizing the African diaspora's resources might entail. We address a fundamental strategic choice that African governments must make as they consider engaging their diasporas; examine specific strategic options that confront African governments in harnessing the African diaspora's resources for enterprise development and wealth creation; consider roles, responsibilities, and the place of collaboration in implementing the strategy; and address continuous learning, evaluation, and adaptation.

Fundamental Strategic Choice: Integrated or Dual?

Although we have already noted that few African governments have incorporated migration and development perspectives into their overall development strategies, this is, arguably, only one of two fundamental strategic choices open to them. The choices are, in essence, to incorporate diaspora resources into an overall development strategy or to pursue a two-pronged, dual strategy.

Aid-dependent African countries typically develop Poverty Reduction Strategy Papers as a multistakeholder process that aims to build a consensus around the country's development priorities and process and to unlock the aid flows to implement the strategies. Some commentators have suggested that Poverty Reduction Strategy Papers are externally driven and lack local ownership in African countries.[7] Given that African diaspora resource flows come with fewer and different conditionalities, it might seem self-evident that African governments should seek to leverage diaspora resources to reduce their aid dependency, to pursue more autonomous policies, or to wrest concessions from their international bilateral and multilateral aid partners. However, the weak state capacity that afflicts most African countries suggests that this two-pronged approach is often a reach too far, and meaningful delivery suffers. Table 9.2 compares the pros and cons of the integrated compared to the dual diaspora engagement strategies.

Specific Strategic Options

Table 9.3 presents options in both policy and programmatic terms. Table 9.4 presents strategies specific to the characteristics of a country's particular diaspora population. Once again, this reinforces the importance of each country understanding its diaspora and matching these characteristics to its particular needs and priorities.

TABLE 9.2

Pros and Cons of Integrated Compared to Dual Diaspora Engagement Strategies

	Integrated strategy	Two-pronged/dual strategy
Pros	• Makes more effective use of limited state capacity	• Offers opportunities to pursue sophisticated policies radically different from mainstream approaches • Potentially creates space for autonomy in policy making • Scope for move from poverty reduction to wealth creation
Cons	• Presents challenges for addressing two very different audiences—diaspora and development partners	• Failure to integrate into state structures may undermine long-term institutionalization and sustainability • May tend to overemphasize symbolic over substantive initiatives for short-term political gain

Source: Author's compilation.

TABLE 9.3

Specific Policies and Initiatives to Harness African Diaspora Resources

Productivity driver	Diaspora capital	Policy initiatives	Programs/projects
Skills	Intellectual	• Improve linkages among business; vocational, educational, and training providers; and employers to produce workforce with more marketable skills • Revise educational curricula to incorporate critical thinking skills, innovation, and entrepreneurship to help nurture a culture of entrepreneurship	• Develop schemes to build the capacity of small and medium enterprises nationwide using diaspora skills and know-how
Innovation	Intellectual, financial	• Systematize the purposeful search for innovation in firms and organizations and society at large; create incentives to encourage and reward innovation; send strong message to diaspora that the country is open for innovation	• Establish a competition for innovation and entrepreneurship that includes diaspora innovators and entrepreneurs
Investment	Financial	• Pursue investment climate reforms to encourage domestic investment; foreign direct investment; and diaspora direct investment (all investors share similar core concerns). Those issues of specific concern to diaspora investors include land reform; dual nationality (or other means to guarantee property rights for diaspora investors who may now hold foreign citizenship) • Encourage greater financial literacy and inclusion (bank the unbanked) • Develop closer linkages between the remittances economy (e.g., housing and construction) and the local economy to enhance beneficial multiplier effects of remittances • Encourage and regulate innovative financial products and services attractive to diaspora investors	• Restructure investment promotion agencies to attract diaspora direct investment and foreign direct investment • Encourage local chambers of commerce to develop relationships with diaspora chambers of commerce for information exchange, business partnerships, and two-way trading relationships • Launch products such as diaspora bonds to attract diaspora direct investment • Support innovative products to enable remittances recipients to gain access to financial services and business support where the intention is to use remittances for enterprise endeavors

Enterprise	Financial, intellectual	• Reduce administrative barriers to doing business; reduce registration costs for new businesses; implement tax incentives to encourage enterprise • Amend banking regulations to enable "portable" credit histories to allow diaspora entrepreneurs to access credit in local capital markets • Amend employment laws to facilitate easier hiring of African diaspora employees, even when they are not nationals of the country	• Encourage value chain initiatives to promote export of goods and services that target diaspora consumers, particularly where products have the potential to gain wider market access via diaspora channels (e.g., in the same way that "Nollywood" Nigerian movies now enjoy widespread appeal thanks to Nigerian diaspora consumers)
Competition	Political	• Encourage competition in remittances service provision: reduce entry barriers to enable more players to reduce transfer fees; allow other financial institutions (e.g., monetary financial institutions) to provide money transfer services; apply competition policy frameworks to exclusive agreements involving money transfer operators and their distributors	• Use public-private dialogue structures to incorporate the views of diaspora investors and entrepreneurs on necessary reforms

Source: Author's compilation.

TABLE 9.4

Strategies for Matching Diaspora Investors and Entrepreneurs with Possible Actions

High finance capital, low nonfinance capital:	High finance capital, high nonfinance capital:
• Cash rich, time poor, long-term settled individuals with few links with "home" but some emotional connection (i.e., potential investors) **Mechanisms, actions, and policy options:** • Stock exchange • Investment/managed funds • Hands-on trade missions and virtual mentoring to harness resources and strengthen emotional bonds	• Highly skilled individuals in senior positions in management, corporate finance, etc. • Successful owners of well-established medium and large businesses • Strong links with/interest in "home" affairs **Mechanisms, actions, and policy options:** • Venture capital instruments/funds • Stock exchange • Private equity/managed funds • Joint venture investments • High-profile, focused networks/think-and-act tanks for action-oriented initiatives • Diaspora appointments on government advisory boards
Low finance capital, low nonfinance capital:	**Low finance capital, high nonfinance capital:**
• Marginalized, trapped in low-skilled/low-paying jobs • Undocumented migrants (cannot travel back and forth) • Asylum seekers barred from working • Refugees unable to secure jobs commensurate with their skills and experience • People remitting significant portions of even meagre income to relatives at home **Mechanisms, actions, and policy options:** • Research to understand investment portions of remittances • Channel remittances via formal structures • Small-scale business development initiatives, e.g., microfranchising • Seek linkages between remittances expenditure and local economy • Tax relief on remittances for development • Negotiate for recognition of rights for migrants in host countries	• Owners of small enterprises • Young/female entrepreneurs • Members of hometown and other associations • Highly skilled individuals in paid employment **Mechanisms, actions, and policy options:** • Match diaspora entrepreneurs to small and medium enterprise partners • Business development support and networks • Trade initiatives linking home and host countries • Business plan competitions • Harnessing skills via virtual business peer support/mentoring and hands-on skills-sharing trade missions

Source: Author's compilation.

We now consider approaches that African governments might adopt in implementing the above strategies.

Roles and Responsibilities: Collaborative Approaches

This transnational age of migration demands that migrant-sending and receiving countries cooperate if they want to harness the benefits of migration for development (GCIM 2005). Geographer Giles Mohan (2002) argues that the following three interrelated aspects of diasporas' engagement with the world need to be considered:

- *Development in the diaspora*, that is, the circumstances under which diaspora communities operate in the host country (jobs, housing, welfare, and so forth)
- *Development through diaspora*, that is, the ways that globally dispersed diaspora networks support each other, engage in trade, and so forth
- *Development by diaspora*, that is, the support that diaspora communities provide to sending communities, ancestral home communities, or both, through remittances, lobbying, and so forth.

Clearly, there is a symbiosis between conditions in the host countries of diaspora settlement and the capacity of members of the diaspora to contribute to Africa's development. This provides a context for bilateral and multilateral partnerships and collaboration between African governments and countries of diaspora settlement.

In addition to government-to-government relations and collaboration in the context of mobilizing African diaspora resources for development, African governments should also consider relations with the private sector, particularly where private-sector-led development and jobs are desired outcomes.

The growing consensus surrounding the central role that business must play in the achievement of the Millennium Development Goals is significant because of the evolving partnership between diasporas and business around development.[8]

Recent deliberations have identified ways in which businesses can contribute to poverty reduction.

First, businesses can contribute to economic growth through:

- Advocacy for improvements in investment climate and business environment
- Investment in infrastructure
- Facilitating international and regional trade.

Second, businesses can also contribute to poverty reduction through their core business activities by:

- Involving small and medium enterprises in value chains as suppliers and distributors

- Creation of decent, productive employment (including transferring skills to Africa through hiring Africans in the diaspora for roles on the continent)
- Provision of goods and services for consumers at the base of the economic pyramid.

Most important, of course, is a collaborative approach with the African diaspora.

If African governments can devote sufficient time and energy to getting their thinking, strategies, and policies right, partners—other governments, the private sector, and members of the diaspora themselves—can take responsibility for much of the implementation. This approach has the potential, therefore, to address one of the key constraints hampering effective development in Africa—that is, inadequate state capacity.

Learning and Growing

Engaging the African diaspora in contributing to Africa's development in the systematic way outlined in this chapter is still relatively new terrain for African governments, and there are many unknowns. That is why clarity of purpose, with clear goals, targets, and milestones, is so important to enable progress to be measured and periodic adaptations made.

African governments, however, are not alone in their journey. Many Asian and Latin American countries have in recent years made significant strides in developing productive relations with their diasporas in an effort to harness their resources for development. African governments could develop agreements to share learning and experiences with counterparts in these regions and to adapt them to the contexts specific to different parts of Africa.

Conclusion

While the growing interest of African governments in engaging the African diaspora as a development resource is logical, the diaspora is neither the silver bullet of development nor a panacea for all Africa's ills. Indeed, tapping into the African diaspora's resources does not reduce the need for home-grown solutions, sound leadership, effective management, and good governance as the absolute cornerstones of development in the

21st century. Rather, if anything, reinforcing the contributions of diasporas to development and taking them to a new level makes new and additional demands on African governments.

Nonetheless, as democratic governance improves in Africa and elected officials accountable to their peoples for effective service delivery becomes the norm, the outlook for a productive relationship between Africa and its diverse diasporas appears promising.

In considering an overall strategic framework, this chapter has highlighted the fundamental choice that African governments face. While many African governments have in recent years reached out to their diasporas as development partners, they have not in general incorporated migration and development concerns into their overall development strategies. Although this might imply that they have been deploying a highly sophisticated dual-pronged strategy of engaging diasporas as separate development partners from their more conventional partners, this does not seem to be the case, not least because of the additional demands on limited state capacity (in most cases) that this makes. Indeed, for relatively weak states, integrating diaspora components into their main poverty reduction strategy may be the more pragmatic choice for many African governments.

Although this chapter has focused on the role of African governments—which still bear the prime responsibility for national development—in reinforcing the African diaspora's contributions to development, there remains a critical role for regional bodies such as the African Union and even the regional economic communities. As explained, not all of the African diaspora identifies strongly with the nation-state as their primary entry point to development. For some, it is a subnational ethnic or regional identity (or even a gender or professional identity). For others, it is Africa as a whole to which they relate. The African Union, therefore, has a comparative advantage in structuring the symbolic and symbiotic relationship between Africa and its diverse diasporas.

On a more practical level, the African Union could and should do more to help improve standards of democratic governance across the continent. Although all African countries have the right to be members of the African Union based on geographic position alone, the African Union could tier this base-level entry with more nuanced and gradated levels of membership based on, for example, a country's commitment to principles such as free and fair elections, term limits on elected office, and respect for the rule of law. This could go a long way toward building a more direct relationship between the African Union and citizens in Africa and the diaspora.

Finally, the limited capacity of state structures within Africa is, arguably, for many countries, the main constraint hampering a more strategic and systematic approach to reinforcing the African diaspora's contribution to the continent's development. It requires a reasonably well-organized state to effectively engage its diaspora to achieve development outcomes. What, then, is the overworked African policy maker and decision maker to do on the proverbial Monday morning, in taking forward the ideas outlined in this chapter?

The diaspora itself can serve as a resource to help African governments devise and implement such strategies. While use of such a resource on a pro bono basis is one option, the World Bank has developed its strategy of engagement with the African diaspora as a development resource. Within that framework, the World Bank has developed eConsult, a mechanism for diaspora consultants to register and be available for Bank-funded projects. The Bank has also established the African Diaspora Facilitation Engagement Fund. The Bank is even considering organizing a study tour of India for African officials to learn how that country transformed its relationship with the Indian diaspora for mutual gain. Lack of resources, thus, can no longer be an adequate explanation for not taking a systematic and strategic approach to harnessing the African diaspora's contributions to Africa's development.

Notes

1. Olaudah Equiano, also known as Gustavus Vassa, was one of the most prominent Africans involved in the British movement for the abolition of the slave trade (wikipedia.com).
2. Although the focus of this chapter is on enterprise development, the same would be true for other areas of development, such as in the education or health sectors, community development, and so forth.
3. Circular migration is defined as "a continuing, long-term, and fluid pattern of human mobility among countries that occupy what is now increasingly recognized as a single economic space" (Newland, Rannveig Agunias, and Terrazas 2008).
4. Scholars have subjected the concept of social capital to sustained criticism (see, for example, Franklin [2004]), and its meaning is highly contested. Nonetheless, it retains some utility in capturing the messy, fuzzy range of factors at play in motivating diasporas to do what they do vis-à-vis development.

5. See, for example, Nielsen and Riddle (Undated).
6. As the Economic Commission for Africa points out, "The response of African Governments to migration challenges has been very limited and fragmentary. Few countries have implemented international conventions and related policies on migration. International migration barely features in national development plans and strategies, and has not been adequately addressed in any of the regional development frameworks such as the NEPAD [New Partnership for Africa's Development], MDGs [Millennium Development Goals], and PRSPs [Poverty Reduction Strategy Papers]" (ECA 2006b).
7. Former Eritrean finance minister, Gebreselassie Y. Tesfamichael believes that Poverty Reduction Strategy Papers are aimed at extracting the most aid possible (Tesfamichael 2005).
8. This point was driven home in a report (InWent 2006) presented at an Internationale Weiterbildung und Entwicklung (Capacity Building International, InWEnt)-sponsored conference in Bonn, Germany in 2006. The conference was significant not only for its focus on the role of business in contributing to achievement of the Millennium Development Goals, but because it was the first major conference to bring together business investors in Africa and the African diaspora to explore ways of integrating combined efforts in achieving the Goals.

References

Argunias Rannveig, Dovelyn, and Kathleen Newland. 2007. "Circular Migration and Development: Trends, Policy Routes, and Ways Forward." Migration Policy Institute, Washington, DC. April.

Boon, Martin. 2006. "BME Remittance Research Report Prepared for Department for the International Development." ICM Research, London. July 27.

ECA (Economic Commission for Africa). 2006a. *Economic Report on Africa 2005: Meeting the Challenges of Unemployment and Poverty in Africa.* Addis Ababa: United Nations Economic Commission for Africa.

————. 2006b. *International Migration and Development: Implications for Africa.* Addis Ababa: United Nations Economic Commission for Africa.

Franklin, Jane, ed. 2004. *Politics, Trust and Networks: Social Capital in Critical Perspective.* London: London South Bank University. April.

GCIM (Global Commission for International Migration). 2005. "Migration in an Interconnected World: New Directions for Action—Report of the Global Commission on International Migration." Global Commission for International Migration, Geneva.

InWEnt (Internationale Weiterbildung und Entwicklung [Capacity Building International]). 2006. "Business and MDGs—The Business Challenge Africa: Report of the 11th International Business Forum." Bonn, October 8–10.

Lubkemann, S. C. 2008. "Remittance Relief and Not-Just-for-Profit Entrepreneurship: The Case of Liberia." In *Diasporas and Development: Exploring the Potential,* ed. J. Brinkerhoff. Boulder, CO: Lynne Rienner Publishers.

Mohan, Giles. 2002. "Diaspora and Development." In *Displacement and Development,* ed. J. Robinson. Oxford: Oxford University Press, in association with the Open University.

Ndofor-Tah, Carolyne. 2000. "Diaspora and Development: Contributions by African Organisations in the UK to Africa's Development." A report commissioned by the African Foundation for Development as part of the Africa21 Project, "Target Africa 2015: Development Awareness, Networking and Lifelong Learning among African Organisations in London." September. http://www.afford-uk.org/resources/download/.

Newland, Kathleen, Dovelyn Rannveig Agunias, and Aaron Terrazas. 2008. "Learning by Doing: Experiences of Circular Migration." *Migration Policy Institute Insight.* http://www.migrationpolicy.org/pubs/Insight-IGC-Sept08.pdf.

Nielsen, Tjai M., and Liesl Riddle. Undated. "Diaspora Homeland Investment Motivation in Post-Conflict Economies: Evidence from the U.S. Liberian Community." Unpublished manuscript. George Washington University, Washington, DC.

Tesfamichael, Gebreselassie Y. 2005. "In Africa, Just Help Us To Help Ourselves." *Washington Post,* July 24. http://www.washingtonpost.com/wp-dyn/content/article/2005/07/22/AR2005072202226.html.

UNCTAD (United Nations Conference on Trade and Development). 2006. "Least Developed Countries Report: Developing Productive Capacities." United Nations Conference on Trade and Development, Geneva.

World Bank. 2006. *Global Economic Prospects: The Economic Implications of Migration and Remittances.* Washington, DC: World Bank.

Zan, Samuel. 2004. "One Nation, One People, One Destiny? The Ghanaian Diaspora's Contribution to National Development Using Diverse Channels." London: African Foundation for Development. http://www.afford-uk.org/resources/download/one_nation.pdf.

CHAPTER 10

Migration and Productive Investment: A Conceptual Framework

Valeria Galetto

The dominant view of the relationship between migration and development has changed significantly over the past three decades. Prior to the 1990s, the view was that migration had overall negative effects on migrants' communities of origin. However, in the 1990s, the view was that the effects of migration were large and positive. Currently, the consensus among researchers is that the effects of migration on development are not invariably positive or negative but, rather, are *contingent on a set of factors that vary over time and across locales.* De Hass, for instance, writes:

> *Suggesting an automatic mechanism in which migration leads to more development (or the contrary) would be to ignore the accumulated evidence pointing to the differentiated nature of the spatial, temporal, social and sector-specific impact of migration. . . .Migration impacts are therefore highly context-sensitive* (De Hass 2006:579).

Likewise, after conducting an extensive literature review on migrants' remittances and development, Ghosh (2006:70) concludes that, "to sum up, remittances can contribute to investment and output growth, but this is not automatic, and should not be taken for granted."[1]

A closer look at the studies that lend empirical support to the current view reveals that multiple factors may shape the relationship between migration and development. These factors range from fiscal and socioeconomic policies (for example, exchange rates, interest rates, employment), to local infrastructure and natural resources (for example, schools, health clinics, roads, public transportation, running water, electricity, availability and quality of land), to migrants' household and individual characteristics (for example, assets, number of dependants compared to earners, total months of U.S. experience). In practice, researchers work with different combinations of explanatory factors; for instance, some look at community- and national-level variables, others analyze community- and household-level variables, and others study community- and individual-level variables. As a result, when these studies are taken together, they show a great deal of variation in terms of the factors that facilitate (or impede) migration-driven development.

One goal of this chapter is to examine whether the large variability of findings reported in the literature since the mid-1990s has more to do with the multiple aspects and dimensions of analysis considered in studying the association and less to do with the nature of the association between migration and development. To this end, the chapter focuses on one particular aspect of economic development—*productive investment.*[2] The selected studies have three characteristics in common: (a) they investigate the relationship between migration and productive investment, (b) they assess the level of investment, and (c) they advance an explanation for the observed findings. The systematic comparison of these studies shows that, indeed, they tend to focus on several goals, include different sets of explanatory factors, and use diverse methodologies, all of which contributes to the great diversity of findings reported in the literature.

However, the systematic comparison across studies also reveals that there are several common trends among them. In other words, the relationship between migration and productive investment, the development aspect examined here, turns out to be less erratic than an initial reading of the literature suggests. To be sure, the evidence shows that migration has varying effects on development; however, those effects are not randomly distributed across locales.

The second goal of this chapter, then, is to identify general trends across a diverse group of findings and to discuss the implications of these trends for the study of the interactions between migration and productive investment.

The divergent effects of migration on local development have been a central preoccupation in the Mexico-U.S. migration literature since the early

1990s. Moreover, many researchers have argued that the fundamental question regarding the relationship between migration and development is why international migration seems to be associated with positive development outcomes in some communities but not in others. Yet, few attempts have been made to offer a thorough answer to this question. In particular, researchers still lack a comprehensive framework that takes into account the multiplicity of factors that may contribute to development (or the lack thereof) in migrant-sending regions and, at the same time, examines the interactions among those factors and their evolution over time. This chapter contributes to the construction of such a framework.

Specifically, a framework is advanced that conceptualizes the relationship between migration and productive investment. This framework integrates the main findings of the literature, offering an overview of the multiple factors that may contribute to migration-driven investment. The chapter's main argument is that investment is contingent on four main factors:

- A minimum amount of money remitted or saved
- A minimum level of local development
- The presence of suitable investment opportunities
- The existence of specific household arrangements.

These factors are, in turn, the result of other sets of interrelated factors, and some of those interrelations are examined, as well. In sum, the framework identifies a comprehensive set of conditions that account for high or low levels of productive investment in migrants' communities of origin and specifies some of the mechanisms that lead to those outcomes. Accordingly, the chapter:

- Reviews the literature on the relationship between migration and development, particularly as it relates to migration from Mexico to the United States
- Compares a set of studies that report a significant level of productive investment with a set of studies that report a limited level of investment and identifies general trends within and between them
- Outlines a conceptual framework that examines the relationship between migration and productive investment
- Illustrates the proposed framework by applying it to the analysis of investment patterns of two migrant communities in western Michoacán, Mexico

- Examines why investment patterns in these communities have been so different
- Offers concluding remarks.

Literature Review

Academic views on the relationship between migration and development have changed significantly in the last three decades.

From Pessimism to Optimism

In the specific case of Mexican migration to the United States, the dominant view during the 1980s was that migration contributed to increases in migrants' household incomes and standards of living, but it seldom "stimulated production or created new employment opportunities" in their communities of origin (Reichert 1981:63; see also Stuart and Kearney 1981; Wiest 1984). Households with members working in the United States had access to an array of goods and services that made their lives not only more enjoyable but also more productive (for example, access to health care, education, better housing). These tangible improvements among migrant households led other community members to leave for the United States, increasing the share of the local population with migratory experience.

However, consistent with dependency theory and with a historical-structural perspective, many researchers argued that the higher rate of migration, and its concomitant greater flow of remittances and savings entering migrants' communities of origin, did not lead to a significant change in the structural conditions that engendered migration in the first place. Migrant households did increase their levels of consumption, but very few were able to establish, enlarge, or renovate a business and, thus, directly contribute to local employment (including self-employment).[3] Based on these findings, the general consensus among researchers was that:

- Once migration starts, it "perpetuates itself" (Wiest 1984:132)
- As migration to the United States becomes more prominent among the population of a locality, its economy becomes more dependent on, or tied into, U.S. labor markets

- Migration does not contribute to the type of development that ensures "the long range viability and autonomy of sending communities" (Reichert 1981:64).

If, in the 1980s, the prevailing view in the literature on the effects of migration on development was pessimistic, the opposite was true in the 1990s. Articulated as the New Economics of Labor Migration, scholars subscribing to this position claimed that migration had positive and large effects on development. The gist of the argument, which served both as a critique of the previous position and as a foundation of its own, centered around the specifications of the appropriate object of study, the determinants of migration, and the effects of remittances on the economy at large.

New Economics of Labor Migration argues that migration is a household strategy and, consequently, when studying migration the appropriate unit of analysis is not the individual but the household. Also, in contrast with neoclassical economics and the historical-structural perspective of the 1980s, it maintains that migration is not driven primarily by wage differentials between sending and receiving countries, or by the lack of employment or meaningful employment opportunities in migrants' communities of origin. Instead, it is driven by the desire to overcome risk and credit market failures. Migration is seen, therefore, as a household strategy to diversify sources of income, augment capital assets, and provide insurance against risks (Taylor 1999; Taylor et al. 1996).

If this premise is correct, as New Economics of Labor Migration's proponents contend, then migrants' remittances and savings cannot be analyzed independently of other household incomes, as was the practice during the 1980s, with the proliferation of remittances-and-savings use surveys. Rather, household expenditure decisions are made taking into consideration *all* household incomes and assets, whether they are available at present or in the future. In particular, some studies show that having a household member in the United States augments the propensity to invest in Mexico, possibly because it loosens capital constraints or acts as a tacit "insurance policy" against future, unforeseen risks (Taylor and Mora 2006; Taylor et al. 1996).[4] This latter positive effect on development could not be captured with remittances-use surveys and thus remained unnoticed during the 1980s.

New Economics of Labor Migration's main contribution to the migration and development debate, however, has been to draw attention to the indirect or multiplier effects of migrants' remittances and savings on the economy. As Durand, Parrado, and Massey (1996:425) explain:

> By focusing on the small share of migradollars devoted to productive investment, however, prior investigators have ignored the indirect effects that consumer spending has on economic production and income in Mexico. Even though migradollars may be spent largely on consumption, this spending augments the demand for goods and services produced in Mexico, leading ultimately to more production, higher employment, and increased national income. In short, migradollars have potentially strong multiplier effects throughout the Mexican economy.

To be sure, during the 1990s, proponents of this position argued that migrants' remittances and savings had potentially strong multiplier effects not only at the national and regional levels, but also at the community level. They maintained that as the amount of remittances and savings coming from the United States rose, so did "the demand for locally produced goods and services, creating entrepreneurial opportunities for nonmigrant households and raising production, income and employment throughout the community" (Massey and Parrado 1998:12; see also Papail and Arroyo Alejandre 1996:121; Taylor 1999).

In recent years, a number of studies have questioned the magnitude of the multiplier effects of remittances on the economy, showing that they have a limited impact on national growth (Fajnzylber and López 2007; Ghosh 2006; Kapur 2005; Rannveig Agunias 2006). In Latin America, for instance, Fajnzylber and López (2007:xi) find that in the 11 countries included in their sample, an average increase in remittances "from 0.7 percent of GDP [gross domestic product] in 1991–1995 to 2.3 percent of GDP in 2001–2005 is estimated to have led to an increase of only 0.27 percent per year in per capita growth." At the local level, researchers have found that although the multiplier effects of remittances may vary greatly across locales, in general, those effects tend to be small because most of the goods and services demanded by migrant households are not produced or offered locally, but in nearby regional centers (Arroyo Alejandre and Berumen Sandoval 2000; Arroyo Alejandre and Corvera Valenzuela 2003; Arroyo Alejandre, De León Arias, and Valenzuela Varela 1991).

From Uniform Effects to Diverse Effects

As the idea that migration had varying effects on development took hold in the literature, researchers began to look at the circumstances under which the observed effects tended to occur. Further, some scholars maintained that the discussion about whether migration had positive or negative effects on development missed the point. Rather, they argued, efforts should focus on what they considered the fundamental question of this debate: *why* migration is associated with positive development outcomes in some cases but not in others (Durand and Massey 1992; Ghosh 1992:432; Taylor 1999:65). This analytical shift—from describing the effects to investigating their causes—marked a new phase in the study of the relationship between migration and development.

A direct consequence of this analytical shift has been the difficulty in interpreting the large variability in results reported in the literature. In part, this has to do with the fact that many studies tend to look at the conditions that account for a specific outcome without investigating whether those same conditions are present or absent in other studies. Without a systematic comparison across studies, it will be difficult to assess whether there are common trends across different locales and, most important, to advance a thorough answer to the key question mentioned above.

Migration and Investment: A Comparative Analysis of the Literature

As a preliminary step to advancing a general framework that examines the relationship between migration and investment, a systematic review of the literature on this problem was conducted. Two sets of studies were analyzed: (a) studies that report a positive and significant association between international migration and productive investment in migrants' communities of origin, and (b) studies that report a positive but limited association between these two processes. In both cases, the studies' goals, data, methodology, and suggested explanatory factors were investigated. These topics and whether there are some common trends between these two groups of studies are the focus of this section.

Productive Investment in Migrant-Sending Regions

Table 10.1 provides details about a set of studies that report a positive and significant association between international migration, including migrants' remittances and savings, and productive investment in migrant-sending

TABLE 10.1

Studies Reporting a Significant Association between Migration and Productive Investment in Migrant-Sending Regions

Study	Goal	Data and methodology	Explanatory factors				
			National	Regional	Local	Household	Individual
Arroyo Alejandre and Corvera Valenzuela 2003	Identify the conditions that determine the positive impact of remittances on migrants' communities of origin in western Mexico	General Census of Population and Housing, and other economic censuses, Mexico, 1998, 2000 Descriptive statistics			Entrepreneurial structure	*Amount,*[a] uses, and proportion of remittances within total income	
Basok 2003	Study "the link between the impact of migration on local development and the nature of communities in which remittances are spent" (p. 6)	Guest workers survey conducted in 11 communities of Guanajuato and Tlaxcala, Mexico in 1999–2000 Descriptive statistics			Worse-endowed communities greater investment in land Better-endowed communities greater investment in businesses		
de Haan 1999	Identify the conditions that determine the impact of migration on agriculture	Analysis of secondary sources, including the author's previous research, various countries			Context	Assets	*Education* Length of time spent away[b]
Durand et al. 1996	Determine the factors that affect the odds of spending U.S. earnings on production relative to consumption	Household survey conducted in 30 communities of Guanajuato, Jalisco, Michoacán, Nayarit, and Zacatecas, Mexico, 1982–83 and 1987–92, and secondary sources Regression analysis			Presence of an Ejido	Potential family labor Assets (land, business, or a home)	*Education*

Study	Objective	Data and method			Natural resources (high-quality land) / *Infrastructure*		
Durand, Parrado and Massey 1996	Determine the conditions under which farm households tend to use U.S. earnings to finance agricultural production	Analysis of secondary sources, including the authors' previous research, Mexico			Natural resources (high-quality land) *Infrastructure*		
Lindstrom and Lauster 2001	Examine the initial conditions of municipalities that currently offer favorable investment opportunities to migrants	Household survey conducted in 29 municipalities of Zacatecas, Mexico in 1990–91 Regression analysis		Municipalities with early favorable economic conditions			
Massey and Parrado 1998	Identify the factors that affect the likelihood of financing a business with U.S. earnings	Household survey conducted in 30 communities of Guanajuato, Jalisco, Michoacán, Nayarit, and Zacatecas, Mexico, 1982–83 and 1987–92 Regression analysis				*Amount of remittances* Life cycle (married with children are less likely to fund a business, except when they own a home)	Migrant status (currently in the United States) *Total years in the United States*
Papail and Arroyo Alejandre 1996	Identify the conditions that contribute to establishing a firm or business among international migrants	Household survey conducted in four cities of Jalisco, Mexico, in 1993 Descriptive statistics	Policies (low exchange rate) Economic crises				
Sana and Massey 2005	Test hypotheses that remittances are used for risk diversification and investment versus family maintenance or as income supplement; identify conditions when remittances play the former role	Household survey conducted in Costa Rica, the Dominican Republic, Mexico, and Nicaragua between 1999 and 2002 Regression analysis			Minimum level of development *Infrastructure* Commercial opportunities		*Total years in the United States* Labor experience in the United States

(continued next page)

TABLE 10.1 (continued)

Study	Goal	Data and methodology	Explanatory factors				
			National	Regional	Local	Household	Individual
Sofranko and Idris 1999	Study "whether the use of remittance income for business investment was influenced by several extended family measures" (p. 465)	Household head survey conducted in a community in Pakistan, early 1990s Regression analysis				Assets (current or previous business) Support to extended family members	Knowledge of business opportunities
Taylor 1999	Identify the conditions that influence the nested decisions of migrating and allocating remittances and savings to investments	Case studies from Mexico Use of Social Accounting Matrixes	Policies (unspecified)	Access to product markets	Natural resources (unspecified)		
Taylor 2004	Determine the conditions that affect the extent of the positive effects of migrant remittances	Analysis of secondary sources, including the author's previous research, Mexico		Profitability of new production activities or techniques	Profitability of new production activities or techniques	Amount of remittances	
Woodruff and Zenteno 2007	Study "the impact of migration networks in Mexico on the development of microenterprises in the country" (p. 510)	National Survey of Microenterprises, Mexico, 1998 Regression analysis			Access to capital through social networks		

Note: a. The factors that appear in more than one study are in italics.

b. In addition to the factors identified in the table, de Hann (1999) points to the seasonality of migratory flows, and the social structure and institutions allowing women and others to pursue activities previously reserved for men and household heads.

regions. As the table shows, researchers have analyzed very different aspects of this association (see the "Goal" column of the table). In effect, some studies look at the characteristics of the municipalities and communities in which migrants are more likely to invest their remittances and savings (Basok 2003; Lindstrom and Lauster 2001). Some studies investigate the conditions that affect the economic impact of migrants' remittances and savings on their communities of origin (Arroyo Alejandre and Corvera Valenzuela 2003; Taylor 2004). Other studies examine the conditions that contribute to establishing a firm or a business among international migrants (Massey and Parrado 1998; Papail and Arroyo Alejandre 1996; Sofranko and Idris 1999; Woodruff and Zenteno 2007). Other studies analyze the relationship between migration and investment in agriculture (de Haan 1999; Durand, Parrado, and Massey 1996), while the remaining studies have other goals.

Since these studies have such *varying research goals*, it is not surprising that they point to a wide range of explanatory factors to account for their findings (see the "Explanatory factors" column of table 10.1).[5] However, if we only compare studies within the same thematic group outlined above (that is, municipality and community characteristics, remittances' impacts, business and firm formation, and migration and agricultural effects), we still find that they advance *different sets of explanatory factors*. Thus, for instance, the studies that investigate business and firm formation among international migrants suggest that different conditions may contribute to starting a business. Just to take two examples, while Massey and Parrado (1998) claim that the amount of remittances, the life cycle, the migratory status, and the total years abroad affect the propensity to invest U.S. earnings in a business, Papail and Arroyo Alejandre (1996) maintain that the economic crises, the low exchange rates, the labor experience in the United States, and the total years abroad contribute to that end. That is, there is only one explanatory factor common to both studies: total years abroad. In addition, while the former study includes household-level variables in its explanation, the latter study points to national-level variables.[6,7]

Finally, the other aspect that may contribute to the large variability of findings is the use of *different data sources and methodological approaches*. As table 10.1 shows, studies employ a large diversity of sources. Data sources include national censuses; standardized surveys (for example, the National Survey of Microenterprises); customized surveys (designed by the study's authors); and secondary sources, which usually include qualitative studies.

To use the same comparison as above, Massey and Parrado (1998) and Papail and Arroyo Alejandre (1996) use different data sources to study migration and business formation in Mexico; each uses their own household survey. The surveys differ in terms of the content and representativeness of the data; the former was conducted in 30 communities distributed across five states, while the latter was carried out in four cities within a single state. In addition, these studies differ in terms of methodological approaches—a regression analysis in one case and a descriptive statistical analysis in the other. The use of different data sources and methodologies may certainly contribute to different findings.

Limited Productive Investment in Migrant-Sending Regions

Table 10.2 presents a set of studies that report a *limited* or *very limited* association between international migration and productive investment in migrant-sending regions. In contrast to the studies in table 10.1, most of these studies have a *similar goal*: to identify the conditions that tend to be associated with low levels of productive investment in migrants' communities of origin (Arroyo Alejandre, De León Arias, and Valenzuela Varela 1991; Basok 2000; Delgado Wise and Rodríguez Ramírez 2001; Gundel 2002; Pedraza Rendón, García García, and Ayvar Campos 2004; Taylor et al. 1996).[8] The remaining studies focus on various aspects (Arroyo Alejandre and Berumen Sandoval 2000; Durand, Parrado, and Massey 1996; Durand et al. 1996; Zárate-Hoyos 2004).

Table 10.2 also shows that researchers in these studies advance *similar types of explanatory factors* to account for low levels of productive investment in migrants' communities of origin. In effect, with the exception of Arroyo Alejandre, De León Arias, and Valenzuela Varela (1991), Basok (2000), and Delgado Wise and Rodríguez Ramírez (2001), who include household-level factors, individual-level factors, or both, in their explanations, all of the studies in table 10.2 point to unfavorable conditions that operate at the national, regional, and local levels. At the local level, two factors are consistently mentioned—the lack of basic infrastructure and public services, and the lack of high-quality land. Finally, with respect to data and methodology, researchers use a wide range of sources (national and regional household surveys, interviews, secondary literature, and so forth), and methodological approaches (quantitative and qualitative analyses) to obtain these findings.

TABLE 10.2
Studies Reporting a Limited Association between Migration and Productive Investment in Migrant-Sending Regions

| Study | Goal | Data and methodology | Explanatory factors | | | | | |
			National	Regional	Local	Household	Individual
Arroyo Alejandre and Berumen Sandoval 2000	Identify the characteristics of the municipalities or regions that tend to be associated with low levels of productive investment (buy, establish, or enlarge a business)	Survey on Migration in Mexico's Northern Border, 1995 Descriptive statistics		Metropolitan municipalities Regions with low migration rates			
Arroyo Alejandre, De León Arias, and Valenzuela Varela 1991	Examine the main factors responsible for the low utilization of remittances in the development of the rural and semi-urban communities of the study	Household survey conducted in 69 localities of Jalisco, Mexico; interviews; and other secondary sources, 1988–89 Regression analysis			*Lack of infrastructure[a] Poor natural resources* Low profitability of agriculture		*Lack of experience in organizing, financing, and administering a business*
Basok 2000	Study the "problems" associated with the low propensity of Canada-bound migrants to invest remittances productively	Interviews with participants of the Canadian Seasonal Agricultural Workers Program conducted in Canada and Mexico in 1996–98 Descriptive statistics	Decline of subsistence agriculture in Mexico because it is considered a nonviable activity			Composition—temporal absence of males Low income	Low level of education

(continued next page)

TABLE 10.2 (continued)

Study	Goal	Data and methodology	Explanatory factors				
			National	Regional	Local	Household	Individual
Delgado Wise and Rodríguez Ramírez 2001	Identify the "structural features" that account for migrants' low levels of productive investment of remittances	National surveys and secondary sources including the authors' previous research, Mexico Descriptive statistics	Economic difficulties (shrinking of the domestic market) Institutional difficulties (lack of support to small businesses)		Lack of a dynamic economy (limited multiplying benefits of remittances on the local economy)	Low amounts of remittances and savings (excessive fragmentation of resources for funding projects)	*Lack of business experience* Limited vision for investment options in migrants' communities
Durand et al. 1996	Identify the factors that "simultaneously generate high rates of out-migration and low rates of investment" (p. 250)	Household survey conducted in 30 communities of Guanajuato, Jalisco, Michoacán, Nayarit, and Zacatecas, Mexico, 1982–83 and 1987–92 and secondary sources Regression analysis		*Limited access to regional product markets*	Shortage of arable land Small and poorly educated workforce *Poor transportation and communications*		
Durand, Parrado and Massey 1996	Determine the conditions under which farm households are less likely to use U.S. earnings to finance agricultural production	Analysis of secondary sources, including the authors' previous research, Mexico		*Limited access to product markets*	*Poor-quality land* Limited infrastructure (few roads, schools, sewage plants, electricity, phones, etc.)		

296

Study	Objective	Data and method		Regional-level factors	Local-level factors
Gundel 2002	Identify the circumstances that prevent the Somali diaspora from investing in productive activities	Analysis of secondary sources, Somalia	*Lack of political stability* Lack of a favorable economic environment		Lack of a favorable investment climate at the local level
Pedraza Rendón et al. 2004	Study the factors that account for the very limited use of remittances with productive ends	Survey conducted in Michoacán, Mexico Descriptive statistics	Lack of economic stability *Lack of political stability*	Lack of a favorable investment climate at the regional level	
Taylor et al. 1996	Determine "the obstacles to the effective promotion of development through emigration" (p. 402)	Analysis of secondary sources, various countries		Lack of well-functioning factor markets—mainly rural credit markets	*Poor public services and infrastructure* *Poor-quality land, fragmented tenure system, and unequal land distribution*
Zarate-Hoyos 2004	Examine why remittance-receiving households from rural areas are less likely to invest in productive activities than households in urban areas	National Household Income and Expenditures Survey, 1989, 1992, 1994, and 1996, Mexico Regression analysis			*Lack of basic infrastructure and little or no availability of public services in rural areas*

Note: a. The factors that appear in more than one study are in italics.

Accounting for Differences in Productive Investment: A Comparison Across Studies

A closer look at the factors that tend to promote and hinder productive investment (tables 10.1 and 10.2) reveals some interesting trends.

First, different levels of productive investment tend to be associated with *different types* of explanatory factors. In the case of a positive and significant correlation between migration and productive investment (table 10.1), most studies identify diverse combinations of structural and individual factors. Investment tends to occur, in general, when there are certain national-, regional-, or local-level conditions or a combination thereof (structural factors) *and* when individuals or households have certain characteristics (individual factors). In other words, these studies seem to indicate that a favorable investment structure, however defined, is a necessary but not sufficient condition for productive investment to occur.[9] On the other hand, most studies that show a positive but limited association between migration and productive investment (table 10.2) point to structural factors alone. That is, the presence of an unfavorable investment structure seems to be a sufficient condition for observing low levels of productive investment in migrant-sending regions.

Second, similar levels of productive investment tend to be associated with *multiple sets* of factors. The evidence suggests that, indeed, a particular level of investment (low or high) may occur under multiple conditions. However, the observed diversity of factors among studies primarily results from including different groups of variables. That is, the variables present in one study are, in general, partially absent in another study. An example from each table will illustrate the point. Arroyo Alejandre and Corvera Valenzuela (2003) and Taylor (2004) study the conditions that affect the economic impact of migrants' remittances and savings on their communities of origin (see table 10.1). The former argue that the impact depends on the entrepreneurial structure of migrants' communities of origin, and the amount, uses, and proportion of remittances within total household incomes, while the latter maintains that it depends on the profitability of the new production activities or techniques and the amount of remittances.

As we can see, only the amount of remittances (the higher, the greater the impact) is common to both studies. Likewise, Arroyo Alejandre, De León Arias, and Valenzuela Varela (1991) and Durand, Parrado, and Massey

(1996) agree that a limited infrastructure and poor natural resources are associated with low levels of productive investment in migrant-sending regions (see table 10.2). However, they also identify other factors: the former study recognizes the low profitability of agriculture and the lack of experience in organizing, financing, and administering a business, while the latter study recognizes the limited access to product markets.

Third, the identification of different sets of factors does not represent, in general, competing explanations of the same problem. In effect, when we consider comparable studies (that is, studies that examine similar research problems), their explanations do not tend to conflict with each other. Instead, they focus on different aspects, offering complementary accounts of the same reality. Take, for instance, the last example. As we have seen, Arroyo Alejandre and his colleagues find that one of the factors that contributes to the low levels of investment in migrants' communities of origin is the low profitability of agriculture, while Durand and his associates point to limited access to markets. Although several elements contribute to the low profitability of agriculture in Mexico, a limited access to product markets is certainly one of them. People from rural areas with poor roads, high transport costs, limited market information, and scant technical assistance face enormous obstacles to selling their products at a competitive price (IFAD 2006). This example illustrates how, in general, the different explanations advanced by these studies tend to offer complementary accounts of the same problem.

This analysis of the literature provides new grounds for revising the current position on the relationship between migration and development. Specifically, it suggests that although some of the factors that facilitate (or impede) investment may vary across migrant-sending areas, there are clear regularities linking explanatory factors and levels of productive investment.

Also, the previous analysis sheds some light on the nature of the relationship between migration and development. De Hass (2007:70), for instance, maintains that the large diversity of findings reported in the literature shows the "fundamentally heterogeneous nature" of migration/development linkages. However, the empirical evidence discussed here casts some doubts on that conclusion. The diversity of findings seems to be less related to the nature of the linkages between migration and development and more to the multiple aspects, explanatory factors, and methods of analysis considered in studying these linkages.

Finally, the systematic analysis of investment patterns in migrants' communities of origin speaks directly to the central question of why remittances seem to be associated with positive development outcomes in some communities but not in others. According to the studies just examined, migration is less likely to be associated with productive investment (the aspect of development considered here) when migrants come from communities that have poor public services and infrastructure (roads, schools, banks, and so forth), poor natural resources (in particular, agricultural land), and a rudimentary economic structure. The reverse situation, however, does not seem to be a sufficient condition for investment to occur. In addition to a minimum infrastructure and rich natural resources (in the case of rural areas), studies point to individual and household characteristics for productive investment to occur.

Research on the differential effects of migration has contributed to a better understanding of the complex relationship between migration and development. Still, there are two aspects that have received very little attention: (a) the identification of the *mechanisms* through which certain conditions lead to certain results, and (b) the study of the *interactions and feedback loops* among groups of variables and their evolution over time. The few studies that have focused on these aspects offer more nuanced and compelling accounts of how multiple interconnected conditions contribute to produce certain outcomes. Building on these studies and the literature findings outlined above, the next section advances a conceptual framework to examine a specific aspect of the relationship between migration and development—the relationship between migration and productive investment in migrants' communities of origin.

Migration and Investment: Toward a New Conceptual Framework

Most studies that focus on the conditions that tend to facilitate productive investment in migrants' communities of origin assume that these conditions have independent and unidirectional effects on the outcome. The following example nicely illustrates this type of explanation:

> *Migrants with access to resources such as education, potential family workers, a migrant spouse,* ejidos, *[collective landholding units] and real assets such as land, businesses, and housing are far more likely to channel their migradollars into*

productive investments than are persons without access to such resources, who tend to devote their earnings to consumption (Durand et al. 1996:261).

A minority of studies, however, adopt a different approach (de Haas 2006, 2007; Ghosh 1992, 2006; Lindstrom 1996; Rionda Ramírez 1992; Zachariah, Mathew, and Irudaya Rajan 2001). The authors of these studies propose that the conditions associated with productive investment are interdependent and have feedback effects—the interactions among conditions affect the outcome and, in turn, the outcome affects those interactions. The most important contribution of these studies is the idea that the *interactions among factors*, rather than the factors per se, are what create favorable and suitable conditions to invest. Consequently, the same combination of explanatory factors may lead to different results if there are differing interactions among these factors.

Lindstrom's model of trip duration (1996) is a good example of this type of explanation. His main argument can be summarized as follows: The character of capital markets and investment opportunities in migrants' communities of origin determine the options available for investing foreign earnings. These options, in turn, determine the extent to which migrant earnings will be used to satisfy long-term as opposed to short-term needs. The more the opportunities for local investment, the greater the incentives migrants have to accumulate capital and remain abroad. The evidence shows that migrants from economically dynamic communities are more likely to prolong the duration of their trips and to invest in productive activities than migrants from economically depressed communities (Lindstrom 1996).[10]

As illustrated in this example, the proposed explanatory factors are closely interconnected and tied to one central issue—the availability (or lack thereof) of investment opportunities in the place of origin. Similarly, the studies identified above focus on other central, interconnected aspects. Taken together, they not only complement each other but also offer a comprehensive view of the multiple components that may affect the relationship between migration and investment. Based on these studies and the extensive body of secondary literature, four primary "nodes of interaction" are identified to account for migration-driven investment outcomes. These nodes are the building blocks of a reference framework that aims to (a) offer a synopsis of the main interactions among key sets of variables, and (b) capture the extremely complex and dynamic nature of the relationship between migration and productive investment in migrant-sending regions. The four primary nodes of interactions are as follows.

The first node: Investment is contingent on the amount of money remitted[11]
Investment is contingent on the amount of money remitted, which "fundamentally depends on the migrants' social and economic position at the destination" (de Haas 2007:15). Migrants' positions abroad are the result, in turn, of several factors. Chief among them are social networks, which play a fundamental role in the way migrants are incorporated into the labor market of the receiving country. Because recently arrived migrants generally find jobs through other network members, the larger and longer-standing the community of people from the same place of origin living abroad, the greater a migrant's chances of accessing a better-paying job (Light 2006; Massey and García España 1987; Zahniser 1999).[12] Two additional factors directly affect migrants' earning capacity: legal status and total time spent abroad (Reyes 1997). Using data from the March 2004 Current Population Survey, Passel (2005) finds that "incomes for unauthorized migrants are low compared to legal immigrants and the native born, but they increase somewhat the longer an individual is in the country."

At the same time, social networks have a large impact on the total time migrants spend abroad, particularly among undocumented workers. Indeed, as shown elsewhere (Galetto 2008), migrant networks may encompass very different levels of social capital—that is, the set of resources, information, and support that an individual is able to mobilize by virtue of his or her social relations. A large and well-established migrant network is usually better equipped to handle and, sometimes, partially reduce, the risks, fears, and sense of vulnerability that most undocumented workers confront in the country of destination. Experienced migrants are an invaluable source of information and emotional support to help negotiate and succeed in an unfamiliar and hostile environment. Thus, as migrants and, in particular, recently arrived migrants, are able to tap into these network resources, they are far more likely to find a job, withstand the hardships of being an undocumented worker, extend the duration of their trips and, ultimately, save money to invest in a productive activity.

Other factors that tend to be associated with migrants' earning capacity abroad are:

- The general economic situation in the country of destination
- The economic sector in which migrants find employment
- Migrants' human capital.

The second node: Investment is contingent on a
minimum level of local development

The decision of how and when to use savings earned abroad depends on the investment conditions in the country and, specifically, the community of origin of migrants (de Haas 2007:15). The conditions that favor investment are many and vary according to geographic and socioeconomic context. However, in the case of rural areas, there is a set of local conditions that seems to be critical. They are:

• The provision of basic services such as education, electricity, running water, and phones lines
• The availability of passable roads year-round
• The existence of a minimum level of commercialization
• The accessibility of markets (which is often conceptualized as the relative proximity to commercial centers)
• The availability of natural resources within or near the locality, in particular high-quality land.[13]

Investment conditions may vary over time as a result of the migration process itself. Communities with minimal development may alter the conditions of investment through three basic types of interventions: individual, collective, and joint (private-public) actions. Individual actions that directly affect the investment conditions of a locality include initiating activities that are profitable and nonexclusive. At first, few people are willing to take the risk of investing in a new activity, but once it proves to be profitable, a significant number of people from the same community, migrants and nonmigrants alike, begin to adopt it. The key point is that the activity is profitable *and* nonexclusive—that is, that the demand for the products and services offered is large enough to support a considerable number of suppliers without affecting its profitability.

When a considerable number of people adopt a new activity it creates new demands for goods and services, thereby stimulating other economic sectors. For instance, when avocado production began to grow steadily in the State of Michoacán, Mexico in the 1970s, so did the industries that were related to the production, transportation, and commercialization of this crop. As a result, migrant communities strengthen and diversify their economic structures. The few studies that offer detailed accounts of the conditions that allowed a significant share of the population to invest in an economic activity show that people invested in the production of commercial crops that were profitable and nonexclusive. In all cases, these migration-driven investments contributed to the transformation of the economic structure of those communities (see Galetto 1999 for avocado production; Mestries 1994 and Nichols 2004 for peach production; and Rionda Ramírez 1992 for lentil production).[14]

In addition to individual actions, the investment conditions of a locality may improve through collective actions. Of particular importance are those actions carried out by U.S.-based hometown associations and their counterparts in the country of origin. Hometown associations vary greatly in terms of size, organizational capacity, fundraising, and number and magnitude of projects managed per year. However, they primarily focus on the development of basic infrastructure in migrants' communities of origin. Some of the most common projects they carry out are the construction and paving of roads; the remodeling of schools; and the provision of water, sewerage, electricity, and street lighting (Alarcón 2002; Kapur 2005; Levitt 1997; Orozco 2000; Zabin and Escala Rabadan 1998). As a result of these actions, migrant organizations "directly help to set the stage for future investments in these communities" (IADB 2006). The study of investment patterns in migrant-sending regions should not only investigate, then, the type of investment (individual vs. collective), but also how these two types of investments evolve and influence one another over time.

Finally, a third way of improving the investment conditions of a locality is through the joint action of the public and private sectors. In Mexico, the quintessential example of this type of intervention is the so-called "Programa 3 x 1." The program is based on the principle that for each dollar contributed by the migrants, the government contributes three dollars—one each from the federal state, the provincial state, and the municipal state. Since its inception in 1999, "the priority in allocating funds has been the development of basic infrastructure" including the provision of water and electricity, and the building or remodeling of schools, parks, and squares (García Zamora 2004:187; Urciaga García 2004; World Bank 2001). Although collective and joint actions focus on the same types of projects, in practice they are substantially different. The main difference lies in the magnitude of the projects carried out in partnership with the state—they tend to be significantly more costly, larger, and more complex. On the other hand, securing the support of the state requires considerable levels of community organization among members on both sides of the border, and the right political connections between local and provincial-level authorities (García Zamora 2004; World Bank 2001). Hundreds of communities that do not meet those conditions are at a serious disadvantage because they cannot request desperately needed resources to improve the basic infrastructure and, consequently, the local investment conditions. [15]

The third node: Investment is contingent on suitable investment opportunities

Investment is contingent on the availability of suitable investment opportunities in migrants' communities of origin. It is not enough that communities offer attractive opportunities for investment. In addition, those opportunities have to be suitable *for the local people*, that is, opportunities must have entry-level requirements (capital, labor, skills, and a general knowledge of the activity) that can be met by a significant proportion of the population. When people are confronted with new opportunities, previous experience in that field is very helpful. For example, when a commercial crop is introduced in a rural area, having previous experience in agriculture helps both to minimize the risks and uncertainties associated with starting this new activity and to increase the likelihood of succeeding at it.[16]

The notion of suitable investment opportunities partially explains why people invest in certain sectors of the economy and, within those sectors, in certain types of businesses. At a more general level, it also partially accounts for low levels of productive investment in communities with a long-standing and well-extended migration tradition. Some researchers have argued that the low level of investment constitutes proof of migration's failure to contribute to economic development (for a full version of this argument, see Binford 2003; for a critical response, see Cohen, Jones, and Conway 2005). Decades of migration experience may have contributed to the development of a locality by, for instance, channeling collective remittances into basic infrastructure projects. However, better investment conditions do not automatically translate into concrete investment opportunities suitable for that particular population. Investment conditions, therefore, should be clearly distinguished from investment opportunities.[17]

At the same time, the availability of suitable investment opportunities in migrant-sending regions affects the migration process itself. In particular, when migrants have such investment opportunities in their communities

of origin, they have a greater incentive to accumulate capital and, therefore, to prolong their migratory careers. As we have seen, Lindstrom (1996)
shows that Mexican migrants from economically dynamic communities
tend to stay in the United States longer and invest more in productive activities compared to migrants from economically depressed communities.

The fourth node: Investment is contingent on household arrangements

Investment is contingent on household arrangements that support the
establishment of new enterprises. Households confronted with investment
opportunities that require significant amounts of capital or long waiting
periods to generate a regular income usually depend on the joint efforts of
household members to seize them. In a typical household arrangement,
the household head continues working abroad after initiating a business in
the hometown, while the wife or partner stays behind to manage the business. Another, less common, arrangement takes place when single sons or
daughters invest in a business that is supervised by a close relative, usually
a parent; upon return, the business is "transferred" to the owner.

In practice, the decision to invest in a new business and the rearrange-
ment of roles within the household are deeply influenced by social norms.
De Haan, for instance, points out that the impact of migration on the local
economy depends on, among other variables, the "social structures and
institutions allowing—in case of single male migration—women and
others to pursue activities previously reserved for men and households
heads" (De Haan 1999:29). In Mexico, where there is a strong *machista* culture, men tend to embark on investment projects with little or no consultation with their wives or partners, even though women often play a
fundamental role in ensuring the success of the investment while men are
abroad (Galetto 1999).[18] In comparison, Gulati (1993) finds that in a rural
town in southwestern India where women are strongly discouraged from
working outside the domestic unit, male migrants are less inclined to start
a business while they are abroad because they would have to ask a close
male friend or relative to manage it. Migrants prefer to invest in a business
at the end of their migrant careers, when they return to their communities
of origin permanently.

Favorable household arrangements are, therefore, the household
views, decisions, and practices that tend to facilitate the adoption of new
investment opportunities. This node has received the least attention in
the literature. Specifically, we still know very little about how households

make decisions about whether to invest in a new business (for instance, how and from whom they gather information about a new investment opportunity), and how households reconcile social, economic, and family obligations (for instance, when parents migrate to maximize their saving capacity and leave their children in the care of a relative). In sum, the examination of household arrangements forces us to consider migration-driven investments (or the lack thereof) within the households' overall livelihood strategies.

These four nodes of interactions are highly interrelated. Migration-driven investments tend to occur when people are confronted with suitable investment opportunities in their communities of origin and when household arrangements favor their adoption. These opportunities become suitable for some people when, among other things, they can meet their capital requirements. The greater the amount of money a household member remits from, or saves in, the country of destination, the more likely the household is to meet those capital requirements and invest in an economic activity. Also, these opportunities tend to arise in localities that have a minimum level of local development.

In the next section, this framework is used to analyze investment patterns in two migrant communities of Michoacán. The goal is to illustrate the type of analysis that results from examining the interactions and feedback loops among multiple sets of explanatory factors.

Investment and Avocado Production in Two Mexican Migrant Communities: An Application of the Proposed Framework[19]

San Juanico and Xhániro are located in the municipality of Tingüindín, in northwestern Michoacán, Mexico. They are good cases for a comparative analysis of migration-driven investment patterns for several reasons.

First, they are similar in size and ethnic composition. In 2005, the populations of San Juanico and Xhániro were 375 and 421, respectively, and only a handful of people in each community reported that they spoke an indigenous language (INEGI 2005).

Second, San Juanico and Xhániro are located about 15 kilometers from one another, possess similar natural resource endowments, and have agriculture-based economies. Agriculture was largely a subsistence activity until the commercial production of avocados began in the mid-1960s. The production of avocados as a commercial activity developed steadily after that. Today, both communities are part of Michoacán's avocado-producing region, which has a highly dynamic and fast-growing economy and houses 84 percent of Mexico's estimated 117,000 hectares planted with avocados (SIAP 2007). This region almost solely accounts for Mexico's position as the main avocado producer in the world (FAOSTAT 2007).

Third, people from Michoacán have been migrating to the United States since the end of the 19th century (Durand 1994). As a result, international migration has become a widespread and entrenched phenomenon across the state. In 2000, 63 percent of its municipalities scored "high" or "very high" (on a scale also including "very low," "low," and "medium") on the index of intensity of migration to the United States, developed by Mexico's National Population Council (Tuirán 2002:81).[20] The municipality of Tingüindín rated "high" on the index. Most important, labor migration to the United States started at the same time, the beginning of the Bracero Era (1942–64), in both communities.

Despite these similarities, avocado production has become a central economic activity for a large number of households in San Juanico, but not in Xhániro; while one in four households obtained a substantial share, if not all, of their income by growing avocados in San Juanico, only 1 in 10 households in Xhániro did so. The following subsections briefly explain why a significant number of households were able to accumulate capital in the United States and invested it in avocado orchards in San Juanico but only a handful of households did so in Xhániro.[21]

San Juanico

The production of commercial avocados in the municipality of Tingüindín started in the mid-1960s, when entrepreneurs from outside the municipality came to the area to buy land to establish the first orchards.[22] Although the average rate of return was uncertain at the time, they invested considerable amounts of capital and used the latest technology.[23] After they obtained the first harvest and sold it locally for a good price, producing avocados rapidly became a salient investment opportunity in the area.

Growing avocados is a relatively long-term project that requires, on average, five years of continuous investment. It requires a large initial investment to establish the orchard. Capital is necessary to purchase the land (if the household does not own a plot), to clean and prepare the site for planting, and to buy and plant the avocado trees. Subsequently, periodic investments are required to maintain the orchard. In general, it is only at the five-year mark, when the trees are in full production, that the orchard becomes self-sustaining and profitable. A significant number of San Juanico's migrants were able to seize this investment opportunity. How is it that these migrants were able to become engaged in avocado production when most of them were experiencing serious economic deprivations?

Most producers followed a three-step strategy of migrating to the United States, accumulating capital, and establishing avocado orchards. To examine the timing of and relationship among these events, the migration prevalence ratio, that is, the proportion of the population of San Juanico that had traveled to the United States, was estimated for each year between 1950 and 2005 (for more information on how to estimate this ratio, see Massey, Goldring and Durand 1994).[24] As figure 10.1 illustrates, between 1950 and 1969 the percentage of the population that migrated to

FIGURE 10.1

Migration Prevalence Ratio, San Juanico and Xhániro, 1950–2005

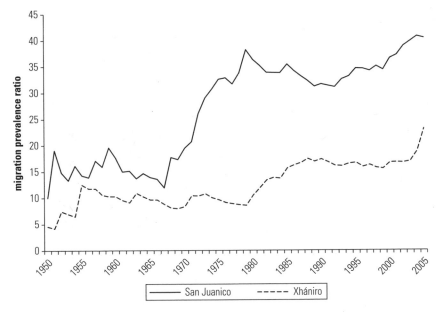

Source: Author's analysis of Mexican Migration Project data.

the United States was low, which is common when the process of migration is in its first stages. However, this share soared during the 1970s—the migration prevalence ratio increased from 17 percent in 1969 to a peak of 38 percent in 1979. The proportion of the population with migratory experience declined slightly in the following two decades, and began to expand again in the first years of the 21st century, reaching a historically high 41 percent in 2004.[25]

Working in the United States was the central means by which individuals accumulated the capital required to produce avocados—a full 80 percent of avocado producers worked in the United States. Even more important, almost *80 percent* of the hectares planted with avocado trees in 2005 were established with at least some capital earned in the United States, while almost *60 percent* of the avocado hectares were established *exclusively* with that kind of capital. In addition, as shown in figure 10.2, both having worked in the United States and the amount of time the migrant worked abroad are clearly associated with the establishment of avocado orchards. Indeed, there is a direct relationship between the number of years in the United States and the likelihood of becoming an avocado producer. For instance, while only 30 percent of those who worked in the United States for less than five years became avocado producers, 75 percent of those who worked 15 or more years did so.

FIGURE 10.2

Share of Avocado Producers among Household Heads, San Juanico, 2005

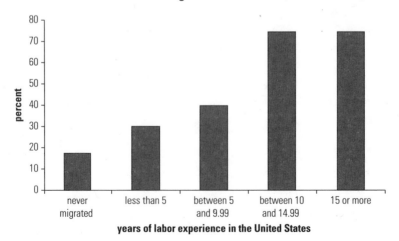

Source: Author's survey data.

Migrants who invested in avocado orchards continued working in the United States for long periods of time until they were able to earn a living from their orchards. The long waiting period was due not only to the nature of the economic activity, but also to the household strategies adopted to produce avocados. In effect, most producers of San Juanico could only afford to grow avocados by establishing their orchards in phases. For instance, if a producer established the orchard in three phases, he or she first planted one-third of the plot with avocado trees and waited until they started to produce fruit. Then, with the revenues obtained by selling that fruit, he planted the second third of the orchard. He repeated this procedure one more time, at which point the entire plot was covered with avocado trees. Therefore, migrants continued working abroad until the orchard was in full production or was large enough to support the family expenses and cover its own operating costs.[26]

To carry out this strategy, households depended heavily on the joint efforts of their members. Two types of household arrangements, each associated with a specific migration pattern and avocado production phase, were the most common. The first arrangement took place during the period in which Mexican migration to the United States was dominated by men.[27] Consistent with this national trend, the prevailing pattern in San Juanico was that men migrated and the rest of the family stayed behind. Most men were engaged in seasonal migration—they usually left for the United States in March and returned to Mexico in November. Once the orchard was established, the typical arrangement was that the household head worked "in the north" for most of the year, while his wife or partner and usually an eldest son took close care of the family business.

After the 1960s, there was a major shift in the demographic composition of the migration stream from Mexico to the United States when women and children began to migrate in significant numbers. This change, which also took place in San Juanico, gave rise to a second household arrangement in which the entire family migrated to and resided in the United States while a nonimmediate family member remained in the community to manage the orchard.[28] This arrangement became vital during the 1980s, when the costs of producing avocados increased significantly (particularly the cost of land) due to an unprecedented expansion of the activity. Households in which the entire family was living in the United States (and which usually had two earners) were in a much better position to accumulate the required capital to invest in avocado production. However, the household also needed someone in the community who could look after the business. This person usually was the household head's father or other close relative, who personally supervised and managed the orchard. When the orchard was in full production and generated a steady income, many families returned to San Juanico for good.

The time at which people started growing avocados was critical. The new commercial crop was very well received among Michoacán growers. The area planted with avocado trees grew explosively—it increased 43 times between 1960 and 1981. During the initial years, when avocado production was starting in the area and the demand for the product was beginning to develop, capital entry barriers were relatively low and, therefore, a larger share of the population could afford the costs of producing avocados. Almost two-thirds of all the orchards owned by the people of San Juanico were established between 1960 and 1989 (71 percent of them between 1969 and 1986). After that, there was a sharp decline in the establishment of new orchards in the community.[29]

In effect, a significant number of San Juanico residents were able to invest in commercial avocado production because they had the right resources at the right time. Two factors largely contributed to this outcome: (a) the rapid accumulation of social capital stocks within migrants' network, and (b) the availability of high-quality, affordable land in the locality. Each is briefly explained below.

The nature of migration flows to the United States changed dramatically during the 1970s:

- The number of people who migrated to the United States for the first time was five times greater in that decade than in the 1960s
- Upon arrival in the United States, migrants overwhelmingly settled in a single area. Before 1970, San Juanico's migrants were distributed evenly between different locations in the state of California and the city of Chicago. However, during the 1970s, 9 out of 10 new migrants arrived in Chicago
- There was a substantive change in the gender composition of migration streams. Migration shifted from being a male-dominated phenomenon to one in which women participated broadly.

These changes were mainly the result of the undertakings of two experienced migrants from the community who, throughout the 1970s, regularly helped other migrants get into and remain in the United States.

As a significant number of people from San Juanico found jobs and set-tled in Chicago, they accumulated resources, established a strong commu-nity abroad, and developed a solid social infrastructure to receive subsequent migrants and help them succeed in the new destination. Indeed, many people from San Juanico joined them there. These newly arrived migrants, in turn, accumulated resources that others in Mexico could use, maintaining and boosting the process of social capital accumu-lation within the network. Thus, the rapid accumulation of high volumes of social capital within the network contributes to explaining why a con-siderable number of residents of San Juanico were able to migrate and secure investment capital during the 1970s and 1980s.

In addition, land access was critical to investing in avocado production. In the case of San Juanico, land became particularly affordable as a result of a land dispute. At the beginning of the 1960s, a group of residents from the community initiated a formal petition for land to the Secretary of the Agrarian Reform. The piece of land they proposed to expropriate to form an *ejido*[30] belonged to a wealthy storekeeper from the municipal seat. The filing of this petition and the constant threats of an imminent land occupa-tion led the landowner to start selling the land that presumably would be expropriated by the state at below the market price. In addition, by the early 1970s, the first avocado producers of the municipality of Tingüindín had shown that avocado production was an economic activity worth con-sidering. As a result, a significant share of the population of San Juanico bought land and began planting avocados.

Although growing avocados radically transformed the way people prac-ticed agriculture—from subsistence to a market-oriented approach—it was consonant with people's labor experience. Having agricultural experience facilitated migrants' investment in avocado orchards in two ways:

- The migrants' agricultural know-how provided them with many of the skills and the knowledge required to successfully carry out the new activity
- Having agricultural experience made the goal of establishing avocado orchards easy to articulate within the migrants' worldview.

Finally, San Juanico had a basic economic infrastructure that facilitated the adoption of this economic activity. In particular, the town's proximity to the municipal seat (it is 4 kilometers north of Tingüindín) and its loca-tion on a state highway that connects two important regional hubs in the northwestern portion of Michoacán (Zamora in the north and Los Reyes in the south) offered great advantages, allowing residents to transport and sell the produce at a competitive price.

Xhániro

The residents of Xhániro did manage to grow avocados over the years, albeit to a very limited extent. In 2005, 60 percent of the households produced some avocados. However, the great majority of households (67 percent) owned less than 1 hectare. Most of these orchards were "backyard orchards" where the trees were planted close to each other and without following any neat pattern (many of them were literally in the backyard of the house). Also, their owners tended to use low levels of technology and invest few economic resources in the production of this crop. Hence, for most households, growing avocados was a very small-scale enterprise, done to supplement other sources of income.

Most households engaged in very small-scale avocado production due to their limited capacity to accumulate financial capital. If we examine the capital used for growing avocados, we find that a full 83 percent of the hectares were established exclusively with capital generated in Mexico. However, the majority of the population worked as agricultural laborers in the avocado orchards established by other producers; therefore, their saving capacity in Mexico was very limited. Only 9 percent of the total hectares of avocados owned by the people of Xhániro were established exclusively with capital generated in the United States. This raises the question of why, unlike in San Juanico, so few hectares of avocados were established with capital earned in the United States. Modest rates of migration, restricted access to U.S. labor markets, and the relatively short time migrants spent abroad, all limited migrants' capacity to accumulate capital that could be used for avocado production. These points are briefly discussed below.

Xhániro's residents began to migrate to the United States in the 1950s. Yet, for almost three decades the share of the population with migratory experience was negligible. The incidence of migration only began to grow in the 1980s, reaching a peak of 17 percent in 1988. The percentage of residents with migratory experience remained in the upper teens during the 1990s and the first years of the 21st century and then achieved a historic high of 23 percent in 2005 (see figure 10.1).

Thus, although migration to the United States was a relatively long-standing phenomenon, only a modest share of the population of Xhániro resorted to this livelihood strategy.

The low rates of international migration were largely associated with the nature of Xhániro's migrant networks in the United States—they tended to be extremely small and geographically dispersed. People summarize it well when they say "estamos todos regados," which loosely translates as "we are all over the place." To a great extent, this settlement pattern had to do with migrants' great difficulty in gaining control over employment opportunities abroad. Many migrants worked either for small firms that only occasionally hired workers (family restaurants, convenience stores, landscaping businesses, and so forth), or in larger firms where employees from Xhániro had very little control over vacancies. Also, migrants residing in the United States tended to have sporadic interactions with people outside the circle of family and friends from their hometown. Consequently, they had very few contacts outside their workplaces they could tap into to help other people from Xhániro to get jobs in the United States.

In general, the few network members already in the United States had such limited resources that they could not usually provide recently arrived migrants with the minimum assistance needed to stay where they resided. When people from Xhániro went to one of these destinations, they typically stayed there for a few days and then moved somewhere else, leaving both the size of the network and the volume of social capital in the network unchanged. Because network resources remained very limited, when other migrants from Xhániro showed up at the same U.S. destination at a later time, they confronted the same adverse conditions and, like those before them, they moved someplace else. As a result, migrants from Xhániro went to many different destinations in the United States, reinforcing an already scattered settlement pattern.

Between 1950 and 1979, although migration flows were small, first-time migrants went to six different locations in Arizona, California, and Illinois. The destination that attracted the largest number of migrants received one-third of them. During the 1980s, half of those who left Xhániro for the United States arrived in Stockton, California. The remaining half, however, went to eight different localities, six of which were new destinations for Xhániro's migrants. Geographic dispersion increased even more in the 1990s; about one-third of first-time migrants went to Stockton, while the rest distributed themselves evenly among eight localities, four of which were new destinations. Between 2000 and 2005, people continued to migrate to new destinations, and over half of all locations attracted less than 12 percent of migrants each. During this period, Stockton continued to become less important, while Las Vegas, Nevada received the highest proportion of migrants, 34 percent of the total. Overall, California has been the main destination state throughout Xhániro's migration history; within that state, only Stockton attracted a good proportion of migrants at some point, although too few to trigger a sustained settlement process.[31]

In most U.S. destinations people from Xhániro used to find short-term, low-paying jobs. Because they usually had access to very limited network resources (in particular, job contacts, housing, and emotional support), after a short time in the United States they tended to return to Mexico. Many of the Xhániro migrants tried their luck in "the north" a few more times; however, unable to significantly alter their labor situation, most of them returned to Xhániro permanently.

The low levels of social capital within the network directly affected migrants' capacity to remain abroad. Most people from Xhániro had relatively short migrant careers: the average number of months that a household head with migratory experience had spent in the United States was 25 in 1970, 27 in 1990, and 38 in 2005. In comparison, a household head from San Juanico had spent, on average, 77, 123, and 127 months, respectively, in the United States in the same years.[32]

In addition, the rapid expansion of avocado production throughout the 1970s and early 1980s created an unprecedented demand for agricultural land in the region. A significant number of people from outside the community bought large tracts of land to establish orchards in or near the locality during those years. As time passed and the price of land soared, it became increasingly difficult for local residents to invest in commercial avocado production. Given these conditions, most migrants from Xhániro were unable to meet the minimum capital requirements for producing a *significant volume* of avocados—only a handful of households, some with migratory experience and some without, were able to seize this investment opportunity and earn a living from it.

Discussion: Migration and Local Development

The comparative analysis of San Juanico's and Xhániro's investment patterns contributes to a more nuanced understanding of several aspects regarding the interactions between migration and development. Four comments are in order.

First, as mentioned, the more time an individual spent working abroad, the more likely he or she was to become an avocado producer. However, the direction of causality, at least at the beginning of the process, was the opposite of that reported by Lindstrom (1996). Rather than a dynamic economy creating incentives to migrate and accumulate capital, in San Juanico a stagnant economy led people to migrate in the first place. Later, when the opportunity to grow avocados emerged in the community as a result of broader agricultural changes in the region, the individuals who had been migrating for some time invested in it and continued migrating for many years.

Second, local conditions may change as a result of regional transformations. Indeed, the investment conditions of a community may improve due to geographic proximity to areas that are undergoing major economic changes, such as the creation of a business district, the construction of a manufacturing plant or, in this case, the introduction of a profitable commercial crop. Thus, while the economic conditions in San Juanico and Xhániro before the mid-1960s did not favor investment in general, these economic conditions began to change when producing commercial avocados in the *region* became a viable and profitable way of earning a living. However, to capitalize on regional transformations and reap their benefits, communities need to have the right resources at the right time. San Juanico and Xhániro not only offered excellent conditions for producing avocados, but also had a land tenure system, the small private property that allowed people to freely buy and sell land. These two characteristics attracted many people to invest in the so-called "green gold" of Michoacán. Among such investors were many of those in San Juanico who had migratory experience.

Third, although growing avocados was not a suitable investment opportunity for most people of Xhániro, including those who had U.S. migratory experience, it was certainly suitable for other people who were able to meet this crop's entry-level requirements. Individuals from outside the community—most of them from outside the municipality—bought large tracts of land to produce avocados. Moreover, Xhániro was one of the two localities with the highest share of large avocado orchards in the entire municipality of Tingüindín (JLSVT 2004). The production of this crop created a significant number of permanent jobs in and near the town. Workers were needed so badly during a time when most of the tasks performed in an orchard were not yet mechanized that producers hired women to work side by side with men—a highly unusual practice in the region.

Finally, as local economic conditions change over time, so do the determinants of migration. The first generation of migrants, that is, those who migrated before the avocado era, uniformly mentioned that they left for the United States because, with the exception of a few weeks per year, there were no jobs available in the local area. The structural conditions of the municipality improved with the expansion of avocado production; its production and commercialization for the national and international markets have become Tingüindín's main economic activity, creating hundreds of local jobs.[33] However, despite a sustained labor demand, people from San Juanico and Xhániro have continued to migrate to the United States. Chief among the reasons for this continued migration is that the prospects for improving household living conditions are much greater in the United States than in Mexico.

Conclusions

This chapter discusses the standard view of the relationship between migration and development. It argues that the large variability in results reported in the literature since the mid-1990s seems to lend little empirical support to the proposition that the nature of migration is highly diverse. Rather, it shows that according to the studies examined here, the large variability in results has to do with the fact that the studies focus on several goals, include varying sets of explanatory factors, and use diverse methodologies.

In addition, the chapter contends that the variability in the results reported in the literature is less erratic than many researchers seem to suggest. An examination of studies according to their reported level of productive investment (low or high) reveals several clear trends. One of the most important is that migration-driven investments are less likely to occur in communities that have poor public services, substandard infrastructure (lack of passable roads, schools, banks, and so forth), few natural resources (in particular, agricultural land), and a rudimentary economic structure. However, the inverse conditions do not seem to be sufficient for investment to occur; in addition to a minimal infrastructure and rich natural resources (in the case of rural areas), residents tend to invest in their communities of origin when they meet certain individual and house-holds characteristics.

Although the identification of these trends may improve researchers' understanding of the relationship between migration and productive investment (the aspect of development considered here), few attempts have been made to systematically analyze the multiple and dynamic inter-actions between these two processes. Moving toward that goal is the main contribution of this chapter, which advances a framework that examines the relationship between migration and productive investment in migrants' communities of origin.

This framework has four main characteristics:

- It integrates a large body of findings from the literature into a consistent whole. This is particularly relevant because, as explained above, studies tend to focus on very different aspects of the relationship between migration and productive investment.
- It identifies four primary nodes of interaction: (a) the amount of money remitted or saved; (b) the availability of a minimum level of local devel-opment; (c) the presence of suitable investment opportunities; and (d) the existence of specific household arrangements. Thus, instead of pointing to isolated individual variables, this framework encom-passes sets of highly interconnected variables. As a result, it is better equipped to account for the complex interactions between migration and development—an issue that most researchers acknowledge but that few have actually addressed.
- It incorporates a temporal dimension of analysis. Specifically, it sug-gests several feedback loops among the primary sets of variables. That is, far from assuming that variables have one-time and unidirectional effects on the outcome, it illustrates specific ways in which the primary nodes of interactions affect, and are affected by, migration-driven investments over time.
- It advances a thorough and systematic method for examining why some communities exhibit high levels of migration-driven investments while others do not. Each node suggests certain aspects that might con-tribute to a given outcome; they represent, so to speak, lines of inquiry. And, because they are highly interrelated, the examination of one primary node leads to the others. The comprehensive character of this

framework reveals, in turn, some of the mechanisms through which certain conditions result in certain outcomes.

It should be clear that this framework is, nevertheless, a first attempt to systematize the main results in the literature on the relationship between migration and productive investment. It was advanced in the hope that researchers will continue to complete, refine, and improve it in further research.

Notes

1. See also Rannveig Agunias (2006:43).
2. The term "productive investment" refers to investments that are made to start, expand, or operate a business that generates employment (including self-employment).
3. Reichert points out that migrants tended to invest in "economic activities that supplement, but rarely replace, migrant labor" (1981:63).
4. Adams, Jr. (1998) reports a similar finding for rural Pakistan. Using five-year panel data from 469 rural households, he finds that the availability of remittances "helps to increase investment in rural assets by raising the marginal propensity to invest for migrant households" (1998:170). The author argues that the higher propensity to invest among households receiving remittances—especially remittances from abroad—has to do with a tendency to treat such earnings as temporary shocks to income that should be invested.
5. For heuristic purposes, tables 10.1 and 10.2 list the explanatory factors according to their main level of operation or influence—national, regional, local, household, and individual.
6. As we can see from this example, table 10.1 does not show the specific value for each factor. Factors are listed in order to maximize the level of comparability across studies. The same criterion applies to table 10.2.
7. Whether the advanced explanatory factors used to account for similar outcomes are, indeed, alternative sets of factors or simply different sets of variables is discussed below.
8. Two of these studies (Arroyo Alejandre, De León Arias, and Valenzuela Varela 1991; Taylor et al. 1996) have more comprehensive goals than the one pointed out above: they focus on the conditions that tend to limit the *development* of migrants' communities of origin. However, because limited investment in productive activities affects the prospects for development, they are grouped together for the sake of the argument.
9. Studies that focus on issues that rule out the possibility of including structural or individual factors as part of their explanations are not considered here.

They are Basok 2003; Lindstrom and Lauster 2001; Sofranko and Idris 1999; and Woodruff and Zenteno 2007.

10. Lindstrom finds that "[i]n communities with high levels of female economic activity [the proxy used for high/low levels of economic development], 19.1% of households used remittances to purchase productive capital, compared with only 5.5% of households in communities with low levels of female economic activity" (1996:362).

11. As discussed above, New Economics of Labor Migration rightly maintains that unless remittances are explicitly earmarked for a particular end, they are added to the pool of household incomes; consequently, in analyzing migrants' spending decisions, researchers should take into account all income sources and assets, not remittances alone. This proposition is incorporated below. For recent publications on remittances earmarked for particular uses and their implications for development, see Grigolini (2005) and World Bank (2001).

12. Family migration increases both the size and level of integration of the "daughter" community abroad (see Galetto 2008).

13. In addition to the references listed in tables 10.1 and 10.2, see Ballard 2005; Binford 2003; Durand and Massey 1992; Lindstrom 1996; and Rapoport and Docquier 2005.

14. Avocado production is discussed in the next section.

15. In addition to the above references, other sources used here are interviews conducted by the author with Nino Andrade, an ex-municipal president of Tingüindín, Michoacán. While he was in office (2002–04), the municipality supported several "3 by 1" programs, including remodeling a church and constructing a square.

16. In effect, when people are confronted with investment opportunities similar to the type of activities in which they used to participate, they are more likely to take risks. However, Ghosh (2006:65) argues that "[g]iven the socio-cultural and educational background of the majority of migrant households in developing countries, it is not surprising that in general they feel unaccustomed and ill-equipped to be involved in risk-taking activities."

17. The proposition that investment is contingent on suitable investment opportunities is fully compatible with one of the main literature findings discussed in the previous section. Indeed, previous studies show that investment tends to occur when communities have favorable investment conditions *and* when migrants and their households have certain characteristics.

18. This practice was fairly common among the first migrant households that invested in avocado production in San Juanico, a northwestern rural community of Michoacán, Mexico. Indeed, when avocado production was new to the area, in the mid-1960s, men invested in avocado orchards without their wives' consent. Further, women strongly opposed it because they thought that their husbands were wasting the household savings—they did not believe that one day they could earn a living as avocado producers. Also, wives opposed

investing in avocado production because it required making huge sacrifices and postponing other basic needs. However, avocado production turned out to be a profitable activity, and a large majority of the migrants who first became avocado producers did very well. As one woman commented 30 years later, "thank God he [her husband] did not listen to me."

19. This section draws on research conducted by the author between October 2004 and August 2005, using a combination of archival, ethnographic, and survey methods. For a full description of the data and methods used, see Galetto (2008).

20. The migration intensity index is obtained by combining four quantitative indicators; this summary measure is then transformed into the five-point ordinal scale described in the text (CONAPO 2007).

21. See Galetto (2009) for details.

22. These entrepreneurs bought land in two specific places: between San Juanico and the municipal seat, and in Xhániro itself.

23. Considering the orchards' average size in this avocado-producing district of Michoacán, these producers established large-sized orchards (seven or more hectares). One of them was the first to use irrigation in the municipality. Not only that, he invented a dripping irrigation system to water the trees.

24. The ratio is defined as the number of people older than 14 with international migratory experience divided by the total number of people in that age range. It can be calculated retrospectively for any year using the date of birth and the date of the first foreign trip of every community member.

25. The migration prevalence ratio was advanced to standardize the units of analysis, allowing researchers to compare communities with different socioeconomic characteristics and migration histories. Massey and his coauthors identify five stages of migration prevalence: in the first stage, 1 to 9 percent of the adult population has traveled to the United States; in the second, 10 to 19 percent; in the third, 20 to 29 percent; and in the fourth, 30 to 39 percent. The fifth stage "constitutes a situation of mass migration with overall prevalence ratios above 40 percent" (Massey, Goldring, and Durand 1994:1513).

26. The great majority of San Juanico's orchards were small: 37.5 percent were less than 2 hectares, 35 percent were between 2 and 3.9 hectares, 10 percent were between 4 and 5.9 hectares, and 17.5 percent were six hectares or more. Although migrants weighed many factors to decide when to stop migrating (size of the family, number of dependants, total household incomes, legal status, labor opportunities in the United States, and so forth), most of them continued migrating until at least two-thirds of their orchards were in full production.

27. This period went from the late 19th century to the late 1960s (Durand 1994).

28. This arrangement coexisted with the first one.

29. Most of the hectares (65 percent) acquired between 1990 and 2005 were located outside the municipality of Tingüindín. They belonged to three producers that started growing avocados in the early time period and are today among the better-off residents of San Juanico.

30. Article 27 of the 1917 Mexican Constitution established three types of land tenure: pequeña propiedad (small private property), ejido (collective landholding units), and tierra comunal (collective, indivisible land).

31. Most people who in 2005 were planning a trip to "the north" mentioned that they would go to Las Vegas, Nevada. And they had good reasons to choose that destination. A Mexican agronomist from a neighboring town showed up in Xhániro to recruit people for his cattle ranch near Las Vegas. He offered them employment and housing and, as a result, many people started to go there. Note that even in this case, early migrants had little to do with the settlement process in this specific U.S. destination.

32. The previous section argued that when migrants are confronted with investment opportunities in their communities of origin, they have a greater incentive to accumulate capital and, thus, to extend their migrant careers. The case of Xhániro does not contradict this general statement. In effect, most migrants from Xhániro were unable to secure "long-term" employment in the United States. Therefore, they were not in a position to choose how long they wanted to stay abroad.

33. In 2004, there were 16 packing houses for fresh fruit and one processing plant producing guacamole operating in the municipality of Tingüindín; three of these (including the processing plant) were oriented exclusively to international markets.

References

Adams, R. H. Jr., 1998. "Remittances, Investment, and Rural Asset Accumulation in Pakistan." *Economic Development and Cultural Change* 47 (1): 155–173.

Alarcón, R. 2002. "The Development of the Hometown Associations in the United States and the Use of Social Remittances in Mexico." In *Sending Money Home: Hispanic Remittances and Community Development*, ed. R. de la Garza and B. L. Lowell. Lanham, MD: Rowman & Littlefield Publishers.

Arroyo Alejandre, J., and S. Berumen Sandoval. 2000. "Efectos subregionales de las remesas de emigrantes mexicanos en Estados Unidos." *Comercio Exterior* 50 (4): 340–49.

Arroyo Alejandre, J., and I. Corvera Valenzuela. 2003. "Actividad económica, migración a Estados Unidos y remesas en el occidente de México." *Migraciones Internacionales* 2 (1): 136–58.

Arroyo Alejandre, J., A. de León Arias, and M. B. Valenzuela Varela. 1991. *Migración rural hacia Estados Unidos: Un estudio regional en Jalisco*. México, D.F.: Consejo Nacional para la Cultura y las Artes.

Ballard, R. 2005. "Remittances and Economic Development in India and Pakistan." In *Remittances: Development Impact and Future Prospects*, ed. S. M. Maimbo and D. Ratha. Washington: DC: World Bank, pp. 103–18.

Basok, T. 2000. "Migration of Mexican Seasonal Farm Workers to Canada and Development: Obstacles to Productive Investment." *International Migration Review* 34 (1): 79–97.

———. 2003. "Mexican Seasonal Migration to Canada and Development: A Community-based Comparison." *International Migration* 41 (2): 3–26.

Binford, L. 2003. "Migrant Remittances and (Under)Development in Mexico." *Critique of Anthropology* 23 (3): 305–36.

Cohen, J., R. Jones, and D. Conway. 2005. "Why Remittances Shouldn't Be Blamed for Rural Underdevelopment in Mexico: A Collective Response to Leigh Binford." *Critique of Anthropology* 25 (1): 87–96.

CONAPO (Consejo Nacional de Población). 2007. "Anexo C. Metodología del índice de intensidad migratoria México–Estados Unidos." http://www.conapo .gob.mx/publicaciones/migra4.htm. Accessed May 5, 2007.

de Haan, A. 1999. "Livelihoods and Poverty: The Role of Migration—A Critical Review of the Migration Literature." *The Journal of Development Studies* 36 (2): 1–47.

de Haas, H. 2006. "Migration, Remittances and Regional Development in Southern Morocco." *Geoforum* 37 (4): 565–80.

———. 2007. "Remittances, Migration and Social Development: A Conceptual Review of the Literature." United Nations, Research Institute for Social Development, New York.

Delgado Wise, R., and H. Rodríguez Ramírez. 2001. "The Emergence of Collective Migrants and Their Role in Mexico's Local and Regional Development." *Canadian Journal of Development Studies* XXII (3): 747–64.

Durand, J., W. Kandel, E. A. Parrado, and D. S. Massey. 1996. "International Migration and Development in Mexican Communities." *Demography* 33 (2): 249–64.

Durand, J. 1994. *Más allá de la línea. Patrones migratorios entre México y Estados Unidos.* México: Consejo Nacional para la Cultura y las Artes.

Durand, J., and D. S. Massey. 1992. "Mexican Migration to the United States: A Critical Review." *Latin American Research Review* 27 (2): 3–42.

Durand, J., E. A. Parrado, and D. S. Massey. 1996. "Migradollars and Development: A Reconsideration of the Mexican Case." *International Migration Review* 30 (2): 423–44.

Fajnzylber, P., and J. H. López. 2007. "Close to Home: The Development Impact of Remittances in Latin America." World Bank, Washington, DC.

FAOSTAT (Food and Agriculture Organization of the United Nations Statistical Database). 2007. http://faostat.fao.org. Accessed March 22, 2007.

Galetto, V. 1999. "Aguacate y Migradólares: Un estudio sobre la migración a Estados Unidos y la transformación de la economía agrícola de San Juanico, Michoacán." Master's thesis, Universidad Iberoamericana, Mexico City.

————. 2008. "Migration Dynamics in Two Rural Mexican Communities: Virtuous and Vicious Cycles of Social Capital Formation." Unpublished manuscript.

————. 2009. "International Migration, Capital Formation, and Avocado Production in Two Rural Communities of Western Mexico." Unpublished manuscript.

García Zamora, R. 2004. "Migración internacional y desarrollo local: una propuesta binacional para el desarrollo regional del sur de Zacatecas." In *Nuevas tendencias y desafíos de la migración internacional México-Estados Unidos*, ed. R. Delgado Wise and M. Favela. México, D.F.: CEIICH-Porrúa, pp. 175–94.

Ghosh, B. 1992. "Migration-Development Linkages: Some Specific Issues and Practical Policy Measures." *International Migration* 30 (3–4): 423–56.

————. 2006. *Migrants' Remittances and Development: Myths, Rhetoric and Realities.* Geneva: International Organization for Migration and The Hague Process on Refugees and Migration.

Grigolini, S. 2005. "When Houses Provide More Than Shelter: Analyzing the Uses of Remittances within Their Sociocultural Context." In *Migration and Economy: Global and Local Dynamics*, ed. L. Trager. Lanham, MD: Altamira Press, pp. 193–223.

Gulati, L. 1993. *In the Absense of Their Men: The Impact of Male Migration on Women.* New Delhi: Sage Publications.

Gundel, J. 2002. "The Migration-Development Nexus: Somalia Case Study." *International Migration* 40 (5): 255–81.

IADB (Inter-American Development Bank). 2006. "Pooling Resources through Hometown Associations." http://www.iadb.org/news/articledetail.cfm?Language =EN&artid=3077&artType=WS. Accessed July 15, 2008.

IFAD (International Fund for Agricultural Development.) 2006. "Finding New Ways to Access Markets." In *Update*. http://www.ifad.org/newsletter/update/ 2/9.htm. Accessed June 29, 2008.

INEGI (Instituto Nacional de Estadística y Geografía). 2005. *II Conteo de Población y Vivienda*. Aguascalientes, México: Instituto Nacional de Estadística y Geografía.

JLSVT (Junta Local de Sanidad Vegetal del Municipio de Tingüindín). 2004. "Reconocimiento como zona libre de barrenadores del hueso del aguacatero (Conotrachelus perseae y Conotrachelus aguacatae Barber; Heilipus lauri Boheman y Stenoma catenifer Walshingham) al municipio de Tingüindín, Michoacán." Junta Local de Sanidad Vegetal del Municipio de Tingüindín, Tingüindín, Michoacán.

Kapur, D. 2005. "Remittances: The New Development Mantra?" In *Remittances: Development Impact and Future Prospects*, ed. S. M. Maimbo and D. Ratha. Washington, DC: World Bank, pp. 331–60.

Levitt, P. 1997. "Transnationalizing Community Development: The Case of Migration between Boston and the Dominican Republic." *Nonprofit and Voluntary Sector Quarterly* 26 (4): 509–26.

Light, I. 2006. *Deflecting Immigration: Networks, Markets, and Regulation in Los Angeles.* New York: Russell Sage Foundation.

Lindstrom, D. P. 1996. "Economic Opportunity in Mexico and Return Migration from the United States." *Demography* 33 (3): 357–74.

Lindstrom, D. P., and N. Lauster. 2001. "Local Economic Opportunity and the Competing Risks of Internal and U.S. Migration in Zacatecas, Mexico." *International Migration Review* 35 (4): 1232–56.

Massey, D. S., and F. García España. 1987. "The Social Process of International Migration." *Science* 237 (4816): 733–38.

Massey, D. S., L. Goldring, and J. Durand. 1994. "Continuities in Transnational Migration: An Analysis of Nineteen Mexican Communities." *American Journal of Sociology* 99 (6): 1492–533.

Massey, D. S., and E. A. Parrado. 1998. "International Migration and Business Formation in Mexico." *Social Science Quarterly* 79 (1): 1–20.

Mestries, F. 1994. "Migración internacional y agricultura campesina en Zacatecas." In *Campo y ciudad en una era de transición. Problemas, tendencias y desafíos,* ed. M. Bassols. México: UAM-Iztapalapa, pp. 171–97.

Nichols, S. 2004. "Technology Transfer through Mexican Migration." *Grassroots Development* 25 (1): 27–34.

Orozco, M. 2000. "Latino Hometown Associations as Agents of Development in Latin America." Inter-American Dialogue and the Tomás Rivera Policy Institute, Washington, DC and Los Angeles.

Papail, J., and J. Arroyo Alejandre. 1996. *Migración mexicana a Estados Unidos y desarrollo regional en Jalisco.* Guadalajara: Universidad de Guadalajara.

Passel, J. S. 2005. "Unauthorized Migrants: Numbers and Characteristics." Pew Hispanic Center, Washington, DC. http://pewhispanic.org/reports/report.php?ReportID=46. Accessed June 12, 2006.

Pedraza Rendón, O. H., J. O. García García, and F. J. Ayvar Campos. 2004. "Ahorro migrante y proyectos productivos: ¿Opción para el desarrollo de Tacámbaro Michoacán?" In *Migración internacional y remesas en México,* ed. J. I. Aguirre Ochoa and O. H. Pedraza Rendón. Morelia, México: Universidad Michoacana de San Nicolás de Hidalgo / Universidad Autónoma de Zacatecas, pp. 331–59.

Rannveig Agunias, D. 2006. "Remittances and Development: Trends, Impacts, and Policy Options. A Review of the Literature." Migration Policy Institute, Washington, DC.

Rapoport, H., and F. Docquier. 2005. "The Economics of Migrants' Remittances." Institute for the Study of Labor Development Paper No. 1531. Institute for the Study of Labor, Bonn.

Reichert, J. S. 1981. "The Migrant Syndrome: Seasonal U.S. Wage Labor and Rural Development in Central Mexico." *Human Organization* 40 (1): 56–66.

Reyes, B. I. 1997. "Dynamics of Immigration: Return Migration to Western Mexico." Public Policy Institute of California, San Francisco.

Rionda Ramírez, L. 1992. *Y jalaron pa'l norte … Migración, agrarismo y agricultura en un pueblo michoacano: Copándaro de Jiménez*. México: Instituto Nacional de Antropología e Historia.

Sana, M. and D. S. Massey. 2005. "Household Composition, Family Migration, and Community Context: Migrant Remittances in Four Countries." *Social Science Quarterly* 86 (2): 509–28.

SIAP (Servicio de Información Agroalimentaria y Pesquera). 2007. http://www.siap.gob.mx/. Accessed September 15, 2007.

Sofranko, A. J., and K. Idris. 1999. "Use of Overseas Migrants' Remittances to the Extended Family for Business Investment: A Research Note." *Rural Sociology* 64 (3): 464–81.

Stuart, J., and M. Kearney. 1981. "Causes and Effects of Agricultural Labor Migration from the Mixteca of Oaxaca to California." Working Papers in U.S.-Mexican Studies No. 28. University of California-San Diego, La Jolla, CA.

Taylor, J. E. 1999. "The New Economics of Labor Migration and the Role of Remittances in the Migration Process." *International Migration* 37 (1): 63–86.

———. 2004. "Remittances, Savings, and Development in Migrant-Sending Areas." In *International Migration: Propects and Policies in a Global Market*, ed. D. S. Massey and J. E. Taylor. Oxford: Oxford University Press, pp. 157–73.

Taylor, J. E., J. Arango, G. Hugo, A. Kouaouci, D. S. Massey, and A. Pellegrino. 1996. "International Migration and Community Development." *Population Index* 62 (3): 397–418.

Taylor, J. E., and J. Mora. 2006. "Does Migration Reshape Expenditures in Rural Households? Evidence from Mexico." World Bank Policy Research Working Paper No. 3842. World Bank, Washington, DC.

Tuirán, R. 2002. "Migración, remesas y desarrollo." In *La situación demográfica de México*, ed. E. Zúñiga Herrera and V. Partida Bush. México, D.F.: Consejo Nacional de Población, pp. 77–87.

Urciaga García, J. 2004. "Las remesas: Una opción estratégica para el financiamiento del desarrollo local." In *Migración internacional y remesas en México*, ed. J. I. Aguirre Ochoa and O. H. Pedraza Rendón. Morelia, México: Universidad Michoacana de San Nicolás de Hidalgo / Universidad Autónoma de Zacatecas, pp. 101–14.

Wiest, R. E. 1984. "External Dependency and the Perpetuation of Temporary Migration to the United States." In *Patterns of Undocumented Migration: Mexico and the United States*, ed. R. Jones. Totowa, N.J.: Rowman and Allanheld, pp. 110–35.

Woodruff, C., and R. Zenteno. 2007. "Migration Networks and Microenterprises in Mexico." *Journal of Development Economics* 82 (2): 509–28.

World Bank. 2001. "Migrants' Capital for Small-Scale Infrastructure and Small Enterprise Development in Mexico." World Bank, Washington, DC.

Zabin, C., and L. Escala Rabadan. 1998. "Mexican Hometown Associations and Mexican Immigrant Political Empowerment in Los Angeles." The Aspen Institute, Washington, DC.

Zachariah, K. C., E. T. Mathew, and S. I. Rajan. 2001. "Impact of Migration on Kerala's Economy and Society." *International Migration* 39 (1): 63–87.

Zahniser. S. S. 1999. *Mexican Migration to the United States: The Role of Migration Networks and Human Capital Accumulation.* New York: Garland.

Zárate-Hoyos, G. A. 2004. "Consumption and Remittances in Migrant Households: Toward a Productive Use of Remittances." *Contemporary Economic Policy* 22 (4): 555–65.